Mexico's
Political
Awakening

Recent Titles from the Helen Kellogg Institute for International Studies

Scott Mainwaring, *general editor*

Roberto Bouzas and Jaime Ros, eds.
Economic Integration in the Western Hemisphere (1994)

Luca Meldolesi
Discovering the Possible: The Surprising World of Albert O. Hirschman (1995)

Mark P. Jones
Electoral Laws and the Survival of Presidential Democracies (1995)

Dimitri Sotiropolous
Populism and Bureaucracy: The Case of Greece under PASOK, 1981–1989 (1996)

Peter Lester Reich
Mexico's Hidden Revolution: The Catholic Church in Law and Politics since 1925 (1996)

Michael Fleet and Brian H. Smith
The Catholic Church and Democracy in Chile and Peru (1997)

Robert Pelton, C.S.C., ed.
Small Christian Communities: Imagining the Future Church (1997)

A. James McAdams, ed.
Transitional Justice and the Rule of Law in New Democracies (1997)

Carol Ann Drogus
Women, Religion, and Social Change in Brazil's Popular Church (1997)

Victor E. Tokman and Guillermo O'Donnell, eds.
Poverty and Inequality in Latin America: Issues and New Challenges (1998)

Brian H. Smith
Religious Politics in Latin America, Pentecostal vs. Catholic (1998)

Tristan Anne Borer
Challenging the State: Churches as Political Actors in South Africa, 1980–1994 (1998)

Juan E. Méndez, Guillermo O'Donnell, and Paulo Sérgio Pinheiro, eds.
The (Un)Rule of Law and the Underprivileged in Latin America (1999)

Guillermo O'Donnell
Counterpoints: Selected Essays on Authoritarianism and Democratization (1999)

Howard Handelman and Mark Tessler, eds.
Democracy and Its Limits: Lessons from Asia, Latin America, and the Middle East (1999)

Larissa Adler Lomnitz and Ana Melnick
Chile's Political Culture and Parties: An Anthropological Explanation (2000)

Kevin Healy
Llamas, Weavings, and Organic Chocolate: Multicultural Grassroots Development in the Andes and Amazon of Bolivia (2000)

Ernest J. Bartell, C.S.C., and Alejandro O'Donnell
The Child in Latin America: Health, Development, and Rights (2000)

For a complete list of titles from the Kellogg Institute for International Studies, see
http://www.undpress.nd.edu

Mexico's Political Awakening

Vikram K. Chand

University of Notre Dame Press
Notre Dame, Indiana

Vikram K. Chand received his Ph.D. in political science from the
Department of Government at Harvard University in 1991. He held
research fellowships at the Center for U.S.-Mexican Studies at the University of California, San Diego, during 1990–91 and the Watson Institute for International Studies at Brown University during 1994–96; he
taught courses on Latin American and Mexican politics, democratization, and the political economy of development at Brown University
and Wesleyan University. He served as the principal consultant to the
Carter Center's Mexican elections program for most of the 1990s and
was its field representative during the 2000 Mexican presidential elections. He was also a member of several small international delegations
sent by the Carter Center to assess the electoral process in Mexico in
1993, 1994, 1997, and 2000. He has been an Associate Research Professor at the Center for Policy Research, New Delhi, and is currently
Public Sector Management Specialist with the Poverty Reduction and
Economic Management Team at the World Bank in New Delhi.

Library of Congress Cataloging-in-Publication Data

Chand, Vikram K., 1959–
    Mexico's political awakening / by Vikram K. Chand.
        p. cm.
    "From the Helen Kellogg Institute for International Studies"—CIP ser. t.p.
    Includes bibliographical references and index.
    ISBN 0-268-03458-3 (cl : alk. paper)—ISBN 0-268-03459-1 (pa : alk. paper)
        1. Chihuahua (Mexico : State)—Politics and government. 2. Mexico—
    Politics and government—1988– 3. Democratization—Mexico. I. Helen Kellogg
    Institute for International Studies. II. Title

JL 1299.C53 C53 2000
320.972´16—dc21   00-056455

∞ *This book was printed on acid-free paper.*

To my parents

Contents

Acknowledgments

Several people and institutions helped nurture the development of this project from its inception as an idea for a doctoral dissertation to its eventual transformation into a book. I first visited Mexico as a Harvard graduate student in January, 1986, and spent the next four and a half years living in the country and conducting research on political change in the north, particularly Chihuahua, as well as the nation as a whole. I continued visiting Mexico many times during the 1990s to deepen my understanding of the complex and gripping picture of democratization as it unfolded in the country during the decade.

My first debt is to several people in Chihuahua who opened their doors to an outsider and shared their story with me. I am particularly grateful to the late Guillermo Prieto Luján, then president of the PAN state committee, and Antonio Morales Mendoza, then the state party's secretary general, both of whom aided my research in ways too multifaceted to mention here. Francisco Barrio, Antonio Badía, and Luís H. Alvarez were among some of the key PAN members in Chihuahua who spared time from very busy schedules to talk at length with me about the party in the state and nationally. Several Catholic Church leaders in the state were also very generous in sharing their time with me: I am particularly grateful to Bishops Adalberto Almeida and Manuel Talamás for facilitating my work as well as Father Camilo Daniel for many long discussions about the role of the Church in the process of change. Humberto

ix

Ramos and Salvador Cortés spent much time with me discussing local politics and civic associations in Chihuahua. I also learned much about the process of internal change in the PRI in Chihuahua from Mario Tarango, and Artemio Iglesias. For my understanding of the history of Chihuahua, I am deeply indebted to Zacarías Márquez Terrazas, who spent endless agreeable hours with me sharing his insights over numerous cups of coffee in Chihuahua City.

For the national story, Carlos Castillo Peraza, Felipe Calderón, Cecilia Romero, Juan Landerreche Obregón, Bernardo Bátiz, and the late José Angel Conchello, among many others, helped me understand the changes underway in the PAN during the 1980s and 1990s, and the party's long history. Sergio Aguayo was crucial in helping me grasp the role of civic associations in the democratization process, particularly the Civic Alliance. Alfonso Castillo helped me refine my knowledge of Church-State relations and the growth of social movements linked to the Church over several discussions at his home in Tequisquiapan; Father Joel Padrón took me under his wing when I visited the town of Simojovel in Chiapas a long time ago. I am also grateful to Cuauhtémoc Cárdenas for granting me a lengthy personal interview during the height of the 1988 presidential campaign, despite the extraordinary pressures on his time, the first of several interactions with him over the years.

Several academics also facilitated the development of this book: Jorge Domínguez was an excellent adviser, always ready to point out a flaw in an argument and the way out at the same time. Samuel Huntington provided valuable insights for the development of the theoretical argument. I also received many useful suggestions from Alberto Aziz, John Bailey, Thomas Biersteker, Ilan Bizberg, Roderic Ai Camp, Wayne Cornelius, Nguyen Dong, Rodolfo O. de la Garza, Yuen Foong Khong, Joseph Klesner, Juan Molinar, Robert Pastor, Peter Uvin, and Jeffrey Weldon. Any remaining errors in the book are obviously mine alone.

Institutionally, I am grateful to the Center for U.S.-Mexican Studies at the University of California, San Diego, for awarding me a predoctoral Visiting Research Fellowship in 1990–91, and to its director at the time, Wayne A. Cornelius, for his generous support of my work. I am also grateful to the Watson Institute for International Studies at Brown University, which awarded me a two-year postdoctoral fellowship from 1994 to 1996 that enabled me to begin turning a doctoral dissertation into a book. Thomas J. Biersteker, the director of the Watson Institute, was a source of many stimulating conversations on democratization in general and Mexico in particular. I must also thank the Carter Center of Emory University: As the principal consultant to the Carter Center's Mexican Elections Project for most of the 1990s and the center's field representative for the 2000 presidential elections, I had an opportunity to observe the process of political and electoral change in Mexico at very close quarters. I also served as a member of several small delegations sent by the Carter Center in 1993, 1994, 1997, and 2000 to assess the Mexican electoral process. I am particularly grateful to Robert Pastor, the director of the Carter Center's Latin American and Caribbean Program for most of that period, for his support of my work as well as his many penetrating insights into Mexican politics, U.S.-Mexican relations, and electoral processes more generally.

Several friends made the process of completing the book much more pleasant especially Robert Arida, Sathi and Prema Clarke, Elias Flores, Hal Obayashi, Daniel Philpott, and Jim and Vera Shaw. Ashutosh Varshney very much encouraged my work on Latin America. Ruth Melkonian-Hoover offered to track down a few citations as the final revisions came down to the wire, and I was by then in India, very far from a library on Mexico. Leopoldo and Gabriela Chavarín taught me much about Mexico by their friendship, as did Francisco Fonseca. I remember many good evenings spent discussing the intricacies of Mexican politics and other subjects in the home of Leticia Barraza and Ilan Bizberg.

I am also grateful to Jeffrey Gainey, the associate director of University of Notre Dame Press, and Jeannette Morgenroth, my editor, for shepherding this book through the publication process, and to Scott Mainwaring, the general editor of the Helen Kellogg Institute for International Studies series of which this book is a part. I would also like to thank Carlos Salazar, the secretary of international relations of the PAN, and Mireya Domínguez, his assistant, for providing the photograph that appears on the cover of this book.

Finally, I would like to thank my father, a former Indian diplomat, and my mother, who together opened my mind to the world. This book is dedicated to them.

Lodi Estate, New Delhi
November 18, 2000

NEW MEXICO

El Paso

Ciudad Juárez

TEXAS

Rio Grande River

SONORA

Madera

Ciudad Guerrero

★ CHIHUAHUA

COAHUILA

Cuauhtémoc

Delicias
Saucillo

Sierra Madre Occidental Mountains

Ciudad Camargo

Ciudad Jiménez

Parral

SINALOA

DURANGO

1

Introduction

This book is about the process of institutional transformation in Mexico at the regional and national levels. Mexican institutions changed dramatically between 1982 and 2000: the traditional dominance of the one-party state yielded to a more democratic structure marked by the emergence of vibrant opposition political parties, the rise of the Catholic Church as an important player in politics, growing decentralization of Mexico's regions, the proliferation of civic associations, the adoption of fairer election rules and procedures, and the democratization of the official Institutional Revolutionary Party (PRI) itself. In 2000, the National Action Party (PAN) won the presidency, decisively ending seventy-one years of one-party rule at the national level.

What explains these institutional shifts? One critical factor was the eruption of citizen involvement in politics during the 1980s and 1990s, or what I call *the political awakening of society*. Elections grew increasingly competitive, with the PRI losing important state and municipal races throughout the country to opposition parties. In many cases, the government responded to its declining electoral fortunes by resorting to fraud, and the electoral process became the focal point of a deepening clash between society and the state. Disgruntled Mexicans also signaled their disaffection by joining civic associations dedicated to promoting clean elections and joining opposition parties on the left and the right of the political spectrum. Abstention rates declined significantly between 1982 and 1997

1

relative to the 1960s and 1970s, and public opinion surveys revealed growing support for a more open political system.

The political awakening of society was the product of three factors: the availability of political space, rapid social and economic change between 1940 and 1980, and the role of the economic crisis of the 1980s in triggering social protest. The political awakening in turn nourished the growth from below of non-state institutions that had been relegated to the periphery of Mexican politics.

The other major source of institutional transformation was the leadership of social organizations. Long before the political awakening began, Church leaders and the leaders of the main opposition party, the PAN, were engaged in a slow and difficult battle to pry open political space that dated back to the 1930s and 1940s. Leaders reshaped their organizations to appeal to society. In the 1970s, for example, PAN leaders chose to focus more on elections; the party could therefore profit from the political awakening of society that occurred in the 1980s. Leaders also harnessed rising civic engagement in the 1980s and 1990s for the benefit of their institutions and brought pressure to bear on the regime to negotiate reforms. In most cases, social leaders became politicized for reasons that were exogenous to the political awakening of society. Clergy, for instance, were influenced by the doctrinal reforms sweeping Catholicism in the wake of the Second Vatican Council (1962–65); business people became involved in politics, in large measure as a response to the nationalization of the banking system in 1982; and PAN elites had long supported a stronger society as an alternative to state dominance. The political awakening of society, however, encouraged social leaders to take bolder steps in favor of democracy by giving them a reservoir of support that they had never possessed before.

CHIHUAHUA: A REGIONAL CASE STUDY

This book focuses on a regional case study and the national implications of institutional development in the state of Chihuahua. Mexico's largest state, Chihuahua, borders Texas and New Mexico to the north, Sinaloa and Sonora to the west, Coahuila to the east, and Durango to the south. Chihuahua has played an important role in Mexican history, providing refuge to the liberal leader,

Benito Juárez, during the civil war of the 1860s, serving as Francisco Villa's base in the revolution, and emerging as a harbinger of democratization in the 1980s and 1990s. Chihuahua is also one of Mexico's wealthiest states, falling in the top third of Mexican states in per-capita income.

The political awakening of society in Chihuahua initially took the form of an electoral rebellion against the state—marked by sweeping opposition victories in municipal elections in 1983, massive protests against election fraud in the disputed gubernatorial elections of 1986, and a swelling of membership for the PAN and several civic associations seeking democracy. A highly competitive two-party system emerged in the 1990s that produced a truly competitive PAN victory in the governor's race in 1992 and a PRI victory in 1998. Chihuahua thus offers an example of political awakening and its impact on institutions over a period of fifteen years in one of Mexico's most important states.

Social leaders also played a gripping role in Chihuahua: Nowhere else in Mexico did Church leaders play such a visible part in supporting democracy as in Chihuahua, with lasting consequences for national Church-State relations. The state's business community also became active in supporting the PAN and the reform wing of the PRI. The combination of political awakening from below and the actions of social leaders propelled the PAN to prominence in Chihuahua, greatly strengthened the Church and civic associations as societal actors, and ultimately led to the extraordinary democratization of the PRI in Chihuahua.

Chihuahua also had a profound impact on national politics. The main institutions active in Chihuahua—the PRI, the PAN, and the Church—were all important actors at the national level as well. The process of politicization in Chihuahua thus had a major impact on these institutions nationally by percolating upward to their national decision-making centers, and by spreading laterally to these same institutions in other states. PAN leaders in Chihuahua, for example, were able to construct a new party more capable of winning power that quickly became a model for the transformation of the party nationally and in other states, while the decision of Chihuahua's bishops to condemn election fraud in 1986 triggered the formation of a national movement of bishops in favor of clean elections. The fact that a democratized PRI was able to win the 1998

gubernatorial elections in Chihuahua also set the stage for the transformation of the ruling party nationally along the lines of the party
in Chihuahua, culminating in the holding of an open primary to
determine the party's presidential candidate in November, 1999. Two
other factors magnified the national impact of Chihuahua: (1) the
intrinsic importance of Chihuahua, which makes it a highly watched
state and a source of national trends; and (2) the fact that the political awakening of society had by 1988 become a national phenomenon, thus creating conditions for the transmission of the political
and institutional innovations in Chihuahua to the national stage.
Chihuahua thus represents a pivotal case in the analysis of Mexican democratization in the 1980s and 1990s.

THEORETICAL ISSUES

Several theoretical issues go to the heart of debates about the
reasons that people become involved in politics, the impact of growing citizen activism on institutions, and the much-neglected role of
institutions in democratization. The twin themes of political culture and the role of institutions in democracy are addressed by Robert
Putnam in his study of Italian regions, *Making Democracy Work*.[1]
Putnam seeks to explain differences in institutional performance
by regional governments across Italy between 1978 and 1985. He
argues that the superior institutional performance of regional governments in the north relative to the south can be explained primarily by the higher level of civic community in the north and not
by differences in the level of socioeconomic modernity.[2] Putnam
measures his concept of civic community through indexes of civic
engagement, social trust, political equality, and the density of associational networks. He discovers that there is a strong correlation
between those regions that had high levels of civic community between 1860 and 1920, and those with high levels of socioeconomic
development in the 1970s.[3] In addition, he finds that there is an
almost perfect correlation between those regions that possessed a
civic community between 1860 and 1920 and those that have one
today.[4] Putnam traces the origins of these differences in the level of
civic community between the north and the south back to the twelfth
century, when civic republicanism began to flourish in northern

Italy while southern Italy became subject to the feudal yoke of the Norman conquest.[5]

The inescapable logic of Putnam's argument is that good citizens are not made but born. Whether a society has good citizens depends on whether it had them in the past. Civic tradition determines civic community. This argument underestimates, however, the effect of more dynamic factors in affecting political participation and awakening, such as political space, socioeconomic change, and economic crisis. Putnam also pays surprisingly little attention to such major institutions in Italian politics as the Catholic Church, trade unions, and political parties. He treats associations as a key component of civic community and the generation of what he calls *social capital*, yet he has a very narrow view of what constitutes an association, and the criteria that he uses to include or exclude particular associations from his civic community are not clear. Neither the Church nor political parties nor trade unions seem to be included. This impoverished view of civic community would ignore the pivotal role of the Church in reconstituting civic community and promoting democratization in a host of countries such as the Philippines, Chile, Brazil, and Poland. The exclusion of opposition political parties from the civic community is also problematic, particularly in explaining democratic outcomes in Latin America and Asia in the last two decades. In Mexico, both the Church and opposition political parties have played major roles in the process of democratization.

This book seeks to explain not only why citizens become politically active but also what impact they have on institutions. It makes the claim that one reason that active citizens are good for democracy is because of their effect on the institutional structure of society. As people become more politically aware they tend to participate more, whether by going to the polls in growing numbers, or by attending political demonstrations, or by enlisting in political parties and civic organizations. This in turn affects institutions. Political scientists have in the main tended to be pessimistic about the effects of increased democratic participation on institutions. Samuel Huntington argues that rapid surges in participation place excessive demands on institutions, force institutions to engage in populist and ultimately destructive policy shifts in order to appease public clamor, strain organizational coherence, and lead to a generalized distrust of institutional authority. The result is political decay, violence, and disintegration.[6] The only antidotes to this situation are either a reduction in the level of participation, or an expansion of institutions to soak up excess participation, or a combination of the two. Sidney Verba and Gabriel Almond, in their classic study of political culture in five nations including Mexico, *The Civic Culture*, implicitly concur with Huntington's analysis.[7] They argue that society consists of three types of citizens: parochials, subjects, and participants, depending on their level of involvement with the political system.[8] The ideal civic culture will include a higher proportion of participants relative to parochials and subjects, but parochials and subjects are needed to give balance and equilibrium to the system.[9] In short, if too many people become involved in politics too fast, chaos will follow and democracy itself could be imperiled.

My study of the Mexican experience challenges Huntington's thesis about heightened participation's destabilizing effects on institutions. The increases in participation in the 1980s and 1990s in Mexico seem to have revitalized the institutional fabric of Mexican society in ways that were highly beneficial to democracy. Rising citizen activism significantly strengthened opposition political parties, the Catholic Church, and independent civic associations, thereby enhancing the institutional capacity of society to extract democratic reforms from the Mexican state.

Huntington and Almond and Verba pay little attention to the strategic choices that established institutions and institution builders make to take advantage of the opportunities presented by increases in political participation. The effects of increased participation on institutions is seen as a one-way causal arrow, but rational choice theorists and resource mobilization theorists have shown that institutions play a crucial role in channeling and molding social mobilization to fulfill their own objectives.[10] Any analysis that seeks to empirically assess the effects of increased participation on institutions must look at both sides of the equation: the effects of new citizen preferences on institutions and the reaction of institutions to these changed preferences. Growing citizen participation might not have strengthened non-state institutional actors and helped produce a democratic response on the part of the Mexican state without the strategic choices made by key institutional elites in response to their changed social environment. One goal of this study is to probe those strategic choices by leaders across institutions in a systematic and comparative way.

Central to this book's argument are two related propositions: (1) strong social institutions are important for the development of democracy; and (2) increases in political participation play a vital role in strengthening social institutions. An early example of the view that well-developed social institutions are important for democracy is Alexis de Tocqueville's classic study of *Democracy in America*. In Tocqueville's analysis, hierarchically ordered institutions at all levels of the societal pyramid—such as political parties, associations, churches, vigorous municipal governments, and townships—gave form and structure to American society, strengthened society's ability to check the dictatorial powers of the modern intrusive state, undid the leveling effects of the inexorable trend towards equality, provided arenas for people to develop their potential as citizens, and helped generate frameworks of personal meaning. Tocqueville linked the development of these institutions to the existence of an active citizenry. For him, virtuous citizens were necessary for these institutions to work well. Civic virtue, or "self-interest rightly understood," was itself the product of mores, which Tocqueville saw as being shaped in large measure by religious values.[11] Curiously, Tocqueville himself was skeptical about the prospects for democracy in Mexico and Latin America generally. Latin America and the United States possessed vast natural resources and impeccable constitutions, but Latin America, encumbered by the authoritarian legacy of Spanish colonialism, lacked the mores for democracy to take root and flourish.[12] Yet, in the 1980s and 1990s, Latin America has become overwhelmingly democratic, and the region no longer seems bound by Tocqueville's pessimism. In Mexico today, many of the institutions that Tocqueville regarded as important for democracy—churches, civic associations, opposition political parties—have become important actors on the Mexican political stage, creating powerful counterweights to the traditional hegemony of the one-party state.

Previous studies of democratization in Mexico have focused mainly on top-down analyses of political change.[13] From this perspective, democratization in the highly centralized Mexican political system was said to flow from the president and his cohort of reform-minded politicians. This view of Mexican politics is not necessarily wrong, but it distorts what is happening in Mexico in two ways. First, it ignores crucial social and political processes at the regional and local levels that have been gnawing at the foundations of Mexico's authoritarian political system.[14] These processes involve growing political consciousness among ordinary citizens; increasingly competitive elections; stronger opposition political parties; a more vigorous associational life; and growing activism by the Catholic Church after many decades of quiescence. Second, the top-down perspective fails to come to grips with the role of bottom-up pressures in compelling the president and his allies to promote political opening. One could make a persuasive case that the decisions to recognize opposition victories in key gubernatorial races during the Salinas *sexenio*, such as Baja California Norte in 1989 and Chihuahua in 1992, and to reform Mexico's election codes in 1993, 1994, and 1996 were fundamentally responses by the president to increasing societal pressure. The fact that political reform happens to be initiated by the president is therefore not prima facie evidence for the top-down view of Mexican politics.

THE METHODOLOGY OF THIS STUDY

This study uses data from Chihuahua and the nation as a whole to probe the sources of the political awakening of society, the impact of the political awakening of society and the role of leaders on critical institutions, particularly the PAN, the Church, civic associations, and the PRI, and the consequences of these institutional transformations for democratization. The fact that opposition parties did well in states other than Chihuahua, and nationally as well, indicates that the processes occurring in Chihuahua were not unique to Chihuahua but extended to other regions and the country as a whole. For example, the first state to come under opposition rule was not Chihuahua; Baja California Norte, located on the border with San Diego, California, fell to the PAN in 1989. Since the PAN's victory in Chihuahua in 1992, the party has won power in four central Mexican states as well—Guanajuato, Jalisco, Querétaro, Aguascalientes; the party also held on to power in Baja California Norte and captured the industrial state of Nuevo León. In 2000, in addition to winning the presidency, the party won the state of

Morelos and retained Guanajuato by wide margins. The PAN also won control of many important municipalities throughout the country in the 1990s, including major southern cities such as Tuxtla Gutiérrez, Oaxaca, and Mérida. At the national level, the intense competitiveness of the federal elections of 1988, 1994, 1997, and 2000, and the dramatic gains of the country's two main opposition parties, the PAN and the Democratic Revolutionary Party (PRD), in these four electoral processes relative to previous contests support the thesis that the political awakening of society is a country-wide phenomenon.

This book is thus far broader than a single case study in the conventional sense of the term. A systematic effort has been made to increase the number of observations in this study in order to enhance the scientific validity of the study's arguments about causality and process in general.[15] Units of analysis range from the study of politics in one state, Chihuahua, to in-depth comparisons with several other states and the country as a whole. This study also analyzes a series of elections in various states and the country between 1982 and 2000 and compares them to elections held in prior decades to demonstrate the changing role of elections in the 1980s and 1990s. In addition, the book studies a variety of important institutions through time, in Chihuahua and nationally, including the official party, the PAN, the Church, and a host of civic groups. This study's three main analytical units—geographical entities, elections, and institutions—thus vary spatially and across time, and yield a rich mine of multiple observations for the researcher.

It may be helpful to define terms that are crucial to grasping the theoretical argument of this book. Most theories of civil society make no distinction between individual acts of participation and social institutions; civil society is taken to be a discrete whole comprising both individuals and institutions.[16] The concept of civil society thus fails to capture the crucial relationship between the development of civic consciousness at the micro-level of the individual and its impact on institutions. The vast political science literature on participation, however, makes a sharp distinction between political participation at the individual level and the effects of such participation on institutions.[17] In this book, the term *political awakening of society* refers to individual acts of participation by citizens, such as going to the polls in increased numbers, voting for an opposition party, voting for different parties in quick succession, joining an opposition party or civic association, or demonstrating for democracy. These acts of participation by ordinary citizens have profound consequences for institutions, including the state, but are analytically distinct from the institutions themselves. This book seeks to demonstrate the effects of increasing civic involvement among citizens on institutions because it contends that these effects are important for the development of democracy.

The book distinguishes between two kinds of institutions: the regime and social institutions. The term *regime* consists of the ruling bureaucratic elite and the former state party, the PRI. The term *social institutions,* on the other hand, includes all institutions not directly controlled by the regime, such as opposition parties, churches, independent trade unions, civic associations, opposition-run municipalities, and the like. Social institutions in some way represent society in its confrontation with the erstwhile one-party regime (hence the term *social).* Obviously, the distinction between the regime and social institutions is not always clear cut. All social institutions have to deal with the regime in one way or another or face irrelevance; and, in practice, their level of independence from the regime can vary significantly across institutions and time periods. Nevertheless, we can distinguish institutions that can act independently of the regime and possess social representativeness from those that do not.[18] The term *social leaders* refers to opposition party elites, clergy and bishops, and newly politicized business people who in one way or another sought to promote democracy.

This book is based on two hundred ninety-three interviews conducted by the author with ruling party politicians, opposition party leaders, Church leaders, civic activists, and government officials over the fourteen-year period between 1986 and 2000. These interviews were conducted in both the state of Chihuahua and the federal capital of Mexico City. This study also relies on documents obtained by the author from the institutions that he studied, as well as press accounts. Chapter 2 examines the sources of the political awakening of society, focusing on political space, socioeconomic change, and the impact of the economic crisis of the 1980s. Chapters 3, 4, and 5 study how social leaders and the political awakening of society transformed institutions in Chihuahua and nationally, particularly the opposition National Action Party (PAN), the

Catholic Church, and a variety of civic associations. Chapter 6 focuses on the reaction of the Mexican regime, particularly the democratization of the PRI in Chihuahua and nationally, and the enactment of pathbreaking electoral reforms. Chapter 7 provides a summary of the main argument and its implications for democratization in Mexico. The epilogue provides an analysis of the 2000 Mexican presidential election and its importance for the central thesis of this book.

2

The Political Awakening
of Mexican Society

The most dynamic change in Mexican politics during the 1980s and 1990s was the emergence of the citizenry as a driving force for the democratization of Mexico's authoritarian political system. The availability of political space, economic and social development in most parts of the country before 1980, and the economic crisis of the 1980s contributed to the political awakening of Mexican society. In turn, Mexican electoral politics in the 1980s and 1990s reveal the far-reaching effects of this awakening. Chihuahua's elections from 1983 to 1998, the national elections of 1988, 1994, 1997, and 2000, and regional elections from 1988 to 1998 show major gains by opposition parties, strong protests against electoral fraud, rapidly shifting voter preferences from one party to another, and increasing competitiveness of elections generally. Further change can be seen in citizens' increased interest in political campaigns, growing willingness to discuss politics openly, and rising dissatisfaction with authoritarianism. The political awakening of society was also a crucial factor encouraging social leaders to become more active politically.

THE "OLD" MEXICAN POLITICAL SYSTEM

The old Mexican political system that has now effectively broken down emerged from the chaos and carnage of the Mexican

Revolution (1911–17) in which nearly one million Mexicans lost their lives. The response of Mexican leaders to the national yearning for political stability and economic growth in the wake of the devastation of the Revolution was to create a highly centralized political system with an extremely powerful president and a dominant state-sponsored political party, whose function was to garner support for the revolutionary elite and ensure that social demands were channeled through the confines of the official party, where they were more easily controlled. The concentration of power in the hands of the president in Mexico City came at the expense of the legislature, the judiciary, and Mexico's far-flung provinces, despite the constitution's express commitment to the principles of separation of powers, federalism, and municipal autonomy.

Yet, if the old Mexican political system was marked by obvious authoritarian features, it also possessed considerable flexibility in adapting to changing conditions. This peculiar mix of authoritarianism and political flexibility, and the constitutional ban on the reelection of the president, explained the extraordinary longevity of the system.

The former official party went through three distinct phases of evolution. Founded in 1929 by President Calles, the main goal of the National Revolutionary Party (PNR) was to create a centralized political party controlled by the chief executive that could check the power of Mexico's revolutionary generals in their regional strongholds and force them to resolve their conflicts within an institutional context rather than on the battlefield. By the 1930s, the regime had entered a phase of mass mobilization and social reform. In 1938, President Lazaro Cárdenas reorganized the PNR as the Mexican Revolutionary Party (PRM). Unlike the PNR, the PRM was organized on corporatist lines, with separate sectors being created for labor, the peasantry, the military, and middle class groups. If the initial goal of the PRM was to provide a framework for the expression of popular demands, the sectors became an instrument of political control and electoral manipulation. The official party could rely on its control over the votes of organized labor and the peasantry to "win" elections in exchange for providing economic and political benefits to the sectors and their leaders. By 1943, the power of the military in Mexican politics had eroded so much that the military wing of the PRM was abolished. In 1946, the PRM experienced another metamorphosis with the creation of the Institutional Revolutionary Party (PRI). The change in nomenclature signaled a turn away from the revolutionary upheavals of the Cárdenas years in favor of political stability and economic development.

While the PRI until relatively recently has remained substantially the same in terms of its organizational structure, there were numerous changes in Mexico's election laws between 1940 and 1980. In 1963, the party deputy system gave the political opposition greater access to the Chamber of Deputies. Under the new law, any minority party winning 2.5 percent of the national vote would automatically win 5 seats in the Chamber plus an additional seat for every half percentage point up to a maximum of 20 seats. This was over and above what a party could win by majority vote. In 1973, the maximum number of party deputy seats allowed to a minority party was raised to 25. In 1977, President López Portillo, embarrassed by having had no opponent in the presidential election of 1976 and seeking to incorporate the left into the political system, expanded the number of minority party seats allocated on the basis of proportional representation to 100 and legalized a host of leftist parties.

These reforms represented gains for opposition political parties but they did not change the authoritarian character of the Mexican state. Indeed, well into the early 1980s, the president continued to wield nearly absolute power during his six-year term, while the legislature, judiciary, and state governments were essentially weak and powerless. Decades of one-party rule completely blurred the distinction between the PRI and the state, making the PRI "the party of the government" rather than just "the party in power." The PRI's official status meant that it enjoyed tremendous advantages over opposition political parties by virtue of its vastly superior access to financial resources, media coverage, and state patronage. There were no opposition senators or governors and only a handful of mayors in the entire 1940–80 period. PRI candidates for elective office, instead of being chosen by party members, were designated by a narrow group of PRI leaders, starting with the Mexican president, who enjoyed the extraordinary privilege of nominating his own successor. If the PRI's candidates floundered at the polls, the regime, more often than not, took advantage of its tight control over the supervision of electoral processes to ensure victory by fraud.

And the PRI's three sectors—the Mexican Workers' Confederation (CTM), the National Peasants' Confederation (CNC), and the National Confederation of Popular Organizations (CNOP)—quickly evolved into powerful political machines that represented major obstacles to democracy.

FACTORS INFLUENCING THE POLITICAL AWAKENING OF MEXICAN SOCIETY

The political awakening of Mexican society was the result of three factors: the prior existence of sufficient political space for democratizing movements to take hold; rapid socioeconomic development between 1940 and 1970; and the impact of the economic crisis of the 1980s. Guillermo O'Donnell and Philippe Schmitter argue that political openings produce civic mobilization and sometimes what they term "the resurrection of civil society."[1] In Mexico, however, the electoral reforms of 1977 produced no civic upsurge at all, although they did significantly widen political space by greatly increasing the number of seats reserved for the opposition in the Chamber of Deputies and by legalizing a host of leftist political parties; the PRI did extremely well in the federal elections of 1979 and dominated the Chamber. Only in the early 1980s when the Mexican debt crisis erupted, did significant civic mobilization against the regime occur. O'Donnell and Schmitter thus ignore the importance of economic crises in stoking bottom-up pressures for democracy and fail to consider the effect of socioeconomic change on the prospects for democracy.[2] The Mexican crisis mobilized a society that already possessed key prerequisites for democracy, including a reasonable level of wealth, education, and urbanization, as well as a large and diverse middle class and business community.[3] The result was a political awakening with democracy as its main goal. An economic crisis occurring in a predominantly rural society with low levels of literacy and a weak middle class and business community might have produced a very different set of outcomes less hospitable to democracy. Mexico's prior social mobilization profile was thus an important factor in determining the political outcomes of the economic crisis of the 1980s.[4] Political space is important but does not necessarily trigger civic mobilization: that depends more on other variables, such as the level of socioeconomic development and the impact of crises.

The Availability of Political Space

Compared to the bureaucratic authoritarian regimes of the 1970s in the southern cone and the communist systems of Maoist China and the Soviet Union, Mexican authoritarianism offered far more political space for potential opposition groups to organize and press their demands. Elections were manipulated, but they occurred with punctual regularity and the possibility existed that they might evolve into genuine occasions for democratic contestation. Occasionally, regional level contests, even in the period 1940–82, could turn surprisingly competitive, such as the gubernatorial elections of 1956 in Chihuahua and of 1968 in Baja California Norte. The holding of elections in turn sparked the formation of political parties, with Mexico's main opposition party, the National Action Party (PAN), being formed as early as 1939. Regular elections constituted an implicit recognition by the political elite that the source of its legitimacy was not limited to the revolution but possessed an electoral dimension as well. Because Mexican elections were so far from the norm of free and fair elections, the regime had a large margin of security in which to make incremental changes in election laws that over time nudged Mexican elections closer to the democratic norm while allowing the official party to retain its grip on power.[5]

The old Mexican political system relied less on repression than a mixture of cooptation, flexibility, and persuasion. The principle of no reelection meant that there was plenty of room to absorb ambitious social leaders into the framework of the governing party. There were moments of repression, such as the crushing of the railway workers' strike in 1958 and the student rebellion of 1968, but the amount of force used to sustain the state was relatively low. While the electronic media was tightly controlled by the state, the print media gradually developed a moderate degree of freedom despite ever-present threats that the government might withdraw advertising, or employ violence against journalists, or place reporters on the official payroll. Nor was the state able to absorb all independent social organizations into its fold. The Catholic Church, while careful not to antagonize the regime during the 1940–80 period, is an important example of an organization that fell outside the control of the state. In addition, unlike the former Soviet Union and pre-1979 China, Mexico was a market economy with a large business community, extensive foreign investment, and the norm of private property (with the important exception of the individually farmed but communally owned rural *ejido*); the surge in state-owned industry occurred only in the 1970s under Presidents Echeverría and López Portillo.[6] The high level of marketization placed major constraints on the power of the state even in the 1940–80 period,[7] and Mexican business would later emerge as an important source of funding for opposition parties, particularly the PAN, in the 1980s and 1990s.[8]

The availability of political space in the 1940–80 period was at least partly the result of the activities of social leaders. As Church leaders deepened their societal role, PAN leaders made efforts to expand political space by pressing for electoral reforms, mounting campaigns (particularly at the local and state levels, with victory as the main objective), and debating the official party in Congress and the media.

The existence of opposition parties, elections, some relatively independent organizations, and a half-free press meant that potentially democratic institutions were already in place to profit from the surge of civic involvement in the 1980s. In addition, there was sufficient political space for society to form new organizations to promote its interests vis-à-vis the state. The relatively low level of repression made it easier for individuals and organizations to press for democracy. Had the political system been more closed, the social pressure unleashed by the economic crisis of the 1980s might have erupted in a far more violent and polarized fashion with negative results for the future of democracy.

These institutional channels toward democracy were initially quite rudimentary—opposition parties at the beginning of the 1980s were weak, elections tightly controlled by the regime, and civic organizations timid—but they were the kind that were needed to build an incipient democracy. From the regime's point of view, these institutional channels, if allowed to operate, could drain away social pressure and reduce the probability of violence. There was also the risk, however, that the electoral process, opposition parties, and civic organizations might become strengthened as they harnessed social discontent into the political arena and slipped out of the government's control.

Social and Economic Development, 1940–80

By 1940, when Manuel Avila Camacho became president, the revolutionary state had successfully consolidated itself. The military had been subordinated to the state, the confrontation with the Catholic Church was over, workers and *campesinos* had been incorporated into the revolutionary fold, the oil and railroad industries were no longer under foreign control, and the institutionalization of the principle of no reelection had created an orderly process of elite rotation and succession for the first time in Mexican history. Political stability, a *sine qua non* of economic development, had thus been reestablished by 1940, after three decades of social upheaval. Other factors favoring rapid economic growth after 1940 were the new dynamism of the agricultural sector as a result of the land reforms of the 1930s, the creation of a structure of corporatist control over labor and *campesinos* during the presidency of Lazaro Cárdenas (1934–40), the stimulus to economic development provided by World War II, and the postrevolutionary state's commitment to rapid industrialization. In addition, high tariffs encouraged foreigners to invest in import-substituting industrialization and discouraged U.S. exports to Mexico.

The north, with its long tradition of entrepreneurship predating the revolution, was very well placed to profit from the return of political stability and the growth of the Mexican economy after 1940. The two most important entrepreneurs of late nineteenth- and early twentieth-century Mexico, Luís Terrazas and his son-in-law Enrique C. Creel, emerged from Chihuahua. They created a vast economic empire around cattle raising, mining, banking, and manufacturing that equaled the American tycoons of the same period.[9] While the Terrazas-Creel family lost political power as a result of the revolution, it survived economically. Today, the Terrazas-Creel family remains a powerful economic force in Chihuahua, with interests in hotels, industrial parks, transportation, real estate, food processing, insurance, and construction. Between 1890 and 1910, a powerful industrial elite revolving around the Garza-Sada family also developed

in the northern city of Monterrey, capital of the state of Nuevo
León, with investments in beer, mining, steel, and construction.
Monterrey's business elite clashed with the Mexican state during
the most populist phase of revolution under Lazaro Cárdenas, particularly over labor policy and the Monterrey Group's ties to international capital. Business pressure forced the state into a moderate
stance by 1940, and the sustained expansion that followed until
the early 1980s strengthened the Group's position as Mexico's most
important industrial conglomerate.[10]

The revolution also fostered the growth of new entrepreneurs
who profited from their ties with the nascent Mexican state. The
rise of the Chihuahua Group, Chihuahua's largest business conglomerate, was closely linked to its connections with the new revolutionary elite. In 1934, Eloy Vallina, Sr., founded the Mexican Commercial Bank as the core of the conglomerate. In 1946, he bought
the foreign-owned Mexico Northwest Railways Company, including its railway installations and vast forest tracts in Chihuahua's
Tarahumara Sierra. Four years later, he sold the railway installations, but not the forests, to the Mexican state at three times the
original purchase price including the forests. At the same time, he
received a fifty year exclusive concession to exploit the region's
forestry reserves and government financial assistance to establish
Latin America's most advanced cellulose producing facility not far
from Chihuahua City.[11] Apart from banking and the wood industry, the Chihuahua Group acquired interests in communications,
insurance, real estate, construction, and the production of cement,
steel, and tires. As a response to the dual shocks of the nationalization of the Chihuahua Group's forestry holdings in 1971 and its
banks in 1982, the Group diversified into new lines of business activity at home and abroad.[12]

Northern Mexico's close proximity to the United States has
given its economy a natural orientation towards exporting goods
and hosting foreign investment. Chihuahua's capacity to export goods
and attract foreign investment in the postrevolutionary period was
enhanced by federal infrastructural investments in irrigation, education, and basic services like water, electricity, and telephone lines.
Chihuahua also profited from favorable central government policies designed to stimulate foreign investment in the state. In the
early 1960s, business leaders in Ciudad Juárez, Chihuahua's largest

city, approached the federal government for assistance in industrializing their border city. They were worried about the specter of rising unemployment and social unrest as a result of the U.S. decision to suspend the *bracero* migrant workers program, and the leaders were unhappy with the city's reputation as a cross-border haven for legalized gambling, lax liquor laws, instant divorces, prostitution, and the like.[13] Business leaders argued that the best way to promote industrial development in the city was to lure foreign investment to produce for the nearby U.S. market rather than the distant internal market.[14] This was an early instance of the growing frustration in northern Mexico with the country's inward-looking development policies, which northern entrepreneurs believed failed, in the name of national sovereignty, to take advantage of Mexico's easy access to U.S. markets.

In 1965, the federal government, responding to a combination of local, national, and international factors, adopted the Border Industrialization Program, which permitted foreign ownership of manufacturing plants situated in the border region and allowed them to import inputs duty free, provided their output was sold only abroad. Finished products entering the U.S. market were taxed on the basis of the value added in the production process in Mexico.[15] Since value added was low because most inputs (except labor) were imported from the U.S., U.S. import levies were low as well. The Border Industrialization Program provided the legal framework for the growth of the multinational assembly or *maquiladora* industry in Mexico. By 1974, there were eighty-nine *maquiladoras* in Ciudad Juárez alone, employing 17,484 people.[16]

Foreign investment by U.S. automobile companies has contributed significantly to economic development in two major northern states, Chihuahua and Sonora. In 1980, the Ford Motor Company built one of its most sophisticated engine-producing facilities in Chihuahua City. This was followed in 1983 by the construction of a highly advanced automobile export plant in Hermosillo, the capital of the state of Sonora. Ford's Chihuahua City plant produces about 500,000 automobile engines annually of which 90 percent are exported to the U.S. and Canada. It employs over 1,000 people directly and receives 40 percent of its inputs from Mexican sources. The Hermosillo plant, which required an initial investment of $500 million, receives 35 percent of its inputs from Mexico.[17]

While Ford's choice of Chihuahua City and Hermosillo as investment sites was clearly the result of localized factors, such as the
high quality of the labor force and geographical proximity to the
United States, it is unlikely that the company would have considered such an investment in the first place without the Mexican
government's prodding. In 1977, the federal government enacted
tougher local content standards for automobile manufacturers, requiring them to balance imports with exports. In order to comply
with the new law, it became necessary for Ford to develop an export-oriented facility in Mexico. The federal government also discouraged the company from setting up the new plant in the Mexico
City area, agreed to construct an industrial park with all services
wherever the company located, and almost certainly instructed the
state-controlled Mexican Workers' Confederation (CTM) to negotiate a labor contract on the company's terms.[18]

The process of economic development unleashed after 1940
had profound social effects in both the country as a whole and the
dynamic northern region. Between 1940 and 1980, the Mexican
economy grew at an average annual rate of over 6 percent and real
per-capita income quadrupled. In the same period, the country's
rural population fell from 65 percent to 34 percent, while the total
population exploded from 20 million to 70 million. The population
active in the secondary and tertiary sectors doubled between 1960
and 1980 and constituted 66 percent of the economically active
population by the late 1980s as compared to just 40 percent in 1960.
Illiteracy slid from 64 percent in 1940 to 17 percent in 1980, and
the university educated population rose fifteenfold. The population older than 15 years with more than a primary school education also rose sevenfold between 1940 and 1980. Individual annual
gasoline consumption increased from 30 liters in 1940 to 307 liters
in 1980, while the number of registered television sets in the country shot up from 1.2 million in 1965 to 8.3 million in 1983, about
the same as in Western Europe in the late 1960s.[19]

In Chihuahua, the rural population plummeted from 63 percent in 1940 to 30 percent in 1980, and the total population rose
from approximately 620,000 to more than 2 million in the same
period. Illiteracy in the state dropped from 34 percent in 1940 to
only 9 percent in 1980. By 1980, 50 percent of Chihuahua's inhabitants were concentrated in its two largest cities, Chihuahua City

and Ciudad Juárez, and the state ranked within the top one-third of all Mexican states in terms of its contribution to the nation's gross domestic product (GDP). In 1980, Chihuahua, like most of the northern region, was thus more prosperous, educated, and urbanized than the nation as a whole.

Economic development gave birth to a new society nationally—and in the north—that was far more oriented towards political participation than before. One important social consequence of economic growth was the dramatic expansion of the middle classes and business community. By 1960, the middle classes amounted to approximately 17 percent of the country's population and were almost evenly divided between the rural and urban sectors. By the 1980s, the middle classes constituted 25 to 30 percent of the national population and had become mainly urban in character.[20] In the north, the middle classes were even more important, given the region's higher levels of urbanization, wealth, and education compared to the nation as a whole. The rise of the middle classes and the business community helped lay the foundations of a society increasingly oriented towards political participation. Indeed, relative to groups lower on the socioeconomic ladder, the middle classes were more likely to have stronger feelings of political efficacy, more access to political information, an increased sense of duty to participate, a greater propensity to join organizations, a higher perceived stake in government decisions, better developed political skills, and the monetary resources to participate politically.[21]

The middle classes, by virtue of their diversity, size, and superior access to key resources such as time, money, and education, were not easily absorbed into the corporatist structure of state control. When in 1938 the Mexican Revolutionary Party (PRM) created four sectors—military, peasant, labor, and popular—the popular sector was meant to attract the middle classes, but the popular sector, represented by the National Confederation of Popular Organizations (CNOP), did not even hold its first convention until 1943 and made inroads only among bureaucrats and public school teachers. In northern Mexico, the relatively small proportion of bureaucrats in the population, the lack of industries sponsored by the state, and business's lower reliance on sales to the public sector because of the region's orientation towards foreign investment and exports meant that the middle classes were even more independent of the regime than were their counterparts in the rest of the country. The north's orientation towards foreign investment also translated into a lower level of state control over labor, particularly in the *maquiladora* industry where less than 20 percent of the assembly plants are unionized.

Empirical research on political participation shows that urbanization by itself does not necessarily cause an increase in participation. Indeed, it has been argued that as cities grow larger they lose their sense of community or "boundedness," causing participation actually to decline.[22] In Mexico, however, urbanization seems to have a positive effect on autonomous participation. In rural areas and small towns, *caciques* or PRI bosses often exercise despotic powers in local affairs and opposition supporters are easily singled out for swift and sometimes brutal reprisals. In larger cities, opposition supporters are much harder to identify, acts of repression are more likely to be scrutinized by public opinion and the press, and the hold of local bosses is weaker.

Medium-sized cities may offer optimal conditions for autonomous participation because they combine a high level of urbanization with a vigorous sense of community. Indeed, one of the most important demographic trends between 1940 and 1980 was the rapid growth of medium-sized cities throughout Mexico, with the population living in cities greater than 100,000 quadrupling between 1960 and 1980. This in turn augured well for the development of a more participatory society.

Another important consequence of socioeconomic change in Mexico between 1940 and 1980 was the development of an increasingly integrated political community for the first time in Mexican history. Rapid urbanization, vastly improved communications systems, the spread of education, the ideology of equality proclaimed by the revolution, the homogenizing triumph of middle-class values among all social classes, and the unifying impact of revolutionary pride and symbols were all vital elements in the development of political community in Mexico. In Chihuahua, a political community shaped largely by the region's own particular historical trajectory already existed before the revolution, but it was greatly strengthened by the new forces working to generate political community throughout the country after 1940.

Social and economic development produced a gradual but

unmistakable erosion of voter support for Mexico's one-party system. Statistical analysis reveals that support for the official PRI between 1967 and 1991 was negatively correlated with industrialization, urbanization, and higher levels of education.[23] The PRI's strongest reservoir of support was concentrated in the less developed countryside and among those without a formal education, although the PRI was still able to poll a majority in urban districts until as late as 1985. The converse was true for opposition parties. Support for the center-right National Action Party (PAN) was positively correlated with urbanization and even more strongly with industrialization. The left also performed better in urban areas but made inroads into the PRI's rural base in the federal elections of 1988, when it won 24 percent of the vote in districts less than 25 percent urban.

The PRI's support in rural areas was partly the result of the perception among older peasants that the Mexican Revolution had fulfilled its promise to satisfy the peasantry's land hunger by creating the *ejido*, a collective unit of agricultural land owned by the state but farmed by individual *campesinos*. Yet, the *ejido* also furnished an excellent basis for control over the impoverished peasantry. Peasants who opposed the regime ran the risk of being denied credit from the state, repressed by local rural bosses, and expelled from the *ejido*; and the largely illiterate peasantry were also much easier to manipulate than more educated city dwellers. The CNC, National Peasant Confederation, provided a powerful mechanism to mobilize rural support, centered in the country's *ejidos*, for the PRI's dominance in rural areas. Under these conditions, opposition parties found it difficult to establish even a foothold in most rural areas. As the country becomes more industrialized and the size of the agricultural sector shrinks, the difficulties of the PRI can only worsen, unless there are real efforts to reform the party to appeal to Mexico's burgeoning population of urban, educated voters.

The Impact of the Economic Crisis of the 1980s

The economic crisis of the 1980s was the pivotal factor affecting the timing of the political awakening of society. During the 1980s, the Mexican economy entered a period of deep crisis and painful adjustment marked by high inflation, severe recession, runaway capital flight, collapsing real wages, drastic cuts in public spending, and sharp devaluations. In part, the crisis reflected structural problems caused by import-substituting industrialization that had become evident by the early 1970s, including a high-cost industrial structure, a weakening agricultural performance, an abandoned export sector, and rising trade deficits.[24] But the crisis was also the result of President José López Portillo's (1976–82) disastrous decision to stake the country's entire economic destiny on the fate of its newly discovered oil reserves. He embarked on a program of massive public spending, backed by the windfall of revenues from petroleum exports, and huge international loans. For López Portillo, the oil boom promised an easy solution to the country's economic ills and obviated the need for structural changes.

When international oil prices fell in 1981, Mexico quickly tumbled into its worst economic crisis since the Great Depression of 1929–32. In 1982, the country registered 100 percent inflation, economic growth shrank to minus 0.2 percent, unemployment doubled to 8 percent, the public sector deficit soared to 18 percent of the Gross Domestic Product (GDP), the government suspended payments on the principal of its $80 billion foreign debt, and the *peso* was steeply devalued, despite López Portillo's pledge to defend it "like a dog."[25] On the eve of leaving office, López Portillo nationalized the banking system and imposed tight exchange controls, including the obligatory conversion into *pesos* of all dollar-denominated accounts held in Mexican banks. His successor, Miguel de la Madrid (1982–88), inherited an economy in ruins and was compelled to follow a course of drastic economic restructuring.

The economic crisis unleashed the underlying social pressures for greater political participation, spurred a major increase in the level of politicization, and galvanized society against the state. The crisis not only posed an immediate threat to the relatively privileged economic and social status that many middle-class people believed was rightfully theirs by virtue of their thrift, hard work, and ingenuity, but also seriously undermined the prospects of continued upward mobility for themselves and their children. For the business community, the nationalization of the banking system starkly revealed the defenselessness of society to the whims of presidential power. Instead of seeking to resolve their differences with the government through traditional channels, like the relatively "nonpolitical" business chambers, many businessmen now opted for direct involvement in opposition politics. The crisis also eroded the historical identification of workers and *campesinos* with the Mexican state, owing to the dramatic fall of real wages, the dismantling of subsidies, growing rural misery, and the complete inability of the CTM and CNC to defend the perceived interests of their members.

By virtue of their proximity to the United States, the northern Mexican states were particularly hard hit by devaluation, for northerners accustomed to making a significant proportion of their purchases in the U.S. were no longer able to do so. The requirement that dollar deposits be converted into *pesos* was also deeply resented in the north, where there were many more such accounts than in the Mexican heartland. Indeed, the combination of devaluation and the banning of dollar-denominated accounts seriously disrupted the complex network of border transactions, particularly between the twin cities of San Diego–Tijuana, El Paso–Ciudad Juárez, and Brownsville-Matamoros. This led to acute shortages of basic commodities as U.S. residents along the border took advantage of the stronger value of the dollar to make an increasing proportion of their purchases in Mexico. On the other hand, the constant devaluation of the *peso* during the 1980s—especially the sharper devaluations of 1982, 1986, and 1987—and the decline of real wages in Mexico stimulated tremendous growth in the *maquiladora* industry throughout the border region. The number of people employed in the industry rose from 127,048 to 447,190, and the number of plants from 585 to 1,760 during the 1980s.[26] And the *maquiladora* industry displaced tourism as Mexico's second largest source of hard currency after petroleum. As in the rest of the country, however, business expansion in the domestically oriented sectors of the northern economy was hampered by the scarcity of credit caused by the soaring interest rates and the erosion of purchasing power caused by inflation, which peaked in 1986.

Social protest against the crisis was initially strongest in the north, particularly in Chihuahua. To some extent this reflected the fact that the interdependent border region was initially worse affected by the crisis even if it subsequently benefited by the growth of the *maquiladora* industry. In addition, the economic crisis rekindled age-old hostility towards central government and sharpened feelings of relative deprivation vis-à-vis the United States. Throughout the north, the crisis interacted with a culture characterized by both a strong regionalism and a deep mistrust of the central government.[27] For example, for much of its history, the distant northern region developed in isolation from the rest of the country. Located more than a thousand miles away from Mexico City, Chihuahua was enclosed on the west by the daunting Sierra Madre Occidental mountain chain, to the east by an extended desert, and to the north by the United States. The political turmoil, social upheaval, and plain banditry marking much of nineteenth-century Mexico all but severed communication between the north and the rest of the country and forced the northern region to strengthen commercial ties with the United States in order to ensure access to basic supplies. The process of integrating the north into the national mainstream would begin only in the 1880s with the construction of railway lines linking Mexico City and major northern centers such as Ciudad Juárez, but the dictator Porfirio Díaz (1880–1911) was unable to dislodge northern elites. In Chihuahua, for example, the Terrazas-Creel family continued to govern the state of Mexico City autonomously.

The result of northern Mexico's isolation was the development of a regional culture quite different from that of central and southern Mexico. Indeed, the north's pattern of social evolution was akin to that of the frontier societies that developed throughout the American West. The boom and bust syndromes characterizing the mining industry, the insecurity of ranching due to Apache raids, and the paucity of Indian labor thwarted the development of a local aristocracy, a subject labor force, and rigid class divisions. The vastness of the northern expanse, the reluctance of clergy to abandon the comforts of central Mexico for the inhospitable north, and the low religiosity of the settlers frustrated the development of a clerical tradition. The lack of intermarriage between the settlers and nomadic Indian tribes that inhabited the region, the existence of a common enemy in the form of the perceived Apache menace, and the low rate of migration from the rest of the country until recently gave the population a high level of homogeneity and social cohesion. On the other hand, the enterprising nature of the settlers, who came north chiefly in search of mineral wealth or to flee the law, the harsh terrain and climatic conditions, and the fact of a small population scattered over a huge area bred a hardy individualism.

Unlike central and southern Mexico, the north lacked a feudal past and its dominant social values were ordered around the idea of egalitarian individualism.

The north's powerful sense of regionalism in turn furnished the basis for the accumulation of resentments against the central government. Historically, the north, particularly Chihuahua, had bitterly resented the refusal of the central government to send military aid to the state during the worst phase of the Apache conflict from 1832 to 1880, which wrecked havoc throughout the region.[28] Politically, northerners were alienated by the central government's cavalier imposition of leaders on the state without even a semblance of popular support and the regime's habitual resort to fraud when such candidates failed to win a popular mandate. Indeed, one of the most important sources of the north's democratic convictions was the desire to reduce the power of the federal government by fighting for the right to choose the state's elected representatives in free and fair elections. Economically, northerners believed that the central government was milking the region through high taxes without spending an equivalent amount in the state by way of federal investment and budgetary support.[29] They accused the central government of ploughing the difference into subsidies to pacify Mexico City. Given northerners' innate dislike of the central government, their blaming the economic crisis of the 1980s entirely on the central government was hardly surprising. For northerners, the crisis had been created by the mistakes of corrupt and power-hungry politicians in Mexico City and artificially imposed on the region, despite an intrinsically healthy economy. Northerners thus reacted to the crisis with an explosion of fury directed mainly at the central government.

The broad exposure of northerners to the workings of U.S. democracy and consumer society also meant that the crisis aggravated an already well-developed sense of relative deprivation. Northerners have always tended to compare themselves with their American neighbor, even if only at a subconscious level. In 1981, 35 percent of those surveyed in Ciudad Juárez and 29 percent of those surveyed in Chihuahua City said they wanted Mexico to be like the United States as compared to 20 percent nationally.[30] This tendency to compare was only natural given their geographical proximity to the United States, their intertwined economies, and the ability of

many northerners to watch television programs, listen to radio stations, and read newspapers from the U.S. on a regular basis. In fact,
Chihuahua has one of the highest ratios of parabolic antennas per
inhabitant in the country. Northerners argued that the lack of democracy in Mexico and the resultant inability of society to control
the state had opened the door to massive governmental corruption,
produced a dangerous concentration of power in the hands of the
president, and ultimately plunged Mexico, a country well-endowed
with natural resources, into economic disaster.

THE IMPACT OF THE POLITICAL AWAKENING
OF MEXICAN SOCIETY ON ELECTIONS

The political awakening of Mexican society in the 1980s and
1990s was captured by five major indicators: (1) the growing competitiveness of elections relative to the 1960s and 1970s, (2) the
surge in opposition electoral gains at the local, state, and national
levels, (3) the increasingly explosive nature of Mexican elections,
with fraud becoming a major point of conflict between society and
the state, (4) the growing tendency of the electorate to swing rapidly from one party to another from one election to the next, and
(5) the higher voter turnout characterizing elections between 1988
and 2000, particularly federal ones. These factors marked an important break with Mexico's long tradition of mostly formalistic elections dating back to the dictatorship of Porfirio Díaz (1880–1911).
Usually, the PRI won by huge margins against a small and demoralized opposition with only a few significant exceptions,
mostly at the state and municipal levels. Nor were elections as a
rule a path to political power. For opposition parties, it seemed
unrealistic to think of elections as a means to power in view of
the state's tight supervision of electoral processes, the use of fraud
to divest opposition parties of electoral triumphs, and the institutional weakness of the opposition parties. As far as PRI candidates
were concerned, elections served mostly as a ritual to ratify their
prior selection from above.

Despite lacking impact on the distribution of political power,
elections did perform a variety of system-strengthening functions.
They bestowed the regime with a measure of democratic legitimacy

that it would otherwise not have possessed. Elections represented a useful safety valve for dissipating social tension, while campaigns offered an opportunity for PRI candidates to acquire a firsthand knowledge of the country's problems. The punctilious observance of the electoral calendar, along with the principle of no reelection, furnished an important mechanism for ensuring the peaceful rotation and renewal of the political elite and ensured that a large number of ambitious PRI politicians would eventually receive some kind of political reward if they waited their turn. The fact that elections were not considered a path to political power helped enforce discipline among the political elite by discouraging those denied the PRI ticket from deserting the party and joining hands with the opposition. Also, the occurrence of elections meant that at least a theoretical possibility existed that they would one day become competitive.

During the 1980s and 1990s, elections were increasingly shorn of their purely ritualistic character and evolved into a real mechanism for the transmission of power among rival contenders. Opposition parties registered significant gains in federal and regional elections around the country and inflicted major defeats on the PRI in several states. The growing significance of elections as a means to power greatly raised the incentives for dissatisfied PRI members to desert the ruling coalition, as occurred in the 1988 presidential election. As the regime responded to the surge of opposition strength by turning to electoral fraud on a major scale, elections became a focal point for confrontation between society and the state. Largely ignored in the past, Mexican elections, even at the state and local levels, began to draw unprecedented international and domestic attention. The electoral calendar, far from being a source of quiet reassurance for the political elite, turned into a periodic nightmare that threatened to sap the legitimacy of the political system. The regime's use of fraud to reverse unfavorable verdicts and the tendency of opposition parties to proclaim the inevitability of fraud, sometimes without proper evidence, seriously undermined the credibility of election results and threatened to depress voter turnout, though the actual effects on voter turnout over time seem to be ambiguous. Towards the late 1980s and 1990s two new additional trends emerged: voters began to shift preferences from one election to the next between opposition parties and the ruling PRI, and between rival opposition parties; and participation rates in federal and several regional elections markedly increased in the 1990s compared to 1988 and earlier.

The growing competitiveness of elections in the 1980s reflected the emergence of a more politically aware society as a result of social and economic change, coupled with the social discontent produced by the economic crisis. In addition, the greater level of contestation characterizing elections in the 1980s reflected the erosion of the corporatist system of interest representation of the middle classes, the workers, and the peasants. As we have seen, the middle classes had been mostly excluded from the ruling party's official structure of control, which had taken shape in the 1930s prior to the onset of industrialization; the CNOP had never adequately represented the middle classes. Only weakly linked to the state in institutional terms and disinclined to violence, the middle classes had few avenues of social protest available to them during the crisis other than the ballot box. The crisis also undermined the ability of the state to funnel money and patronage to union bosses, thereby loosening the glue that had held the system together—and linked the workers to the state—for decades. The subsequent process of economic restructuring and adjustment compelled PRI reformers to dismantle the remains of the inefficient corporatist system in order to develop new forms of labor representation more compatible with the demands of economic modernization and integration with the United States. Further, the 1991 decision to permit the sale of *ejidal* land opened up the countryside to foreign investment and full-scale modernization but potentially lessened the government's control over *campesinos.* Workers and *campesinos,* faced with the CTM's and CNC's unresponsiveness to the collapse of their living standards—with real wages falling by more than 50 percent between 1982 and 1991—thus turned in growing numbers to the ballot box to voice their discontent.

The regime itself was also partly responsible for channeling social discontent into the electoral arena by deciding to hold clean elections at the local level early in President de la Madrid's term; de la Madrid's subsequent decision to return to fraudulent practices in the last three years of his term, 1985–88, dashed the

expectations of fair play that his initial 1983 opening had provoked and transformed elections into occasions of mass mobilization against the Mexican state.

Elections in the State of Chihuahua, 1983–98

Opposition Electoral Gains

Nowhere was the regime's hold on power more threatened in
the early 1980s than in Chihuahua. Ironically, the regime itself had
opened the electoral Pandora's box. In the first few months of his
administration, President Miguel de la Madrid made the decision to
recognize local-level opposition triumphs.[31] De la Madrid's willingness stemmed partly from his program of "moral renovation,"
adopted to restore public trust in government badly shaken by the
scandals of the López Portillo years. More importantly, the decision
reflected the regime's concern that Mexico desperately needed an
electoral safety valve to dissipate the social tension generated by
the crisis.[32]

The abrupt removal of fraud, the upsurge of anti-PRI protest
voting fed by the crisis, and opposition's selection of highly popular
candidates to act as lightening rods of social resentment against the
regime led to an unprecedented series of opposition victories in
municipal elections in various regions in 1983. Between 1946 and
1979, the PAN had never won a single mayoralty in Chihuahua.
Nor had the party fared much better in the competition for the
state's ten federal deputy seats, which come up for election every
three years. In the eleven federal elections held in Chihuahua between 1946 and 1979, the PAN won just four seats by majority vote
in a period spanning more than three decades.[33] Now in 1983, the
opposition National Action Party (PAN) swept to victory in mayoral races in all of Chihuahua's main cities, including the strategic
border city of Ciudad Juárez, the state capital of Chihuahua City,
and other important urban centers like Parral, Delicias, Meoqui,
and Camargo. PAN also did exceptionally well in the elections for
the state legislature, carrying the state's five most important seats,
corresponding to Ciudad Juárez, Chihuahua City, Parral, and
Camargo. In one stroke, over 70 percent of Chihuahua's population
had fallen under PAN jurisdiction. The PAN, alone or in coalition

with various allies, also made significant gains in other parts of the country, winning the mayoralties of major state capitals like Durango, Guanajuato, San Luis Potosí, and Hermosillo.

The PAN's winning streak in Chihuahua continued in 1985, when the party won five of Chihuahua's ten federal deputy seats. Most objective analyses of the 1986 state elections indicate that the PAN would likely have won the governorship had the elections been clean. In 1988, however, the PAN won three federal deputy seats in Congress from Chihuahua. In 1992, the PAN finally captured the state house, with Chihuahua becoming only the second state since 1929 to fall under opposition control after Baja California Norte, which was taken by the PAN in 1989.

Protests against Election Fraud

Mexican elections have never been considered exemplary examples of the democratic process at work. Vote buying, biased election officials and laws, unreliable voter registration lists, slanted media coverage, and the huge financial disparity between the ruling party and opposition parties have marked Mexican elections throughout the postrevolutionary period. But fraud as such rarely became an issue, partly because the PRI was so strong that its victories were rarely questioned and partly because society was unwilling to protest against fraud. There were a few exceptions: Significant protests were lodged against election fraud in the gubernatorial elections held in Chihuahua in 1956, and allegations of fraud surfaced in the 1968 Baja California municipal elections.

By the 1980s, however, electoral fraud emerged as a major issue. The rash of opposition triumphs in 1983 stunned the Mexican political establishment. The election verdicts hammered home the dangers that holding clean elections, especially at a time of grave social distress and painful economic restructuring, posed to the PRI's grip on power. The PAN's victories also infuriated the leaders of the PRI's state, local, and sectoral organizations, particularly the CTM, who were dismayed that their handpicked candidates were not rescued by fraud from defeat. CTM leaders accused de la Madrid and his team of being inexperienced technocrats poorly skilled in the task of political management.[34] The twin fears of losing power and fracturing the party were enough to close de la Madrid's limited political opening. Electoral fraud would now become the main arbiter of Mexican elections for the remainder of de la Madrid's term.

The hardening of the government's attitude towards the opposition was clearly visible in the 1985 midterm elections. Gubernatorial elections that year in the northern states of Sonora and Nuevo León, where the PAN was considered strong, were tarnished by major irregularities, and the overwhelming victories accorded to the PRI by the official count lacked credibility. In Chihuahua, the PAN won four federal deputy seats, including one from Chihuahua City and all three belonging to Ciudad Juárez, despite the annulment of the results of a large number of voting precincts where the PAN had done well. In the seventh district, corresponding to Chihuahua City and its rural hinterland, Jorge Doroteo Zapata, a notorious labor leader, lost to the PAN's candidate but was rescued by fraud as a result of intense pressure from the CTM's national leadership. The results of precincts favoring the PAN were annulled on a grand scale, and PRI votes in rural precincts, where government control is tightest and opposition vigilance virtually nonexistent, were artificially inflated to ensure a victory for Zapata.[35]

In the 1986 state elections in Chihuahua, the PAN was widely expected not only to retain power in the municipalities that it had won in 1983 but to make history by becoming the first opposition political party to gain control of a governorship since 1929, when the state-sponsored National Revolutionary Party (PNR) came into existence. The consensus that the PAN was favored to win the gubernatorial elections stemmed from the party's impressive election victories in 1983 and 1985, the highly successful performance of the PAN mayors—whose honesty, efficiency, and responsiveness to the citizenry contrasted sharply with the preceding PRI municipal administrations—and the tremendous popularity enjoyed by the party's youthful candidate for governor, Francisco Barrio, the mayor of Ciudad Juárez.

There were, however, growing indications that the government was planning to resort to electoral fraud to guarantee that the PRI would win the elections. In September, 1985, Chihuahua's governor, Oscar Ornelas (1980–85), resigned under intense pressure from the central government. An administrator rather than a politician, Ornelas had ignored all the major factions constituting the

PRI in Chihuahua and relied instead on a team of political novices from the Autonomous University of Chihuahua (UACH), where he had served as rector. He had also maintained correct relations with the PAN mayors for the greater benefit of the population.[36] Ornelas was accused of dividing the PRI in Chihuahua, handing the state over to the PAN, and harboring PAN sympathizers in his government. Fidel Velázquez, the geriatric national leader of the CTM, declared that "there has been nothing important that can be praised in the government led by Oscar Ornelas" and demanded its dissolution.[37] Ornelas could clearly no longer be trusted to do what was necessary to assure a PRI victory in the gubernatorial elections. His fall, in the wake of an outbreak of student unrest at the UACH that was probably manipulated by the Interior Ministry, and his replacement by an old-style PRI *político* thus deeply worried the opposition.

Another troubling sign was the regime's decision in December, 1985, to modify the state electoral code, making it much easier to commit electoral fraud.[38] The new code ensured that the state election commission (CEE), which was responsible for supervising and issuing verdicts, would be dominated by government supporters. The regime was guaranteed at least 10 of 18 seats in the CEE, without taking into account the votes of three "satellite" parties that almost always supported the government. The new code also stipulated that no political party would be allowed more than one representative per voting booth or *casilla*. On the other hand, the various election commissions were permitted to nominate an unlimited number of "auxiliary" personnel on election day. The code required that party representatives be residents of the electoral section corresponding to the *casilla* to which they had been assigned and registered as such in the list of voters. This was designed to thwart opposition parties from being able to post representatives in *casillas* located in marginalized urban and rural zones, where the power of local PRI bosses was so intimidating that no resident was willing to risk becoming an opposition party representative. Finally, the new code established that only the copies of election returns in the hands of the CEE, not the copies in the hands of political parties, would determine the validity of the election results.

The government also delayed the delivery of the list of registered voters to political parties until less than three weeks before the elections scheduled for July 6, 1986.[39] This meant that the opposition would not have the time to check the accuracy of the list or verify the inclusion of the names of their *casilla* representatives, without which they could be denied access to the *casillas* on election day. Meanwhile, thousands of voter credentials were indiscriminately delivered to the PRI by the National Registry of Voters (RNE), while ordinary citizens faced long delays before receiving their credentials, and many never received them.[40]

Public school teachers were forced to pressure the parents of their students into voting for the PRI, state-controlled *campesinos*, workers, and bureaucrats were obliged to attend PRI campaign events *en masse*, the pliant electronic media completely ignored the opposition except when criticizing it, and the PRI poured a huge sum of money into the campaign of its candidate for governor, Fernando Baeza.[41] The CEE de-recognized virtually all party representatives from the small Unified Socialist Party of Mexico (PSUM), thus isolating the PAN representatives as the lone opposition in the *casillas*.[42] In a transparent maneuver to reduce voter turnout, the CEE decided to publish only a partial list of the location of the *casillas* in the local newspapers and then changed the location of a number of *casillas* at the last moment. Finally, on the morning of the elections, forged leaflets with the PAN logo were found in churches, cinemas, major streets, and plazas in Chihuahua City and Ciudad Juárez, exhorting people to abstain from voting.[43]

The elections themselves were characterized by almost every conceivable kind of irregularity from ballot box stuffing to expulsion of opposition representatives from polling stations to intimidation by soldiers, among others. [44] Fraud also occurred by manipulating the list of registered voters or *padrón*. One study reveals that Chihuahua's *padrón* grew by 7.3 percent between 1983 and 1986, while the state's population rose by only 0.92 percent.[45] The number of names in the *padrón* exceeded the estimated voting population in 53 of Chihuahua's 67 municipalities. Almost all these municipalities were located in distant rural areas, where vigilance by the opposition was extremely poor and regime control over local inhabitants tightly enforced by local bosses, *caciques*. On election day, the PRI won all 53 municipalities by huge margins in elections marked by extraordinarily high levels of citizen participation, according to official figures. In 17 of the 53 municipalities, the ones located in the isolated Tarahumara mountains, 99.6 percent of 41,000 eligible voters cast ballots; of these, 81.2 percent voted PRI. The PRI's strategy of padding the *padrón* in rural areas paid off handsomely, especially if one considers that the party won the governorship by a modest margin of 167,363 votes.

In the end, the PAN registered 920 complaints of irregularities in 500 of 1,789 *casillas* before Chihuahua's PRI-controlled Electoral College, the final court of appeal in electoral matters in the state.[46] The Electoral College chose to annul the results of only eight of the 500 *casillas* in question and, on August 8, 1986, the PRI's Fernando Baeza was ratified as the official winner of the gubernatorial election, with 395,221 votes as against 227,858 votes for the PAN's Francisco Barrio.[47] The PRI was also declared the winner of mayoral races in all the cities that the PAN had won in 1983.

While it is impossible to prove, PAN would probably have won the gubernatorial election had fraud not occurred. Baeza, while sticking to his claim that he had won the election, admitted that his victory did not have credibility.[48] Curiously, the Electoral College found that many of the irregularities claimed by the PAN did not violate state election law and could therefore not be used to annul the results of any *casillas*.[49] In other words, electoral fraud was perfectly legal.

The massive irregularities characterizing the state elections of 1986 in Chihuahua produced one of the most serious protest movements that the Mexican regime has faced in the postrevolutionary period. Business organizations, the Catholic Church, civic associations, housewives, urban marginals, workers, intellectuals, and opposition political parties of varying persuasions joined hands to condemn the electoral process as fraudulent and to fight for its annulment. At issue was not just the distribution of political power between two rival parties but the right of society to choose its rulers in free and fair elections, the very essence of democracy. Indeed, the traumatic experience of fraud turned many merely discontented citizens into committed democrats. The movement also spawned a variety of highly innovative political tactics in the Mexican context, including nonviolent civil disobedience, charging the regime with human rights violations before international forums, and new technical strategies to make fraud more difficult to commit. Finally, the exhilaration of openly challenging the regime for the first time in decades gave Chihuahuans a completely new sense of confidence and dissipated the fear by which the government had often held the citizenry in check.

The archbishop of Chihuahua announced that all church services would be suspended on Sunday, July 20, 1986, to protest against fraud. The last time the Church had suspended religious services had been in 1926, signaling the eruption of the *Cristero* war, a bloody confrontation between Catholic militants and the revolutionary state. Thus filled with ominous historical meaning, the archbishop's decision to suspend worship services generated a major crisis in Church-State relations that was defused only as a result of the direct intervention of the Vatican, which ordered the archbishop to keep the churches open so as not to imperil the existing *modus vivendi* of Church and state in Mexico.

A hunger strike lasting forty-one days was launched by Luís H. Alvarez, the PAN's mayor of Chihuahua City, Victor Manuel Oropeza, a physician of homeopathic medicine and the founder of the Mexican Workers Party (PMT) in Ciudad Juárez, and Francisco Villareal Torres, a wealthy businessman who belonged to no political party. The nonpartisan tone of the hunger strike and the willingness of the three men to risk death in their struggle for clean elections gave them enormous moral stature. Angry protesters led by Francisco Barrio seized the international bridges linking Ciudad Juárez and El Paso for days at a time. The takeovers of the international bridges ensured that the charges of electoral fraud would receive extensive coverage in the international press, thus severely damaging the regime's carefully cultivated image abroad, undermining its standing with foreign investors, and circumventing the news blockade at home.

The hunger strike and the blockade of the international bridges became focal points of Chihuahua's resistance against the election fraud and inspired other kinds of protest as well, such as consumer boycotts of businesses whose owners were PRI collaborators, plebiscites on whether the elections were fraudulent, massive rallies, silent marches, the obstruction of busy traffic intersections, and blockades of the highway linking Chihuahua to the rest of Mexico. The business community downed its shutters on multiple occasions and disrupted the local banking system by withdrawing deposits in unusually large amounts without prior notice. The Movement for

Electoral Democracy (MDE), an umbrella organization of various civic associations and opposition political parties, formed a "popular jury" to evaluate the electoral process. After documenting the irregularities tarnishing the July 6 elections, the "popular jury," consisting of eight individuals known for moral character and not linked to any political party, unanimously recommended both the abrogation of Chihuahua's election code and the annulment of the elections.

Meanwhile, on July 23, twenty-one of Mexico's most prestigious intellectuals, including Nobel laureate Octavio Paz and the poet Gabriel Zaid issued a joint declaration calling for the annulment of the elections in Chihuahua.[50] Finally, the PAN charged the Mexican government before the Inter-American Human Rights Commission (IAHRC) of the Organization of American States (OAS) with major violations of the American Convention on Human Rights, as a result of election fraud committed in the gubernatorial elections of 1986 in Chihuahua, the federal deputy elections of 1985 in Chihuahua's seventh district, and the 1986 mayoral elections for the city of Durango. On May 17, 1990, almost four years after the charges were filed, the IAHRC concluded that Mexican law offers no protection, recourse, or guarantees against acts that violate political rights and formally requested Mexico to adopt the necessary domestic legislation to "make effective the rights and liberties which the Convention recognizes."[51] The ruling was the first time that the Mexican government had been condemned for violating political rights by an official international organization.

The most intense phase of protest against the fraud spanned about two months from July 6, when the elections were held, to August 10, by which time Barrio had ended his seizure of the international bridges and the sixty-seven-year-old Alvarez his marathon hunger strike. Both men were discouraged by the decision two days earlier of Chihuahua's Electoral College to ratify Baeza as governor of Chihuahua. It was now abundantly clear that the regime was determined to cling to Chihuahua no matter the cost, and there seemed little point in continuing the fight to annul the elections.

Why did the regime refuse to annul the elections in Chihuahua, despite mounting political costs at home and abroad? The most likely explanation is that the government was afraid that a PAN victory in the gubernatorial elections in Chihuahua would have a powerful domino effect on other Mexican states, particularly in the northern region, by undermining the PRI's image of invincibility, emboldening the opposition to seek political power more aggressively, and sending a signal to voters that a ballot cast for the opposition was not a ballot wasted.

The 1988 federal elections in Chihuahua were marked by less citizen interest than the 1986 gubernatorial elections. This was to be expected since it was unlikely that society would have been able to sustain the 1986 fevered level of activity indefinitely. Both the business community and the Catholic Church also kept a lower profile than in 1986. The archbishop of Chihuahua issued only one five-page pastoral orientation regarding the forthcoming elections. Fraud, however, remained an integral part of the electoral process, though less blatantly so. Over 20 percent of the PAN's supporters were eliminated from the list of registered voters in the state. In Chihuahua City alone, 15,000 voters were unable to cast their ballots because their names did not appear in the list. The PRI also mobilized the corporatist vote with thousands of CNC and CTM-affiliated peasants and workers being bused to polling stations and obliged to vote PRI. Many voted more than once because the so-called indelible ink used to stamp their thumbs to indicate that they had already voted was easily washed off.

Yet, despite the lower level of citizen enthusiasm and the pervasiveness of fraud, the PAN still won all three federal deputy seats in Ciudad Juárez. This reflected the successful implementation of a sophisticated organizational strategy to frustrate fraud on election day by the PAN in Ciudad Juárez (see chapter 3). In Chihuahua City, where the PAN had no real organizational strategy to defend the vote, the party did not win a single federal deputy seat. The contrast between the 1988 electoral results in the two cities underlined the importance of organizational strategy for the defense of the vote.

Shifting Voter Preferences

Between 1983 and 1988, politics in Chihuahua were polarized between two diametrically opposed parties, the PRI and the PAN. The PAN acted as an instrument of society in its clash with the Mexican state, represented by the PRI. By the end of the 1980s, this pattern of polarization gave way to the emergence of a two-party system at the regional level with voter preferences shifting rapidly between the PRI and the PAN from one election to the next.

The first indication of this new pattern occurred in the 1989 municipal elections, when the PRI swept all the state's cities and won 17 of the 18 majority vote seats in the state legislature. Apart from an early attempt to manipulate the list of registered voters that was denounced by the PAN and corrected by the regime, the elections were more or less free from fraud and the results quickly accepted by the PAN. One explanation of the dramatic revival of the PRI's electoral fortunes in Chihuahua is that in 1989 the PRI in Chihuahua decided to democratize the selection of its candidates for municipal and state legislative offices and approved a new electoral code that incorporated most of the opposition's demands. A revitalized PRI in turn attracted more votes. A second explanation is that the PRI won in Chihuahua because the PAN was wracked by factionalism in both Chihuahua City and Ciudad Juárez, fielded largely unknown candidates, and made serious blunders in the campaign. These blunders ranged from denouncing electoral fraud early in the campaign, thus depressing voter turnout, to replacing the PAN's highly effective campaign strategy of simply exposing the PRI's errors with a more academic focus on the PAN's own particular solutions to major problems. A third explanation is that society in Chihuahua by 1989 was exhausted and cynical. Chihuahua's voters had after all passed through four highly charged electoral processes in six years (1983, 1985, 1986, and 1988), and the bitter experience of fraud in 1986 and 1988 had predisposed voters not to believe the government's oft-repeated promises of a fair election this time around. The result was an abysmally low voter turnout of only 30 percent of all registered voters; the vote favored the PRI since potential opposition voters stayed at home and thus could not be used to counter the PRI's usual army of captive voters.

That the 1989 municipal elections in Chihuahua marked the beginning of the emergence of a highly competitive two-party system in the state became apparent in 1992, when the PAN won the gubernatorial elections, with Francisco Barrio running as the party's candidate for the second time. In addition to winning the race for governor, the PAN also took all the major cities in the state except the capital and gained a majority of the seats in the state Congress.[52]

By contrast, the PRI in Chihuahua failed to extend its experiment in internal democracy to the gubernatorial elections and instead chose a lack-luster candidate, hand-picked by the president, who lacked the stature to win against Barrio. Interestingly, voters in Chihuahua City and the state's agricultural capital, Delicias, split their tickets by voting for the PAN's candidate for governor and the PRI's candidates for mayor.[53] The 1992 gubernatorial elections were the cleanest on record in the history of the state. The PAN audited the state's voter registration list at government expense and inaccuracies were corrected well in advance of the elections.[54] Further, the PRI's rural vote in the state fell by 12 percent relative to the gubernatorial elections of 1986, mostly because the PAN succeeded in ensuring that almost all rural precincts in the state were monitored by an opposition party representative.[55]

Two years later, in the 1994 federal elections, the PRI won all of Chihuahua's ten federal deputy seats and defeated the PAN's presidential candidate by a margin of almost 2 to 1. In the race for the Mexican Senate from Chihuahua, the former national president of the PAN, Luís H. Alvarez, went down to a humiliating defeat.[56] Some argued that the PRI's victory in Chihuahua was the result of national factors such as the anxiety provoked by the assassination of the PRI's presidential candidate, Luís Donaldo Colosio, and the rebellion in the southern state of Chiapas.[57] Others claimed that the election results signaled a rejection of the PAN's technocratic style of government and the party's unpopular policies of raising property taxes, eliminating subsidies, balancing the state budget, and refusing to engage in traditional pork-barrel politics.[58] From this perspective, the 1994 elections in Chihuahua marked a desire to return to the populist policies of the old-style PRI, even though the PRI's policies at this time were exactly the same as the PAN's. PRI leaders claimed that the party's victory reflected its success in transforming itself into a democratic alternative to the PAN; as a result of the bitter experience of losing the governor's race in 1992, the PRI became in effect an opposition party at the state level.[59]

In the municipal elections of 1995 the PRI won all the municipalities where the PAN had been in power with the exception of Ciudad Juárez, and also gained a majority in the state congress. The result was a state run by a PAN governor with the legislature and all major cities but one under the PRI. In 1997, the PAN rebounded

to win four of Chihuahua's nine federal deputy seats with the remaining five won by the PRI.[60] The 1997 elections were extremely
competitive, with the PRI winning by a margin of 8,004 votes in
the federal deputy races and the PAN by a mere 791 votes in the
race for senators.[61]

The emerging pattern of alternation between the PRI and the
PAN solidified in 1998, when the PRI recaptured the state house.
Its candidate, Patricio Martínez, very much resembled PAN candidates of the past: he came from a business background and had a
close relationship with Barrio during his tenure as mayor of Chihuahua City (1992–95). Martínez was chosen in an open primary
in which all voters were eligible to participate, an important reason
for his ultimate victory. The PAN may also have lost votes because
of a serious crime wave linked to the growth of drug trafficking, the
decline of patronage-based politics under Barrio, and perception
that the PAN's candidate, Ramón Galindo, lacked the support of
Barrio. The result was a victory for the PRI candidate, who won
49.3 percent of the vote against 41.4 percent for the PAN, a margin
of 80,160 votes.[62] Martínez won more votes than Barrio had in 1992.
The PRI retained its control over the state Congress, while the PAN
won mayoral races in three major cities—Ciudad Juárez, Cuauhtémoc, and Parral—but not Chihuahua City, which was won by the
PRI.[63]

In general, the rise of two-party politics in Chihuahua was
a positive development for democracy. Voters had a chance to
exercise greater control over whatever party happened to be in
power at the time by threatening to vote it out of office; this
improved the incentives for good government, for neither party
could afford to take the voters for granted in Chihuahua any
longer. In addition, two-party government generated a system
of checks and balances between the legislature and the executive branches, and between the state government and municipalities, that had previously existed only on paper. Further, the
rise of two-party politics reflected the transformation of the PRI
in Chihuahua into a far more democratic party than the PRI in
most other states. And finally, the level of trust between the PRI
and the PAN has grown considerably in the 1990s in Chihuahua:
neither party can govern without the other and both parties are
willing to function as a loyal opposition while the other is in

power. This is a major advance in Mexican political culture, where suspicion and an unwillingness to compromise have prevented the emergence of a democratic party system.

The Growing Competitiveness of Elections in Chihuahua

Elections in Chihuahua in the 1980s and 1990s were marked by a far greater level of competitiveness than preceding decades in both federal and state elections. Table 2.1 shows the growing competitiveness of elections in Chihuahua for the state's ten single-member federal deputy seats. Between 1961 and 1979, the average difference between the PRI and the PAN over seven successive federal deputy elections was 60 percent, but between 1982 and 1997

TABLE 2.1
Federal Deputy Elections in Chihuahua Majority Districts
(percentage of votes)

Year	PRI	PAN	Other	Margin (PRI:PAN)
1961	82	18	0	64
1964	77	22	1	55
1967	76	23	1	53
1970	84	11	2	73
1973	71	15	4	56
1976	72	8	7	64
1979	66	14	13	52
1982	64	29	7	35
1985	52	37	5	15
1988	55	38	6	17
1991	58	32	9	26
1994	60	28	12	32
1997	41	40	16	1

Sources: For data on Chihuahua elections, see Instituto Federal Electoral, *Memorias del proceso electoral federal de 1991*, tome 4, vol. 4, part 1, p. 37 (Mexico City: Instituto Federal Electoral, 1993); Silva Gomez Tagle, "Los adjetivos de la democracia en Chihuahua," *Argumentos: Estudios críticos de la sociedad* (June, 1987): p. 96; Victoria Rodríguez and Peter M. Ward, *Policy-Making, Politics, and Urban Governance in Chihuahua: The Experience of Recent PANista Governments* (Austin: U.S.-Mexican Policy Studies Program, University of Texas, 1993), p. 41; Instituto Federal Electoral, *Estadística de las elecciones federales de 1994: Compendio de resultados* (Mexico City: IFE, 1995), p. 225; and http://www.ife.org.mx/wwworge/tablas/diputhtm/disthtm/mrhtm/chihd.htm.

TABLE 2.2
Gubernatorial Elections in Chihuahua
(percentage of votes)

Year	PRI	PAN	Other	Margin (PRI:PAN)
1968	74	25	1	49
1974	96	0[a]	1	96
1980	70	14	7	56
1986	59	35	4	24
1992	45[b]	51	4	-6
1998	49	41	5	8

a. Note that the PAN did not participate in the 1974 gubernatorial elections.
b. PRI and allies.

Sources: Alberto Aziz Nassif, Chihuahua: Historia de una alternativa (Mexico City: Ediciones La Jornada, 1994), p. 144; Silva Gomez Tagle, "Los adjetivos de la democracia en Chihuahua," Argumentos: Estudios críticos de la sociedad (June, 1987); and http://www.pan.org.mx for 1998 data.

TABLE 2.3
Municipal Election Results in Chihuahua
(total percentage of votes in municipal elections)

Year	PRI	PAN	Other	Margin (PRI:PAN)
1965	89	7	4	82
1968	74	25	1	49
1971	n.a.	n.a.	n.a.	n.a.
1974	91	3	3	88
1977	85	5	4	80
1980	77	15	8	62
1983	48	45	6	3
1986	58	35	4	23
1989	60	33	1	27
1992	46	46	5	0
1995	48	41	5	7
1998	43	41	10	2

Sources: Alberto Aziz Nassif, Chihuahua: Historia de una alternativa (Mexico City: Ediciones La Jornada, 1994), p. 118; Silva Gomez Tagle, "Los adjetivos de la democracia en Chihuahua," Argumentos: Estudios críticos de la sociedad (June, 1987), p. 97; and Victor Orozco, "Los resultados electorales: Posibles tendencias objectivas," Cuadernos del Norte, no.3 (December, 1992): p. 32; Diario de Juárez, "Proclama Triufo Patricio" (July 6, 1998); and http://www.pan.org.mx for 1998 data.

this difference fell to only 21 percent. The same trend towards increasing competitiveness holds even more strongly in gubernatorial elections, with the margin of victory between the two largest parties shrinking from 49 percent in favor of the PRI in 1968 to just 6 percent in favor of the PAN in 1992 and 8 percent in favor of the PRI in 1998 (Table 2.2). In the four gubernatorial elections held between 1968 and 1982, the margin of victory of the largest party over its nearest rival averaged 67 percent but in the three gubernatorial contests in 1986, 1992 and 1998 this margin fell to an average of barely 13 percent. With regard to municipal elections held in Chihuahua between 1965 and 1980 at intervals of three years, the PRI won by an average margin of 72 percent over the PAN (Table 2.3).[64] On the other hand, between 1983 and 1998, the average difference between the PRI's and the PAN's relative share of the total vote in the six municipal elections held during that period fell to only 10 percent. The 1980s and 1990s in Chihuahua were thus marked by a major jump in the competitiveness of all types of electoral contests—municipal, gubernatorial, and federal.

National Elections, 1988, 1994, and 1997

In 1988, the political awakening of Mexican society, which until then had been largely limited to northern states, became a national phenomenon. In 1988, the PRI faced the most serious electoral challenge to its monopoly on the presidency in the party's history. The presidential elections pitted the PRI's Carlos Salinas de Gortari against the PAN's Manuel Clouthier, an ex-president of Mexico's Business Coordinating Council (CCE), and Cuauhtémoc Cárdenas, the son of Lazaro Cárdenas, who broke with the PRI to launch his own candidacy for the presidency under the banner of the National Democratic Front (FDN), a hastily cobbled coalition of various leftist forces. Cárdenas's decision to leave the PRI resulted from his unhappiness with the economic policies of de la Madrid; the refusal of the PRI's leadership to heed the demands of the Democratic Current (led by Cárdenas himself and former PRI president Porfirio Muñoz Ledo) that the PRI's internal procedures for selecting the party's presidential nominee be democratized; and the unprecedented level of voter discontent with the regime after almost a decade of social and economic decay.[65]

Both opposition presidential campaigns, particularly that of Cárdenas, acquired tremendous momentum among ordinary citizens throughout the country. In the end, Salinas was declared the official winner of the presidential election with only 48.8 percent of the votes cast, which was by far the party's worst showing in a presidential election, representing a more than twenty point erosion in the PRI's share of the presidential vote compared to 1982. Cárdenas did exceptionally well, receiving 29.9 percent of the national vote, defeating Salinas in four states (Morelos, Michoacán, Mexico State, and Baja California Norte), and carrying Mexico City by a margin of four to one. The *cardenista* coalition also elected four senators, thus ending the PRI's long-standing monopoly over the Senate. Clouthier came in third place with 17 percent of the vote, but the PAN's 101 federal deputies made it the largest single opposition party in the Chamber of Deputies. The parties supporting Cárdenas won 139 federal deputy seats. The fact that the PRI won only 261 of the 500 seats in the new Chamber meant that it would no longer have a two-thirds majority to amend the constitution on its own. For the first time, the PRI would have to open negotiations with the opposition if a constitutional path were to be cleared for the new government's policy initiatives, especially in the sensitive areas of electoral reform and the privatization of industries constitutionally limited to state participation only. The major gains registered by the opposition in Congress ensured that for the first time since the presidency of the murdered father of the Mexican revolution, Francisco Madero (1911–13), Congress would not function as a supine instrument of executive power.

The 1988 election was thus nothing short of a "political earthquake" for the PRI. Together, Clouthier and Cárdenas won an unprecedented 48 percent of the presidential vote, and it is likely that the opposition presidential candidates did better than the official count indicated. Indeed, the Federal Election Commission's decision to delay issuing election results until six days after the election—which officials lamely ascribed to computer crashes, heavy voter turnout, and even "atmospheric conditions"—and the refusal of the PRI-controlled Electoral College to release individual tallies for the presidential vote from 24,647 of the 54,646 voting precincts pointed to fraud of major proportions. There was also considerable concern over the 1,762 "Soviet-style" precincts in which Salinas won with 100 percent of the vote; most of these precincts were located in remote areas where opposition parties found it difficult to post a representative to monitor the voting on election day.[66] The PRI did best in the countryside but lost by large margins in Mexico City and other major cities. The PRI won by large margins in the rural southern portion of the country, including some of the areas now controlled by the Emiliano Zapata National Liberation Army (EZLN) in the state of Chiapas, indicating that a significant measure of the PRI's rural support in 1988 was the product of old-fashioned mobilization strategies by the party's official unions and not a voluntary act by individual citizens. Six years later, in 1994, the director of the Federal Election Institute disclosed that the Interior Ministry had decided to suspend the count in 1988 because of the panic caused by early urban returns that indicated that Cárdenas was winning the presidential race.

While the PAN argued that no candidate could in good conscience claim victory, the party did join hands with Cárdenas in protesting election irregularities. Shortly after the polls closed on July 6, Clouthier, Cárdenas, and Rosario Ibarra de Piedra, the presidential candidate of the miniscule Revolutionary Workers Party (PRT), strongly condemned the irregularities marring the voting process and accused the regime of attempting to impose its own candidate at the expense of the will of the electorate. The three opposition candidates declared that if the government did not move to reestablish the "legality of the electoral process in an unequivocal fashion," they would refuse to accept the election results or recognize the new fraudulently elected authorities; the opposition candidates would take steps to defend the right to a clean election using constitutional weapons.[67] That same evening, with the vote count already suspended because of supposed computer failure, Cárdenas, Clouthier, and Ibarra, arriving at the Interior Ministry amid loud cheers from spectators, personally delivered their "Call to Legality" to Interior Secretary Manuel Bartlett.[68]

The protests had no affect on the outcome of the presidential election and the PRI's candidate, Carlos Salinas, was declared the official winner. PAN's Clouthier insisted on the basis of postelection surveys of voter choices that he had been cheated of 2.6 million votes fraudulently credited to Salinas.[69] The same surveys also led Clouthier to claim that he, not Cárdenas, had been the main victim of fraud.[70] According to a PAN-commissioned survey of 14,000 Mexicans, Salinas won the election by a small plurality of 34–35 percent followed by Cárdenas in second place with 31–32 percent, and Clouthier with 29–31 percent.[71] The PAN further claimed, however, that it was impossible to know who had won the election because of the massive fraud that had occurred. Cárdenas insisted that he had won the election with a plurality of 41–42 percent.

Neither Cárdenas nor Clouthier was willing to recognize the legitimacy of the new president, but the PAN later issued a statement acknowledging Salinas's de facto legitimacy and pledged to work with him for democracy. The process of ratifying the presidential results in Congress was marked by blows between PRI and *cardenista* members and talk of ungovernability, while the official inauguration of the new president was repeatedly interrupted by opposition deputies' shouts of fraud that were broadcast live on television to millions of Mexicans.

The trend towards more competitive presidential elections continued in 1994, when the PRI's Ernesto Zedillo faced two strong challenges from the PAN's Diego Fernández de Cevallos and the PRD's Cárdenas. The PRD, Democratic Revolutionary Party, formed in 1989 as the successor of the FDN, consisted of Cárdenas's own breakaway group from the PRI, independent leftist parties such as the Mexican Socialist Party (PMS), and representatives of left-wing social movements. Missing from the PRD were the former state-oriented parties that had supported Cárdenas in 1988 but returned to the PRI fold in 1994, including the Authentic Party of the Mexican Revolution (PARM), the Popular Socialist Party (PPS), and the Frente Cardenista de Reconstrucción Nacional. According to the official count, Zedillo won 48 percent of all valid votes cast while the PAN received 26 percent and the PRD 17 percent. Together the opposition won 43 percent of the vote, giving Zedillo only a 5 percent margin of victory. Under a new election law, the opposition presence in the Senate expanded to include 36 seats, 24 for the PAN and 8 for the PRD, with the remaining 96 seats going to the PRI.[72] In the Federal Chamber of Deputies, the PRI received 300 seats as compared to 119 for the PAN, 71 for the PRD, and 10 for the new Workers Party (PT). The PRI's share of seats in Congress thus declined slightly from 64 percent in the federal elections of 1991 to 59.6 percent in 1994; correspondingly, the PAN's share rose from 17.8 percent in 1991 to 23.6 percent in 1994, and the PRD rose from 8.2 percent in 1991 to 14 percent in 1994.[73]

Participation increased significantly in federal elections between 1988 and 1994. The presidential elections of 1994 were marked by a tremendously high voter turnout (77.7%) relative to 65.4 percent in 1991 and 50 percent in 1988. In certain states marked by tight competition between the opposition and the PRI—in Jalisco, for example—voter turnout crossed the 80 percent mark. Even though official figures on participation rates in federal elections prior to 1988 are not reliable because the government systematically inflated voter turnout to strengthen the PRI's legitimacy, the voter turnout of almost 78 percent in 1994 was the highest recorded for presidential elections held between 1917 and 1994. Further, there was no evidence that turnout was artificially boosted by padding the voter registration list with nonexistent voters in areas where the PRI was strong.

What explains this high turnout? The outbreak of the Chiapas rebellion on New Year's Day of 1994 and the subsequent assassination of the PRI's presidential candidate may have led to a massive turnout in order to preserve the country's stability at a critical moment. Also, the perception among voters that the opposition could win in 1994 may have contributed to the higher rate of participation. This perception intensified greatly after the PAN's Diego Fernández de Cevallos outperformed both Zedillo and Cárdenas in the May 16, 1995, debate, the first televised debate among rival presidential candidates to occur in the history of Mexican elections; so strong was Diego Fernández's performance that the PRI refused to hold a second debate closer to the elections. Finally, the higher turnout may have reflected the growing credibility of the electoral process in the wake of the adoption of new reforms, including the development of a more accurate voter registration list, a new fraud-resistant voter identification card, a dilution of government control over the Federal Elections Institute, an expanded role for domestic observers, and the unprecedented decision to invite foreign observers to view the elections (see chapter 6).

As a result of these reforms, the 1994 presidential elections were probably the cleanest on record in the history of Mexico. The PAN, which had been relegated to third place by Cárdenas in the 1988 presidential elections, now moved back into second place with nine million votes, the best performance in the party's history at the national level. While both opposition parties have a core of committed supporters, the ease with which voters shifted preferences from the PRD to the PAN in 1994 indicates that a significant portion of PAN support came from voters looking for the most credible option to oppose the PRI. Strategic voters who had gravitated to Cárdenas in 1988 now favored the PAN. The 1994 federal elections thus confirmed the impression of a volatile electorate with a large proportion of floating independent voters. In the states governed by the PAN—Chihuahua, Baja California Norte, and Guanajuato— the PRI won the presidential elections by margins of more than 2 to 1.[74] The fact of rapidly shifting voter preferences between opposition parties and between opposition parties and the ruling party means that it will be increasingly difficult to predict the winner of an election with any certainty. The institutionalization of uncertainty in Mexican elections is an important step towards the achievement of democracy in a system where, historically, opposition parties had been perceived as incapable of winning, or even garnering a respectable percentage of votes.

One of the most important innovations characterizing the 1994 elections was the use of quick counts by a variety of organizations to provide fast and accurate results on election night. Quick counts, which involve predicting the results of voting from a small, representative sample of the country's 88,000 precincts, were conducted by the Civic Alliance with assistance from the National Democratic Institute (NDI), the Mexican Employers' Confederation (COPARMEX), the Federal Election Institute, Televisión Azteca, the opposition-leaning newspaper *Reforma / El Norte*, and the *Washington Post*, among others.[75] All these quick counts came close to mirroring the official results of the presidential elections, with the exception of the PRD's own quick count, which showed Cárdenas as the winner. The use of quick counts made it impossible for the regime to delay the counting of votes, as in 1988, and strengthened the credibility of the election outcome. In addition, virtually all the opinion surveys commissioned in the last month prior to the elections came within a few percentage points of predicting the final outcome.[76] This contradicted the assumption that voters would not reveal their preferences to poll takers because of the fear of retribution and the low level of social trust.

The crucial role played by domestic observers in the 1994 elections provided fresh evidence for the development of a more participatory political culture in Mexico. Over 89,000 Mexicans signed up to participate in the process of monitoring the presidential elections throughout the country. In addition, over 1,000 foreigners were officially accredited as international visitors to observe the elections. The sheer number of observers was without precedent in Mexican history and paralleled the massive effort mounted by the National Movement for Free Elections (NAMFREL) in the Philippines in 1986 that led to the downfall of the dictator Ferdinand Marcos.

The national scope of the political awakening of society was underscored by the 1997 midterm elections.[77] The opposition was helped both by bold electoral reforms passed in 1996, which provided for the election of the mayor of Mexico City and virtually eliminated the chances of fraud in federal elections, and by the impact of Mexico's latest economic crisis, which erupted in the wake of the December 1994 devaluation of the *peso* by the incoming Zedillo administration. For the first time in history, the opposition won a majority in the Chamber of Deputies. The PRI received only 239 seats in the lower house with 39.1 percent of the vote, while the PAN won 122 seats with 26.6 percent and the PRD won 125 seats with 25.7 percent. In Mexico City, the PRD, fielding Cárdenas as its candidate, handily won the governor's race with 47.1 percent of the vote compared to 25.1 percent for the PRI and 15.3 percent for the PAN. The PAN, however, won two important governorships: the northern industrial state of Nuevo León and Querétaro. As in 1994, quick counts and almost all opinion surveys commissioned in the last month before the elections proved to be accurate predictors of the final results. The presence of observers was, however, lower than 1994. Rather than showing a decline in politicization, this reflected the greater credibility of the 1997 process, the ability of political parties to monitor elections themselves, and the fact that midterm elections tend to attract less attention. The 1997 elections were an important watershed in Mexican democratization that produced a far more assertive Congress, more autonomy for Mexico's regions, and a significant weakening of the hold of Mexican presidentialism.

Data for federal elections in the 1980s and 1990s reveal trends towards greater electoral competitiveness, major electoral gains by

TABLE 2.4
Patterns of Electoral Competition,
Federal Chamber of Deputies, 1964–1994
(percentage of 300 single-member electoral districts)

Year[a]	Type of Competition					
	PRI Monopoly	Strong PRI Hegemony	Weak PRI Hegemony	Two-Party Competition	Multi-Party Competition	Opposition Victory
1964	28.1	52.2	4.5	14.0	—	1.1
1967	24.2	61.2	3.6	9.7	—	1.2
1970	27.0	53.9	1.7	17.4	—	—
1973	18.7	51.3	4.1	21.8	1.0	3.1
1976	35.8	44.6	6.7	11.9	0.5	0.5
1979	9.4	48.0	12.3	6.3	22.7	1.3
1982	1.3	51.7	6.3	26.1	14.0	0.3
1985	3.3	41.7	9.6	21.0	21.3	3.7
1988	1.0	19.0	15.0	8.3	34.0	22.7
1991	0	32.3	16.0	31.7	17.0	3.3
1994	0	11.7	32.3	25.0	31.0	

a. Figures for 1991 have been calculated by the author using the same the criteria followed by Bailey and Gomez (see source note, below) for 1964–88, with only slight modification. Figures for 1994 are derived from from Gaudalupe Pachecho Méndez,"1994: Hacia un realineamiento electoral"(see source note). Note that her data were obtained by a different procedure, the Molinar index, from the one used by Bailey and Gomez; in addition, Pacheco subsumes districts where the opposition won under her biparty and multiparty headings; opposition parties won in 27 districts or 9 percent of all seats.

Sources: Leopoldo Gómez and John Bailey, "La transición política y los dilemas del PRI," Foro Internacional 31,1 (July–September, 1990): p. 69; Instituto Federal Electoral, Memorias del proceso electoral federal de 1991: Resultados de la eleccion de diputados federales de mayoria relativa, tome 4, vol. 4, part 1a (Mexico City: Instituto Federal Electoral, 1993); Instituto Federal Electoral, Memorias del proceso electoral federal de 1991: Resultados de la eleccion de diputados federales de mayoria relativa, tome 4, vol. 4, part 2a; and Guadalupe Pacheco Méndez, "1994: Hacia un realineamiento electoral," in Germán Pérez Fernández del Castillo et al., La voz de los votos: Un analisis crítico de las elecciones de 1994 (Mexico City: Miguel Angel Porrua, 1995), p. 227.

higher opposition parties, and higher rates of voter participation. As the first three columns of Table 2.4 show, the proportion of the country's 300 single-member federal deputy districts dominated by the PRI fell from 85 percent in 1964 to an all-time low of 35 percent in 1988; the PRI recovered slightly in 1991, when it dominated 48 percent of the districts, but lost ground again in 1994, when it remained dominant in only 44 percent of all districts. At the same time, the number of competitive districts marked by two-party, three-party, or opposition dominance (the last three columns of Table 2.4) climbed from just 14 percent in 1964 to 65 percent in 1988, 52 percent in 1991, and 56 percent in 1994.

More recent data using a different index to measure competitiveness reveal much the same conclusion. As Table 2.5 clearly shows, the number of districts marked by one-party dominance fell dramatically from 242 in 1979 to 25 in 1997, while the number of

TABLE 2.5
Electoral Competition in Midterm Congressional Elections, 1979–97 (number of single-member federal electoral districts by pattern of party competition)

Pattern of Competition	Year			
NP Index[a]	1979	1985	1991	1997
Tripartite (NP > 2.5)	0	3	1	56
Two-party+ (2.0–2.5)	5	27	20	112
Pure two-party (1.5–2.0)	53	71	92	107
One party hegemonic (1.0–1.5)	242	199	187	25
Total	300	300	300	300

a. This classification procedure is suggested by Guadalupe Pacheco Mendez, "Un caleidoscopio electoral: Ciudades y elecciones en Mexico, 1988–1994," *Estudios Sociologicos* 15, no. 44, pp. 319–50. Tripartite districts are marked by effective three-party competition; two-party+ districts are marked by competition between two parties joined by a weaker third; in pure two-party districts, competition is restricted to two dominant parties; and in hegemonic districts, one party dominates. The number of competitive parties (the NP index) uses a measure developed by Juan Molinar Horcasitas, "Counting the Number of Parties: An Alternative Index," *American Political Science Review* 85, no. 4 (December 1991): pp. 1383–92.

Source: Wayne A. Cornelius, *Mexican Politics in Transition*, 5th edition (La Jolla, Calif.: Center for U.S.-Mexican Studies, University of California, San Diego, 2000). Modified from Joseph L. Klesner, "Electoral Politics and Mexico's New Party System," paper presented at the 21st international congress of the Latin American Studies Association, Chicago, Ill., September 24–26, 1998, table 2.

pure two party districts doubled from 53 to 107 in the same period. Clearly mirroring the rise of the PRD as an important player in Mexican politics, the number of tripartite districts marked by three party competition increased from zero in 1979 to 56 in 1997; the number of districts characterized by two-party competition with a significant third force also increased dramatically from 5 to 112 in the same period.

TABLE 2.6
Voting in Presidential Elections, 1934–1994
(percentage of votes)

Year	Votes for PRI Candidate[a]	Votes for Second Place	Votes for Third Place	Margin of Victory[b]	Voter Turnout[c]
1934	98.2	1.1	0.7	96.4	53.6
1940	93.9	5.7[d]	0.4	87.8	57.5
1946	77.9	19.3[d]	1.5	57.1	42.6
1952	74.3	15.9[d]	7.8 (PAN)	50.6	57.9
1958	90.4	9.4 (PAN)	—	81.0	49.4
1964	87.8	11.0 (PAN)	—	76.8	54.1
1970	83.3	13.9 (PAN)	—	69.4	61.7
1976[e]	87.9	3.7 (PPS)	3.1 (PARM)	81.1	64.5
1982	68.4	15.7 (PAN)	3.5	49.2	66.1
1988	48.9	29.9 (FDN)[d]	16.2 (PAN)	2.8	50.0
1994	48.8	25.9 (PAN)	16.6 (PRD)	6.3	77.7

a. PRI and other votes are calculated as a percentage of all votes cast including annulled ones.
b. The margin of victory is the PRI candidate's votes minus the sum of the votes of the second and third place candidates.
c. Turnout for 1934 to 1982 is based on those eligible to vote; for 1988, and 1994, it is based on those registered to vote.
d. In the presidential races of 1940, 1946, and 1952, the official party's candidate faced challenges by breakaway candidates from its own ranks including General Adreu Almazán in 1940 with 5.7% of the vote, Enrique Padilla in 1946 with 19.3% of the vote, and Miguel Henríquez in 1952 with 15.9% of the vote. In 1988, breakaway candidate Cuauhtémoc Cárdenas won almost 30% of the vote.
e. In 1976, the PAN abstained from participating in the presidential race; the second and third places went to two small parties normally allied with the PRI, the Popular Socialist Party (PPS) and the Authentic Revolutionary Party (PARM).

Sources: Juan Molinar Horcasitas, *El tiempo de legitimidad: Elecciones, autoritarismo, y democracia en México* (Mexico City: Cal y Arena, 1991), p. 226; Jennifer McCoy, "The Meaning of the Mexican Elections," *Hemisphere* (November, 1994); Pablo González Casanova, *Democracy in Mexico* (New York: Oxford University Press, 1970), pp. 199 and 221; Rogelio Ramos Oranday, "Oposición y abstencionismo en las elecciones presidentiales, 1964–1982," in Pablo González Casanova, *Las elecciones en México: Evolución y perspectivas* (Mexico: Siglo Veintiuno Editores, 1985), pp. 174–94; and Miguel Angel Granados Chapa et al., "Las elecciones de 1982," in González Casanova, *Las elecciones en México*, pp. 202–4.

With regard to presidential elections held between 1934 and 1994, the official party's share of votes tumbled from 98.2 percent in 1934 to 48.8 percent in 1994, and its margin of victory over the combined votes of the candidates in second and third places shrank from 96.4 percent in 1936 to 2.8 percent in 1988 and 6.3 percent in 1994 (Table 2.6). Between 1934 and 1982, the official party obtained an average of 85 percent of all votes and a margin of victory that averaged 73 percent. In the 1952 presidential election, the most competitive of the eight held between 1934 and 1976, the PRI candidate still won an overwhelming 74 percent of the vote and a handsome margin of 51 percent over his two main rivals, Miguel Henríquez, a PRI dissident, and Efraín González Luna, the PAN's first presidential candidate. In the presidential elections held in 1988 and 1994, however, the PRI's average share of votes declined sharply to 49 percent, one percentage point short of a majority in both cases, while its margin of victory over the country's two main opposition parties fell to a wafer thin 4.6 percent.

Another index of the political awakening of society in the 1980s and the 1990s was the dramatic influx of new members into opposition political parties and civic associations, although accurate figures are not easy to come by because many organizations are secretive about their membership and members are sometimes reluctant to disclose their affiliations for fear of retaliation. As Table 2.7 shows, the PAN's active national membership rose from 49,300 in 1988 to 130,200 in December, 1993, and leveled off at 127,000 by the end of the century. Membership growth figures for the PRD are harder

TABLE 2.7
Active Members of the PAN

Year	Members
1988	49,300
1989	59,600
1990	73,900
1991	77,300
1992	102,700
1993 (December)	130,200
1999	127,000

Source: National Action Party, Research Secretariat, Basic Information about the Party (Mexico City: January, 1994); data for 1999 from http://www.pan.org.mx.

to obtain because the party came into existence only in 1989 and the party is far less organized than the PAN; however, the PRD was able to fulfill the minimum requirement of 65,000 members to obtain legal recognition as a political party in 1989 by merging with the Mexican Socialist Party (PMS) and taking over its registry.[78]

Most of the important civic associations dedicated to promoting democracy, such as the Civic Alliance, the Convergence of Civil Organizations for Democracy, the Citizens' Movement for Democracy, the Higher Institute for Democratic Culture, and the Mexican Human Rights Academy, were all formed in the 1980s and 1990s and thus, by definition, experienced membership growth relative to the 1960s and 1970s. By the time of the presidential elections of August, 1994, Mexican civic organizations had a sufficiently large membership to blanket the country with 89,000 observers on election day. The most important domestic monitoring group, the Civic Alliance, which was formed in January, 1994, as an umbrella organization of hundreds of smaller groups, was alone able to field 11,000 observers by July, 1994.

Regional Elections, 1988–98

At the state and local levels, opposition parties advanced significantly during the Salinas administration. The government's decision to recognize the PAN's victory in Baja California (1989) marked the first time since the foundation of an official party in 1929 that an opposition party had been allowed to take the reigns of power in any of Mexico's thirty-one states.

Meanwhile, the PRD won 52 of 113 municipal presidencies in 1989 in its stronghold of the state of Michoacán, including the three most important cities of the state, Morelia, Pátzcuaro, and the industrial city of Lázaro Cárdenas; the PRD also won 7 of the 18 seats in the state congress.[79] In addition, seven municipalities were eventually subjected to an unwieldy formula of "co-government" by both the PRI and the PRD after prolonged protests against fraud by PRD militants, who were often ordinary peasants. In the 1988 presidential elections, Cuauhtémoc Cárdenas had swept Michoacán, his home state, defeating Carlos Salinas by a large margin, and his National Democratic Front had also won two Senate seats from the state. Prior to the 1988 federal elections, Michoacán had been dominated by the PRI although the PAN had occasionally been able to mount localized challenges to the official party there.[80] By 1991, however, the PRD's support in the state seemed to ebb somewhat and the PRI won all seven federal deputy seats in dispute that year as well as one Senate seat. Then in 1992, the PRI claimed to have won the gubernatorial race in the state by a margin of 59 to 41 percent and took office amid charges of fraud from the PRD, which claimed that it had won the election by a margin of 53 to 47 percent.[81] The PRD claimed that the voter registration list had been inflated in areas where the government could manipulate the vote, such as distant rural areas, and shaved in urban areas such as Morelia, where the PRI was likely to fare poorly.[82] In addition, the PRD claimed that the PRI had spent approximately $50 million on the gubernatorial race as compared to $5 million for the PRD.[83] However, an international team sent by the Council of Freely Elected Heads of Government, based at the Carter Center of Emory University, to witness the work of domestic observer groups in the states of Michoacán and Chihuahua in 1992 disagreed with the PRD's assertion that the conditions prevailing in Michoacán did not permit a free and fair election. The delegation concluded that the voter registration list had an error rate of only 10.7 percent, which was normal for a state like Michoacán, which has high rates of migration, and far below the error rate of 30–37 percent alleged by the PRD.[84] The PRD itself never presented hard evidence to back up its claim of fraud and chose instead to rely on the general lack of credibility of Mexican elections to mobilize public support. The state, however, was so destabilized by the protests against fraud that the Salinas administration forced the new governor to resign and replaced him with a more acceptable PRI leader.

The government's handling of the 1992 state elections in Michoacán replicated a pattern that had developed in 1991 during the gubernatorial elections in the central Mexican states of Guanajuato and San Luis Potosí in which the president would intervene to countermand the results of state elections after prolonged protests against fraud (see chapter 6).[85]

The same pattern obtained in the southern state of Yucatán, where the PAN also did extremely well. In the municipal elections of November, 1991, the PAN managed to wrest all the major cities of the state, including the state capital Mérida, from the PRI despite a climate of fraud and intimidation. Traditionally, the state had been almost entirely dominated by the PRI. The PAN had last won in Mérida in 1967, mostly because of internal divisions in the PRI, and had succeeded in winning only two federal deputy seats from Yucatán between 1946 and 1979.[86] Like Chihuahua, Yucatán possessed a long tradition of hostility towards the central government revolving around its Mayan heritage.[87] In addition, the influx of foreign tourism and the growth of foreign investment has exposed the population to ideas of democracy and created a thriving middle class relatively independent of the Mexican state. In the state elections of November, 1993, the PRI initially claimed to have won both the mayoralty of Yucatán and the governorship, even though the elections were widely believed to have been marred by fraud. One graphic instance was the power blackout that interrupted the vote count in Mérida during which some men made off with ballot boxes. Independent citizens groups, who monitored about 20 percent of the state's polling stations, reported irregularities in more than half of them.[88] A quick count of a representative sample of polling stations conducted by the citizen observer groups showed that the PRI had won the governorship by a margin of 57 percent to the PAN's 38.8 percent but that the PAN had carried the city of Mérida by a margin of 50.46 percent to the PRI's 47.18 percent.[89] The PAN demanded fresh elections and threatened to call for a nationwide civil disobedience movement. After a series of protests including a hunger strike in Yucatán, the federal government intervened to let the PAN take office in Mérida but insisted on allowing the PRI to retain the governorship. The PAN, in turn, suspended its campaign of civil disobedience. What was troubling about this pattern of countermanding disputed election results was that the final outcome of state elections became contingent less on the results of the ballot box than on protests in the streets, backroom negotiations between the ruling party and the opposition, and the direct intervention of the president.

The PRD claimed that the PRI was guilty of practicing "selective democracy," favoring the recognition of PAN triumphs rather than PRD wins because of the PRI's ideological affinity with the PAN, which the PRI believed was no longer a real threat to the system. In fact, the willingness of the Salinas administration to recognize opposition triumphs, particularly those of the PAN, stemmed from a variety of factors. First, the PAN was in a position to destabilize the states in which it was strong: in other words, electoral imposition by fraud was certain to be met with resistance by the local population. Second, the regime was unwilling to let such resistance sully its image in the United States at a time when Congress was considering NAFTA. Messy protests against fraud, particularly in strategic border states like Chihuahua and Baja California Norte, would have given ammunition to congressional critics of NAFTA such as Senator Ernest Hollings (R-SC) who argued that the lack of democracy in Mexico made it an unworthy candidate for free trade. Third, PAN leaders made concerted efforts to reassure the regime that PAN rule in the two states would not disrupt center-state relations. Finally, the decision of the government to recognize the PAN's victory in the gubernatorial race of Baja California in 1989 also made it easier to recognize an opposition victory in Chihuahua since a precedent had already been set.

In Chihuahua and Baja California, the mere possibility of protest was itself sufficient to induce the government to accept opposition victories. In San Luis Potosí, Guanajuato, Michoacán, and Yucatán, a significant level of social protest had to be kindled before the government was willing to consider negotiating a solution with the opposition. In the absence of domestic protests against fraud, it is highly unlikely that the international community would have pressured Mexico to recognize opposition victories for which the opposition itself was not willing to fight. On the other hand, there is little question that Mexico's heightened vulnerability to international pressure increased the incentives of domestic groups to engage in high-profile protests against fraud to attract media and congressional attention in the United States—and encouraged the Mexican government to preempt such protests by recognizing opposition victories.

The PRI's victory in the presidential elections of 1994 did not mark a reversal of the tendency towards opposition gains at the state level. In the elections for mayor of Monterrey, Mexico's most important financial and industrial center, the local electoral commission overturned the PRI's victory by annulling the results of 42 precincts where the PAN alleged serious irregularities had occurred.

The PAN's candidate was allowed to take office, marking the first time that Monterrey would be governed by an opposition party. In February, 1995, the PAN swept to victory in the gubernatorial elections in the important industrial state of Jalisco, located in the west central portion of the country. The PAN won the governorship of Jalisco by a wide margin of 52.71 percent to the PRI's 37.09 percent, with voter turnout reaching 70 percent.[90] The PAN also won 54 of the state's 124 municipal governments, including the mayoralty of Guadalajara, the capital of Jalisco and the country's second largest city. In addition, the PAN won an outright majority in the state legislature, with 24 deputies, while the PRI received 12 seats and the PRD just one.

These events reversed a long tradition of PRI rule. Between 1946 and 1976, Jalisco was dominated entirely by the PRI; during this period the PAN managed to win the mayoralty of only one minor municipality, El Grullo, in 1946.[91] The PAN did better in the federal deputy elections held in Jalisco during the same period electing one federal deputy by majority vote in 1949, 1952, 1964, and 1967; three in 1970; and two in 1973.[92] All these victories were concentrated in metropolitan Guadalajara, which contains 10 of Jalisco's 20 single-member federal deputy districts. The 1988 federal elections represented a quantum leap for the PAN when the party swept 8 of the 10 single-member federal deputy districts in metropolitan Guadalajara. In the 1991 federal deputy elections, the PRI rebounded to win all 20 single-member districts in the state.[93]

The assassination in 1993 of the cardinal of Guadalajara, Juan José Jesús de Posadas, in a mysterious shoot-out at the airport, the emergence of drug-traffickers as a potent force in Jalisco, and a tragic gas explosion that killed hundreds of people set the stage for the PAN's tumultuous victory in 1995 in a state where voters were for the moment alienated from the regime. Despite these setbacks, the PRI's Zedillo carried the state in the 1994 presidential elections by a margin of only 2 percent over the PAN's Fernández de Cevallos.[94] In effect, Jalisco by the mid-1990s had achieved the transition to a two-party system, with voter preferences shifting naturally in response to changing political and economic conditions and no longer subject to artificial manipulation by the PRI's political machine.

In May, 1995, the PAN won the governor's race in the central state of Guanajuato by a wide margin of 58.1 percent to 32.9 percent for the PRI and only 7 percent for the PRD.[95] This marked the first gubernatorial election in Mexico to be held under the supervision of an opposition government. The elections were conducted impeccably under a new election code adopted by the interim PAN government.

The election in Guanajuato contrasted sharply with the results of the gubernatorial elections in Yucatán held at the same time. In Yucatán, the PRI's candidate Victor Cervera Pacheco, a former cabinet minister and leader of the PRI's hard-line faction in Yucatán, claimed to have won the governor's race by a narrow margin of 49.4 percent to the PAN's 43.8 percent.[96] According to the PAN and independent civic associations, the elections were marred by irregularities so serious that they not only threatened to launch a campaign of civil disobedience but asked for the intervention of the OAS.[97] The problems in Yucatán highlighted the danger that well-entrenched local bosses allied to the PRI can pose to the democratization process. Indeed, the Zedillo administration seemed powerless to prevent the irregularities that occurred in Yucatán and proved unwilling to risk chaos in the state and internal divisions in the ruling party by overturning Cervera's questionable victory.

Much the same pattern can be discerned in the southern state Tabasco, a major oil-producing zone since the late 1970s. Historically known for its ferocious anticlericalism during the Mexican revolution, Tabasco had always been very much under the control of the PRI until 1988 when Cárdenas picked up 20 percent of the vote despite a weak campaign by the FDN.[98] The gubernatorial elections held in Tabasco six months later in November, 1988, which were won by the PRI, were marked by extremely serious irregularities and the FDN candidate's call for the elections' annulment went unheeded.[99] In the gubernatorial elections held in November, 1994, the PRD once again claimed that the elections had been fraudulent and launched a series of protests to persuade the federal government to intervene. PRD officials delivered 16 stackloads of receipts, ledgers, and financial reports leaked from PRI headquarters in Tabasco to federal election officials in Mexico City that showed that the PRI had spent U.S. $70 million to win a gubernatorial election in which only 500,000 people had voted.[100] This marked the first time in

Mexican history that an opposition party had been able to furnish detailed documentary proof of the massive diversion of public resources into the coffers of the official party. In February, 1995, President Zedillo agreed in principle to hold new elections in Tabasco, but this decision led to a major rebellion by local PRI leaders who blockaded highways, forced the closure of hundreds of businesses, and seized the state television network to broadcast attacks on Zedillo.[101] Zedillo buckled under the pressure and allowed Roberto Madrazo, the official winner of the election, to remain in office. The strategy of launching protests in order to influence the president to reverse election results, initially developed by opposition parties in response to unfair election verdicts, was now being put to use with considerable success by entrenched interests within the PRI to prevent the president from forcing them out of power, despite the questionable means by which they had gained office.

The handling of elections in Yucatán and Tabasco pointed to a troubling new trend, with conservative forces in the PRI actively seeking to sabotage the federal government's initiatives to promote clean elections in their zones of influence. And as the federal government grew weaker, the danger increased that regime hard-liners might team up with Mexico's powerful drug cartels and its corrupt police and military establishments to derail the reform process.

By 1998 six important states in addition to Mexico City—Baja California Norte, Guanajuato, Jalisco, Nuevo León, Querétaro and Zacatecas—were all ruled by the opposition, whereas in 1988, the PRI had enjoyed an absolute monopoly in all of Mexico's thirty-one states. At the same time, the PRI continued to govern at the presidential level, despite the growing competitiveness of federal elections in the 1980s and 1990s. Democracy thus advanced fastest at the local and state levels.

SURVEY RESEARCH PERSPECTIVES

The political awakening of society in Mexico was captured by numerous survey research studies. The three most important surveys of public opinion in the 1980s were conducted by Enrique

Alduncin in 1981, Miguel Basáñez in 1983 and 1987, and the Gallup Organization in 1988.[102] In addition, research by Jorge Domínguez and James McCann, relying on survey data from Gallup and other sources, also supports the claim that Mexicans became more politicized in the 1980s and early 1990s.[103] These studies portray an increasingly sophisticated society that was dissatisfied with the state of the country, pushing to expand the boundaries of participation in both electoral and nonelectoral arenas, in favor of placing real limits on presidential power, and no longer willing to be taken for granted by the PRI.

In Alduncin's 1981 study, 52 percent of the respondents said they were not satisfied with the nation's achievements, compared to 46 percent who said they were satisfied. At the highest income level, 76 percent said they were not satisfied with the nation's achievements, while only 24 percent said they were satisfied. At the lowest income level, 54 percent were satisfied with the nation's achievements and only 46 percent were dissatisfied.[104] About 66 percent of the respondents felt that Mexico's problems could only be solved by the participation of "all or the majority of the population." Eighty-three percent of those falling in the highest income bracket, 81 percent of those with a professional education, 70 percent of urban residents, and 68 percent of literate individuals felt that participation was necessary to solve the country's problems as compared to only 48 percent of rural laborers, 54 percent of the illiterate, and 56 percent of rural residents.[105] From the lowest to the highest income bracket, respect for politicians declined by 100 percent for men and 233 percent for women, respect for millionaires rose by 60 percent for men and 40 percent for women, and respect for *Gringos* and *Gachupines* (Spaniards) rose by 60 percent and 75 percent respectively for men.[106]

Miguel Basáñez's comparative study of Mexican public opinion in 1983 and 1987 also contains useful findings. While 55.3 percent of those surveyed expressed sympathy for the PRI in 1983, only 29.6 percent did so in 1987. Support for the PRI fell most steeply in central Mexico—from 56.9 percent in 1983 to 26 percent in 1987—though this did not translate into greater support for the PAN in that region. Instead, the number of central Mexicans who said they sympathized with no political party climbed from 24.6 percent in 1983 to 50.1 percent in 1987, thus creating a political vacuum that would be filled by Cuauhtémoc Cárdenas in 1988. In the north, support for the PRI fell less sharply—from 48.2 percent in 1983, then the lowest sympathy level of all regions, to 36.2 percent in 1987.[107] By 1987, the center had thus displaced the north as the region least sympathetic to the PRI.

According to Basáñez, sympathy for the PRI in 1983 was strongest among political leaders (74.9%), followed by peasants (68.1%), bureaucrats (65.3%), professionals (53.7%), workers (52.7%), businessmen (50.9%), employees (50.2%), and urban marginals (44.8%).[108] By 1987, the PRI had lost massive support among all social groups, including those traditionally identified with the party, such as political leaders, *campesinos,* and bureaucrats. Now only 52.1 percent of the political leaders supported the PRI as compared to 33.6 percent of the bureaucrats, 31.7 percent of the businessmen, 29.5 percent of the *campesinos,* 28.5 percent of the employees, 27.4 percent of the professionals, 23.6 percent of the urban marginals, and 21.9 percent of the workers.[109]

Basáñez's data also revealed that the number of Mexicans who no longer sympathized with any political party also rose dramatically; in central Mexico, the number of people claiming no party label increased from 24.6 percent in 1983 to 50.1 percent in 1987.[110] The trend toward a loosening of party identification continued into the 1990s. A poll conducted by Basáñez in July, 1991, found that 56 percent of his respondents expressed no party sympathy, 28 percent each with the PRI and the PAN, and only 6 percent with the PRD.[111] These findings are consistent with the growing tendency of voters to swing rapidly from one party to another in successive elections.

The findings of the Gallup poll, conducted in May, 1988, about five weeks short of the 1988 presidential elections, were also important. Almost two-thirds (63%) of all those surveyed said that "the Mexican political system should be changed so that the candidates of other parties will be able to win more often" and only slightly more than one in four (28%) said "the existing system works well and should be left as it is." This desire for greater electoral competitiveness was not limited to supporters of the two opposition presidential candidates, Manuel Clouthier and Cuauhtémoc Cárdenas. Supporters of the PRI candidate, Carlos Salinas, also expressed a desire for greater electoral competitiveness, but by a much smaller margin, with 50 percent in favor of it and 43 percent saying it was not necessary.[112]

Significantly, very few respondents in the Gallup poll expressed support for the PRI's traditional method of selecting the party's nominee for president, including Carlos Salinas, whereby the outgoing president personally chooses the PRI's presidential nominee, and hence his virtual successor. Only a miniscule 4 percent believed that the PRI's presidential nominee should continue to be chosen by the president, 22 percent felt that the nominee should be chosen by "a national assembly of the PRI, where leaders of the party from the entire country participate," and a clear majority of 61 percent came out in favor of choosing the nominee "by an internal balloting, in which all members of the party are able to vote."[113]

Domínguez and McCann show that the political awakening of society was a national trend, not one limited to the north.[114] Only 15 percent of Mexicans surveyed in Almond and Verba's civic culture study (the baseline for Domínguez and McCann's work) paid close attention to political campaigns. By 1988, the number of people expressing close interest in a campaign had risen to 30 percent and 25 percent in 1991, a drop not unusual for a midterm campaign (Table 2.8). In 1959, campaigns were likely to be followed most closely by residents of Mexico City and least so by northerners. By 1988, all regions were likely to follow campaigns with more or less equal interest, with central Mexicans being the most attentive. The number of Mexicans willing to talk about poli-

TABLE 2.8
Changes in Attentiveness to Political Campaigns
(percentage expressing great interest)

	1959	1988	1991
National	15	30	25
North	9	28	21
Central	12	33	29
South	19	29	33
Federal District	24	30	25

Source: Adapted from Jorge I. Domínguez and James McCann, *Democratizing Mexico: Public Opinion and Electoral Choices* (Baltimore: Johns Hopkins University Press, 1996), p. 32.

tics freely with anyone also rose from 19 percent in 1959 to 27 percent in 1991 (Table 2.9). In the north, the number of people willing to discuss politics climbed from 20 percent in 1959 to 25 percent in 1991; in the Federal District, the figure shot up from only 14 percent in 1959 to 32 percent in 1991. The number of Mexican authoritarians also declined significantly between 1959 and 1991. In 1959, 67 percent of all Mexicans agreed with the statement, "A few strong leaders would do more for Mexico than all the laws and talk," while only 59 percent did so in 1988 and 54 percent in 1991 (Table 2.10). The steepest declines in the preference for strong leaders occurred in the south and the Federal District, although the north remained the region least likely to support them in 1991, followed closely by the south. This find-

TABLE 2.9
Willingness to Discuss Politics
(percent)

	1959	1991
National	19	27
North	20	25
Central	20	23
South	20	30
Federal District	14	32

Source: Adapted from Jorge I. Domínguez and James McCann, *Democratizing Mexico: Public Opinion and Electoral Choices* (Baltimore: Johns Hopkins University Press, 1996), p. 36.

TABLE 2.10
"A few good leaders would do more for Mexico
than all the laws and talk"
(percentage agreeing)

	1959	1988	1991
National	67	59	54
North	62	53	49
Central	68	61	60
South	68	61	51
Federal District	72	64	56

Source: Adapted from Jorge I. Domínguez and James McCann, *Democratizing Mexico: Public Opinion and Electoral Choices* (Baltimore: Johns Hopkins University Press, 1996), p. 41.

ing may reflect a fear of the strong hand of the central government in Mexico's more distant regions. Domínguez and McCann conclude:

> The attitudes of Mexican citizens have changed in important and consistent ways since 1950. By the early 1990s, Mexicans had become much more likely to be interested in politics, attentive to political campaigns, and to discuss politics freely.[115]

RESPONSE OF SOCIAL LEADERS TO THE POLITICAL AWAKENING OF MEXICAN SOCIETY

The 1980s and 1990s were also marked by growing political involvement by important social elites, particularly businessmen and clergy. Unlike the 1970s, when business opposition to the regime had been expressed mainly through the country's non-political business chambers, an increasing number of businessmen in the 1980s openly supported the opposition by joining the PAN, running as PAN candidates, and donating money to opposition causes. Businessmen were also to be wooed by the reform wing of the PRI and contributed to the reformist impulse in the official party as well. Meanwhile, clergy and bishops played an increasingly active role in political affairs by denouncing election fraud. The 1986 state elections in Chihuahua marked the first time since the supercharged environment of the 1920s and 1930s that the Church was willing to risk a direct confrontation with the regime over the issue of democracy. The growing support for free elections in the Church around the country and the spread of liberation theology in southern Mexico, particularly in the states of Chiapas and Oaxaca, revealed a general tendency towards greater Church activism in the 1980s and 1990s.

Social leaders became politically active for two sets of reasons. On the one hand, social leaders were part of the larger society and were influenced by the overall societal thrust towards democracy. If they seized the opportunity to lead the movement for democracy they enhanced their stature in society. Bishops and clergy in Chihuahua chose to respond to intense lay pressure to denounce election fraud rather than risk losing credibility by remaining silent. On the other hand, social leaders were responding to other factors that were largely exogenous to the political awakening of society in the 1980s and 1990s. Clergy and bishops were influenced by the sweeping currents of doctrinal change in the global Church, which stressed a renewed commitment to the redemption of the temporal realm through the achievement of social justice and democracy. Businessmen became involved when they were incensed by the government's sudden nationalization of the banking system in 1982.

Social leaders harnessed the rising tide of citizen activism for institutional growth and used their newfound organizational strength to negotiate reforms with the regime. The role of leaders also predated the political awakening: PAN leaders and clergy, by prying open political space, contributed to the possibility of political awakening, as chapters 3 and 4 demonstrate. Leaders also helped make institutions more acceptable to society by reshaping tactics and ideology. The PAN's decision in the 1970s to emphasize elections, for example, made it possible for the party to serve as a channel for the political awakening of society that occurred in the 1980s.

Social leaders also helped shape the democratic values associated with the political awakening of society. There is no question that all the major segments of Mexican elite opinion had come to view democracy as necessary for the well-being of the country by the 1980s. Businessmen believed that only a democratic political system could provide the necessary checks and balances needed to curb corruption and protect society from such dangerous acts of presidential caprice as the expropriation of vast tracts of farmland in Sonora by Echeverría in 1976 and the bank nationalization of 1982. The best articulator of this ideology was the Mexican Employers' Confederation (COPARMEX), from which a number of PAN candidates for office, including Clouthier, emerged. This negative view of the Mexican state received fresh impetus in the winter of 1994–95 with the eruption of Mexico's second major economic crisis in less than fifteen years, which many felt could have been averted by more transparent economic management by the government. Catholic Church leaders also argued that democracy, for all its imperfections, was the only system of government capable of safeguarding human rights and containing corruption.[116] They were also influenced by the Latin American Bishops Conference held at Puebla in 1979, which had defended the right of ordinary citizens to take part in political decision making and condemned authoritarian governments inspired by the "doctrine of national security." Church leaders also believed that a democratic political system would result in the easing of a multiplicity of anticlerical constitutional laws dating from the time of the Revolution and give the Church more liberty to pursue its mission in society. Finally, PAN leaders since the party's founding in 1939 had stressed the importance of democracy grounded in a strong society capable of checking the state. Among political parties, the PAN also provided the most stinging critique of the economic effects of authoritarianism. The PAN's 1986–92 platform, for example, stated:

> history and common sense tells us that material prosperity depends on the health of democracy; the current state of economic underdevelopment is more an instrument of autocratic domination, than a cause of tyranny.[117]

Untrammeled presidentialism thus caused economic backwardness, not the other way around.

CONCLUSION

This chapter has argued that the political awakening of society in Chihuahua and Mexico was the result of three major factors all of which were present nationally: the prior availability of political space, the effects of social and economic change between 1940 and 1980, and the impact of the economic crisis of the 1980s. One alternative explanation, similar to Putnam's emphasis on deeply rooted civic tradition as the mainstay of civic community in northern Italy,[118] might stress the cultural uniqueness of Chihuahua as the key source of the state's political awakening. From this perspective, the political awakening of society would most likely be strongest in Chihuahua and the north because of its distinctive tradition of egalitarianism, individualism, and community spirit in contrast to the rest of Mexico struggling with its feudal past inherited from the Aztecs and reinforced by three-hundred years of Spanish colonial rule. Yet, this explanation breaks down when one considers the fact that the political awakening of society had by the late 1980s and 1990s become a national phenomenon that extended not only to the north but to much of the central Mexican heartland and significant areas of the south as well, despite major variations in cultural patterns. This trend was confirmed by the PAN's victory in the 2000 presidential elections, discussed in the epilogue. The opposition also performed consistently better in cities than rural areas regardless of region, making regional cultural distinctions less relevant. There is no doubt that the political awakening of society was most apparent first in the north, but this had more to do with the electoral calendar and the fact that the crisis initially had a more disruptive effect on the north than with cultural reasons. In any event, this early gap between the north and the rest of country was soon closed by 1988 when Cárdenas and his FDN scored a series of impressive victories in most of the states located in the central region. It is true that the crisis aroused anti-centralist anger in the north but anti-centralism was by no means limited to the northern region; in fact, virtually all of Mexico's provinces have chafed under the dominance of Mexico City, especially the neglected south. Also, while northerners may have been more susceptible to U.S. democratic and cultural values for reasons of geographical proximity, this should not blind one to the fact that Mexico as a whole is also subject to myriad forms of U.S. cultural influence. The central state of Michoacán, for instance, sends one of the highest proportions of seasonal rural migrants in the country to the United States; such migration can easily function as a mechanism of cultural transmission even in relatively poor regions. In short, the cultural perspective overstates the differences between the north and the rest of the country. Nor does the cultural explanation account for the PRI's long period of hegemony in Chihuahua and the north from 1940 to 1982.[119] If differences in regional cultural traditions were important, one might have expected the PRI's hegemony to be much weaker in Chihuahua and the north during this period relative to the rest of the country but this was patently not the case. Instead, the PRI's hegemony in Chihuahua and the north was part of a national pattern of PRI dominance that remained intact until 1982. Even if one grants that Chihuahua and the north possess a culturally distinctive tradition, this tradition was clearly not a significant factor in explaining the political awakening of society that began there in the early 1980s.

A second alternative explanation put forward by Schmitter and O'Donnell stresses the role of the state in triggering the political awakening of society.[120] Viewed from this angle, the state, by agreeing to recognize the PAN's electoral victories in 1983, set off a cycle of electoral mobilization that eventually spun out of control. The state, by allowing fair elections in 1983, gave voters an incentive to vote for the opposition and encouraged opposition parties to compete with the official party. This explanation is problematic for three reasons. First, the decision of de la Madrid to recognize opposition victories at the local level in 1983 was not widely publicized and came largely as a surprise to opposition parties and the voters. Second, the fact that voters might want to vote for the opposition in the event of a clean election implies an underlying alienation of voters from the regime that the state-oriented explanation takes for granted. Yet, as already mentioned, the regime's first significant political opening in decades in 1977 met with little response from the voters. In 1983, however, de la Madrid's political opening, occurring during a full-blown crisis, led to a spate of opposition victories. The fact that there was a political opening is therefore not sufficient to explain the lack of opposition gains in 1977 or the string of such successes in 1983. Nor does the state-centered explanation provide a satisfactory explanation of why the regime chose political opening in 1983. Most agree that de la Madrid hoped that recognizing opposition victories at the local level would diffuse social tension. De la Madrid's opening was thus a response by the state to the prior accumulation of social dissatisfaction with the regime, and not the other way around. Conversely, the regime's decision to close off the electoral channel by resorting to fraud was a direct response to the growing competitiveness of opposition parties. Nor does the regime's attempt to close off the electoral channel by resorting to fraud seem to have discouraged voters from continuing to support the opposition and demonstrating against election fraud in the state elections of 1986 in Chihuahua, the presidential elections of 1988, and numerous other electoral contests.

The political awakening of society in Chihuahua and nationally in the 1980s and 1990s was reflected in the surge of opposition electoral gains, the increasing competitiveness of elections, the popular outcry against election fraud, significantly higher voter turnout rates, the growing independence of the electorate, and the influx of new members into opposition political parties and civic associations. Survey research also mirrored the political awakening of society. Social leaders, particularly business people and clergy, also became active in the struggle for democracy, condemning fraud, joining opposition parties, and forming civic associations. Social leaders acted partly in response to the broader political awakening of society and partly for their own reasons. Leaders in turn played a vital role in tapping growing civic activism to strengthen opposition political parties, such as the PAN, the Catholic Church, and civic associations as actors capable of pressuring the regime for democratic change. Subsequent chapters focus on the impact of the political awakening of society and social leaders on such institutions, regionally in Chihuahua and nationally, and the ensuing consequences for the development of democracy.

3

The Transformation of Mexico's National Action Party (PAN): From Civic Example to Political Power

The 1980s and 1990s were marked by a dramatic increase in the strength of the opposition National Action Party (PAN), and, by the late 1990s, the PAN had emerged as a serious democratic alternative to the PRI at the national level. From holding almost no elective offices in 1980 at any level, the PAN in 1999 governed six major Mexican states, including Jalisco, Aguascalientes, Nuevo León, Querétaro, Baja California Norte, and Guanajuato. It also ran fourteen of Mexico's twenty most important cities, including the industrial capital, Monterrey; the country's second largest city, Guadalajara; several other state capitals, such as Mexicali, Saltillo, Tuxtla Gutiérrez, Cuernavaca, Oaxaca, San Luis Potosí, and Mérida; the U.S. border cities of Ciudad Juárez and Tijuana; and other towns such as León, Naucalpan, and Tlalnepantla. Overall, the number of municipalities controlled by the PAN increased from only 18 in 1987 to 103 in 1994 to 287 in 1999. The population governed by the PAN also rose from approximately 800,000 in 1988 (1%) to 24.7 million in 1996 (27%) to 32.7 million in 1999 (36%).[1] The number of seats controlled by the PAN in the federal Chamber of Deputies climbed from just 41 in 1985 to 101 in 1988, fell slightly to 89 in 1991, and then rose again to 118 in 1994 and 121 in 1997. In percentage terms, the PAN averaged about 12 percent of the vote in federal deputy elections held in the 1970s, 17 percent in the 1980s, and 23 percent in the 1990s,[2] while the PAN's performance in presidential elections after hovering around 16 percent in 1982 and 1988

75

jumped significantly to 26 percent in 1994. The results of the 2000 presidential elections provided a vivid confirmation of these trends, with the PAN decisively capturing the presidency, winning the state of Morelos and retaining Guanajuato by huge margins, and bagging, in alliance with the Mexican Ecological Green Party (PVEM), 45 percent of the seats in the Chamber of Deputies, thus emerging as the single-largest grouping in Congress.

Previous work on the PAN has focused on its origins and role in the political system. Donald Mabry, for example, stresses the Catholic roots of the party, while Abraham Nuncio sees it as primarily an instrument of the business community to oppose Cárdenas's economic policies.[3] Franz Von Sauer captures the ambivalent role of the PAN in the political system before 1980 when he dubs the party "the alienated 'loyal' opposition in Mexico."[4] More recent work by Soledad Loaeza on the PAN stresses its transformation from a party that initially accepted its secondary role in the political system and functioned as a "loyal" opposition to becoming a channel for protest votes against the system in the 1980s and 1990s.[5]

Historically, the PAN, which was founded in 1939, placed more emphasis on the development of civic consciousness than the achievement of political power. A strategy designed to promote civic awareness was deemed to have positive long-term effects for the development of democracy in Mexico; political power, however, was considered an illusory goal, given the utter dominance of the one-party regime. In the first four decades of its existence, the PAN controlled only a handful of municipalities and federal deputy seats, and the party virtually disappeared from the political scene in the 1970s when internal divisions prevented it from fielding a candidate in the presidential election of 1976.

Yet in the 1980s, the party reemerged, this time with political power as its main objective. The political awakening of society in the 1980s and 1990s fueled voter support for the PAN, increased electoral competitiveness, and propelled the party into power at the local and state levels. The active membership of the PAN also swelled from around 49 million in 1988 to 130 million in 1993, dropping slightly to 127 million in 1999. In addition, the contribution of leaders was important. PAN leaders from the 1940s onward made valiant efforts to pry open political space, which helped lay the basis for one of the conditions for a broader societal upsurge for

democracy. Internal conflict among PAN leaders in the 1970s resulted in a major reshaping of the party that placed the PAN in a
strategic position to profit from the political awakening of society
in the 1980s. Party leaders helped use the growing support for the
PAN in the 1980s and 1990s to transform the party institutionally
in Chihuahua and then nationally, and win reforms from the regime. And leaders, particularly businessmen, provided critical financial support and leadership skills that aided the growth of the
party throughout the 1980s and 1990s.

The transformation of the party occurred first at the regional
level in Chihuahua. Party leaders in Chihuahua succeeded in crafting a new model of political action that placed the winning of power
at the core of the party's mission. This new model was marked by
four crucial elements: mass support; campaigning to win; the development of strategies to counter fraud, including improved party
organization, civil disobedience, and appeals to international public opinion; and ideological flexibility. The example of the PAN in
Chihuahua was quickly transmitted to the PAN nationally. The political awakening of society and social leaders, which was initially
strongest in Chihuahua and northern Mexico, had by 1988 become
a national phenomenon, predisposing the PAN nationwide towards
the adoption of a new strategy designed to wrest power from the
PRI. The high level of democracy inside the PAN also made it easier
for regional proponents of party change, especially from northern
Mexico, to win control of the PAN's national decision-making apparatus and transform the party as a whole.

The central theme of this chapter is the transformation of the
PAN from an organization dedicated primarily to promoting greater
civic consciousness in the first three decades of its existence to one
placing the achievement of political power at the heart of its mission in the 1980s and 1990s. One cannot adequately understand
the transformation that occurred in the PAN in the 1980s and 1990s,
however, without understanding the PAN's prior history as an organization dedicated primarily to stimulating citizen awareness, and
the fundamental changes brought about by the internal crisis of the
1970s. The chapter then analyzes the new model to win power
from the PRI that was developed by the PAN in Chihuahua during
the 1980s; the model's subsequent institutionalization by the party
nationwide; and the development of a dialogue with the regime

under Salinas. The chapter assesses the patterns of internal conflict that developed inside the PAN as the party sought to adapt to the participatory thrust of society and social leaders and integrate the flow of new members into the party. Finally, the chapter assesses the implications of an increasingly robust PAN for democratization in Mexico.

HISTORICAL DEVELOPMENT OF THE PAN TO 1970: BUILDING POLITICAL SPACE

Origins and Early Development

Manuel Gómez Morin

The men and women who gathered in Mexico City in September, 1939, to found the PAN were motivated not so much by a feeling that the principles inspiring the Mexican Revolution were wrong as by the conviction that the Revolution had been betrayed and perverted by its leaders.[6] Indeed, Manuel Gómez Morin, the PAN's principal founder, had come to full intellectual maturity in an atmosphere permeated by revolutionary ideas, and he functioned for a time as an important servant of the Revolution. In 1913, the Chihuahua native arrived in Mexico City, at the height of the Revolution, to complete his studies. As a law student at the National University, Gómez Morin attended the debates of the framers of the Constitution of 1917 as an observer[7] and formed part of a highly gifted group of students known as the "seven sages," which included Vicente Lombardo Toledano, who later became Mexico's foremost Marxist thinker and union organizer.[8]

Gómez Morin and the other "seven sages" were soon called upon to collaborate with the revolutionary governments of generals Alvaro Obregón (1921–24) and Plutarco Elías Calles (1924–28).[9] As undersecretary of finance under Obregón and a top financial advisor to Calles, Gómez Morin helped lay the foundations of some of Mexico's most important economic institutions. He played an important role in the adoption of Mexico's first income tax law in 1921. Four years later, he helped draft the law establishing Mexico's central bank, the Bank of Mexico, and functioned as the first president of its board from 1925 to 1928. Convinced of the pivotal role of agriculture in Mexican economic development, Gómez Morin was also responsible for writing the law establishing the National Bank of Agricultural Credit in 1926.

By the late 1920s, however, Gómez Morin began to feel disillusioned with the Revolution.[10] He argued that without democracy and its handmaiden, the rule of law, society would always be vulnerable to the depredations and ideological fancies of whatever *caudillo* happened to be in power at the time.[11] This situation was highly inimical both to the process of economic development and to institution building. He was especially embittered by the growing corruption in the National Bank of Agricultural Credit and the Bank of Mexico, both of which had been forced to issue major loans to regime influentials and Calles himself with little hope of repayment.[12] For Gómez Morin, the violent destructiveness of the revolution could only be justified if it were superseded by a positive phase of construction.[13] And this hinged on the establishment of a democratic political order.

Yet democracy of any kind was inconceivable in Mexico without the prior organization of society. By 1928, therefore, Gómez Morin had begun to think actively about forming a political party whose goals would be to promote citizen participation in the political process and create institutional checks against the dictatorial abuse of power.[14] He tried in vain to dissuade his old friend and mentor, José Vasconcelos, from running in the 1929 presidential election against Pascual Ortiz Rubio, who was favored by Calles, and to join him in the far more difficult task of forming a political party. If Vasconcelos won and his victory was recognized, Gómez Morin argued, then Vasconcelos in the absence of an organized society would simply become another *caudillo*. If he lost or his victory was not recognized, then his supporters would become disillusioned and the task of forming a political party would receive a mortal blow.[15] Vasconcelos was not persuaded, arguing that if the government did not recognize his victory, he would turn to armed rebellion. Gómez Morin, mainly out of loyalty, agreed to become Vasconcelos's campaign treasurer. In the election, Pascual Ortiz Rubio was declared winner, Vasconcelos went meekly into exile, and Gómez Morin, after a brief period of exile himself, returned to Mexico even more convinced of the need for the establishment of an independent political party.

The National Union of Catholic Students (UNEC)

For the time being, however, Gómez Morin lacked the organizational resources to form a political party. This he would find in the National Union of Catholic Students (UNEC). Gómez Morin first came in contact with the UNEC in 1933, when he was elected rector of the National University. At the time, the university was under severe pressure from the regime to restructure its programs to conform to the new orthodoxy of socialist education. What troubled Gómez Morin most about the attempt to impose socialist education was not so much its content but the threat that it represented to the freedom of thought.[16] In the fight against socialist education in the university, the UNEC not only provided Gómez Morin with a ready base of support within the university, but also succeeded in infiltrating and taking over virtually all the student organizations that had declared themselves in favor of socialist education.[17] The regime, facing growing opposition to its project, reluctantly agreed to exempt the university from the requirements of socialist education, though not without drastically cutting its state subsidies.

The UNEC was founded in 1931. Its main goal was to ensure that a Christian voice would continue to be heard on university campuses at a time when Marxist ideas were rapidly gaining ground.[18] The real importance of the UNEC, however, lay elsewhere. It was the first Catholic organization in Mexico that sought to reconcile what many Catholics had come to regard as polar opposites: the Mexican Revolution and Mexican Catholicism.[19] Instead of simply rejecting the Revolution in its entirety, the UNEC sought to conduct a more balanced assessment from the viewpoint of Catholic social doctrine and modern papal encyclicals. In particular, it praised article 123 of the 1917 constitution, which defines the principles governing labor-capital relations, as "filled with magnificent ideas and animated by a Christian desire for social justice."[20] The UNEC also declared that the *ejido* represented on the whole "a good solution to the agrarian problem" and expressed approval of the constitutional provision allowing the state to expropriate private property and regulate its distribution in light of the public interest.[21] In 1938, after a heated debate, the UNEC decided to support President Cárdenas's decision to nationalize the oil industry, then in foreign hands.[22] On the other hand, it strongly criticized the anticlerical articles of the 1917 constitution and the state's attempt to monopolize education, not on religious grounds, but because they constituted a violation of democratic rights.[23]

The UNEC remained in existence for a short period of time only. Technically, the UNEC constituted a part of the Catholic Association of Mexican Youth (ACJM), which, in turn, formed part of the Catholic Action movement. Both the ACJM and Catholic Action were expected to function as nonpolitical instruments of evangelization at the service of the Church hierarchy. Many members of the hierarchy, however, felt that the UNEC had become overly politicized and could drag the Church into an unwanted conflict with the regime. The UNEC was also far less amenable to control by the hierarchy than other Catholic Action organizations. Its spirit was entirely lay in character, decisions were taken by a vote often after prolonged debate, and the Jesuit priests assigned to the organization acted less as authority figures than as spiritual and intellectual guides.[24] The UNEC had been obliged to affiliate with Catholic Action because the Church was unwilling to permit lay organizations to function outside the ambit of clerical control. But Catholic Action was a reluctant host. The UNEC's nuanced view of the Mexican Revolution was viewed with suspicion by many ACJM and Catholic Action members, and UNEC's positions on social questions were seen as excessively radical.[25] Finally, the ACJM resented the UNEC's monopoly of Catholic Action at the university level. In 1941, all apostolic work at the university level was ceded to the Professional and Student Movement (MEP) of the ACJM, and three years later the UNEC was officially disbanded.[26]

The best of the UNEC lived on, however, in what became the PAN. In 1939, with the presidential elections nearing, the UNEC invited Gómez Morin to run against the candidate of the official Mexican Revolutionary Party (PRM).[27] Gómez Morin warned them of the dangers of staking everything on a brief electoral adventure and instead suggested that together they form a permanent political party to arouse society gradually from its slumber.[28] The most important nucleus of the PAN in 1939 thus consisted of Gómez Morin, most of the UNEC, a number of Gómez Morin's former students, most of whom were now urban middle-class professionals, and some of his former university colleagues.

Efraín González Luna

Another vital source of support for the incipient party came from Efraín González Luna, a prominent Guadalajara lawyer, who would become the PAN's most important thinker. Thoroughly steeped in Catholic social doctrine and the modern papal encyclicals, he later became the president of the ACJM chapter in Jalisco.[29] González Luna not only helped the PAN establish a base in the important industrial state of Jalisco but his presence drew many ACJM and Catholic Action militants into the PAN fold. In view of González Luna's background, one might have expected him to have a single-minded focus on the issue of Church-State relations, but he was able to place the conflict in a wider context.[30] Equally surprising was his relationship with Gómez Morin. González Luna's highly religious and reflective bent contrasted sharply with Gómez Morin, who was far less visibly religious and much more inclined to practical action. Yet both men were strongly drawn to each other and one acted as the perfect counterfoil to the other.[31]

González Luna's greatest contribution lay in the elaboration of the doctrine of the PAN.[32] According to González Luna, all human beings, having been created in the image of God, possessed an eternal destiny and inherent dignity. Since human beings were essentially social creatures, individual realization was possible only in society; the role of social institutions was to help individuals realize their material and spiritual potential. González Luna viewed the state as a prerequisite for the creation of a social order based on the rule of law. The only state, however, that could truly guarantee the rights of individuals and intermediate social organizations and not displace them was the democratic state. Any other type of state would become unresponsive to society and destroy the divinely instituted harmony between the individual, society, and state. Since the natural tendency of the state was to usurp the functions of society, the only way to control the state was to create authentic citizens committed to participating in public affairs. For González Luna, the fulfilling of one's duty as a citizen was thus a supreme moral value on which all other values ultimately hinged, and politics, far from being a lowly activity, was a noble undertaking endowed with all the holiness of a religious sacrament. In his opinion, the waves of religious persecution unleashed during the Revolution in an overwhelmingly

Catholic nation could only be explained by the persistent silencing of society throughout Mexican history and the reluctance of ordinary Mexicans to meet their obligations as citizens.

González Luna's ideas on social and economic policy are equally important for an understanding of the PAN.[33] He regarded the act of work as constituting a form of sharing in the creative power of God. Consequently, workers were to be viewed not as mere mechanical agents in the productive process but human beings with innate dignity. They were entitled to a just salary capable of sustaining not only themselves but their families as well. González Luna also favored the creation of a system of universal social security, which he considered a legitimate mechanism of income redistribution. He rejected both economic liberalism and communism as degrading to the human condition but regarded communism as the greater evil. In his view, the theory of class conflict was morally unacceptable. For him, society was composed of hierarchical, multiclass, cooperative organizations designed to fulfill varying social functions to the good of the individual. The theory of class conflict, by dividing organizations into two antagonistic parts, would paralyze all social organization and transform the state into a tool of factional tyranny. Instead, González Luna stressed the need for greater social communion and solidarity as a means of maximizing the common good. On the whole, his social and economic ideas were more conservative than those of the UNEC and the Christian socialists, who came to dominate the PAN in the late 1960s. The UNEC and the Christian socialists were more willing to recognize the reality of class conflict. They were therefore in favor of stronger medicine to advance the cause of social justice and cure society of the sickness of class division. For his part, González Luna was more willing to recognize the importance of the private sector and less disposed to justify state intervention in the economy, which he viewed as desirable only when there was no lesser organization capable of supplanting the role played by the state.

The Business Community

The new party also attracted support from businessmen. This was in no small measure due to Gómez Morin. Having helped lay the institutional foundations of a modern capitalist state in Mexico during the 1920s, Gómez Morin had turned to the creation of a viable private sector that could take advantage of it. He had lent his technical skills to help organize new private banks such as the Bank of Commerce and was also responsible for bringing about the first joint ventures between Mexican and U.S. companies in Mexican business history, and his advice had even helped save the Monterrey Group of companies from impending bankruptcy and takeover by the Bank of Montreal.[34] Gómez Morin was thus both trusted and respected by the business community. Indeed, Gómez Morin's friends in the business community, long after they had severed all ties to the PAN (if they had them in the first place), continued to donate money directly to Gómez Morin for "his party" simply because they did not know how to refuse him.[35]

How to Direct the Revolution towards Democracy

The foundation of the PAN in 1939 at a time of generalized social discontent in the twilight of the Cárdenas administration has led some to argue that the PAN was a conservative reaction to the radical policies followed by Cárdenas.[36] In my view, this is a superficial interpretation of the PAN's origins. The only group that might have joined the PAN for this reason was the business sector, which was alarmed more by the socialist rhetoric of Cárdenas than by any concrete threat to their interests. In any case, only a minority of businessmen actually entered the new party. In the 1940 presidential election, most businessmen voted for Almazán, the dissident right-wing general running against the official PRM candidate, Avila Camacho, but they refrained from joining the PAN. And of those who did join, many soon abandoned the party after it became clear that President Avila Camacho would follow a more moderate course.

In 1940, the PAN picked up support in northern Mexico, not because of ideological factors, but because the north, which had won the Mexican Revolution and dominated national politics in the 1920s and early 1930s through the famous Sonora dynasty, saw its political influence much reduced during the Cárdenas administration, whose emphasis on land reform and other social issues benefited mainly southern and central Mexico. For his part, Gómez Morin had nursed the idea of creating a political party since 1929 and possibly even earlier.[37] The corporatist transformation of the official party initiated by Cárdenas only confirmed Gómez Morin's preexisting view that it was necessary to create an independent political party. The issue for both Gómez Morin and González Luna was not Cárdenas as such, but the more fundamental problem of how to direct the Revolution towards democracy.

Social Justice

Nor did Gómez Morin or González Luna oppose the goals of greater social justice set by Cárdenas but rather the manner in which they were pursued. For Gómez Morin, the central role of government was to reduce human pain in society through the adoption of rational public policies derived from empirical reality rather than ideology.[38] He regarded the populism, demagoguery, and social chaos unleashed by Cárdenas as profoundly antirevolutionary.[39] In his view, the surest way to combat social oppression was through the creation of better institutions, the efficient execution of technically sound policies, an acceptance of the constraints imposed by reality, and a willingness to continue addressing problems even if progress was painfully slow and the ultimate solution not visible.[40] Gómez Morin's quarrel with Cárdenas was thus not over intentions but methods.

The UNEC not only strongly supported the goal of social justice but even applauded some of Cárdenas's methods as well. While the PAN attracted a number of more conservative Catholics connected mainly with Catholic Action who were upset about the revolution's antireligious policies, this dissatisfaction dated back at least to the time of President Calles (1924–28), and the regime's attitude towards the Church had softened considerably by the late 1930s. The rising tide of opposition to the Cárdenas regime in 1939–40 thus clearly furnished the occasion for the foundation of the PAN, but the PAN itself was not fundamentally the product of a conservative reaction to the radicalism of the Cárdenas years.

Democratic Power

For the PAN's founders, the main goal of the new party was not the acquisition of power as such but rather the creation of conditions that would permit power to be wielded in a democratic fashion.

The party's founders also recognized that it was unrealistic to expect the PAN to acquire significant access to power by way of elections any time soon, since the regime was unlikely to allow the opposition to win. In their view, only a strong and participatory society could provide the necessary conditions for democracy and protect the triumphs of opposition parties. They therefore insisted that the task of organizing and politicizing society had to take clear precedence over the need to gain access to power. Gómez Morin even stated that if the PAN were to suddenly gain power, the party would be unprepared to exercise it alone and would have to form a government of national unity.[41] Indeed, one of the most important factors explaining the remarkable longevity of the PAN spanning over five decades, without real access to power until the 1980s, was the ability of the party's founders to divorce the basic purposes of the PAN from the immediate need to acquire power.[42] Had the founders placed the acquisition of power at the heart of the PAN's mission, the party would have been overtaken quickly by disappointment and frustration and would probably not have survived much beyond its birth.

Electoral Participation

Closely related to the debate over the party's raison d'etre was its dilemma concerning electoral participation. If the main goal of the party was to organize society rather than to gain power, then electoral campaigns were not so much to be won as to be used to enlighten society, and might even be altogether unnecessary. Neither Gómez Morin, who functioned as the party's president during its first ten years, nor González Luna wanted the party to participate in the presidential election of 1940. They feared that this futile electoral entanglement would result only in the imposition of the official PRM candidate, the exhaustion of society, and the legitimizing of an essentially undemocratic regime.[43] Finally, they believed that the party was too weak to launch its own presidential candidate; they were also against endorsing an outsider like Almazán, whom they viewed as an opportunist.[44] But Gómez Morin and González Luna, in an early display of internal party democracy, were overruled by the national convention, which, caught up in the enthusiasm of the moment, voted to participate by endorsing Almazán.

Gómez Morin and González Luna were not by any means arguing for a permanent policy of abstentionism. They understood that electoral participation, even at the risk of legitimizing the regime and without much hope of victory, could nevertheless facilitate the PAN's mission by giving the party an opportunity to shape public opinion, disseminate its doctrine, and stimulate greater political awareness. They did, however, believe that such participation would be most effective if it occurred first at the legislative rather than presidential level.[45] Legislative campaigns would place less burden on the party's limited organizational capacity and victories were more likely to be recognized by the regime. And a presence in the legislature would provide the party with a national platform from which to criticize the regime, present alternative policy proposals, and influence public opinion as well as government decision making. In 1943, the PAN participated in legislative elections for the first time but won no seats. Success would come three years later when the party elected four federal deputies.

The party would not, however, run its own candidate for the presidency until 1952, when the national convention selected González Luna as the PAN candidate. The party's decision to participate in presidential electoral contests helped the PAN gain vital public exposure as well as an organizational presence throughout the country. This in turn paved the way for the party to intensify its participation in state and municipal electoral contests.[46] The concentration of power in the hands of the central government in Mexico City, the abandonment of municipal government to the whims of local PRI bosses, the persistence of strong regionalist sentiments, and the fact that most PAN candidates for state and municipal offices were well-respected members of the local community gave the PAN a fair chance of victory in such hard-fought contests. The emphasis on state and municipal contests marked the beginning of a new strategy to gradually wrest power from the PRI, starting at the local level. And by the late 1960s, the PAN had succeeded in winning control of the cities of Mérida, Hermosillo, and Uruapan. Electoral fraud, however, would rob the party of many potential victories, especially in the gubernatorial elections held in Chihuahua (1956), Baja California Norte (1959), Sonora (1967), and Yucatán (1969), and in the municipal elections in Baja California Norte (1969).

The PAN's Relationship to the Regime

The weakness of the PAN during the first two decades of its existence made it imperative that the party pay special attention to its relationship with the regime. It suited the regime to allow an opposition party to exist as a means of legitimizing the one-party state, but the regime could easily have displaced the PAN in favor of a more pliable opposition party without risking social unrest in the process. The PAN's vulnerability thus required that it avoid undue confrontation in order to ensure its survival and development.

In the 1940s, Gómez Morin's prestige and the fact that the PAN sought to influence government decision making rather than exercise power helped create a grudging acceptance of the party in official circles. By the mid-1950s, however, younger PAN members had become increasingly frustrated over the inability of the party to acquire meaningful power. Matters came to a head during the 1958 presidential campaign of Luís H. Alvarez, a young textile industrialist, who had been selected as the PAN's candidate. Alvarez, who had run for governor of Chihuahua two years earlier, conducted an extremely vigorous campaign in which he attracted huge crowds, visited over 500 towns across the republic, and confronted the PRI with its failure to make good on its promises of greater social justice and democracy. The campaign was interspersed with violent confrontations with PRI supporters. It ended with Alvarez accusing the PRI of having conducted a "gigantic fraud" and characterizing the incoming López Mateos regime as a "de facto government."[47] In order to protest the fraud, Alvarez also persuaded Gómez Morin and the party not to accept the six federal deputy seats that the party had apparently won.[48] In contrast to PAN presidential candidates until very recently, Alvarez conducted his campaign as if his main goal were to win. If he did not personally feel he would win, this was because he had been warned against harboring any such illusions by his mentor Gómez Morin.[49] Indeed, while fraud certainly occurred, there is no doubt that PRI candidate López Mateos carried the election.

The 1958 presidential contest and its bitter aftermath severely strained the PAN's relationship with the regime. PAN president Adolfo Christlieb Ibarrola (1962–68), recognizing the dangers this held for the party, attempted to steer the PAN away from its collision course with the state. One of the first fruits of improved relations with the regime was the introduction of the party deputy system in 1963, which in effect guaranteed the PAN a minimum of twenty legislative seats and any additional seats that it could win by majority vote. Christlieb's decision to initiate a dialogue with the regime stemmed from a simple recognition of reality. As long as the party remained weak, it could not afford to provoke a serious conflict with the regime. On the other hand, a dialogue might strengthen the PAN politically and ultimately lower the costs of challenging the regime.

Tension between Secular Panistas and Panistas for Catholic Social Action

One consistent dynamic throughout PAN history has been the underlying tension between secular *panistas,* oriented towards the business community, and *panistas* representing various shades of Catholic social activism. Both groups have repeatedly clashed with each other over control of the party and its ideological agenda. The pro-business policies of President Miguel Alemán (1946–52) accelerated businessmen's desertion from the party and paved the way for the PAN in the 1950s to become dominated by *panistas* linked mainly with Catholic Action. Gómez Morin's successors as party president in the 1950s had all been members of Catholic lay associations. One of them, José González Torres (1959–62), had served as president of the ACJM, Mexican Catholic Action, and Pax Romana, an international organization of Catholic university students.

While members of the party remained committed to the concept of the PAN as a secular political party, albeit inspired by Catholic social doctrine, the party nonetheless acquired an overtly religious tone that it had not possessed earlier. In 1951, the PAN national convention selected González Luna as the party's candidate for the Mexican presidency over the less religious Antonio Rodríguez, a Monterrey financier, and Roberto Cossío y Cosío, PAN secretary general under Gómez Morin.[50] While González Luna himself eschewed religious issues in his highly pedagogical campaign, he received thinly veiled support from Catholic Action and a formal endorsement from the National Synarchist Union (UNS), a fundamentalist organization with a large rural following in central Mexico.[51]

Ideologically, the departure of businessmen freed the party to adopt an increasingly vociferous stance in favor of Catholic social justice as an alternative to the menace of communism. This in turn brought the PAN much closer to the recently formed Christian Democratic parties of Latin America and Western Europe, some of whose leaders were personal acquaintances of *panistas* like González Torres. And by the late 1950s, younger PAN members became increasingly vociferous in their demand that the PAN turn itself into a Christian Democratic party as well. They had participated with great enthusiasm in the 1958 Alvarez presidential campaign and had believed that victory was possible.[52] Bitterly disillusioned when this did not occur, they turned to Christian Democracy as a means of duplicating at home the success enjoyed by such parties abroad and linking the PAN to an increasingly prestigious international movement.

Most of the PAN's leadership, however, felt that such an explicitly religious identification would do grave damage to the party's image in Mexico, and Christlieb expelled those who still clung to the idea of turning the PAN into a Christian Democratic party. Christlieb also moderated the anticommunist rhetoric that had characterized the party in the 1950s, guiding the PAN towards the adoption of even stronger positions concerning social justice based on the new thinking emanating from Vatican II and the papal encyclicals of the 1960s. In 1965, Christlieb proposed that a supplement be added to the party's original *Principles of Doctrine*, in order to reflect the PAN's changing agenda. The supplement advocated the participation of workers in the ownership, profits, and management of business enterprises; urged that female workers receive equal treatment in the labor market; and demanded only the democratization of the *ejido* rather than its elimination.[53] The document also expressed the party's lack of faith in the invisible hand of the free market to guarantee just social outcomes and declared that economic growth should not occur at the cost of economic distribution and human rights.[54]

By the end of the 1960s, the party moved further to the left, responding to the Conference of Latin American Bishops held at Medellín and the explosion of student unrest in Mexico in 1968.

The task of reinterpreting party doctrine from a Christian socialist viewpoint fell to Efraín González Morfín, the son of González Luna and a disciple of Christlieb. González Morfín had returned to Mexico in 1959 after ten years of studying abroad. By the late 1960s, he had emerged as the PAN's most important thinker. In February 1969, the PAN national convention approved the document, *Democratic Change of Structures,* written mostly by him. The document declared that the party was in favor of a revolutionary change of unjust political, social, and economic structures from below; rejected the idea of gradual reform from above; accused the private sector of being in cahoots with the regime; and condemned the institutionalized violence of existing social arrangements.[55] It also criticized the regime for suppressing the reality of class conflict through the imposition of political controls on labor unions.[56] For González Morfín, the confrontation of antagonistic social classes presented a natural opportunity to remedy injustice and forge new social relationships that could transcend the earlier situation of conflict and lead to greater social solidarity.[57] González Morfín also stressed that the right to private property was not absolute but subject to the requirements of the common good; he also criticized the growing concentration of private property in fewer hands and accepted the right of the state to appropriate property for its own use.[58] By 1970, when González Morfín ran as the PAN candidate for the Mexican presidency, the PAN's social agenda had become more radical than at any time in its history; conservative *panistas,* especially from Catholic Action, had been largely displaced, and business support for the party had all but dried up.

THE CRISIS OF THE NATIONAL PAN IN THE 1970s

In the 1970s, major changes in the political and social environment that were set in motion during the terms of Presidents Luís Echeverría (1970–76) and José López Portillo (1976–82) brought the PAN's underlying contradictions to the surface and plunged the party into its worst internal crisis ever. The crisis forced the PAN to choose between two radically different conceptions of the party. While the crisis almost destroyed the PAN in the 1970s, the resulting redefinition of the party contributed significantly to the PAN's ability to harness social discontent in the 1980s and 1990s all over Mexico.

New Trends in the PAN

In February 1972, José Angel Conchello, a relatively unknown figure, was elected party president with the support of González Morfín. The emergence of Conchello as party president coincided with a period of growing polarization in Mexican politics. Echeverría's populist measures and leftist-sounding rhetoric, coupled with his defense of Salvador Allende, had alienated middle class opinion as well as the business community. For Conchello, the main goal of the PAN was to capitalize on existing discontent and create a broad front of opposition to the socializing tendencies of the Echeverría regime.[59] This in turn would allow the PAN to transform itself from a small band of well meaning but ineffectual Catholic intellectuals into a mass political party for the first time in its history. Conchello therefore actively wooed the support of the middle classes and the business community, where he enjoyed a level of credibility unmatched by earlier PAN presidents with the exception of Gómez Morin. A native of Monterrey, Mexico's most important industrial center located in the northern state of Nuevo León, Conchello had worked for the Confederation of Industrial Chambers, the Moctezuma Brewery Company, and the National Association of Advertisers. As party president, Conchello mostly ignored the PAN's anticapitalist ideological positions of the late 1960s, though he did not openly renounce them. Instead, he accused Echeverría of seeking to create a Marxist-Leninist dictatorship, distorting the humanistic and libertarian ideals of the Mexican revolution by viewing it as socialist, and aligning Mexico with the Soviet Union in foreign affairs.[60] Conchello also attacked Echeverría for a lack of evenhandedness in condemning human rights violations in Chile but not Cuba.[61] In economic policy, he criticized the president for deliberately trying to frustrate economic growth, "communizing" agricultural property, saddling the country with a huge public debt, promoting inefficient state industries, creating a costly regime of subsidies, and ruining the middle classes.[62]

Along with guiding the PAN towards an open advocacy of market economics and reviving the anticommunist rhetoric of the

1950s, Conchello recast the party's view of the role of elections. He regarded electoral participation not as a vehicle of civic education but, rather, as the occasion for mass mobilization against the regime and the party's only available means for gaining access to power. Conchello was hostile to the idea of electoral abstention, which he felt would force the PAN to choose between two unacceptable options: fade gracefully into political oblivion or resort to violence, in which case the party would be easily crushed by the overwhelming power of the Mexican state.[63]

Consistent with his desire to gain more public offices for the PAN, Conchello had few reservations about sacrificing the subtleties of party doctrine in order to improve the party's electoral performance and make its ideological positions more accessible to voters. One of Conchello's first acts as PAN president was to eliminate the requirement of subjecting all prospective members to a course of several weeks duration on party doctrine before they could officially join.[64] The new leadership also attempted to popularize PAN doctrine by printing thousands of copies of the party's *Principles of Doctrine* for mass distribution free of charge.[65] Intellectual qualifications became less important than popular appeal for those seeking to represent the party in electoral contests for public office. And Conchello himself discarded the high sounding tone of traditional PAN discourse in favor of a more colorful and colloquial style.[66] The changes introduced by Conchello were vindicated in the federal deputy elections of 1973, when the party received a record number of votes compared to earlier such elections.

Conflict within the PAN

These same changes, however, angered González Morfín and his supporters. In March, 1975, González Morfín decided to challenge Conchello in his bid for reelection as party president. Predictably, the election was an extremely tight affair, with González Morfín being declared the winner only on the fifth ballot. González Morfín accused Conchello of transforming the party into a tool of corporate interests and undermining the PAN's commitment to social justice. Conchello's blunt rejoinder was that his successful courtship of the business community represented a positive achievement for the party in light of the fact that most businessmen had other institutional channels to make their voices heard and did not necessarily need the PAN as much as the PAN needed them.[67]

The primacy of Christian socialism was reasserted in the 1976–82 party platform written under the auspices of González Morfín. The platform called for both electoral democracy and socioeconomic democracy, as well as radical changes in the pattern of property distribution, the suppression of internal colonialism, and reduced cultural and economic dependence on transnational organizations.[68] The 1976–82 platform, the most radical in the party's history, led to accusations that González Morfín and other likeminded party leaders had been "infected by Marxism."

Electoral Participation

Directly linked to the debate over ideology was the question of the party's attitude towards electoral participation. González Morfín understood that Conchello's desire to transform elections into a vehicle of access to power depended on the PAN's ability to tap existing social discontent for electoral gain. Since social discontent was concentrated in the middle classes and the business community, González Morfín feared that electoral compulsions would force the party to dilute its commitment to Christian socialism and betray the PAN's true mission of fighting for social justice in Mexico.[69] Conchello's electoral rabble-rousing ran contrary to González Morfín's belief in the overriding importance of doctrine in shaping meaningful political action rather than being helplessly driven by the whirlpool of society.[70]

For González Morfín, the marginal benefits that could be obtained by the party's electoral participation were outweighed by the disadvantage of legitimizing the one-party state by giving it a democratic veneer. He regarded the regime-manipulated electoral process as too tainted to function as a credible means of access to power.[71] Not surprisingly, González Morfín concluded that the best course for the PAN would be to abstain from the electoral process altogether. In 1970, he had agreed to run as the PAN's candidate for the Mexican presidency only as a matter of party discipline, since the party convention had voted by a narrow margin against abstaining in order to protest the electoral frauds of the late 1960s. During the campaign, González Morfín had pointedly avoided asking people to vote for him since he could not morally bring himself to do so.[72] González Morfín, however, never clearly indicated what the future role of the party would be if it opted for electoral abstention, an omission implying that he had in fact lost faith in the viability of the PAN as a political party under existing circumstances. For his part, Conchello sought to win more public offices for the party, even if the rules of electoral competition were biased in favor of the PRI. Both Conchello and González Morfín were thus frustrated with the PAN's traditional approach to electoral participation, though the solutions they favored were diametrically opposed.

Party Leadership and the Presidential Election of 1976

Another important factor in the conflict between Conchello and González Morfín was the issue of the over-centralization of power at the expense of rank and file PAN members, particularly those from the provinces. In part, this was the result of an anomaly in the electoral laws then in effect, which required that all party deputy seats assigned to the PAN in the Federal Chamber of Deputies be distributed in order of priority to those PAN candidates who had polled the greatest number of votes but failed to actually win any seats, a formula that obviously favored Mexico City over the less populated interior.[73] This situation was made much worse by the fact that the PAN during the late 1960s had fallen under the control of a very select group based in the capital that had always enjoyed close ties to the party's founders and boasted many of their offspring as enthusiastic members. Its undisputed leader was González Morfín, whose intellectual charisma had made him the center of a personality cult without precedent in the PAN's history.[74] When Conchello was elected party president, it had been assumed that he would follow González Morfín's lead in most matters.[75] Though a member of the PAN since 1955, Conchello had never formed part of its directive elite and owed his election as party president mostly to the fact that it was González Morfín who had proposed him for the post.[76]

It soon became clear, however, that González Morfín had underestimated the outsider from Monterrey. One of Conchello's first challenges to González Morfín was to assert his authority over party finances. After the death of Gómez Morin in 1972, the task of raising money for the party had been taken over by González Morfín and his supporters. In order to break their stranglehold over the

PAN's purse strings and gain the financial independence needed to bring his own policies to fruition, Conchello introduced a new system of automobile raffles and may even have bypassed the party treasury altogether by raising money directly from his friends in the business community, though he denies doing so.[77]

Conchello's defiance of González Morfín's leadership escalated dramatically after the latter was elected PAN president. By custom, Gómez Morin had enjoyed the right to propose his own candidate for nomination as the party's choice for the Mexican presidency.[78] Only after he had done so was it considered proper for others to announce their own candidacies, and the final decision was then taken by secret ballot at the party's national convention. González Morfín believed that as PAN president he had inherited this right from Gómez Morin and was infuriated when Conchello and his supporters preempted him by launching Pablo Emilio Madero, a business executive from Monterrey and nephew of Francisco Madero, as their preferred candidate for the PAN nomination in the upcoming presidential election of 1976.[79] Madero's candidacy was enthusiastically received by PAN militants outside Mexico City, in spite of the fact that many of the party's regional committees were controlled by González Morfín loyalists. At the party's convention held in October, 1975, neither Madero nor his principal opponent, Salvador Rosas Magallón, who was backed by González Morfín and his National Executive Committee (CEN), were able to secure the required 80 percent of all votes cast in order to be declared the party's presidential nominee. After three inconclusive ballots, González Morfín, amid angry protests from the floor, declared the convention closed and abandoned the hall. A month later at a meeting of the National Council—the party's highest body of oversight, comprising the presidents of state PAN units, regional delegates, and CEN appointees—González Morfín accused Conchello of creating a parallel organization with its own "financial maintenance, ideology, organization, hierarchy, loyalties, and communications at the margin and against the legitimate and statutory PAN."[80] When the councilors refused to censure Conchello by name, limiting their condemnation to his acts only, González Morfín resigned as party president.[81] His ill-starred presidency of the party had lasted only nine months, the shortest ever in the history of the party.

González Morfín was replaced by Manuel González Hinojosa,

a founding member and past-president of the PAN, who was unanimously elected to a second term by the National Council with the express mission of restoring party unity, even though his ideological orientation and political style were much closer to González Morfín than to Conchello. González Hinojosa, bowing to regional sentiment, immediately scheduled another convention to be held in January, 1976. The second convention was even more dismal than the first. After seven inconclusive ballots in which neither Madero nor Rosas Magallón showed the slightest willingness to withdraw in favor of the other, González Hinojosa suspended the balloting and announced that the PAN would not present a candidate for the Mexican presidency in 1976.

Faced with González Hinojosa's refusal to call a third convention, Conchello and Madero attempted to enlist the support of at least five regional committees, which was required to convoke the National Council, which in turn could overrule the president and his CEN. With nine regional committees supporting Conchello,[82] González Hinojosa realized that a meeting of the National Council was inevitable and called it into session himself rather than risk an open split in the party. The National Council, however, voted overwhelmingly against convoking another convention, thus sealing the party's decision not to participate in the 1976 presidential election. While the PAN participated in some of the federal deputy races held in the same year, it did so with a singular lack of enthusiasm and organization. Not surprisingly, the number of votes received by the party plunged almost 40 percent, from 2.3 million in 1973 to 1.4 million in 1976.

The Defeat of the González Morfín Faction

This showing, poor as it was, did nothing to temper party divisions. González Morfín and his supporters could hardly conceal their satisfaction at the party's decision to abstain from participating in the presidential election. For their part, Conchello and Madero harped on the disastrous effects of such abstentionism on the PAN and continued to flout González Hinojosa's authority.

This stalemate might have lasted for some time, had the regime not decided to approve a new electoral law in 1977. The LOPPE, as the new law was known, was at least partly a product of López

Portillo's embarrassment about having been left without an opponent in the presidential race of 1976. It greatly increased the access of
the opposition to the Chamber of Federal Deputies by reserving a
hundred seats for "minority parties" to be distributed on the basis
of proportional representation; further, the LOPPE legalized a host
of leftist political parties that had previously been relegated to
the fringes of the political system and instituted state subsidies for
political parties (which the PAN refused to accept). In a remarkable speech delivered to the National Council on February 25, 1978,
González Morfín categorically denied that the LOPPE represented a
positive step towards democratization. Instead, he saw it as a trap
designed to co-opt and fragment the opposition and strengthen the
regime's own legitimacy by creating the image of power sharing
without the substance of it. He declared that any electoral participation within the framework of the LOPPE would be contrary to
the "good of Mexico and the party" and demanded that the PAN
not abandon its abstentionist course.[83]

When it became clear that the majority of councilors did not
share his opinion, González Morfín abruptly announced his resignation from the party. His own resignation was quickly followed by
those of his principal supporters including, among others, Raúl
González Schmal, PAN secretary general under González Morfín;
Mauricio Gómez Morin; younger son of Gómez Morin; Miguel
Estrada Samano and Fernando Estrada Samano, sons of PAN founding member Miguel Estrada Iturbide; Julio Sentíes, former member of both the CEN and Mexico City regional committee; and José
Herrera Marcos, former president of the PAN in Jalisco.[84]

The mass resignations of González Morfín and his supporters
finally ended the internal conflict that had dogged the party since
1970. The crisis had been nothing less than a desperate battle for
the soul of the party in which compromise was virtually impossible. The triumph of Conchello's vision of the party ensured that
the PAN of the 1980s would be less doctrinaire than flexible, more
oriented to the middle classes and the business community than
ever before, firmly anchored in the electoral process as the principal means of access to power, and internally more open to the demands of rank and file members from the provinces, especially those
located in northern Mexico.

The defeat of the González Morfín faction also marked the

end of the long-standing hegemony of Catholic militants inside the PAN, who would find themselves displaced by more secular elements as the party broadened its base. Indeed, Conchello was the first PAN president, with the exception of Gómez Morin, who had never held a prior membership in a religious association. Interestingly, Conchello once remarked that during the decades preceding his presidency, the entry of Protestants into the PAN would have been considered blasphemous and unthinkable, whereas now the party has a significant number of them.[85] The triumph of Conchello's vision of the party in effect ensured that the PAN in the 1980s would be less a party of Christian inspiration than a nonreligious party of the modern right, though the PAN would never fully overcome its basic ideological schizophrenia.

The victory of the Conchello forces placed the PAN in a strategic position to profit from the political awakening of society and social leaders in Chihuahua and elsewhere that began in the 1980s. This political awakening was initially strongest in the highly secular region of northern Mexico and took the form of an electoral revolt against the state; strongly supported by the middle classes and the business community, the awakening lacked a clear ideological agenda apart from an elemental desire for democracy. In retrospect, the crisis of the 1970s for all its immediate disastrous consequences, may have been a blessing in disguise for the PAN.

The Importance of Internal Democracy

The PAN was in a favorable position to profit from the political awakening of society in the 1980s and 1990s by virtue of its strict adherence to democratic mechanisms for choosing candidates for public or party offices. All those wishing to represent the PAN in electoral contests for public office must first face an internal election at a convention in which all registered members of the corresponding PAN unit are eligible to vote. The national convention consisting of active members and party adherents elects the party's candidate for the presidency; state conventions elect candidates for governor, local deputy, and senator; district conventions elect candidates for federal deputy, and municipal conventions elect candidates for mayor.[86] As a result, PAN candidates, precisely because they are democratically elected, enjoy greater credibility inside and outside the party and are therefore able to mount more effective campaigns. Also, an open selection process makes it easier for natural leaders with little previous activity in the party to win nomination as PAN candidates. Party elites find it harder to foist their own candidates on rank and file members, and the base of PAN members is more likely than the party leadership to be influenced by broad societal trends. This in turn greatly improves the PAN's own chances for electoral success, since such homespun candidates can often act as lightening rods for regionalist resentment against the imposition of outsiders by the PRI.

All major party offices are likewise subject to election. The national party president is chosen by the National Council, most of whose members are elected by the party's national assembly. The president of each PAN state committee is elected by the Regional Council, which in turn is chosen by the state assembly, while the presidents of PAN municipal committees are chosen by party members in the municipalities concerned. This means that new groups in the PAN are not marginalized; they have a realistic chance of actually winning control of the party apparatus in a relatively short time, as long as they have the numerical strength to do so.

The high level of democracy inside the PAN translates into a greater sensitivity towards society at large. Democracy within the party also gave it a distinct advantage over the PRI, which until recent reforms had a tradition of selecting candidates for party and elective offices at the behest of party notables rather than through a competitive process (see chapter 6).

THE PAN IN CHIHUAHUA

Regional Factors in the Success of the PAN in Chihuahua

The explosive growth of the PAN in Chihuahua in the 1980s was in part the result of general factors affecting the PAN nationwide, particularly the changes effected by the crisis of the 1970s and the high level of internal democracy in the party. In addition, the PAN's ability to ride the wave of social discontent that developed in Chihuahua in the 1980s was enhanced by the PAN's previous trajectory in the state.

The fact that the PAN's principal founder, Gómez Morin, was a native son certainly enhanced the party's prestige in Chihuahua. It also meant that the task of creating a strong party organization in Chihuahua would not be neglected. Indeed, Gómez Morin's frequent personal visits to the state played a critical role in boosting the PAN's morale and institutional strength and in attracting fresh leadership talent to the party. In 1940, Chihuahua overwhelmingly supported Almazán, giving the PAN an early head start in the state.

In the 1950s, the PAN gained great momentum in Chihuahua as a result of the gubernatorial and presidential campaigns of Luís H. Alvarez. Proud of his strong northern roots, impressed by the workings of American democracy, which he had a chance to observe as a student at the University of Texas at Austin and the Massachusetts Institute of Technology, and sickened by the elaborate courtesanry and sycophancy habitually accorded to public functionaries, Alvarez's political baptism occurred in 1953, when he emerged as the natural leader of a civic movement in Ciudad Juárez that protested the imposition of outsiders designated by the central government to fill the posts of mayor and governor.[87] Three years later, he agreed to run as the PAN's nominee for governor against the PRI's Teófilo Borunda, who enjoyed the personal support of President Adolfo Ruiz Cortines (1952–58). Alvarez's skillful appeal to regionalist sentiment, as well as his local popularity and tireless campaigning, generated enormous enthusiasm across the state. While the official results gave Borunda a comfortable overall lead, the narrow margins of his victories in major urban centers like Chihuahua City and Ciudad Juárez and the not credible low voter turnout reported by the regime pointed to the use of fraud to alter what would otherwise have been an extremely close election.[88] Alvarez's gubernatorial and presidential campaigns, however, had raised expectations to unrealistic heights, and when these were later painfully dashed, the PAN in Chihuahua slid into disillusionment and relative decline for much of the 1960s.[89]

By 1969, the PAN's electoral prospects in the state suffered a new setback, mainly because most of the PAN's top leadership in Chihuahua were drawn to abstentionism. Alvarez himself urged González Morfín to abstain from the presidential campaign of 1970 in order to protest corrupt electoral laws and to avoid legitimizing the one-party system at home and abroad. Alvarez never viewed abstention as a long-term strategic choice, however; instead, he saw it as a limited tactic to be used only under specific conditions, such as when the party was relatively strong and therefore capable of delivering a meaningful blow to regime legitimacy.[90] In 1970, González Hinojosa, then in his first term as PAN president, suspended all but one member of the party's entire municipal committee in Ciudad Juárez for rebelling against the national convention's decision to continue participating in elections.[91] For most of the 1970s, the PAN in Chihuahua participated in only a handful of unimportant electoral contests, mostly to satisfy a small minority of grassroots members who did not wish to abstain. Otherwise, the party failed to field any candidates for mayoral office in the larger municipalities and the more important federal and local deputy seats. Nor did it participate in the race for governor in 1974. Most of the party's stalwarts in Chihuahua were not displeased when the PAN proved unable to nominate a presidential candidate in 1976.[92]

By the end of the 1970s, the PAN had all but vanished from the political landscape in Chihuahua, and the state party leadership reluctantly concluded that abstentionism had in practice been a costly error that had starved the party of media attention, financial resources, new members, and, most seriously, political goals for which to strive. Alvarez acknowledged that one important reason for the failure of abstentionism was that the PAN was unable to retain significant access to the largely state-controlled print and electronic media, which tend to cover opposition parties mainly during elections in order to improve the credibility of the electoral process.[93] For Guillermo Prieto Luján, president of the PAN state committee in Chihuahua from 1980 to 1988, the main lesson of the 1970s was that an abstentionist strategy was unworkable unless all opposition political parties agreed to abstain simultaneously.[94] Otherwise, the PAN would simply lose support to other rival opposition political parties and the regime's legitimacy would suffer little damage. In 1979, the PAN in Chihuahua voted for full participation in the federal deputy elections to be held that year, and although it secured only 14 percent of the vote, the decision to participate at all represented an important first step towards the party's subsequent electoral successes in the state.

The trajectory of the PAN in Chihuahua was uneven. In the 1940s and 1950s, the party established a firm organizational base in the state, emerged as a champion of regional feeling, fielded candidates known for their integrity and competence, and won the trust of large sectors of the population. While the PAN's relative decline in the 1960s and the subsequent phase of abstentionism in the 1970s undermined the party's institutional structure, the positive image of the PAN that was embedded in the popular psyche and the political skills that the party developed over decades remained alive. When the party returned to the electoral arena in 1979, the task of rebuilding the party organization was therefore not as difficult as it seemed at first glance. The abstentionism of the 1970s may even have helped the PAN in two important ways: First, it convinced the state party leadership of the folly of abstentionism and made them more committed to the electoral process than they might otherwise have been. Second, society's natural leaders, as they sought to take over leadership positions inside the party and become PAN candidates for public offices, encountered less resistance than they would have, had the PAN had a strong party structure in Chihuahua with well-established figures.

An analysis of federal deputy election data between 1961 and 1985 reveals that the PAN has always done significantly better in Chihuahua than in the nation as a whole, except in the 1970s when the state party leadership favored abstentionism. Presidential election data for 1964, 1970, 1982, and 1988 show an even stronger tendency in the same direction. While the average difference between the votes received by the PAN in Chihuahua as compared to the nation as a whole for federal deputy elections is 7 percent, the gap widens to 12 percent in the case of presidential elections.[95] These data probably reflect the PAN's advantages: an early start in Chihuahua, the party's ability to channel anticentralist resentment against Mexico City, and the inherent appeal of democracy in Chihuahua's liberal society.

The Development of a New Model

The combination of the surge in bottom-up support and political crafting by state party leaders spawned a "new" party that constituted a model not only for the PAN nationally but for other parties like the PRD. The new PAN in Chihuahua was marked by four elements: (1) the existence of mass support cutting across

divisions of social class; (2) campaigning to win; (3) the development of new strategies to defend the vote against electoral fraud;
and (4) ideological flexibility. The overriding purpose of these
changes was to create an efficient party instrument capable of winning political power by electoral means. While Conchello had already predisposed the PAN to this conception of the party, his had
been essentially a victory of principle. Making the actual leap from
ideas to practice was a task first undertaken by the PAN in Chihuahua in the 1980s.

Mass Support

The term mass support is used here to indicate the presence of
a high magnitude of voluntary support for the PAN on the part of
individual citizens, not the more vitiated concept of the "mass party"
based on the obligatory incorporation of undifferentiated social sectors into hierarchically ordered units and subordinated to the party.
The fact that mass support for the PAN in Chihuahua was manifested in the form of individual citizens freely turning to the party
to further their own goals gave the PAN an inner strength and
resilience that it would never have possessed otherwise. On the
other hand, the PRI's greatest weakness was precisely an acute lack
of such committed citizen participation in its own ranks, making a
mockery of the official party's vastly greater financial resources and
elaborate political machine. Indeed, the clash between society
and the state in Chihuahua can also be seen as a confrontation
between two divergent visions of politics, one elevating the citizen
to the center of the political sphere and the other reducing him or
her to the status of a passive subject of manipulation by the one-
party state.

The essence of the PAN's success in Chihuahua lay in its ability to forge a broad coalition that transcended class barriers and
effectively reduced the PRI to the status of a minority party in the
state. Miguel Basáñez's study of Mexican public opinion shows that
the PAN in 1983 had proportionally more support among workers
than businessmen in northern Mexico and nationally. In 1987, the
PAN had proportionally more support among both workers and
urban marginals than businessmen, in northern Mexico and nationally. In 1983 in northern Mexico, 22.4 percent of the workers

surveyed said they sympathized with the PAN as compared to 20.2 percent of the businessmen and 16.2 percent of the urban marginals.[96] At the national level in 1983, 14.9 percent of all workers surveyed said they sympathized with the PAN as compared to 13.5 percent of the businessmen, and 10.9 percent of the urban marginals.[97] In 1987 in northern Mexico, 30.1 percent of the urban marginals said they sympathized with the PAN as compared to 29.6 percent of the workers, and 15.1 percent of the businessmen.[98] At the national level in 1987, 14.7 percent of the workers said they sympathized with the PAN as compared to 12.4 percent of the urban marginals, 11.6 percent of the employees, and 11 percent of the businessmen.[99] In 1989, a *Los Angeles Times* poll revealed that 12 percent of low-income voters supported the PAN, 17 percent the PRD, 26 percent the PRI, and 32 percent no party; by contrast, 44 percent of all high-income voters supported the PRI, 21 percent the PAN, and 5 percent the PRD.[100]

The multiclass support for PAN in Chihuahua was also underlined by the fact that almost all the party's victories in the 1983 municipal elections occurred in major urban areas marked by high levels of social heterogeneity. In Ciudad Juárez, whose booming multinational assembly industry has made it a powerful magnet for migrant workers, the PAN won by a margin of over 30,000 votes. The party's next highest margin of victory of almost 20,000 votes was registered in the municipality of Chihuahua, which includes Chihuahua City, the state's second largest urban center with an important concentration of working-class popular colonies, and its rural hinterland. The PAN won in half of the *ejidos* in the rural section of the municipality as well,[101] a major achievement, since in rural areas regime control was tightest, the fear of retaliation against potential dissidents most pervasive, and the presence of opposition parties weakest. Interestingly, much of the PAN's electoral support in 1983 in the municipality of Chihuahua was derived from voters who had previously abstained from voting. An analysis by polling station of these new voters has revealed that they were a cross section of the population as a whole.[102]

Most of the party's leaders, however, were drawn from the middle classes and the business community. The fact that the PAN in Chihuahua was led by the middle classes was not surprising in view of their superior access to education, income, and spare time, their greater levels of political sophistication, and their lower vulnerability to government reprisals. Indeed, all political parties and institutions in Mexico suffer from a bias towards the middle classes in their leadership structures. A survey of 100 PAN leaders, mostly legislators, reveals that 85 percent were middle or upper class in origin and 15 percent working class, while the PRI's leadership was 70 percent middle class and 30 percent working class.[103] The fact that the PRI has a higher proportion of working-class leaders probably reflects the role of the party in the country's official labor movement through the CTM. What made the PAN in Chihuahua unusual was its ability to combine a predominantly middle-class leadership with a strong popular following. The party's success in building a coalition of social forces can be partially explained by the fact that the economic crisis, rather than dividing society into mutually antagonistic social classes, actually unified it by sparking an outpouring of Chihuahua's latent resentment toward the central government. Major roles in this coalition were played by women, popular colony residents, and businessmen.

Women   One top PAN official in Chihuahua estimates that approximately 50 percent of the party's membership in the state is composed of women.[104] The high rate of female participation in the party in Chihuahua reflects the higher status enjoyed by women in Chihuahua. The scarcity of labor in Chihuahua meant that women were allowed to play an active role outside the home. Apache wars left many women in Chihuahua widows and forced them to develop independent sources of income to support their children.[105] And the absence of a well-developed aristocratic and clerical tradition frustrated the development of rigid sexually defined roles that placed women in an inferior position. The higher status of women in Chihuahua can also be deduced from the fact that the state's population is richer, more educated, and growing at a slower rate than the country as a whole. Finally, the explosive growth of multinational assembly or *maquiladora* industry in Chihuahua during the 1980s is likely to have had a politicizing impact on the industry's predominantly female workers by inducting women into the industrial labor force, widening their intellectual horizons, and exposing them to major urban settings.[106] The impact of *maquiladoras* on women has been concentrated in the lower strata of Mexican society, since their workers are drawn mostly from low-income families. The relative equality of the sexes in Chihuahua ensured that politics would not be seen as an exclusively male activity; that women participating in political parties could usually count on the support of their families; and that women's views would be taken seriously.

The high rate of female participation in the PAN in Chihuahua also reflects the PAN's openness to women nationally. The PAN was the first political party in Mexico to propose the extension of suffrage to women, introducing bills to enfranchise women in municipal elections (1946) and federal elections (1948).[107] The PRI, however, did not introduce its own bill granting suffrage to women in federal elections until as late as 1953, partly because it feared that women would vote conservative. The PAN has always fielded a high number of female candidates for public offices, and women have occupied important posts in the party's internal organizational structure. In 1964, Mexico elected its first female deputy by majority vote on the PAN ticket from Parral, Chihuahua.

There are several explanations for the openness of the PAN as a national organization to women. The party's early conception of itself as mainly a civic organization and its overwhelmingly middle-class composition fostered a positive environment for female participation. Women, who in Mexico tend to be more religious than men, may have been especially attracted to the PAN by virtue of its Christian inspiration, though this phenomenon was probably most evident in central Mexico during the 1940s and 1950s, when religious tensions and memories of past Church-State conflicts were still very much alive in that region. Also, opposition politicians in Mexico often faced social rejection, ridicule, and reprisals directed at their sources of livelihood. Since the burden of these risks inevitably affected their families as well, a *sine qua non* of individual involvement in opposition parties was family support. This, coupled with the PAN's emphasis on the family as an outward-looking unit of service to the community rather than as a place of egotistical refuge from the troubles of the world, made participation in the PAN very much a family affair and many *panistas* saw their wives and children become prominent party figures in their own right. Finally, the party's relatively small membership until the 1980s may have furnished a major incentive for recruiting women and giving them a real voice in decision making.

While women professionals and female *maquiladora* workers in Chihuahua may have voted for the PAN in great numbers, they lacked the time to become involved in party affairs directly. Those women professionals who did get involved normally had more time to devote to the party or were willing to sacrifice career advancement for the party. The overwhelming majority of female activists in the PAN in Chihuahua, however, consisted of housewives, usually but not exclusively from the middle classes. Housewives made up the majority of the PAN's representatives at the polling stations on election day. They provided the main impulse for the crucial task of organizing party subcommittees in their respective colonies. Such subcommittees were almost always chaired by them as well.[108] Housewives also constituted an important channel of communication between the PAN and society; the party often relied on them to publicize major events, mobilize supporters quickly, and circumvent the news blockade imposed by the state-controlled media. Finally, housewives, often with children, were a major presence at the PAN's numerous rallies, protest meetings, and civil disobedience acts, and this may have helped discourage violent repression by the police.

Housewives participated in the PAN for a variety of reasons. Husbands employed by the state directly or indirectly, belonging to official trade unions, or whose supervisors were PRI supporters feared becoming victims of reprisals if they expressed sympathy for the opposition. Instead, they simply encouraged their wives and children to participate in the PAN in their place. The control that the regime could exercise over the family breadwinner was thus more often than not subverted by the alienation of all the other members of the household. Also, the economic crisis confronted housewives responsible for managing household finances with the difficult challenge of making ends meet on their husband's shrinking income.

While some housewives participating in the PAN would have liked to see female activists occupy more leadership positions inside the party state committee,[109] they did not have an explicit agenda for women as an interest group. They focused instead on issues affecting their families and society as a whole, although their involvement in the PAN nevertheless had an impact on the status of women in Chihuahua.[110] Women who had once related to the outside world almost entirely through their husbands could now do so through the party. Housewives who had rarely read a newspaper in the past suddenly began poring over the front page for the latest political news and flocked to PAN meetings devoted to the study of party doctrine and strategy. The constant exposure to new ideas and people, the experience of taking on the regime in the streets and elsewhere, the long hours spent organizing the PAN in the colonies, and the conviction that what they were doing was important combined to give women in Chihuahua a greater sense of self-confidence, a higher level of political and social awareness, and an enhanced ability to command the respect of the men in their families. Female participation in the PAN in Chihuahua had the unintended effect of promoting the democratization of family life too.

Popular Colony Residents   Unlike the PAN in some other parts of Mexico, the PAN in Chihuahua received significant support from residents of popular colonies as well. The flow of immigrants drawn to the state by the boom in the *maquiladora* industry and Chihuahua's closeness to the United States has greatly exceeded the ability of state and municipal governments, already crippled by drastic budgetary cuts, to cope with the influx. Also, popular colony residents, who rarely possess much of a security cushion in the best of times, have borne the brunt of the impact of economic crisis and its social consequences, including gang violence, family disintegration, drug addiction, and youth unemployment. Social frustration directed at the regime was the principal reason why popular colony residents voted overwhelmingly for the PAN in 1983, even though they knew little about the party's ideology and the PAN's organizational base in popular colonies was very weak at the time.

Some credit must also be given to the PAN's campaign strategy, which focused entirely on attacking regime incompetence and malfeasance as the main culprits of the economic crisis. The party also chose self-made, appealing, and dynamic individuals such as Francisco Barrio and Gustavo Villarreal Posada, a onetime *bracero* in his youth, as its candidates for mayoral office in Ciudad Juárez and Parral, respectively. Both Barrio and Villarreal Posada quickly developed a movie-star-like rapport with the urban underclass and emerged with massive personal followings in popular colonies, particularly among marginalized youth. The presence of large numbers of poorly educated, rebellious, and frustrated youth, in turn, constituted a volatile element at PAN rallies and protest meetings that party leaders feared could easily slip out of control and erupt into violence.

The PAN also used the 1983 campaign to take the PRI to task for failing to solve some of the most pressing problems of the state's popular colonies. In Parral, mayoral candidate Villarreal Posada made a crippling water shortage that had affected the city for years the main issue of his campaign.[111] The shortage was most acute in the popular colonies, which tended to be located in elevated zones around the city and to which water could not be pumped because of a lack of adequate water pressure. The enterprising Villarreal began extracting water from the subsoil of his own ranch, located close to a river, rented a truck with a tank of 4,000 liters, and started delivering water to the city's colonies. The PRI, not to be outdone, began delivering 8,000 liters of water to the affected colonies as well. Villarreal then escalated to a tank of 22,000 liters which was immediately matched by the PRI. The PRI's hopes of winning the competition were, however, shattered when Villarreal disclosed that the water supplied by the PRI in its tanks had simply been taken out of the city's water purification plant. This meant that the PRI, far from increasing the city's net water supply, had actually reduced it, unlike Villarreal, whose water had come from his own ranch.

The fact that the PAN held the reins of municipal government in all of Chihuahua's major cities between 1983 and 1986 also helped the party win the support of popular colony residents. The PAN mayors were reluctant to channel municipal services through PRI-linked organizations, preferring to create alternative institutional networks, such as neighborhood committees or other representative bodies, to act as the principal link between popular colonies and the municipal authorities. Another motive for the formation of the neighborhood committees was to help mobilize popular colony residents against the Popular Defense Committee (CDP). The CDP, a powerful semi-co-opted organization that functioned as the PRI's main conduit for channeling services to popular colonies in Chihuahua City and Ciudad Juárez, was now being used by the regime to wreak havoc in the two municipalities in order to discredit the

PAN mayors and furnish the PRI-dominated state congress with the necessary pretext to dissolve the PAN municipal governments.[112] In spite of the PAN leanings of the neighborhood committees, municipal services channeled through them were distributed without regard to the beneficiary's political affiliation, in a sharp break from past PRI practice. Indeed, the neighborhood committees generated support for the PAN, not by the use of strong-arm tactics, but because they furnished popular colony residents with a representative mechanism to freely express their needs to the municipal authorities.

The PAN mayors, who ran their municipalities as they might run a business, also won support in popular colonies and among the citizenry as a whole by providing better quality services more efficiently as a result of transparent and dexterous financial management, improved tax collection systems, and a refusal to tolerate corruption.[113] This achievement was all the more remarkable given the fact that the PAN mayors had fewer resources at their disposal than their PRI predecessors due to the state and federal government's decision to channel discretionary funds directly and not through the PAN-controlled municipal governments. The PAN administrations, reflecting the party's old belief that private property ownership should be as widely diffused as possible, also granted property titles to *colonos* or settlers who had often been in a state of legal limbo for years. The preceding PRI administrations had tolerated land invasions and the establishment of illegal urban settlements but avoided issuing property titles since this would have lessened the regime's control over the *colonos,* who, no longer facing the threat of eviction, could then freely support the PAN or any other opposition group. The CDP was equally reluctant to provide property titles, fearing that its supporters would simply desert the organization once they tasted the security of legal ownership.[114] The granting of property titles to *colonos* was one of the most significant actions of the PAN mayors because its effects, negative for the PRI and CDP and positive for the PAN, transcended their limited three-year terms.

Fortunately for the PRI, the PAN mayors were unable to regularize the situation of some of the most needy settlers who resided in colonies outside their respective city limits and were by law subject to the control of the state government.[115] The constant flow of migration to Chihuahua also ensured that the PRI would be able to replace those *colonos* that had escaped from its clutches with new ones in a relatively short span of time. And the PRI administrations that took office in the wake of the disputed 1986 state elections completely ignored the neighborhood committees and other representative bodies set up by their PAN predecessors.[116] While these groups, starved of municipal recognition, began to atrophy, the CDP and other PRI-affiliated organizations were able to regain much of the clout that they had earlier lost. As a result, the PAN's support in Chihuahua's popular colonies, which had grown steadily since 1983 and reached its peak in the protests that followed the 1986 state elections, now began to show signs of ebbing. In cities like Ciudad Juárez where an alternative structure of party subcommittees was developed to replace the officially nonpartisan neighborhood committees, the PAN was able to offset this trend for a time. In Chihuahua City, where such subcommittees existed mainly on paper, the PAN proved unable to staunch the loss of support in popular colonies. The decline of the PAN's influence among popular colony residents once the party ceased to exercise power in the state's major cities was not unexpected, since such support had been motivated primarily by pragmatic considerations of material improvement rather than by principle, reflecting both the high economic vulnerability and low level of politicization characteristic of popular colonies.[117]

Businessmen   Another major plank of support for the PAN in Chihuahua was furnished by the business community.[118] State industries producing for the internal market have always played a less important role in the economic development of Chihuahua than in the Mexico City metropolitan area because of the orientation of Chihuahua's economy towards exports and foreign investment and the abundance of entrepreneurial talent in the state. As a result, Chihuahua's business community is less connected to the Mexican state and possesses a greater margin for independent political action. Within this overall context, however, the PAN's support in the business community was likely to vary in intensity according to the size of the business concerned. Much of the PAN's support came from small and medium-sized businesses. Such businesses were less likely to be beneficiaries of major government contracts, being ill-equipped to handle large orders; more capable of securing their inputs from private sources in view of their limited needs; and harder to identify as potential targets for reprisals. Also, smaller businesses usually possessed too few employees to justify unionization by state-controlled labor federations. On the other hand, large businesses often owed more to the state for their success, had greater interests to protect, and had a direct stake in exercising continuing influence over macro-economic policy. As a result, major businessmen usually supported the PRI, except in the 1983 state elections, when the nationalization of the banking system led to a temporary fallout between some of their number and the regime.

Indeed, the growth of Chihuahua's largest conglomerate, the Chihuahua Group, can hardly be separated from its connections with the new revolutionary elite. Echeverría's decision in 1971 to expropriate 256,000 hectares of forests belonging to the Chihuahua Group, now led by Eloy Vallina, Jr., jolted this cozy relationship with the Mexican state. An even bigger jolt occurred in 1982, when López Portillo nationalized all privately owned banks, including the Mexican Commercial Bank, which by now had become one of the nation's most important financial institutions and represented approximately half of the Chihuahua Group's assets. While Vallina, Jr., admits that he was angered by bank nationalization, he denies having supported the PAN in Chihuahua in 1983.[119] Local press reports, however, claim that on being informed of the bank nationalization, Vallina, Jr., declared: "They [the PRI] took my banks from me, I will take Chihuahua from them."[120] His wife also attended some meetings of the National Civic Feminine Association (ANCIFEM), an organization that leans towards the PAN.[121] If Vallina, Jr., supported the PAN in 1983, he probably did so in order to strengthen his bargaining position vis-à-vis the Mexican state over the issue of compensation for the loss of the banks. Indeed, once President Miguel de la Madrid (1982–88) had announced a handsome package of indemnification for the former bank owners, Vallina, Jr., publicly declared that he was a *priísta* and extended his enthusiastic support to the PRI's Fernando Baeza.[122]

Another major business figure who supported the PAN in 1983 was Jaime Bermúdez, the creator of the *maquiladora* industry in Ciudad Juárez and the owner of various industrial parks in the city. Bermúdez helped finance the campaign of Francisco Barrio, a former employee, for mayor of Ciudad Juárez. While Bermúdez was not personally affected by bank nationalization, he was no doubt worried about the impact of Mexico City's strident economic populism

on the future of the *maquiladora* industry. In 1986, however, much
to the surprise of his relatives and friends, Bermúdez agreed to run
as the PRI's candidate for mayor of Ciudad Juárez. The most plau-
sible explanation for this about face is that Bermúdez believed that
he could unite the city around a program of rapid infrastructural
development fueled by generous financial assistance from the central government,[123] which had been made nervous by the strength
of the opposition there. Such a program would be good for himself
as an industrial promoter and his city as well.

The fact that the PAN was initially supported by major businessmen like Vallina, Jr., and Bermúdez has led some to argue that
the rise of the PAN in Chihuahua was simply the result of the machi-
nations of a handful of capitalists eager to protect their interests.
This may explain the personal motives of Vallina, Jr., and Bermúdez
in supporting the PAN in 1983 and the PRI in 1986, but it does not
explain the 1983 electoral victories of the PAN in Chihuahua, which
were the result of a spontaneous outburst of social discontent covering virtually all sectors of society. Also, had antiregime sentiment
in Chihuahua in 1983 been simply the result of an orchestrated
plot hatched by Vallina, Jr., and Bermúdez, then such feelings should
have subsided during the 1986 electoral process, by which time
both men had openly proclaimed their PRI sympathies. Instead,
the very opposite occurred. Finally, the conspiracy theory is unsatisfactory because it ignores the pivotal role of owners of small and
medium-sized businesses.

While most small and medium-sized businesses were directly
affected by the economic crisis through sluggish demand, rising costs,
and lack of credit, it was not adversity per se that led them to support the PAN but rather their perceptions of the underlying causes
of the crisis. Most businessmen started with the premise that Mexico
was an inherently rich country that was poor because of its system
of government. For them, the central causes of the crisis were corruption and mismanagement. The ease with which López Portillo
had nationalized the banking system simply underscored the vulnerability of society to a political system in which presidential caprice could
in one stroke become the law of the land. Nor would Mexico have
fallen so deep into foreign debt had the constitutional provision
requiring the government to seek the consent of the legislature
before contracting international financial obligations been strictly

observed. The only way to save Mexico from further economic disaster was therefore to establish a genuine democracy based on a system of checks and balances among the three branches of government, on clean elections supervised by an impartial body, and on a new respect for the federal nature of the Mexican constitution.

Chihuahua's businessmen were also extremely anticentralist in their ideology. For them, the central government served no useful role except to strangle the productive energies of the state by superimposing a layer of bureaucratic control utterly insensitive to local conditions and aspirations. They never tired of repeating the fact that of all the immense tax revenues collected by the central government in Chihuahua, only a fraction was returned to the state, the rest apparently being ploughed into subsidies to pacify Mexico City. Many businessmen in Chihuahua were deeply influenced in their political and economic thinking by the Mexican Employers' Confederation (COPARMEX), a voluntary association of business employers from whose ranks have sprung in recent years some important PAN figures, and the Technological and Higher Studies Institute of Monterrey (ITESM), a private university system that has educated many of northern Mexico's business leaders and some of whose faculty members, particularly on its Chihuahua City campus, have been sympathizers and informal advisors of the PAN.[124]

The business community in Chihuahua grew increasingly politicized as the 1986 state elections neared. In Chihuahua City, the local branches of the National Confederation of Chambers of Commerce (CONCANACO), National Chamber of Transformation Industries (CANACINTRA), and the Entrepreneurs' Center—as the local branches of COPARMEX are known—issued a joint statement on July 1, 1986, demanding that the upcoming elections be conducted in a "clean and impartial manner" and that the regime respect the results.[125] A few days after the elections, they declared that the electoral process had been marred by grave irregularities and called on their members to pull down the shutters of their businesses on July 10 for twelve hours as a mark of protest. About 1,600 businesses participated in the strictly voluntary shutdown.[126] Another such closure was organized on July 14, but fewer businesses chose to participate this time. The three business organizations also urged their members to withdraw their money from the state-owned banking system in the largest amounts possible and declare their taxes using zeros only.[127] Finally, the Entrepreneurs' Centers of Chihuahua City and Ciudad Juárez jointly called on President de la Madrid to annul the elections and convoke new ones.

When it became clear that the regime would not annul the elections, the business organizations retreated, declaring that while they would continue to question the electoral process, they would now focus on pressing for the adoption of a new electoral law that would reduce the likelihood of future conflicts.[128] The participation of CONCANACO and CANACINTRA in the mobilization of the business community was indicative of the extreme doubt surrounding the election results, since both organizations were established by law to represent the corporate interests of their obligatory membership and were usually less inclined to become involved in a confrontation with the regime than the Entrepreneurs' Centers, which did not face the same constraints. Apart from protesting election irregularities, businessmen also supported the PAN by becoming party candidates for public office (almost all the party's candidates who won mayoral races in Chihuahua in 1983 had business backgrounds); providing generous financial contributions to the party, especially during election campaigns (one party leader estimates that roughly half of the PAN's budget in the state for 1986 came from business donations);[129] and lending their administrative skills to the task of party organization.

Campaigning to Win

For the first time since the latter half of the 1950s, the PAN in Chihuahua enjoyed the mass support necessary to make winning elections a feasible proposition. The swelling of the PAN's popularity in the state was also reflected in a major leap in the party's financial and organizational resources. The party's small size in Chihuahua, made still smaller by the years of abstentionism, its democratic procedures for candidate selection, and the willingness of old-time *panistas* to step aside in favor of newcomers not burdened by the image of being perpetual losers enabled the PAN to field candidates who, in most cases, had hardly any previous record of involvement with the party but were generally recognized as natural leaders in their communities. They were willing to expose their businesses and families to potential government reprisals and to invest considerable resources of their own into their campaigns because they were convinced that they could defeat the PRI machine at the polls.

The overriding determination of the PAN's candidates in the 1983 municipal elections translated into hard-hitting campaign tactics. Constant attacks on the regime were designed to capture the protest vote. Support was garnered by saturation advertising in the press and electronic media, personal visits to offices and private homes, mass rallies, and spectacular actions like Villarreal Posada's dramatization of Parral's water supply crisis. An unprecedented television debate was held between rival candidates for mayor of Chihuahua City. Many of these tactics were quite new in the Mexican context and reflected the influence of U.S.-style campaigning and the enterprising nature of the PAN's candidates.

Defending the Vote

The wave of PAN victories in the 1983 elections, the prestige of the PAN municipal administrations, and the enormous popularity enjoyed by Francisco Barrio, the party's candidate for governor of Chihuahua, led to widespread expectations that the PAN would win the state's gubernatorial election in 1986. Yet there were equally troubling signs that the PRI was planning to resort to unfair means to block the PAN's path to the governorship. In such a situation, merely having the votes to win would not be enough to ensure the acceptance of PAN triumphs by the regime, unless the party could simultaneously develop strategies to defend those votes against probable electoral fraud. The PAN defended the vote through civil disobedience, improving party organization, and appealing to international public opinion.

Civil Disobedience The adoption of civil disobedience as a strategy to defend the vote in the 1986 elections in Chihuahua was formally announced by Barrio on April 18, a few months before the July 6 elections.[130] The reason for initiating the civil disobedience movement before the elections was to discourage the regime from carrying out what the PAN believed was a detailed plan to steal the elections by fraud.[131] After the elections, the focus of civil disobedience shifted to protesting election irregularities and demanding that the government respect the popular will. Barrio also regarded civil disobedience as a means of reducing political apathy.[132] In his view, the high rate of abstention marring Mexican elections was the result of a feeling of profound impotence and cynicism among voters tired of seeing their verdicts overturned by electoral fraud and resigned to the inevitability of a PRI victory by any means. Civil disobedience, by giving voters hope that they could actually do something to combat electoral fraud, would encourage a higher voter turnout, helping the PAN since new voters usually voted against the PRI.

Civil disobedience was also a strategy designed to empower the PAN in its relationship with the regime.[133] Opposition political parties in Mexico have always been faced with the problematic choices of functioning within the rules set by the regime, abstaining, or turning to violence. Violence was not an option for the PAN because it would give the regime an excuse to use its monopoly over the means of force to repress the party, and using violence would contradict the party's oft-stated mission of fighting for a just social order based on the rule of law. At the same time, the experience of the 1970s showed that abstentionism was not a viable option under existing conditions. As a result, the PAN has tended to operate within the limits created by the regime, though it engages in a constant tug of war to have those limits expanded. Politically, civil disobedience guaranteed that any fraudulently elected PRI officials would take office under a cloud of illegitimacy. In the long run, however, civil disobedience, by delegitimizing the electoral process, could also depress voter turnout, even if it might provoke a greater short-run interest in politics.

Among the civil disobedience actions initiated before the elections were the nonpayment of water bills, covering automobile license plates with stickers identifying the motorist as a member of the civil disobedience movement, and stamping currency notes with slogans such as "In Chihuahua we demand respect for the vote."[134] Such measures, which did not inflict any real damage on the regime, the participants, or third parties, familiarized the population with the notion of civil disobedience and fostered solidarity among PAN supporters, eroding their fear of challenging the government and providing visible proof of the party's popularity in Chihuahua. Indeed, by the middle of May, over 25,000 motorists in Ciudad Juárez had covered their license plates with the coveted stickers.[135]

Far more worrisome to the regime was the hunger strike initiated on July 1, six days before the elections, by Luís H. Alvarez, then mayor of Chihuahua City; Victor Manuel Oropeza, founder of the Mexican Workers Party (PMT) in Ciudad Juárez; and Francisco Villareal Torres, a successful businessman who belonged to no party. All three chose easily accessible public parks as the venue for their hunger strikes. Having failed in their initial goal of preventing the regime from rigging the elections on July 6, the hunger strikers, in a statement issued on July 21, characterized the elections as the "most violent injury, the most filthy fraud, and the most vile robbery suffered by the people of Chihuahua" at the hands of "the delinquents of the Mexican political system."[136] They then announced that they would continue their fast "to the end" unless the regime ceased to "mock the popular will."[137]

The nonpartisan tone of the hunger strike was underlined by the fact that neither Villareal Torres nor Oropeza were supporters of the PAN while Alvarez had made it clear that he was undertaking his fast because he considered it incumbent on him as mayor to protect the rights of the citizenry.[138] Their insistence that they were defending democracy, not the PAN's particular victories, and their willingness to risk death in nonviolent struggle against electoral manipulation gave them enormous moral authority. Huge crowds collected daily around the hunger strikers, who became the main source of inspiration for the protests sweeping the state, which included repeated blockades of the Pan American Highway linking Chihuahua to the rest of Mexico, consumer boycotts of businesses collaborating with the PRI, the seizure of international bridges connecting Ciudad Juárez and El Paso, plebiscites on whether the elections were fraudulent, silent marches, and the deliberate obstruction of major traffic intersections. As the three men, particularly the sixty-seven-year old Alvarez, began to weaken physically, the public pressure on the regime to annul the official results grew even more intense. Villareal Torres warned the regime that it would not be able to govern Chihuahua over their corpses, and Guillermo Prieto, president of the PAN state committee, declared that the death of the hunger strikers "would set the state ablaze."[139]

The regime, however, remained steadfast in its decision not to

annul the elections, and on August 7, Chihuahua's PRI-controlled
Electoral College ratified the official elections results. By then, it
was clear that the regime was going to cling to Chihuahua at any
price and would allow the hunger strikers to die regardless of the
political costs. Alvarez himself feared that his death might lead to
an eruption of violence across the state that would be counterproductive and inconsistent with his political values.[140] Meanwhile,
Herberto Castillo, national president of the PMT, visited the hunger
strikers and urged them not to give up their lives in vain but to
place the "ethical and political capital" that they had accumulated
at the service of the continuing struggle for democracy.[141] He warned
them that their deaths would not inflict major damage on the federal government, which could depend on the relatively low level of
politicization in other Mexican states to isolate Chihuahua.[142] Castillo
then proposed the formation of an unprecedented alliance of opposition political parties and civic associations across the political
spectrum to launch a "crusade" for electoral democracy throughout Mexico.[143]

On August 9, national leaders from the PAN, the PMT, the
Unified Socialist Party of Mexico (PSUM), the Social Democratic
Party (PSD), and Revolutionary Workers Party (PRT) met in Ciudad
Juárez under the auspices of the Committee for the Democratic
Struggle (COLUDE), a well known local civic association.[144] They
announced the formation of a National Democratic Movement (MDN)
and the convocation of a National Forum for Effective Suffrage to
be held in early September; the hunger strikers were invited to join
hands with the MDN's quest for democracy.[145] On August 10,
Alvarez, Villareal Torres, and Oropeza reluctantly agreed to suspend
their forty-one-day hunger strike and declared their willingness to
participate in the MDN.[146] While opposition unity represented by
the MDN was short-lived, that it occurred at all was an extraordinary achievement. The exercise in unity gave national credibility
to accusations of fraud in Chihuahua, laid the groundwork for future alliances between ideologically divergent parties to defend the
vote, and ensured that the hunger strikers would not come away
from their fast without a victory.

Another major action to defend the vote was the seizure of
the international bridges linking Ciudad Juárez and El Paso, which
ensured that the PAN's charges of electoral fraud in Chihuahua

would receive extensive media coverage in the international press. This dealt a major blow to the regime's image abroad at a time of considerable stress in U.S.-Mexican relations and on the eve of an important visit by President de la Madrid to Washington. The three bridge takeovers created panic in the *maquiladora* industry, which imports almost all its inputs and supplies critical components to U.S. companies.[147] The fact that the PAN was not regarded as a leftist party hostile to foreign investment[148] and Barrio's astute decision not to seize all the bridges at one time calmed the *maquiladora* industry's fears, but the takeovers nonetheless succeeded in exposing the inherent instability of the Mexican political system to foreign investors. Nor could the regime simply use force to dislodge the cheery multitude holding the bridges without doing so in full view of U.S. television cameras. There was also the risk that any Mexican police or military units sent to clear the bridges might find themselves chasing the protesters onto the U.S. side of the bridges, provoking a major international incident as a result.

On August 9, Barrio ended the third takeover of the bridges, which had lasted for almost a week. He was discouraged by the regime's decision to ratify the election results and reluctant to demand further sacrifices from the residents of Ciudad Juárez and El Paso for nothing.[149] Barrio's decision to end the takeover of the bridges, coupled with the suspension of the hunger strike the next day, sapped the energy of the civil disobedience movement; both measures had become important symbols of resistance in Chihuahua but now they had to be abandoned. Nevertheless, while civil disobedience failed to overturn the election verdicts, it raised the cost of electoral fraud by generating unwanted international publicity, causing economic disruption, and attracting the wider attention of intellectuals, the business community, and the Catholic Church. It also further eroded the credibility of the PRI's claims of victory, furnished the occasion for a rare spirit of opposition unity, and kept the protests against fraud alive for much longer than the regime could have anticipated.

Improved Party Organization   One of the main defects of Mexican opposition parties has been their lack of organization. Indeed, the PAN in Chihuahua was, from an organizational standpoint, unprepared to respond to the eventuality of fraudulent elections in

1986, choosing instead to rely on civil disobedience as its principal means of defending the vote. Guillermo Prieto had assumed that the sheer magnitude of the PAN's triumphs would, as in 1983, be sufficient to deter the regime from stealing the 1986 elections. The party's traumatic encounter with fraud in 1986 led to a major questioning of its approach to defending the vote. Nowhere was this more apparent than in Ciudad Juárez, where the strategy of civil disobedience was criticized for having exhausted society without achieving the reversal of the election verdicts.

The top priority of Gustavo Elizondo, who was elected president of the PAN in Ciudad Juárez in November, 1986, was to develop an organizational strategy to defend the vote in the upcoming 1988 elections for federal deputies and president. Elizondo assembled a team of highly trained individuals who saw themselves more as political managers than politicians. As secretary general of the PAN municipal committee, he appointed Antonio Badía, a shrewd political strategist, who had once worked as an engineer in the *maquiladora* industry. For Badía, the optimal use of the party time lay in devoting 80 percent to organizational activity and only 20 percent to campaigning.[150] A full-time employee of the PAN, Badía was a strong advocate of the professionalization of all aspects of party management.[151] In his view, the efforts of amateur volunteers, who could give the party only their spare time, were woefully inadequate. As a result, the PAN in Ciudad Juárez began hiring record numbers of full-time employees, overcoming both financial limitations and the reluctance of talented individuals to put promising careers on hold for an uncertain future in the PAN. During the 1988 campaign, the PAN in Ciudad Juárez had twenty-three full-time employees, more than even the CEN.[152]

The heart of Badía's strategy to rejuvenate the PAN's organizational ability to combat fraud lay in his plan to develop party subcommittees in the city's approximately 350 electoral sections, each section containing a voting precinct. On the eve of the 1988 federal elections, over half of all the electoral sections had functioning subcommittees, which made it easier for the PAN to verify the accuracy of voter registration lists prepared by the regime.[153] By acting as micro-level units of proselytization, the subcommittees also helped boost PAN votes. They performed routine but time-consuming functions, like distributing PAN propaganda, that would otherwise have fallen to party headquarters, allowing top leadership to focus on more strategic issues. Subcommittees also enabled the party to enhance its ability to raise financial contributions from ordinary citizens.

Another important innovation instituted to defend the vote in the 1988 federal elections in Ciudad Juárez was the practice of visiting at home those whom the government had selected to serve as presidents of the city's voting precincts, or *casillas*. These functionaries enjoyed near dictatorial powers in their respective *casillas*, which they often used to perpetrate fraud. House calls were usually organized by the relevant subcommittee and occurred in groups of approximately two hundred people.[154] If the *casilla* president was an incumbent with no previous record of fraud, he was congratulated for his honesty and offered the support of his community in resisting pressures to commit fraud. If the *casilla* president was an incumbent with a previous record of fraud, he was asked to resign. If he chose to refuse, he was informed that he was under close public observation and that if he betrayed the community on election day, the community would make life impossible for him economically, socially, and legally. The weight of this threat was such that some *casilla* presidents resigned, others failed to turn up on election day, and most of the rest made sure that their conduct was beyond reproach. House calls thus constituted an unusual but simple mechanism of empowering society in relation to the electoral process.

The PAN in Ciudad Juárez also completely restructured its approach to defending the vote on election day itself. In 1986, the organizational chain of command to respond to electoral fraud in progress had been centralized: Party representatives in individual *casillas* were responsible to a smaller number of "general" representatives, who in turn relied on instructions from party headquarters. In 1988, the chain of command was reversed: Party representatives were empowered to make on-the-spot decisions on how to respond to fraud in progress, general representatives were to act only as aids to party representatives, and headquarters was practically deserted on election day.[155] The PAN's ability to organize a well-coordinated defense of the vote on election day was enhanced by an agreement with the leftist opposition political parties allowing the PAN to nominate their respective party representatives.[156]

The PAN in Ciudad Juárez created and trained an elite corps

of party representatives or "commandos," who were assigned to particularly sensitive *casillas* where large-scale fraud had occurred in the past.[157] The "commandos" were well educated, articulate, and successful individuals who enjoyed high status in the community and were therefore in a position to intimidate and undermine the authority of *casilla* presidents. The "commandos" were given instructions to disrupt voting if they saw fraud occurring and the *casilla* president refused to put a stop to it. Under federal electoral law, the violent disruption of voting, when it undermines the secrecy of the ballot and changes the election results, is sufficient cause for declaring the results from the *casilla* concerned null and void. The rationale for disrupting voting was to foil the regime's strategy of selectively committing massive fraud in a small minority of *casillas*, usually located in marginalized areas under tight PRI control, thus altering the results in the entire electoral district. PAN representatives including the "commandos" were assisted by Vote Defense Groups, collections of colony residents, usually assembled by the party subcommittees, who were stationed outside the *casillas*. If irregularities were apparent, the party representative would give the signal for the Vote Defense Group to mount a vigorous protest, placing the *casilla* president under intense psychological pressure to correct the abuses. If this failed, the "commando" would then order the Vote Defense Group to disrupt the voting by invading the *casilla*, throwing away ballot boxes, and provoking the police or army to intervene.[158]

The party's organizational barriers against electoral fraud in Ciudad Juárez were greatly strengthened by the acquisition of a modest computer system.[159] The party was now able to identify which incumbent *casilla* presidents had committed what type of irregularities and when. This made it easier for the PAN to exercise its legal right to petition the regime to replace such corrupt functionaries; and the PAN could identify which *casilla* presidents to visit and what to say to them. Computerization also enabled the party to analyze the pattern of voting in particular *casillas* over time. If the pattern of voting in a given year varied significantly from the normal trend, this was taken to indicate that fraud had probably occurred and that the party should post a "commando" at the *casilla* rather than a party representative. Computerization also helped the PAN determine which of its party representatives had a poor track record in preventing fraud in their *casillas* so they could be replaced. Further, the party could rapidly compare the number of registered voters in a particular *casilla* with the number of votes cast and, if the latter exceeded the former by more than 10 percent, file a petition for annulment before the legal deadline to do so had expired. Finally, computerization ensured that the PAN would be able to deliver its own tally of the election results to the press in record time, thus conditioning public expectations of the election results and making it more difficult for the PRI-controlled electoral district commissions to issue contrary verdicts without losing credibility in the process.

The PAN's decision in Ciudad Juárez to eschew loud and noisy campaigning as well as the spectacular actions typical of civil disobedience in favor of quieter organizational strategy, which took 18 months to design and implement, led to tension with the campaign committee of PAN presidential candidate Clouthier. The local PAN, however, was more than vindicated by the results of the 1988 elections, in which the party won all three federal deputy seats assigned to Ciudad Juárez. Without the party's organizational ability to frustrate fraud on election day, it is unlikely the PAN would have won in Ciudad Juárez. Over 20 percent of the party's supporters had already been eliminated from the government-elaborated electoral rolls before the elections,[160] thus making it all the more crucial that the PAN be able to defend the remainder of its votes against further fraud on election day itself. The narrowness of the PAN's victories in the third federal deputy district, where it officially won by a mere four votes, and the eighth district, where it won by 754 votes, confirmed the importance of being organizationally prepared.[161] In Chihuahua City, where there was virtually no organizational strategy in place, the party failed to win any seats.

Appealing to International Public Opinion   One way of raising the price of committing electoral fraud was to ensure that incidents of fraud received widespread publicity abroad, thereby damaging the regime's carefully cultivated international image. This could be achieved by inviting foreign observers to witness the electoral process, actively courting the international press, and filing formal accusations against the regime before international organizations citing human rights violations. Historically, however, Mexican opposition parties were reluctant to bring international pressure to bear on the regime, fearing that they might be labeled unpatriotic. The regime had always sought to strengthen its legitimacy by cloaking itself in the mantle of nationalistic virtue. For years, state-influenced media, schools, universities, trade unions, and cultural institutions sought to foster a direct link between being a "good" Mexican in the widest sense of the term and supporting the PRI. Those Mexicans who did not accept the dominant myth and supported opposition parties were cast as social misfits with sinister intentions.

The electoral process in Chihuahua provided the occasion for the first major break with the long-standing tradition on the part of opposition parties not to criticize the regime at the international level. To some extent this reflected the fact that Chihuahua, as a border state, is especially open to the foreign news media and the fact that northern Mexicans have always been less likely to confuse love of country with automatic support for the PRI. The willingness of the PAN in Chihuahua to criticize the government abroad also reflected structural changes in the nature of Mexican politics, including the decay of the regime's legitimacy at home in the 1980s. The effectiveness of open criticism of the regime further pointed to the government's heightened sensitivity to international opinion as a result of Mexico's growing dependence on the international economy and the deepening isolation of its authoritarian political system from the global trend towards democracy. The intense foreign press coverage of irregularities in the 1986 state elections by seasoned reporters not only from the United States but Japan and Western Europe as well, the seizure of the international bridges, and the appearance of a group of angry *Chihuahuenses* protesting electoral fraud outside the White House during de la Madrid's visit to Washington in August, 1986, all undermined the government's credibility abroad.[162]

An even more serious threat to the regime's international reputation came from the decision of three PAN candidates, including Barrio, to charge the Mexican government before the Inter-American Human Rights Commission (IAHRC) of the Organization of American States (OAS) with major violations of the American Convention of Human Rights arising out of election fraud committed in the gubernatorial elections in Chihuahua in 1986, the federal deputy elections in Chihuahua City's seventh district in 1985, and the elections for mayor of the city of Durango in 1986. Specifically, the regime was accused of having violated Article 23 (the right to vote and be elected in authentic elections which guarantee the free expression of the will of the electorate) and Article 25 (the right to effective judicial protection against violations of human rights) among other rights.[163] It was the first time in history that an opposition party formally accused the Mexican government of violating political rights before an international body.

The Mexican government, in response, accused the Commission of violating Mexican sovereignty and the principle of nonintervention.[164] It argued that, while the right to vote and be elected was an individual right of "immediate enforceability," the right that elections be conducted honestly was a collective right, not within the Commission's competence, that was to be achieved over time according to "the circumstances and conditions in each country."[165] Finally, the government, in a thinly veiled threat, hinted that it might withdraw from the Convention if the IAHRC issued an opinion on Mexican electoral processes.[166] None of these arguments dissuaded the Commission, which issued a final report on May 17, 1990, though the lapse of four years between the filing of the complaints and the Commission's ruling may have been due to pressure from Mexico.

The report provided a detailed summary of the allegations of election irregularities filed by the PAN petitioners and the abortive steps taken by them to seek legal redress inside Mexico. While the Commission chose not to accept nor deny the truth of the specific allegations of fraud, on the ground that it had been unable to observe the electoral processes concerned directly, it did conclude that Mexican law offered no protection, recourse, or guarantees against acts that violated political rights and requested the Mexican government to adopt the necessary domestic legislation to "make effective the rights and liberties which the Convention recognizes."[167] The Commission reminded the Mexican government that it was under a statutory obligation as a party to the Convention to provide judicial protection for the "free and full exercise of political rights" and to keep the Commission informed of the measures being taken to achieve this end.[168]

The report of the Commission—composed entirely of members

from countries with democratically elected governments (Venezuela, Brazil, United States, Jamaica, Argentina, Barbados, and Honduras)[169]—deeply embarrassed the Mexican government. For the first time, the Mexican government had been condemned for violating political rights by an official international organization. Worse still, the OAS Permanent Council voted to turn over the report for open discussion at the organization's next General Assembly meeting.[170] The Commission's ruling encouraged others to take their case against human rights violations to international bodies; the PRD, for example, charged the Mexican government before the Human Rights Center of the United Nations with violations of political rights in the elections held in Guerrero and Michoacán in 1989.[171] By choosing to appeal to international public opinion, the PAN in Chihuahua thus pioneered a highly effective way to punish electoral fraud and defend the vote.

Ideological Flexibility

The long exclusion of Mexican opposition political parties from meaningful political power forced them to turn to ideology as their main cementing force. Such a criticism cannot, however, be leveled against the new PAN in Chihuahua, which showed a rare capacity for ideological flexibility. The fact that most of the PAN's leaders in Chihuahua had only entered the party recently meant they were largely unfamiliar with the party's ideology but highly attuned to society. Barrio, for example, saw the PAN more as an instrument in the struggle for democracy than an end in itself and believed that the creation of alliances between different social forces and political organizations to overcome the atomization of Mexican society and offer a united challenge to the regime was a prerequisite for the achievement of democracy.[172] The explosive growth of the PAN's membership in Chihuahua between 1983 and 1986 shattered the notion that the PAN belonged only to a select group of initiates and diluted the importance of ideology as veteran *panistas* struggled to school the flood of new entrants in the rudiments of PAN doctrine in order to transform citizen alienation from the regime into long term support for the PAN based on conviction. The PAN's emphasis in Chihuahua on winning elections and defending the vote helped create a new party culture that was geared more towards pragmatic action than doctrinal reflection. This pragmatic orientation was reinforced by the PAN's victories in the 1983 mayoral races in the state, which placed the party in the position of having to resolve municipal problems that know no ideology, meet the soaring expectations of the citizenry, and hammer out compromises with local organizations of various political persuasions.

THE NATIONAL PAN:
INSTITUTIONALIZING THE NEW MODEL

The unifying goal of the model of political action that was developed by the PAN in Chihuahua was the acquisition of power by electoral means. The election of Alvarez as PAN national president in February, 1987, meant inevitably that winning power would become the main priority of the national PAN as well. Three days before his election as PAN president, Alvarez stated that fifty years of promoting civic consciousness was enough and the party should focus on obliging the regime to open the doors to democratic participation.[173] The fact that the PAN possessed a high level of internal democracy made it possible for Alvarez and his northern supporters to capture the party leadership and reshape the national party in the image of the Chihuahua PAN. The growth of the PAN's membership and voter support at the national level, as well as the decline of the regime's image throughout the country, also provided favorable conditions for generalizing the example of the PAN in Chihuahua to the PAN as a whole.

Alvarez was an excellent choice to preside over the transformation of the PAN at an important moment in Mexican history. As a veteran *panista* who played a major role at critical junctures in the party's history, he enjoyed the respect of older party members. As a central actor in the Chihuahua drama, he had won the admiration of new PAN supporters who wanted the party to take more vigorous actions in favor of democracy. A retired businessman, he was also a firm believer in social justice. During the crisis of the 1970s, he supported González Morfín and remained critical of the "economic liberalism" favored by Conchello.[174] A broadminded lay Christian, Alvarez shied away from clericalism, religious smugness, and institutional piety. Indeed, when Girolamo Prigione, the Vatican's

Apostolic Delegate, condemned his hunger strike as a form of suicide, Alvarez took the view that it was entirely a matter of "individual conscience."[175] As a former PAN gubernatorial and presidential candidate with a highly successful term as mayor of Chihuahua City behind him, Alvarez possessed considerable political experience, personal prestige, and administrative talent. A curious if not unique synthesis of the PAN, Alvarez offered both change and continuity. These qualities gave Alvarez the maneuvering space necessary to introduce major changes during his first term as PAN president (1987–90) that were designed to transform the PAN into an alternative to the PRI at the national level.

One of Alvarez's priorities as party president was to increase the number of full-time salaried professionals in the party. This decision was not as straightforward and uncomplicated as it may seem at first glance. The PAN's founders saw political activity as a civic duty rather than a career, and voluntarism has always been a hallowed tradition. The religious roots of the party were such that many older *panistas* viewed their participation in the PAN as a calling and felt that it was morally wrong to claim remuneration for the privilege of serving the party.[176] The corruption and greed of many ruling party politicians provided a grim reminder of the dangers of political careerism, as did the bureaucratization of socialist parties around the globe.[177] On the other hand, the presence of political professionals was necessary if the party was to give structure and coherence to its swelling membership, eliminate the advantage possessed by wealthier though not necessarily qualified *panistas* in staking out party posts, and defend the vote in numerous elections. In order to guard against the real though often exaggerated dangers of professionalization and to mollify party purists, Alvarez declared that a maximum of 20 percent of all leadership posts at any given level of the party would be held by political professionals and that only those individuals who needed a salary to occupy a party post would be offered one.[178]

Another goal of Alvarez's tenure as party president was to broaden the party's base in popular colonies and rural areas. The overwhelmingly middle-class nature of the PAN's founders and leaders, the scarcity of full-time party workers dedicated to organizing the party in marginal zones, the unwillingness of party leaders to make promises of material fulfillment that they might not be able to keep later, and the high level of regime control traditionally exercised over urban workers and *campesinos* hampered the PAN's ability to win support among the underprivileged.[179] The impressive performance of Cárdenas in Mexico City, which has a large working-class population, and in neighboring poverty-stricken states like Morelos, in the 1988 presidential elections provided a reminder to many *panistas* of the importance of expanding the party's following beyond the middle classes.[180]

During the 1980s and 1990s, the PAN made significant gains among urban working-class elements nationwide. In northern Mexico, the PAN's ability to win support among popular classes reflected the region's ethic of social equality, which reduced the psychological distance separating urban workers and party leaders. The PAN's electoral gains among the urban working classes were a direct result of the steady erosion of the PRI's corporatist mechanisms of control over labor. In the 1988 elections, for example, several important labor leaders from the official CTM went down to defeat, particularly in the country's urban metropolises. Subsequent PAN victories in important state elections, like Chihuahua, Baja California Norte, Guanajuato, and Nuevo León, and some of Mexico's largest cities, like Monterrey, Guadalajara, Hermosillo, and Ciudad Juárez, could not have been secured without significant working-class support. The fact that the PAN in the wake of the 1997 elections governed 42.3 percent of the population placed it in an excellent position to resolve popular demands directly, and indirectly by pressuring the regime through PAN legislators and municipal councilors, although PAN leaders have normally shied away from making political support a condition for urban services. Finally, the professionalization of the PAN, along with the formation at Alvarez's instance of a specialized unit devoted exclusively to strengthening the PAN's links with popular colonies and rural areas, also facilitated the PAN's bid for popular support nationwide.[181]

Another watershed in Alvarez's presidency was the PAN's decision to accept the public cash subsidy to which it was entitled by law.[182] While the PAN was always willing to accept public assistance in kind, including free postage, tax exemptions, state supplied paper, and free radio and television time, it was the only party to reject the cash subsidies that were extended to political parties under the 1977 electoral reform law (LOPPE).[183] The LOPPE left the formulation of precise guidelines for the distribution of cash subsidies to the PRI-controlled Federal Electoral Commission (CFE). In the absence of clear legal criteria, the PAN feared that the CFE would distribute cash subsidies according to political compulsions on the basis of negotiations shrouded in secrecy. Some also argued that accepting cash subsidies would damage the party's hard-won reputation of independence and lead to internal party corruption. The issue of whether to accept cash subsidies was reopened when a new electoral law was approved in 1987 that had clearer guidelines for their disbursement.

In May, 1987, the PAN National Council, still smarting from the events in Chihuahua and gearing up for a confrontation with the regime in the 1988 elections, decided to reject the subsidy. Eighteen months later, with the 1988 elections past and a new political situation prevailing, the National Council reversed its decision and accepted it. Based on the PAN's performance in the 1988 federal deputy elections, the party would receive over three years a total of 23 billion *pesos*, the equivalent of over $10 million at October, 1988, exchange rates.[184] The acceptance of public financing freed the PAN from having to depend excessively on financial contributions from businessmen and allowed the party to compete on the same footing as the strengthened leftist opposition parties, which had showed no hesitation in accepting public money. So as to avoid becoming addicted to public financing, which the regime could then slash, the PAN limited subsidy-derived income to a maximum of 25 percent of the party's total revenues.[185] The party also decided not to use the subsidy to meet current expenses.[186] Instead, the PAN used the subsidy to make long-term investments in improved communications equipment, to develop courses in party doctrine for new members, and to institute training sessions for the party's growing number of elected officials.[187]

If the organizational changes introduced by Alvarez revealed the PAN's new orientation towards winning real power, so did Manuel Clouthier's 1988 presidential campaign. Clouthier was a good example of the new model of PAN activism emerging in regions of rapid growth for the party like northern Mexico. A highly successful agricultural entrepreneur from the northern state of Sinaloa and a graduate of ITESM, Clouthier had been president of COPARMEX (1978–81), as well as Mexico's most important business organization, the Business Coordinating Council (CCE) from 1981 to 1983, during the nationalization of the banking system. Underlining the orientation of his own businesses towards exports, Clouthier also served as president of the Mexican side of the Bilateral Committee of U.S.–Mexican Businessmen. Though not directly affected by bank nationalization, Clouthier was nonetheless one of the fiercest critics of the decision, which he felt illustrated the terrible flaws of a political system in which presidential power could run amok totally unchecked. Skeptical, until stunned by bank nationalization, of politics as a way to resolve Mexico's problems, Clouthier entered the PAN in October, 1984. Having sold most of his fourteen businesses to minimize his vulnerability to government reprisals, and abandoned by many of his more fearful colleagues, Clouthier's emergence was indicative of a new tendency for more independent-minded businessmen to participate directly in opposition politics instead of seeking to settle their differences with the regime through institutional channels like the CCE. In 1986, Clouthier conducted a fiery campaign as the PAN's candidate for governor of Sinaloa in an election marred by serious irregularities in favor of the PRI candidate, who was later declared the official winner.[188] On November 22, 1987, the PAN national convention chose Clouthier as the party's candidate for the Mexican presidency in 1988, reflecting the changing outlook of the party's base composed mostly of recent members, especially from northern Mexico. Clouthier won over 70 percent of all votes cast at the convention, overwhelming on the first ballot his opponent, Jesús González Schmal, a respected party member of more than twenty years standing.[189]

Unlike any previous PAN presidential candidate, Clouthier believed that he could defeat the regime at the polls in 1988. For Clouthier, the division of the ruling elite marked by the departure of Cárdenas and much of the PRI's left wing, coupled with unprecedented civic unrest after almost a decade of social and economic decay, had created new conditions that justified a bolder approach.[190] Like Barrio, Clouthier viewed the PAN as an instrument for the achievement of the higher goal of democracy.[191] During his campaign, Clouthier made a number of important and politically courageous proposals concerning the economy, such as granting autonomy to the central bank, slashing the bureaucracy by 10 percent a year, awarding property titles to *ejidatarios*, giving tax breaks to investors, and instituting an austerity plan to curb the budgetary deficit.[192] Yet the thrust of his message focused on unmasking the failures of authoritarianism, sparking an outpouring of civic consciousness, and advancing democracy as the only real solution to the country's problems.[193] Clouthier's obvious sincerity and persistence as well as his inimitable style won him considerable sympathy.[194]

Having paid a heavy price for his defiance of the Mexican state, Clouthier was not willing to become yet another passive victim of electoral fraud. Instead, early in his campaign, Clouthier invited the public to join the PAN in a movement of civil disobedience to ensure respect for the vote.[195] Clouthier was deeply impressed by the role of passive resistance in the overthrow of Ferdinand Marcos in the Philippines. Indeed, a top collaborator of Clouthier and Alvarez visited the Philippines to study the issue firsthand, and a Catholic bishop from the Philippines was invited to give a series of conferences on the theory of civil disobedience to important PAN leaders.[196] Meanwhile, a prominent *panista* from Ciudad Juárez invited an American authority on the politics of nonviolence to visit Mexico, and a Spanish summary of his work was published.[197]

This summary served as the basic manual for the party's new two-day courses on civil disobedience to prepare society to resist any attempt by the regime to rob the 1988 elections.[198] The courses, held over the weekend in major cities, were open to PAN activists as well as the general public, following the logic that no successful civil disobedience movement is sectarian in nature. The courses had both a politicizing and pedagogical impact. Participants were reminded that since all authority ultimately rested on consent, the Mexican regime could be dealt a mortal blow if such consent were peacefully withheld through civil disobedience. They were then asked to enumerate the ways in which they personally might be cooperating with the "unjust" Mexican regime and what steps they could take to avoid doing so. The courses also analyzed the main characteristics of authentic civil disobedience, including strict adherence to nonviolence, and provided a physical demonstration of the body positions most likely to protect vital organs in the event of violent repression. Finally, groups of participants were assigned the task of planning a particular civil disobedience action of their own, to be critiqued by the rest of the class. The PAN's highly visible embrace of civil disobedience deeply troubled the regime, which accused Clouthier of attempting to destabilize the country.

In the end, none of the civil disobedience actions so meticulously planned by the PAN were executed. Not that the election results were free from suspicion (see chapter 2). But with the PAN officially relegated to third place in the presidential election, Clouthier stating that the manipulation of the election results had made it impossible to determine the winner and demanding the annulment of the election, and Cárdenas claiming that he had won the presidency but lacking a strategy to defend his alleged triumph, the PAN was not in a position to launch civil disobedience unless it was also willing to underwrite Cárdenas's claims of victory.[199]

The PAN, reflecting its greater openness to tactical alliances with ideologically divergent forces to defend the vote, joined hands with Cárdenas in protesting election irregularities while refusing to support his claim to victory. In a rare demonstration of opposition unity at the national level, Clouthier, Cárdenas, and Rosario Ibarra de Piedra, the candidate of the miniscule Revolutionary Workers Party (PRT), met in Alvarez's home to draft the document *Call to Legality*.[200] The document, which was written shortly after the polls closed on July 6, condemned the irregularities gravely marring the voting process, accused the regime of attempting to impose its own candidate at the expense of the will of electorate, and declared that if the government did not move to reestablish the "legality of the electoral process in an unequivocal fashion," the three opposition presidential candidates would refuse to accept the election results or recognize the new fraudulently elected authorities and take steps to defend the right to a clean election using constitutional weapons.[201] That same evening, with the vote count already suspended because of supposed computer failure, Cárdenas, Clouthier, and Ibarra arrived at the Interior Ministry amid loud cheers from spectators to personally deliver their *Call to Legality* to Interior Secretary Manuel Bartlett, who asked them not to prejudge the electoral process.[202]

That Clouthier was upstaged by Cárdenas should not cloud the fact that his campaign was a successful one. The 1988 elections saw the PAN gain a record 101 federal deputy seats, making it the largest single opposition party in the new Chamber. Also, even though Cárdenas won more support from popular classes than Clouthier, Clouthier nonetheless won significant support from them

as well. Finally, PAN leaders claimed that the official election results understated the number of votes actually won by the PAN.[203]
The PAN, citing postelection voter surveys, saw itself as the primary
target of fraud. According to PAN, the regime from the start of the
campaign had considered the PAN as its chief enemy and sought to
use Cárdenas's candidacy in order to divide the opposition, channel
protest votes away from Clouthier, and dilute the impact of any
postelectoral charges of fraud.[204] For many *panistas,* the fact that
Cárdenas was supported by three satellite parties of the PRI, including the one that registered him as a presidential candidate without consulting its members, and the greater attention given to
Cárdenas in the state-controlled media confirmed their suspicion
that the regime was deliberately fanning Cárdenas's candidacy.[205]
Unfortunately for those who hoped that Cárdenas's candidacy would
serve merely as a convenient weapon against the PAN (and the
PAN agreed that it is unlikely that Cárdenas was a party to this),[206]
Cárdenas quickly acquired a snowball-like momentum, joined hands
with the PMS, captured much of the protest vote in major areas of
the country, made significant inroads in the regime's traditional vote
banks, and then refused to let himself be co-opted and vanish into
obscurity after the election.

In any event, there is no doubt that Clouthier's campaign—
involving an unabashed drive towards power, ideological pragma-
tism, mass support, novel tactics like civil disobedience and limited
alliances with the left, and a prominent role for businessmen—constituted a major change in the culture of the national PAN. The
party's decision soon after the election to create Mexico's first-ever
shadow cabinet not only gave the PAN a new public platform from
which to monitor government policies and propose alternatives but
also sent a signal that the party was competent to govern at the
national level.

THE POLICY OF DIALOGUE, 1988–94

The policy of dialogue with all political forces initiated by the
PAN in the wake of the 1988 elections indicated the party's desire
to hasten the pace of democratization and make it easier for the
opposition to gain access to new political spaces.[207] Though superfi-

cially a departure from the confrontational style evolved by the PAN in Chihuahua, the strategy of dialogue, insofar as it sought to bring the PAN closer to power, was in harmony with the essence of the PAN in Chihuahua. The fact that Alvarez was nationally known for his defiance of the regime through his hunger strike in Chihuahua also gave him the necessary credibility to open a dialogue with the regime. Such a dialogue seemed warranted by the new political conditions ushered in by the 1988 elections. The highly questionable manner in which Salinas was elected had undermined his legitimacy and compelled the new president to issue an unprecedented call in his inaugural address for a "national agreement to expand democratic life."[208] The 1988 elections had provided a clear mandate for democratic change and greatly strengthened the opposition, which could no longer be ignored by the government without provoking serious political instability in the process. The strategy of dialogue was therefore a means of taking optimal advantage of the opposition's new strength in order to wrest real advances towards democracy from the regime. Also, for the first time in its history, the PRI lacked the necessary two-thirds majority required to amend the constitution on its own. The PRI would therefore have to open authentic negotiations with the opposition and incorporate at least some of its suggestions if a constitutional path was to be cleared for the new government's policy initiatives, especially in the sensitive areas of electoral reform and the privatization of economic activities constitutionally limited to state participation only.

Indeed, the 1988 elections had created three more or less equal political forces—the PRI; the PAN; and Cárdenas's National Democratic Front (FDN), which later evolved into the PRD—none of which was in a position to act unilaterally. For Alvarez, the only solution was for the three main political parties to negotiate a pact or series of pacts setting in motion a phased but irreversible transition to a fully competitive polity.[209] He believed that Spain provided an excellent example of otherwise irreconcilable politicians temporarily choosing to set aside their differences in order to establish new rules of democratic competition.[210] As a result of the enmity that surfaced after the elections between the PRI and the FDN / PRD, the PAN was fated to become the guardian of the balance of power, the government's principal interlocutor, and even a channel of communication between the PRI and the PRD.

The need for Salinas to acquire legitimacy at home and abroad by taking concrete steps towards democracy, as well as the president's own apparent commitment to reformist ideas, ran counter to the vested interests encrusted in the PRI. The PAN therefore saw itself as negotiating mainly with the president rather than the PRI. By bringing pressure to bear directly on Salinas, the PAN not only believed that it would encounter a more sympathetic ear but also hoped to furnish the president with the necessary pretext to introduce changes highly unpopular with the bulk of his party, and provide him with the security of popular support for doing so. In short, the PAN hoped to nudge the president away from his identification with the PRI towards the role of a more neutral arbiter of democratization.[211] The traumatic experiences of the 1986 Chihuahua state elections and the treatment of Clouthier in 1988 may have helped convince the PAN's leadership under Alvarez of the limits of confrontation for its own sake and predisposed the party towards a more subtle and less inflammatory approach.

The PAN's decision to open a dialogue with the president produced positive results. Salinas's recognition of the PAN's victory in the gubernatorial race of Baja California Norte in 1989, despite massive opposition from his own party, vindicated the PAN's strategy. Dialogue may also have helped reassure Salinas that recognizing a PAN victory at the gubernatorial level in an important border state would not provoke a crisis in center-state relations with foreign policy implications. In 1992, Salinas also recognized the PAN's victory in the race for governor of Chihuahua. In Baja California Norte and Chihuahua, the policy of dialogue was a prudent way of facilitating the recognition of the PAN's victories. In Guanajuato, however, dialogue produced an agreement between the PAN and the regime to divide power that clearly violated democratic norms. There, the PRI's candidate, Ramón Aguirre, had been declared the winner of the 1991 gubernatorial election amid accusations of serious irregularities by the PAN candidate Vicente Fox. Discussions between PAN leaders and Salinas resulted in a political compromise to break the deadlock in the state. Aguirre was obliged to resign; the PAN's mayor of León, the state's most important industrial center, took over as interim governor, despite the fact that he was not the PAN's official candidate for governor; and a PRI stalwart was named secretary general, the number two post in the state government. In 1995, the PAN's Vicente Fox won the governorship in a fresh election.

Obviously, dialogue was not the only factor in the president's willingness to recognize PAN victories. The growing institutional capacity of the PAN to mount serious protests against fraud through civil disobedience and other means raised the cost of fraud. The party's improving ability to monitor elections also made rigging more difficult. Salinas's desire to ensure passage of the North American Free Trade Agreement (NAFTA) predisposed the administration to recognize PAN victories to prevent fraud from becoming an obstacle to congressional ratification of the treaty. The regime also hoped that recognizing the victories of the ideologically more compatible PAN might take pressure off to accede to possible PRD victories in Michoacán and elsewhere.

The other main product of the dialogue between the PAN and the regime—and PRD pressure—was a series of electoral reforms from 1989 to 1996, which resulted in a major opening of the electoral system (see also chapter 6). The willingness of Salinas to intervene directly or indirectly through Interior Secretary Fernando Gutiérrez Barrios at critical junctures when the PRI's intransigence threatened to derail the reform process seemed to provide further evidence of the president's benevolent intentions.[212] The 1989 / 90 electoral reform process was divided into two stages, involving first the reform of the constitutional provisions relating to elections on the basis of a two-thirds majority followed by the passage of a new secondary electoral law on the basis of an absolute majority only. In both phases, the PAN chose to vote with the PRI, thus helping the PRI acquire the necessary two-thirds majority to reform the constitution and lending the PAN's moral credibility to the new secondary electoral law. While the reforms fell far short of assuring free and fair elections, they still constituted a significant step in that direction.

The most controversial aspect of the reforms was the "governability" clause, which allowed the party winning a minimum of 35 percent of the votes and the greatest number of seats by majority vote to automatically receive 251 out of a total of 500 federal deputy seats. In addition, such a party could claim two seats for every percentage point of the vote won by it from 35 percent to 60 percent. The governability clause was a direct reaction to the PRI's slipping control of the Chamber of Deputies and was designed to ensure that the PRI would retain control over the Chamber even if it won only a plurality rather than an absolute majority in the 1991 congressional elections.

The other criticism of the 1989 reform package is that it maintained the regime's control over electoral organs by allowing the president to nominate six Magistrate Councilors to the General Council of the Federal Election Institute (IFE), a newly created body charged with supervising elections. The presidential nominees were to have no ties to political parties and be approved by a two-thirds majority of the Chamber of Federal Deputies, thus requiring the president to make his choices carefully. IFE's Director-General would be nominated by the Interior Minister but approved by a two-thirds vote of the General Council. The Interior Minister would, however, function as IFE's President.

In return for acceding to the PRI's demands for overrepresentation and regime control over electoral organs, the PAN was able to wrest significant gains in other areas in the electoral reforms. The most important of these was the government's agreement to compile a new voter registration list in collaboration with the opposition, and to create a "fraud-proof" voter identification card with a photograph. In addition, the regime agreed to provide political parties permanent computer access to the new voter registration list; this enabled them to monitor any additions and deletions, and such changes could be made only with the written permission of the affected parties, including their signatures, fingerprints, and photographs, or on the basis of other documentary evidence such as death certificates.

The regime also agreed that a two-thirds rather than an absolute majority of the Electoral College, composed of incoming federal deputies, would be required to certify the validity of the presidential election results. The importance of this change becomes evident when one considers that had it been in effect in 1988, Salinas would not have been declared elected as president. In addition, the government committed itself to releasing preliminary election results immediately, permitting political parties to have two *casilla* representatives instead of one, and diluting its control over the selection of *casilla* presidents by choosing them from a group consisting of 20 percent of all voters in each electoral section selected by

lottery. It agreed to permit ballots to be signed by a *casilla* function-
ary chosen by lottery before the start of voting in order to prevent
ballot box stuffing and other abuses. The regime suppressed the
infamous practice in large electoral sections of dividing *casillas* into
two or more units but continuing to use the same voter list for all of
them, thereby making it possible to vote more than once. In the
future, the list would be alphabetically divided among each sub-
unit. Other significant reforms included prohibiting political parties
from engaging in corporatist methods of affiliation, opening the
sessions of electoral organs to the presence of the media, requiring that all ballot boxes be transparent, installing screens to allow for greater secrecy at the time of voting, and making those
responsible for committing electoral law violations liable to criminal prosecution.

Despite these gains when compared to the previous electoral
code, the PAN was strongly criticized by the PRD for accepting reforms
that failed to root out the government's control over electoral processes.[213] While the PRD voted against the constitutional amend-
ments as well as the secondary electoral law, it still enjoyed their
benefits without having to pay the political price of negotiating with
the PRI. Alvarez himself was also criticized by some members of his
own party for compromising the PAN's image of independence for
what they felt were only small advances, and a significant number
of PAN deputies chose not to vote in favor of the new electoral
reforms. A deepening of internal party divisions, a more tense relationship with the PRD, and possibly some temporary damage to the
PAN's image were thus the inevitable costs of the strategy of dialogue. But the critics, whether disgruntled PAN members or the
PRD, were unable to show that their "all or nothing" approach would
have produced better results than Alvarez's strategy of negotiating
partial but real advances towards democracy. Indeed, the inevitable
decline of civic enthusiasm in the wake of the 1988 elections, the
acute growing pains of the newly born FDN/PRD, the differences
between the PAN and the PRD particularly over economic policy,
the improvement of Salinas's image, and the highly technical nature of the subject of electoral reform made it implausible that the
opposition would have been able to extract sweeping changes from
the regime in 1989/90. In such a situation, Alvarez's strategy of
negotiating incremental changes with the regime appears to have

been a better alternative to doing nothing at all, but the costs paid by the PAN revealed the limits of the strategy of dialogue.

In 1993, a new round of constitutional reforms suppressed the "governability" clause; established a Federal Election Tribunal to certify the elections of federal deputies; expanded the opposition's presence in the Senate by raising the number of seats in the Senate from two to four per state, with the fourth seat being allocated to the party in second place; and barred any party from holding more than 63 percent of the seats in the Chamber of Deputies, in order to prevent the majority party from reforming the constitution on its own. Once again the constitutional reforms were complemented by changes in the Federal Code of Election Procedures and Institutions (COFIPE). The government agreed to permit the posting of election results by precinct, release official copies of precinct results to political parties on the same day as the election, and select precinct officials by two successive lotteries rather than one. Campaign finance limits were accepted for the first time, but the formula by which ceilings were to be determined was left to IFE. Political parties were required to submit a formal statement of campaign expenditures to IFE after the elections. The government remained in control of IFE, although it was agreed that in the future the directors of IFE's specialized organs dealing with the voter registration list, coalitions, political party finances, and other areas would be selected by a two-thirds vote of the General Council instead of being appointed by the Director General. Finally, the new law legalized domestic election observers but failed to clarify the role of international observers.

The 1993 reforms were incremental in character but they represented an advance over the 1989 / 90 reforms. The state's control over electoral processes was left basically untouched. The reforms were the product of extensive negotiations between the PRI, PAN, and PRD. In the end, the PRD voted against the constitutional portion of the reforms and abstained from the vote on the changes to COFIPE, while the PAN voted in favor of both sets of reforms, though not without demurring at first. With the presidential elections approaching, the party was increasingly aware of the political dangers of being too closely associated with the regime.

In 1994, the regime agreed to commit itself to much bolder steps to bolster the credibility of the electoral processes. The Chiapas rebellion and the assassination of the PRI's presidential candidate stoked fears that a disputed election outcome could lead to a violent explosion. International observers were officially permitted to observe all phases of the electoral process for the first time. IFE's magistrate councilors were replaced by six citizen councilors chosen by consensus among all major political parties and approved by a two-thirds vote of the Chamber of Deputies. The General Council was presided over by the new Minister of the Interior, Jorge Carpizo, who was well known for his personal integrity and concern for human rights. The regime also agreed to expand the penalties for election fraud, widen the definition of electoral crimes, and establish a special office to prosecute such crimes. Finally, the regime agreed to conduct two external audits of the voter registration list.

In 1994, the PAN and PRD used dialogue as a mechanism to translate the growing social pressures for democracy into new, more serious, reforms. PAN leaders had by then become extremely skilled at negotiating electoral reform and were able to take full advantage of the regime's vulnerability. Dialogue also made it possible for the regime to involve opposition parties in the reform-making process, thereby legitimizing both the reforms and the election outcome. This time the reforms were approved by the PRI, PAN, and a portion of the PRD's parliamentary delegation. The reforms represented a major breakthrough that set the stage for Mexico's fairest presidential election ever.

THE PRICE OF CHANGE: PATTERNS OF INTERNAL CONFLICT IN THE PAN DURING THE 1980s AND 1990s

The main cause of internal party conflicts during the 1980s and 1990s was the dramatic growth of the PAN itself. New members brought their own styles and convictions with them, lacked the institutional memory and loyalty of long-time members, and often preferred their own natural leaders to party leaders. Not surprisingly, they clashed with PAN traditionalists unwilling to shed their own agendas, old ways of thinking and acting, and cede power to new groups. The growth of the PAN's support and membership also helped accelerate the pace of change within the party by making it possible to adopt bolder strategies and institute major organizational reforms. But the quickened pace of change left some older *panistas* feeling uncomfortable. The process of growth also altered the composition of the party's membership, leading to a much stronger presence of businessmen often linked to organizations like COPARMEX and Integral Human Development and Citizen Action (DHIAC); this caused a de facto realignment of the party's ideological orientation in favor of the business community, to the dismay of some PAN old-timers. Older *panistas* were divided in their response to the newcomers. One group regarded the infusion of new blood as a blessing for the party and a vindication of their past sacrifice. Another group viewed the changes brought about by the newcomers with misgivings but chose to retire from active party involvement rather than confront them. And a third group, the bulk of whose members had held important leadership positions inside the party in the period directly preceding the entrance of the newcomers, felt displaced and were determined to resist neophyte pretensions to change the party to their liking. Finally, the question of dialogue with the regime heightened party divisions.

As the PAN struggled to absorb the flow of new entrants, internal party conflicts manifested themselves in three successive stages. In the first stage, internal party conflicts were most apparent at the level of the PAN in Chihuahua and northern Mexico, where the party's growth was initially fastest and the process of adjustment most telescoped. In the second stage, with the successful consolidation of a new model of the PAN in Chihuahua and northern Mexico, the locus of internal party conflict shifted, pitting the regional PAN in northern Mexico against the national PAN with Madero as party president. In the third stage, the election of Alvarez as the party's national president in 1987 and Clouthier as the PAN's 1988 presidential candidate opened the door to transforming the national PAN in the image of the PAN in northern Mexico but also produced a highly negative reaction from those who disliked the northern project and felt marginalized by it.

While this sequence of events at first glance suggests an internal party division along regional lines, the gap between the PAN in northern Mexico and the national PAN was mainly the result of the lopsidedly rapid growth experienced by the party in northern Mexico during the 1980s. The real challenge was not regionalism but absorbing the torrent of new members. Indeed, as the PAN's voter support and membership in central and southern Mexico expanded during the 1990s, particularly in Yucatán, Jalisco, and Guanajuato, the phenomenon of clashing regional perspectives inside the party fueled by asymmetrical growth patterns diminished accordingly. Nor is the party dominated by northerners any longer. Alvarez was succeeded as PAN national president in 1993 by Carlos Castillo Peraza, a well-know PAN intellectual from the state of Yucatán. In March, 1996, Castillo Peraza was succeeded by Felipe Calderón Hinojosa, the son of a prominent *panista* from Michoacán and the PAN's candidate for governor of the state in 1995.

In the first stage, the period of early PAN growth in northern Mexico, a classic pattern of conflict was the constant feuding between PAN mayors and local party organizations. The PAN mayors, particularly Barrio in Ciudad Juárez and Villarreal Posada in Parral, had been only recently inducted into the party and saw themselves as leaders of society and resisted being identified with the PAN. They had their own sources of support, especially among civic groups unconnected with the PAN, and tended to bypass the party structure during their 1983 campaigns for mayoral office. Once elected, they appointed mostly figures from outside the PAN to key administrative posts. Indeed, Barrio had accepted the PAN ticket only on the condition that he would be free to select his own collaborators without intervention from the party.[214] Barrio's decision to hire only two *panistas* deeply angered the intermediate generation of *panistas* who controlled the party in the 1970s and early 1980s, but not the party's oldest members, who were delighted by the PAN's electoral success.[215] Barrio argued that he was mayor of all citizens and not only those who had voted for the PAN and that the PAN in Ciudad Juárez was too small to provide the pool of talent necessary for the smooth functioning of his administration.[216] As a result, channels of communication between the local party and the Barrio administration broke down, with the party publicly attacking the apparent inefficiency of the Barrio administration and Barrio studiously ignoring them.[217] Finally, PAN old-timers, fearing that constant feuding would hurt the PAN's electoral prospects, allied themselves with Barrio and persuaded Guillermo Prieto, the state party president, to suspend the local party chief, Bulmaro Márquez, who was replaced by a PAN stalwart.[218]

While the PAN mayors chose their own collaborators, the party succeeded in nominating most municipal councilors or *regidores*, who are elected on the same ticket as the party's mayoral candidates. Traditionally, the PRI mayors simply ignored their municipal councilors, even though constitutionally *regidores* are supposed to observe all aspects of municipal government, approve executive decisions, and generally act as a mini-parliament. The PAN's *regidores*, however, had been chosen to ensure that the new PAN mayors, especially in Ciudad Juárez and Parral, who were only weakly identified with the party, would not betray the PAN's interests and principles.[219] As a result, PAN *regidores* did not hesitate to question executive actions when necessary, raise issues for discussion not included in the mayoral agenda, and even form occasional alliances with the minority of PRI *regidores* when divided among themselves.[220] The divide between the party and the PAN mayors had two salutory consequences: it guaranteed the separation of party and government functions in the PAN-controlled municipalities (though this would have probably occurred anyway, given the PAN's rejection on principle—as lethal to democracy—of interlocking party and government structures) and ensured that the PAN-run municipalities would serve as singular examples of grassroots democracy at work.

As the new contours of the PAN in Chihuahua took shape, the tension between the PAN in Chihuahua and the national PAN escalated. Barrio had considerable difficulty persuading Madero and his National Executive Committee (CEN) to accept the strategy of civil disobedience. The CEN argued that civil disobedience, insofar as it required systematically violating the law, roundly contradicted the PAN's oft-stated mission of implanting the rule of law in Mexico.[221] They also feared that Barrio's civil disobedience strategy might cause the PAN to be regarded as an anarchist or subversive organization, thus providing the government with the pretext to cancel the PAN's registration as a political party.[222] In Barrio's view, the strategy of civil disobedience clashed with the deepest values of most CEN members whose sense of moral duty and civic virtue made them highly respectful of the law even when they disagreed with it.[223] And Barrio as a relatively new figure in the party lacked the moral weight to convince them to break the law in the name of the party.[224] Finally, an unsatisfactory compromise was worked out: the strategy was accepted, provided it would not explicitly involve violating the law.

In the end, Madero and his CEN were completely marginalized from the civil disobedience actions taken in Chihuahua after the elections. The CEN was not consulted by Barrio when he took over the international bridges, and Madero, even though he was personally opposed to the takeover of the bridges, was not in a position to criticize the move, in view of the climate of popular protest in Chihuahua.[225] Indeed, Madero and his secretary general, Bernardo Bátiz, were forced to spend one night at the bridges to manifest their solidarity with Barrio. There is no question that Madero was infuriated by Barrio's decision simply to ignore him, seize the bridges, and present the CEN with a *fait accompli.* The CEN also believed that the PAN in Chihuahua had allowed itself to be swept up by the euphoria of the moment, had failed to measure its real strength in relation to the state, and had engaged in an excessively radical confrontation with the government that had almost spilled over into violence. In Bátiz's opinion, what most frightened the regime, causing it to panic and slam the door tightly shut on the party's gubernatorial aspirations in Chihuahua, was the PAN's menacing language.

The true extent of the divorce between Madero and the PAN in northern Mexico was illustrated in 1986, when the regional presidents of the PAN in northern Mexico held a joint meeting to which Madero was invited only at the last moment and "arrived almost as an intruder." While some of the tension between the CEN and the PAN in Chihuahua was undoubtedly attributable to the greater emotional distance of the CEN from the state, a large part of it was also the result of Madero's anger both at seeing his authority flouted by PAN leaders of recent entry who felt that their primary loyalty was to society in Chihuahua and not to the CEN and at the widely differing mentality and *modus operandi* of new PAN members and leaders in Chihuahua.

The election of Alvarez as party president frustrated Madero's bid for reelection, and Clouthier as PAN presidential candidate turned the national PAN into the main center of internal party conflict. The most trenchant opposition to the implantation of the Alvarez / Clouthier project, with exceptions like José González Torres, who was president of the PAN from 1959 to 1962 and the party's presidential candidate in 1964, came from *panistas* who had played important roles in the party during the 1970s and 1980s, including Madero (PAN presidential candidate in 1982 and party president from 1984 to 1987), Bernardo Bátiz (PAN secretary general from 1972 to 1975 and 1984 to 1987), Conchello (party president from 1972 to 1975 and president of the PAN in Mexico City from 1987 to 1993), Jesús González Schmal (PAN secretary of international relations from 1984 to 1987, parliamentary coordinator from 1985 to 1988, and Clouthier's main opponent for the 1988 presidential nomination), and Gabriel Jiménez Remus (former state party chief in Jalisco and Alvarez's only opponent for reelection as party president). To some extent their opposition stemmed from a sense of frustration at being marginalized by the sudden eruption of new PAN members who "feel that the party began only with them," though it also reflected real concern about the new direction of the PAN under Alvarez's stewardship.[226]

In their view, the large-scale entry of business elements linked to COPARMEX and DHIAC caused the party to take on a right-wing hue at odds with the PAN's doctrine.[227] They alleged that certain businessmen used the party to advance their own interests rather than those of the PAN. They believed that Clouthier's image as a wealthy businessman had cost the party votes in the 1988 elections, especially among the popular classes, and that he should not have been the party's candidate.[228] They felt that full-time party employees should not be given a voice in major policy decisions and should be formally barred from seeking the PAN ticket for elective office. With one or two exceptions, they were against the party's decision to accept public financing, which they feared might undermine the PAN's image of independence and lead to corruption inside the party.[229] They were also highly critical of the PAN's decision to vote with the PRI to approve the 1989 / 90 electoral reforms, which they felt seriously compromised the PAN's credibility as an independent opposition party. Not unexpectedly, they strongly opposed Alvarez's successful bid for reelection in February, 1990, refused to participate in his newly constituted CEN, and formed their own Democratic and Doctrinal Forum (FDD) as an intra-party organization dedicated to achieving greater internal democracy inside the party and defending PAN principles. The CEN under Alvarez refused to officially recognize the FDD as a vertical organization inside the party.

By 1992, the situation had become intolerable for the FDD. In October, 1992, Bátiz, Madero, González Torres, González Schmal, and other members of the FDD announced their withdrawal from the PAN. In a statement explaining their decision, the FDD accused the PAN leadership of "entering a pragmatic stage, one of symbiosis with the system … contrary to the spirit of the founders."[230] The FDD leaders announced that they would consider the formation of new political party based on Christian social doctrine. This new party was never formed, and the FDD has faded into history. Bátiz ran as the PRD's candidate for senator of Mexico City in 1994. The departure of the FDD did not provoke major party divisions at the state and local levels.

The emergence of Conchello, Madero, and Bátiz as Alvarez's main opponents contains a number of ironies when one considers their positions in the 1970s. Then, they were the ones being accused by González Morfín of playing fast and loose with the party's doctrine and pandering to the business community. They were the outsiders protesting the overcentralization of the party in the hands of a tiny elite. They were the reformers striving to reorient the PAN towards pragmatic action to win office. And they were the ones who opposed abstentionism and favored participation within the LOPPE, despite that law's flaws. The profound changes that occurred in the PAN in Chihuahua and nationally in the 1980s and 1990s would have been inconceivable without the prior transformation of the party in the 1970s that had been unleashed by Conchello, Madero, and Bátiz. In a sense, they were overtaken by the consequences of the processes of change that they themselves had set in motion two decades earlier.

CONCLUSION

Over time, the main goal of the PAN evolved from promoting civic consciousness to seeking to win political power. The goal of stimulating civic interest in politics predominated from the founding of the party in 1939 to the election of Conchello as party president in 1972, even though the PAN conducted a number of spirited campaigns during this phase, especially at the municipal and gubernatorial levels. For the PAN, the 1970s was a period of soul searching and definition marked by a bitter struggle between those who wanted the party to remain faithful to its mission as a source of civic consciousness and those who believed that the time had come for the PAN to make the achievement of political power its primary objective. In the end, Conchello's pragmatic vision prevailed, thus placing the PAN in an excellent position to profit from the political awakening of society and social leaders that began in 1982. Conchello's triumph, however, was only one of principle, since as an institution the PAN had been diminished after a decade of internecine party warfare.

The task of constructing a new party with the achievement of power as its central objective fell first to the PAN in Chihuahua. The election of Alvarez as PAN national president and Clouthier as PAN presidential candidate meant the new model pioneered by the PAN in Chihuahua would be applied to the PAN nationally as well. The trend towards the hiring of full-time personnel, the acceptance of public financing, the strengthening of the party's base in popular colonies, Clouthier's presidential campaign, and the strategy of dialogue were all part of the national PAN's drive towards the achievement of power sooner rather than later. The rapid institutionalization of the Chihuahua model by the PAN nationally facilitated the PAN's bid for power in several state and local elections around the country. The price of these changes was wrenching internal debates, a loss of the security and innocence of less challenging times, severe criticisms from the PRD, and a party split. The PAN's victory in the 2000 presidential elections becomes comprehensible only in the light of these preceding institutional changes that allowed the party to become a real contender for power at the national level by at least the late 1990s.

The transformation of the PAN has had a profound impact on Mexico's prospects for democratization. As Victoria Rodriguez and Peter Ward note, the success of the PAN in winning office at the local and state levels invigorated the principles of federalism and municipal autonomy simply because the PAN was an opposition party within a federal system long dominated by a single party.[231] PAN governors reformed state election codes to make fraud virtually impossible in their states; eliminated corrupt practices that inhibited freedom of the press; challenged inequitable revenue allocation procedures between the state and federal governments; undermined the PRI's corporatist structures; and pursued conservative fiscal policies that have curtailed dependence on the federal government.[232] The growing strength of the PAN has also transformed Congress into a much more independent body, challenging executive domination of the legislative branch for the first time in decades. During the Salinas presidency, the PRI was compelled to consult with the PAN on a host of parliamentary issues, particularly electoral reform, privatization, and the reform of the *ejido*.[233] Finally, the PAN's greatest asset, according to Luís Rubio, is its democratic culture, "demonstrating that democracy is not necessarily alien to Mexican culture."[234] He could also have mentioned the party's growing governing experience, parliamentary skills, and capacity for negotiation. All these skills will stand the party in good stead as it takes over the reigns of national power after decades of one-party rule and seeks to consolidate democracy at all levels of the Mexican political system.

4

The Catholic Church and Democratization in Mexico

For most of the postrevolutionary period between 1940 and 1980, the Mexican Catholic Church showed a strong aversion to becoming involved in political questions. In 1926, the Catholic hierarchy had responded to government persecution by suspending Mass, which was then followed by the eruption of the *Cristero* war, a savage confrontation between Catholic militants and the regime. The bitter clash between the Church and the revolutionary Mexican state during the 1920s and 1930s gave way to a cautious accommodation between Church and state after 1940. The basis of this *modus vivendi* rested on a mutual compromise: the state would not interfere with the business of the Church provided the Church refrained from becoming involved in matters that the state considered "political." This compromise, which provided security for both Church and state began to unravel seriously in the 1980s and 1990s. During the 1980s, electoral fraud in the state of Chihuahua led to a crisis in Church-State relations not seen since the 1920s. Not only did the state's bishops condemn election fraud but the archbishop of Chihuahua took the extraordinary step of calling for the suspension of church services to protest the massive irregularities marking the 1986 state elections. The Chihuahua Church's defense of electoral democracy had major ramifications for national Church-State relations. It severely disrupted the *modus vivendi* between the Church and the state and generated a major crisis in Church-State relations that subsided only

153

when the Vatican intervened to countermand the archbishop's decision to close the churches.

Even more significantly, the actions of the Chihuahua Church sparked the formation of a new activist coalition of Mexican bishops in support of democracy. By the late 1980s and 1990s, the Mexican Church as a whole developed an activist profile. The government's attempt to win over the Church by legalizing its activities in 1992 did nothing to dampen the Church's growing involvement in political questions ranging from supporting clean elections to mediating negotiations between the Zapatista rebels and the government in the state of Chiapas. In the 1980s and 1990s, the Mexican Church thus broke free of its cautious mold to become one of the most activist Churches in all of Latin America.

The transformation of the Mexican Catholic Church provides an occasion to theorize about how churches as organizations change in response to different variables, such as ideological shifts, societal pressures, and historically shaped constraints and opportunities. This chapter explains this remarkable transformation from the perspective of a key group of social leaders, clergy and bishops. It argues that clergy and bishops became politicized partly in response to doctrinal changes initiated by the Second Vatican Council (1962–65) and partly as an institutional response to the growing pressure from Mexican society to intervene in favor of clean elections and other social issues. Like Daniel Levine's work on Venezuela and Columbia, this chapter stresses the importance of linkages between the hierarchy and society and examines the reciprocal impact of one on the other.[1] While Levine deemphasizes the role of class,[2] I find that the fact that society in Chihuahua was largely middle class effectively undermined efforts by the Church to promote social justice while making it easier to support democracy. The class composition of the diocese can thus be an important factor in the success or failure of episcopal initiatives.

There were major regional variations in the stance of the Church, with the Chihuahua Church being in the forefront of Church activism for much of the 1980s. This chapter assesses the reasons why the Chihuahua Church was initially more involved in electoral questions than the rest of the Church; probes the impact of the Chihuahua Church on the Mexican Church as a whole; and analyzes parallel developments in the Church in other regions and nationally. Finally, the chapter analyzes the sources of Salinas's decision to normalize Church-State relations in 1992 and its impact on the Church and the political system. The main result of the decision of Mexican bishops and clergy to take up societal concerns like election fraud was to strengthen the Church as an institution by reinforcing its ties to society. The Church's growing social prestige in turn gave it more capacity to challenge the state and thereby weaken it.

THE HISTORICAL DEVELOPMENT OF THE CHURCH IN MEXICO: BATTLING FOR POLITICAL SPACE

Church-State relations in the nineteenth and twentieth century oscillated between periods of intense conflict and uneasy accommodation. The Church in the Spanish Colony enjoyed vast influence, in no small measure because of its organic ties to the state. The history of independent Mexico for much of the nineteenth century was thus marred by factional conflicts between liberals and conservatives over the issue of ecclesiastical privilege. This conflict climaxed in 1857, when a liberal regime under Benito Juárez approved a new constitution that prohibited the Church from owning property not destined directly for religious worship, banned special religious tribunals, and failed to refer to the Church as the official religion of the state. The Constitution of 1857 provoked a civil war in Mexico, the intervention of the French on the side of the conservatives, and the ultimate execution of Emperor Maximilian by the victorious Juárez forces. A new phase in Church-State relations began when Porfirio Díaz seized power in 1876. As part of a strategy of national reconciliation, Díaz chose not to implement the anticlerical legislation, though it remained on the statute books. The overthrow of Díaz by Madero and the onset of the revolution reignited the Church-State conflict. Ironically, this new phase of Church-State conflict occurred when the Church had shed much of its previous reactionary image and had become a more progressive force in society.[3] The new independent ties of the Church to various segments of the urban working classes were perceived by the state as a threat to its monopoly on revolutionary loyalties. Revolutionary leaders like Carranza also accused the

Church of supporting the hated De la Huetra regime, which had overthrown Madero.

The new Constitution adopted by the Constitutionalists in February 1917 came as a great shock to the Church. It declared all public and private elementary education secular and prohibited religious associations or clergy from establishing or directing religious schools (Article 3). All religious orders were banned from Mexico, and the swearing of monastic vows was outlawed (Article 5). Public worship outside the confines of Church buildings was disallowed (Article 24). Religious bodies were prohibited from acquiring, holding, or administering real estate or making loans on such property, and all real estate owned by the Church, including places of worship, was declared to be the "property of the nation" (Article 27). By far the most radical piece of legislation contained in the Constitution was, however, Article 130, which denied the Church legal personality and empowered the federal government to "exercise in matters of religious worship and external discipline such intervention as designated by law." In addition, it reserved the ministry to Mexicans by birth, permitted state legislatures to determine the number of clergy in their states, and forbade the clergy to criticize public officials, the government, or the fundamental laws of the nation. Clergy were also denied the right to vote, hold public office, or assemble for political purposes. Finally, all religious publications were prohibited from commenting on public affairs, and political parties bearing names indicating a religious affiliation were banned.

The logic underlying the Constitution of 1917 was that the separation of Church and state could only be achieved by the subordination of the Church to the state. Yet, the constitutional articles relating to religion were not enforced until 1926, when President Plutarco Elías Calles (1924–28) ordered their application as a response to the rising tide of Catholic opposition to the revolution. In protest, the Church decided to suspend all religious services indefinitely as of Sunday, August 1, 1926. It was the first time in the history of Mexico since the Spanish conquest that the Church had taken such an extreme step.[4] The clergy's abandonment of their churches, in turn, was seen as a signal to many Catholic faithful to turn to armed rebellion against the state. The impulse to rebellion was strongest in rural central and western Mexico. For many *campesinos*, the rebellion was nothing short of a holy war against a regime that had provoked the disappearance of the priest from the village parish, thereby depriving them of the center of their moral universe and placing the salvation of their souls in jeopardy.[5] The declarations of President Emilio Portes Gil that the regime had no intention of destroying the Catholic Church or "intervening in any manner in its spiritual functions" marked the effective end of the *Cristero* war after three years of fighting, and Church services were resumed on June 27, 1929.

The clash between the Church and the state received another impetus in 1934 when the government, under Calles's influence, announced that all future public education would be socialist in content. The conflict over socialist education created instability in the country, becoming a focal point for the mobilization of middle-class opposition to the Cárdenas regime, which chose to downplay the issue. The stage for an accommodation was thus set in the twilight of the Cárdenas administration. President Avila Camacho's public admission of his Catholic faith in 1940, the abandonment of any attempt to enforce the anticlerical constitutional articles, and the repeal of the constitutional amendment promoting socialist education marked the inauguration of a new *modus vivendi* between Church and state. Both sides recognized their inability to achieve complete victory and the ruinous consequences of continued confrontation. The new administration's goals of rapid economic development with political stability were simply incompatible with prolonging the crisis in Church-State relations. By fostering a new amity towards the Church, the regime also hoped to convert the Church into a source of legitimacy for the regime.

The Church had also derived important lessons from its past that rendered it more disposed towards cooperation with the state. The intense conflict between the Church and the state that had characterized the preceding twenty-five years confirmed the need for the Church to develop a strong presence at all levels of society, without a hidden political agenda. The intensification of the Church's presence in society would not only respond to the older problem of seeking an alternative basis of influence and protection outside the ambit of the state but would also address the newer problems of ideological competition from the state and the secular ideals of modern society. Church involvement in society would not, however, be permitted to provoke a crisis in Church-State relations.

The Church would refrain from using the influence derived from involvement in society to increase its institutional power vis-à-vis the state. Power accruing to the Church in this fashion would remain strictly latent and unexpressed. The Church would also refrain from supporting social groups in conflict with the state, even if their cause was justified in Christian terms. In short, Church involvement in society was to remain more or less apolitical. If the Church were to overrun these limits, it ran the risk of not only jeopardizing progress towards the repeal of the anticlerical articles but even of provoking the state into attempting to enforce them again.

The *modus vivendi* proved highly beneficial to the Church, which thrived under the new benignity of the state. The short-term cost, mainly the limits placed on the Church's freedom of action in political matters, was viewed as necessary in order for the Church to strengthen its long-term capacity for autonomy vis-à-vis the state. The recovery was notable. Between 1940 and 1982 the number of functioning churches more than doubled, from 1,600 in 1940 to 3,982 in 1982.[6] The number of seminaries rose from only 57 in 1950 to 99 in 1977 when they enjoyed a total enrollment of 9,379 students.[7] There was also a significant expansion of the private Catholic school system. In 1980, for example, over 6 percent of the total student population was enrolled in Catholic educational institutions.[8] The number of priests, including those belonging to religious orders, also nearly tripled, from 3,863 in 1940 to 9,602 in 1982.[9] The ratio of priests to total population remained relatively stable between 1945 and 1977, deteriorating only slightly from one priest for every 5,380 inhabitants in 1945 to one priest for every 5,791 inhabitants in 1977.[10] The growth in the number of priests between 1945 and 1977 therefore almost matched the very rapid population growth during the same period.

The obvious fruits of the Church's policy of nonintervention in political questions may have helped to reinforce further the hierarchy's desire to avoid any confrontation with the state. Apart from the conflict produced by the Church's opposition to the decision of President López Mateos to introduce state-sponsored obligatory textbooks for all elementary schools in 1960 and the controversy over their updating in 1973, relations between Church and state were extremely cordial.[11] The extent of the Church-State rapprochement was underscored by President Luís Echeverría's visit to the pope on February 9, 1974, and the president's strong support for the construction of a new basilica honoring the Virgin of Guadalupe, the completion of which in October, 1976, was strategically timed to coincide with the final weeks of his administration. A new height in the Church-State relationship was reached when President José López Portillo extended an official welcome to Pope John Paul II on his visit to Mexico in 1979.[12] The massive displays of Catholic faith throughout the pope's tour provided a powerful reminder of the depth of religious feeling in Mexico and gave the Church a new feeling of self-confidence. The welcome and the logistical support for the visit amounted to an all but official recognition of the Church's existence in the eyes of the state.

Yet, despite its new dynamism, the majority of Mexican bishops remained unwilling to risk a conflict with the state by politicizing its role in society. They feared that a fresh outbreak of Church-State tension would threaten the gains achieved by the Church as a result of the *modus vivendi.* Also, they were acutely conscious of the fact that the position of the Church in Mexico was still legally a precarious one and would remain so until the Constitution was reformed. They hoped that the rapprochement between Church and State would culminate in the reform of the anticlerical articles of the Constitution and the granting of official recognition to the Church. Only then would the position of the Church be assured. The Mexican Church, profoundly steeped in the bitter history of Church-State relations, thus deliberately sought to develop a role in society that would not provoke conflict with the state.

THE RISE OF AN ACTIVIST CHURCH IN CHIHUAHUA

During the 1980s and 1990s, however, the Mexican Church shed its fear of confrontation with the state and became increasingly involved in a range of social and political issues ranging from election fraud to social justice. The most important event that disrupted the *modus vivendi* in Church-State relations was the explosive involvement of the Chihuahua Church in defending democracy and clean elections during the 1980s. Why did the Church take such a strong stand in favor of these issues? The most obvious explanation for the Church's involvement is that it was responding to the broad societal pressure to intervene; bishops and priests took their cue from the citizenry. Election fraud had become a major issue in Chihuahua, and the Church felt that it had to become involved or would risk losing credibility by remaining on the sidelines. Three additional factors predisposed the Chihuahua Church to support the movement for clean elections sweeping the state: the historical trajectory of the Church in northern Mexico; the impact of doctrinal change on the state's bishops; and the church's organizational structure in the region.

The Historical Trajectory of the Church in Northern Mexico

The contemporary Chihuahua Church comprises the Archdiocese of Chihuahua, the Diocese of Ciudad Juárez, the Prelatures of Madera and Nuevo Casas Grandes, and the Apostolic Vicarage of the Tarahumara. The overwhelming majority of the state's population is concentrated in the highly urbanized Archdiocese of Chihuahua—which includes the cities of Chihuahua, Cuauhtémoc, Ojinaga, Delicias, Camargo, Jiménez, and Parral—and the Diocese of Ciudad Juárez, strategically located on the border with El Paso, Texas. The other ecclesiastical jurisdictions are, by comparison, much smaller in size and population and were created to respond primarily to specialized concerns of little relevance to the broader pastoral mission of the dioceses.

The Church in northern Mexico and Chihuahua developed largely in isolation of the major crises wracking Church-State relations. As a result, the Chihuahua Church's involvement in society was not conditioned by the desire to avoid conflict with the state. In contrast, the broader Mexican Church, steeped in the legacy of past Church-State conflicts, was more wary of engaging in a confrontation with the state and therefore was more willing to limit its role in society to one unlikely to provoke conflict with the state. Survey research also underlines the same point: states where the *Cristero* war was fought were more likely to favor pacific relations with the state than other regions in the country. For instance, priests in the central states of Guanajuato, Zacatecas, and Querétaro—focal points of conflict in the *Cristero* war—were less likely to support the use of violence as a last resort to correct governmental abuse than their counterparts in Chihuahua, Veracruz, and Mexico City. In Querétaro and Guanajuato, only 22 percent and 36 percent justified violence, respectively, in contrast to 69 percent in Veracruz, 55 percent in Mexico City, and 53 percent in Chihuahua.[13]

The Chihuahua Church's greater "permeability" to society, compared to the Mexican Church as a whole, reflects the Chihuahua Church's distinct history. The Chihuahua Church was largely spared the traumatic experiences of the Reform and the *Cristero* War. As a result, the Chihuahua Church is considerably less fearful of confrontation with the state and more willing to contemplate a role in society that might lead to conflict with the regime.

The Church in Chihuahua and northern Mexico was successful in insulating itself from the upheaval characterizing Church-State relations in no small measure because the presence of the Church in northern Mexico was always weaker than elsewhere in the country. The Church established itself as a formal institution in the northern region as late as 1620 when the Diocese of Durango was formed. Due to the small size of the diocese and the reluctance of clergymen to abandon the comforts of the center for the inhospitable north, the presence of the Church in the region was extremely limited.[14]

The weak organizational structure of the Diocese of Durango inevitably meant that it was unable to assert much control over the small number of clergy dispersed throughout its territory. Most clergy came from wealthy families native to the region, since outsiders were hard to attract. It was not unusual for clergy to combine their priestly duties with other more lucrative activities, such as cattle raising. Many clergy also failed to observe celibacy.[15] Nor did the Church hold much sway over the religious practices of the lay population. The Church sought to assert its control over both clergy and laity by establishing the Diocese of Chihuahua in 1891. Neither the first bishop of Chihuahua, José de Jesús Ortiz (1893–1901), nor the second, Nicolás Pérez Gavilán (1902–19), was able to organize the diocese in a satisfactory manner. It was only in 1921, with the arrival of Bishop Antonio Guizar Valencia, that an acceptable measure of Church control was established.[16] In his long career from 1921 to 1962, first as bishop and then as archbishop of Chihuahua, Guizar Valencia, a native of the state of Michoacán, was finally to begin the process of consolidating and integrating the Diocese of Chihuahua into the mainstream of national Church life.

If the presence of the Church in northern Mexico was historically weak, there was arguably little social need for a stronger Church.[17] Missionary activity, in sharp contrast to central Mexico, was relatively unimportant. The Indian tribes in the north were small in number, largely nomadic in nature, and lacked a competing system of religious belief. Some were willing to accept Christianity fairly quickly and those who were not simply disappeared into inaccessible areas. As a result, the syncretism between indigenous religious traditions and Spanish Catholicism that occurred in central and southern Mexico—and the attendant displays of massive acts of popular devotion, ancestor worship, elaborate temple adornment, worship of idols, and deification of priests—remained almost completely alien to the north. As for the settlers, their main goal was not to win souls for the Church in order to justify conquest but rather to seek the promise of rich mineral wealth or to escape the law by fleeing north.

The role of the Church in the north was thus minimalist in nature both because of its organizational incapacity and the low perceived social need for it. The weakness of the Church in the north meant that it was unable to acquire the fabulous wealth of its counterpart in the center. As a result, when President Benito Juárez sought refuge in the city of Chihuahua during the war with the imperialist forces, the impoverished local Church offered little to be had by the liberals.[18] Since the clash between the liberals and conservatives in central Mexico had been fundamentally over power, there was no reason for the conflict to be repeated in Chihuahua, where the Church was essentially powerless. In a sense, the model of Church-State relations that Juárez had sought to implant in the rest of Mexico, even at the cost of provoking civil war and foreign intervention, already existed in Chihuahua as a natural outgrowth of the pattern of social evolution peculiar to northern Mexico.

The upsurge in Church-State conflict in the 1920s and 1930s had a somewhat greater impact on Chihuahua than earlier conflicts, reflecting the growing integration of Chihuahua into the fabric of national life, a process that had been initiated by Porfirio Díaz and intensified by the revolution. Still, in contrast to the situation in central and southern Mexico, the repercussions of the national crisis in Church-State relations in Chihuahua were slight. The closure of the churches in Chihuahua did not represent the same tragedy for its residents as it did in central and southern Mexico. Most *Chihuahuenses* had long been accustomed to living without a strong religious presence in their midst. Chihuahua was therefore completely untouched by the ravages of the *Cristero* War. When the National League for the Defense of Religious Liberty (LNDLR) attempted to organize a rebellion in the state, it was openly condemned by the bishop of Chihuahua, Antonio Guizar Valencia, who formally prohibited the LNDLR from executing its plan in Chihuahua and threatened to excommunicate the organizers if they disobeyed.[19] The bishop was thus able to win the confidence of the government and went on to play a major role in paving the way for the agreement between Church and state that effectively ended the *Cristero* War. The second wave of religious persecution that began in 1934 had a more significant impact, although the Church in Chihuahua was largely spared the worst of the depredations visited on the Church elsewhere. In 1941 the diocese was able to organize its first Eucharistic Congress, celebrating the diocese's fiftieth year of existence, in an atmosphere of complete liberty marked by the clanging of Church bells, public acts of worship, and extensive press coverage.[20]

The Impact of Doctrinal Change

The Second Vatican Council (1962–65), the 1968 Latin American Bishops' Conference at Medellín, and the 1979 Latin American Bishops' Conference at Puebla stressed the importance of the Church's temporal mission in society. While the Mexican hierarchy accepted Vatican II's liturgical reforms, many bishops resisted a greater temporal role for the Church for fear of upsetting Church-State relations. The full impact of doctrinal reform, particularly with regard to invigorating the Church's role in society, was felt most strongly in regions whose bishops were personally committed to a doctrinal vision that emphasized the temporal dimensions of faith.

Vatican II conceived of the Church as an institution of divine inspiration embedded in human reality,[21] which in turn implied that the Church's mission was both spiritual and temporal. The council also emphasized the interdependence between the individual and society.[22] In its view, sinful social arrangements would inevitably produce individuals inclined towards sin. The Church was thus obliged to seek the transformation of such social systems. Vatican II also emphasized that the legitimacy of political systems depended on the extent to which they promoted human rights, but the council avoided proposing any particular model for that purpose.[23]

The council also acknowledged that the temporal realm was governed by laws which, though emanating from God, functioned autonomously of the Church.[24] This opened up the possibility of the Church actually learning from the temporal realm and incorporating the insights of the social and natural sciences into the framework of Catholic thinking. The Church could also establish alliances with non-Christian groups that could be guided by the hand of God without being aware of it.[25] Instead of conceiving of the Church as a perfect, and therefore static, institution, the Council advanced a more dynamic vision of the Church as a "People of God" conducting a pilgrimage through history that would end only with the establishment of the Kingdom of God.[26] The admission of the Church's historical imperfection provided legitimation for change within the Church.[27] The acceptance of change made it easier for the Church to shed links to conservative elites and placed the Church on the side of rising social forces, with a mission in society.

Vatican II's endorsement of a greater temporal role for the Church went together with a new recognition of the importance of the laity. Given their daily responsibilities in the secular domain, lay Christians were pivotally placed to plant the seeds of the sanctification of the temporal world from within.[28] In this task, the laity was no longer to be viewed as a passive subject at the service of the hierarchy but as an equal partner in the Church's division of labor between priestly and non-priestly functions. Since the temporal world responded to its own inner logic, priests were not always in a position to advise lay Christians on their temporal mission.[29] Instead, lay Christians were expected to rely on their own discernment in the formulation and discharge of their temporal roles. Since the laity constitutes the main bridge between the Church and society, the improvement in the status of the laity implied a greater permeability of the Church to the concerns of society.

Vatican II also reaffirmed the importance of bishops through the principle of collegiality. Divinely invested authority within the

Church was said to emanate only from the union of bishops, with the pope as its supreme head.[30] The application of the principle of collegiality greatly increased the participation of bishops in Church decision making, often at the expense of the Roman curia. Bishops were invited to extend the principle of collegiality to their own dioceses, and priests were urged to do the same in their churches. Episcopal collegiality both stimulated greater national and international coordination between bishops and promoted the decentralization of Church authority at all levels. Bishops found that in this way they could both respond more flexibly to the needs of their particular dioceses and insert their pastoral work more easily into the context of the universal Church. The ability of bishops both to mold society in the image of the ideals of the universal Church and to have those ideals reciprocally molded by society in the image of its own autonomously set priorities was thus greatly enhanced.

The first major opportunity to apply the principles of Vatican II to Latin America came in 1968 at the second General Conference of Latin American Bishops, held at Medellín. As if to stress the importance of the Church's temporal mission, the starting point for theological reflection at the conference was the historical and social context of Latin America. The bishops extended the concept of sin to include not merely situations of individual morality but entire social systems marked by injustice and oppression.[31] In characterizing existing social arrangements as institutionally violent, the Church appeared to be justifying the attempt to change them as an act of religious liberation from social sin, even if this meant resorting to counterviolence in the process. The conference recognized the "autonomy of the temporal" by supporting alliances between the Church and outside groups in the common pursuit of social justice.

The rapid emergence of the theology of liberation in the wake of the Medellín conference generated a counterreaction within the Church that made itself felt at the third General Conference of Latin American Bishops held at Puebla, Mexico, in 1979. At issue was not the Church's commitment to social justice but the strategy employed to achieve it. The bishops at Puebla worried that the Church since Medellín had become identified with overtly Marxist approaches to social change, including violent revolution, that not only went against the grain of the faith but also diluted the Church's message with ideas alien to it. In his address, Pope John Paul II criticized those who saw Jesus mainly as a politician or revolutionary struggling against Roman domination.[32] This may have been the charge made against Jesus by his accusers, but Jesus' own understanding of his mission was very different. The bishops outlined an "integral" conception of liberation that could only be achieved by actions of Christians motivated by the Spirit of Christ and not by recourse to violence of any type or the dialectic of class struggle.[33] They condemned both the institutionalized violence of oppressive social systems and the counterviolence of would-be revolutionaries with the same fervor, in effect equating the two.[34]

If the bishops distanced the Church from Marxism without condemning liberation theology, they also strongly reaffirmed and deepened the Church's understanding—emanating from Vatican II and Medellín—of the importance of its temporal role in the transformation of Latin America. The bishops assembled at Puebla denounced the persistence of widespread poverty in Latin America, supported the right of poor people to organize to defend themselves, and called for a "preferential option for the poor" in the mission of the Church.[35] The bishops did not limit the scope of their temporal concerns to the pursuit of social justice alone but extended it to embrace the political sphere as well. They were, however, careful to distinguish between "politics in the broad sense" and "politics in the narrow sense."[36] Politics in the broad sense, involving the articulation of the fundamental values that ought to orient political activity in all communities, was declared to be a vital part of the Church's mission to evangelize all facets of human existence. Politics in the narrow sense, involving the organization of citizens into political parties for the realization of concrete goals, was restricted to the laity. In defining the content of these "fundamental values," the bishops were quick to condemn the existence of authoritarian regimes inspired by the "doctrine of national security" in Latin America and to defend the right of citizens to participate in the making of political decisions.[37] The conference thus offered a political vision that was clearly democratic in nature.

The progressive expansion of the Church's understanding of its temporal role, beginning with Vatican II, carries with it an increased risk of conflict with the state, given the fact that Church and state often hold clashing visions of society and politics. While Vatican II was generally optimistic about the possibility of avoiding such conflict, Medellín openly warned that any "truly effective" or "audacious" action by the Church in society would inevitably lead to conflict, if not with the state then with vested interests, and the conference exhorted Christians to overcome their passivity, which reflected both a fear of sacrifice and a reluctance to shoulder personal risks.[38] The Church's assertion at Puebla of its right to participate in politics, even if only in a broad sense, and its unequivocal condemnation of authoritarian regimes further heightened the possibility of conflict with the state. The exigencies of doctrinal change in the universal Church thus favored the development of a new role for the Church in society fraught with the danger and even inevitability of conflict with the state.

Dioceses with a higher proportion of clergy ordained after Vatican II were more likely to be open to a postconciliar perspective on the Church's role in society. In the more conservative pastoral zones of the states of Zacatecas, Guanajuato, and Mexico, the number of priests ordained before 1964 stood at 73 percent, 55 percent, and 46 percent, respectively; in the more progressive zones of the states of Chihuahua and Veracruz, the number of priests ordained prior to 1964 fell precipitously to only 33 percent and 25 percent, respectively.[39] Obviously, this is not a hard and fast rule: older priests can change with the times—but they are less likely do so.

Bishops who had attended Vatican II were also more likely to be open to the new currents of doctrinal change. And in 1963, younger bishops influenced by Vatican II formed the Bishops Mutual Aid Union (UMAE).[40] The importance of the UMAE lay in the fact that it created a network of bishops open to new theological trends.

Chihuahua's two major bishops, Adalberto Almeida y Merino and Manuel Talamás Camandari, had attended all four sessions of Vatican II.[41] A few years after Vatican II, Almeida, then bishop of Zacatecas, and Father Pedro Vázquez, director of the Mexican Social Secretariat (SSM), a dependency of the Mexican episcopate, helped draft the pastoral letter, "The Development and Integration of our Country," issued on March 26, 1968, in the name of the Mexican bishops.[42] The letter marked the first time in almost twenty years that the Church was willing to address directly controversial social questions. The pastoral letter denounced the marginalization of the majority of Mexicans from the development process and urged the adoption of a more participatory development strategy, not only in its material benefits but also in its design and execution.[43] Both

Talamás and Almeida were also present at the Medellín Conference, where Almeida played a significant role in the drafting of the documents on justice and peace.[44] In July, 1971, Almeida participated in a month-long retreat of fifty-three Latin American bishops to discuss the reality of Latin America in light of the conclusions reached at Medellín.[45] The retreat was also attended by a number of bishops identified with liberation theology, such as Sergio Méndez Arceo, Samuel Ruíz García, the late Oscar Romero, and the theologian Gustavo Gutiérrez. Also in 1971, Talamás was one of the three Mexican delegates representing the Mexican hierarchy at the third international synod of bishops held in Rome to study the situation of justice in the world.[46] Prior to their departure, Talamás and his fellow delegates had prepared a controversial study of the state of justice in Mexico. Talamás also attended the Puebla conference and served on one of its most important drafting commissions alongside the legendary Brazilian archbishop, Helder Camara, and Oscar Romero, archbishop of San Salvador.[47] While at Puebla, Talamás joined some of his episcopal colleagues in writing a public letter of support for Romero, who would later be assassinated.

The intimate involvement of Almeida and Talamás in the overall process of doctrinal change had a profound impact on how they viewed their pastoral roles in their respective dioceses. Both bishops were strongly inclined towards an understanding of faith that translated itself into temporal action in the economic, social, cultural, and political spheres.[48] Both believed in mounting a vigorous defense of human rights, including the right to free elections. Both bishops were acutely conscious that their defense of human rights could lead to clashes with the state. Almeida believed that conflict with the state was inevitable as the Church intensified its commitment to the defense of human rights in an environment of growing injustice, including what the bishop characterized as:

> a dictatorial system that maintains itself in power on the basis of a high percentage of frauds ... considers that the best democracy in the world is its own ... is managing the economy of the country from a political point of view, that is, its party interests and is not looking for the good of the nation.[49]

In defending human rights, both Talamás and Almeida insisted that they were defending principles, not particular secular ideologies or political parties. In the 1970s, when they had focused on the need for greater socioeconomic rights for the underprivileged, they had been accused of Communist leanings. Now, in the 1980s, when they were championing the cause of clean elections, they were labeled PAN sympathizers. Yet, the bishops themselves did not see any inconsistency between their actions in the 1970s and 1980s, since they sprang from a common religious perspective enunciated at Vatican II, Medellín, and Puebla, that seeks the promotion of full human dignity and the illumination of all aspects of temporal existence in the light of the Gospel, even if this means conflict with the state or other groups.

Organizational Structure

The Chihuahua Church's openness to society was also enhanced by its organizational structure. Unlike the first three bishops of the Diocese of Chihuahua, who were drawn from the states of Jalisco, Durango, and Michoacán respectively, both Talamás and Almeida were from Chihuahua. Neither Talamás nor Almeida was significantly touched by the religious conflicts of the 1920s and 1930s. They were separated by only one year in age, had attended seminary together in Chihuahua, and proceeded to Rome for further studies at about the same time. The two bishops were thus able to achieve an unusually high level of communication and coordination between their respective dioceses.

Talamás and Almeida were also deeply concerned with the implications of Vatican II for the internal organization of the Church. Both bishops therefore sought to stimulate greater participation at all levels of their dioceses. The Archdiocese of Chihuahua was one of the few dioceses in the country to act on the recommendation of Vatican II that the position of the permanent lay deacon, carrying with it functions hitherto reserved for priests, be reinstituted.[50] By 1985 there were six permanent deacons functioning in the archdiocese.[51] Both bishops sought to encourage the growth of lay spirituality by stressing the importance of a personal conversion experience, drawing attention to the underlying religious meaning of the sacraments, and encouraging lay people to integrate their faith autonomously into their temporal lives.

Talamás and Almeida also sought to develop collegial relationships with the priests in their dioceses, though Talamás was more successful in this regard than Almeida. Greater openness to clergy in turn translated into greater openness to lay society because it meant that lay parishioners could communicate more easily with the bishops through their priests. Talamás was made bishop of the new diocese of Ciudad Juárez in 1958. Almost the entire clergy of Ciudad Juárez was personally trained by him.[52] Predictably, relations between Talamás and his presbytery were exceptionally close. The small size of the diocese meant that it was possible for the bishop to hold a weekly meeting with clergy to discuss problems and make decisions usually by consensus.[53] So strongly did Talamás feel about the need for granting priests a greater voice in episcopal decisions that in 1971 he proposed the creation of organizational structures specifically for priests that would defend their interests and facilitate greater coordination.[54] The proposal was, however, rejected by the Mexican bishops.

The Archdiocese of Chihuahua is much larger in area, has a greater number of priests, and has more diverse pastoral needs than the Diocese of Ciudad Juárez. The opportunities for regular face-to-face interaction between Almeida and the priests under his charge were more limited. The archdiocese is divided into five zones, each represented by a single individual on the Presbyterial Council, which meets once a month and acts as an intermediary body between the archbishop and his presbytery. General meetings of all clergy are rare, occurring only once or twice a year. The structure of decision making in the Archdiocese of Chihuahua is thus more centralized than in the Diocese of Ciudad Juárez. Still, the level of communication between archbishop and clergy improved under Almeida, whose arrival in 1969 signaled the end of a period of great confusion for the archdiocese after the retirement of Guizar Valencia in 1962. Almeida, for instance, ensured that the Presbyterial Council functioned without interruption during his tenure as archbishop.[55]

CHIHUAHUA'S BISHOPS, SOCIAL JUSTICE, AND ELECTORAL DEMOCRACY

The activist trajectory of Chihuahua's bishops may be divided into two distinct phases. In the first phase, during the 1970s, the bishops' main concern was the problem of the transformation of unjust social structures rather than the achievement of electoral democracy. The actions of Chihuahua's bishops during this period were deeply influenced by the Medellín Conference, the upsurge in student unrest in Mexico that began in 1968, and the emergence of Latin American liberation theology. Their attempts to promote social justice in Chihuahua aroused great opposition, however, among major segments of society as well as their own clergy. The bishops, particularly Almeida, found themselves isolated and were obliged to modify their militant stance in favor of social justice. In the second phase, during the 1980s, the bishops addressed themselves to the problem of electoral democracy. The response was electrifying. The bishops were applauded by all sectors of society. They received virtually the unanimous support of their presbyteries, and messages of support poured in from their episcopal colleagues in other parts of the country. The repeated failures that had marred the Chihuahua Church's attempts to promote social justice in the 1970s were thus followed by a series of resounding successes in the 1980s.

The 1970s: The Issue of Social Justice

On January 15, 1972, a group of urban guerrillas led by former student leader Diego Lucero Martínez, simultaneously held up three banks in Chihuahua City. Diego Lucero was taken into police custody and apparently shot to death. Another guerrilla was reported to have hanged himself in his cell, and a third was killed by police while allegedly resisting arrest. The bank assaults and the response of the police polarized society in Chihuahua. The middle classes and the business community deplored the robberies and demanded that the guerrillas be severely punished, while students, independent unions, and some popular colonies vigorously denounced the brutal treatment of the guerrillas and formed an umbrella organization, the Popular Defense Committee (CDP), to coordinate the struggle for social justice.[56]

In this highly charged atmosphere Almeida and Talamás decided to express the Church's own interpretation of the situation. Almeida's views were set out in a public document, "Declaration of the Archbishop and Priests of Chihuahua about the Violent Events

Registered There," issued on January 28, 1972, and published in all of Chihuahua City's major newspapers and the Mexico City daily *Excelsior.* The declaration reproached the official media for failing to discern the deeper significance of the guerrillas' actions. Instead, the document viewed the violence of the guerrillas as a response to the institutionalized violence of the rich.[57] The document defined institutionalized violence as

> the violation of constitutional rights ... the unjust and anti-evan-
> gelical stratification of society ... the explicit disdain and disguised
> racism that exists in the most educated classes towards the less
> qualified sectors ... the use of threats to muzzle those who wish to
> speak the truth, physical torture to oblige the victim to confess even
> falsehoods, and bribery to buy consciences and complicit silences,
> especially in the communications media ... [and] all types of power
> structures—political, economic, and religious—which, with an in-
> sulting paternalism, give to those "from below" as charity what is
> owed to them as justice.[58]

In a rare moment of institutional criticism, the declaration criti-cized the Church for favoring elites, for neglecting its mission to the marginalized and those "without a voice," and for being complicit in the perpetuation of unjust power structures.[59] The declaration also stated the intention of the archdiocese to reorient its mission towards the achievement of social justice and the transformation of the existing violent society into one based on love and solidarity.[60] The government was urged to "alter the structures propitiating in-stitutionalized violence in order to avoid worse and more painful violence," while the business community was asked to shun eco-nomic transactions based on "egoism, avarice, and the lack of par-ticipation."[61] The declaration concluded with a warning that true peace would not be possible without the achievement of justice.

In Ciudad Juárez, a "Declaration of the Bishop and Priests of Ciudad Juárez about the National Situation" was issued simulta-neously and also appeared in both the local newspapers and *Excel-sior.* The Ciudad Juárez declaration was broadly similar to the one issued in Chihuahua. Talamás and his presbytery also viewed the recent violence as the result of justice denied.[62] They argued that injustice in Mexico stemmed fundamentally from the lack of ade-quate spaces for participation in the political, economic, and cultural spheres. The situation was one of "permanent sin frustrating God's plan and demanding from us a serious commitment to liberate man from all that makes him less human."[63] Talamás and his presbytery thus replaced the concept of institutionalized violence with the less provocative one of social sin. Still, regardless of how Talamás and Almeida chose to characterize unjust social arrangements, both viewed violence as a natural consequence of injustice. For Talamás and his presbytery,

> The dramatic events to which we refer are therefore an urgent call from God for us to conduct a profound and honest review of our political, social, economic, cultural, and religious institutions. We must discern in them all that is obsolete, vitiated, and putrid; and, once discovered, have the courage to change it even if this goes against our own egotistical interests.[64]

The implication was that without such an overhaul of Mexican institutions, the violence afflicting Mexican society would continue unabated and might even intensify. Finally, the document urged Christians to be sensitive to the liberating word of Jesus and translate their faith into concrete action for the sake of justice.

The declarations issued in Ciudad Juárez and Chihuahua City provoked an extremely negative reaction among Chihuahua's middle classes. The theory of institutionalized violence was widely seen as justifying attacks on homes, property, businesses, and even people.[65] Most of the middle-class recognized the importance of alleviating poverty but viscerally rejected what it considered to be Marxist-inspired solutions to the problem.[66] It was feared that the bishops had allied themselves with Marxism and betrayed the Church's true mission.[67] Rumors spread that Almeida had allowed himself to be misled and manipulated by a small clique of radical priests. Many important sectors of the laity felt that Almeida should take steps to discipline all such priests; when the archbishop failed to do so, he found his authority and credibility further eroded.[68] The bishops had underestimated the strength of Chihuahua's middle classes and overrated the importance of the student movement. The middle classes were inevitably the dominant social element in a state as urbanized and commercialized as Chihuahua. This was even more so in the Church, where the middle classes were in a far better position than other social groups to participate in Church-sponsored activities, by virtue of their superior access to resources such as time, money, and education. The most visible, active, and influential portions of the laity were, therefore, drawn almost exclusively from the middle sectors. Meanwhile, the coalition of students, independent unions, and popular colonies that had originally constituted the CDP, after a relatively brief period of effervescence, began to splinter because of its own heterogeneity.[69] By 1974, the only major group left in the coalition, from the popular colony Francisco Villa in Chihuahua City, had decided to ally itself with the government in exchange for becoming a favored conduit for urban services and property titles. The bishops thus found themselves isolated from the mainstream of lay society in Chihuahua.

Almeida's stance in favor of social justice also generated serious conflicts with his presbytery. In Ciudad Juárez, however, relations between Talamás and his presbytery remained good. To some extent this reflected the great esteem in which most priests in the diocese held their bishop and the high level of communication between Talamás and his presbytery. Also, Ciudad Juárez, by virtue of its position as a major border city, has attracted a flood of migrant workers from other parts of Mexico. This, in turn, has led to a proliferation of makeshift popular colonies around the city, often lacking the most elementary services, and in response a significant proportion of the priests in Ciudad Juárez have chosen to dedicate themselves to the task of serving the urban poor.[70] Talamás's call for social justice was therefore well understood by the majority of his presbytery. This, however, was not so in the Archdiocese of Chihuahua, where only a small fraction of the presbytery was engaged in pastoral work with marginalized groups, and where the majority of priests, as in the rest of Mexico, were hostile to any pastoral strategy even vaguely linked to liberation theology. Initially, most priests in Chihuahua supported Almeida's declaration, albeit reluctantly, but once the anger of their mostly middle class parishioners became clear, they quickly distanced themselves from him.[71] Almeida and a small group of radical priests were thus left to face the ensuing storm of criticism alone.

The increasingly tense relationship between Almeida and his presbytery was highlighted by the murder of Father Rodolfo Aguilar, who had been particularly close to the archbishop. Aguilar was one the few priests in the diocese totally committed to working with the poor; he was appointed a parish priest in the popular colony, Nombre de Dios, on the outskirts of Chihuahua City. In 1975, he led a movement of local squatters to prevent their being dislodged by the authorities, who had earmarked the area for the future site of a major industrial development project. In 1976, Aguilar's residence was set on fire by arsonists and a smear campaign launched against him in the press. It was widely rumored that Aguilar had developed links with the feared guerrilla organization, League of the 23rd of September, and was even learning to shoot.[72] As the controversy mounted, Almeida withdrew Aguilar's appointment as parish priest in Nombre de Dios. The decision was taken under fierce pressure from the government, business community, and Chihuahua's middle classes, as well as from Almeida's own presbytery, which had never approved of Aguilar's activities.[73] Then, on March 21, 1977, Aguilar was found murdered. Some speculated that his murder had been ordered by the government or powerful business interests that he had offended. Others felt that he had been eliminated by the League of the 23rd of September because he had come to know too much about the internal functioning of the organization.

On March 25, 1977, Almeida issued a public declaration protesting the murder of Aguilar and defending his pastoral work; the declaration was signed by the archbishop alone without the support of his presbytery. Many sympathizers of Aguilar openly blamed the presbytery of Chihuahua for being indirectly responsible for his death; Almeida himself probably shared this opinion. Indeed, an official document issued by the Team of Pastoral Reflection for the Northern Zone stated that Aguilar might not have died if more priests in the diocese of Chihuahua had been committed to the line of pastoral work favored by Aguilar.[74] The Aguilar affair most certainly worsened the relationship between Almeida and his presbytery and probably further undermined his standing among many influential sectors of society, which were dismayed by the archbishop's support of Aguilar.

The close of the 1970s was marked by still another controversy of vital importance to all of Chihuahua's bishops and their clergy: the nature of seminary education. The second Vatican Council had strongly supported the creation of regional seminaries that cut across dioceses, both for reasons of economies of scale and to foster a greater sense of solidarity between dioceses. The Regional Seminary of the North's philosophy section opened in Ciudad Juárez in 1970, and the theology section in Chihuahua City in 1973.

In 1976, Father Camilo Daniel of the Archdiocese of Chihuahua was appointed rector of the section of theology. Camilo Daniel felt that the new conception of the role of the priest, articulated at Vatican II, Medellín, and Puebla, could become a reality only if seminary education was restructured in such a way as to promote the emergence of a new kind of priest, capable of exercising a powerful pastoral option in favor of the poor.[75] For him, the best way to train seminary students for the vocation of temporal service was to insert them into the concrete reality of a particular community and stimulate them to reflect deeply on their daily experiences in the light of the Gospel. For Daniel, seminary education had to be conducted "in, with, by, and for the Christian community."[76] In 1979, the bishops, with strong support from Almeida, Talamás, and José Llaguno, the bishop of the Tarahumara, approved an alternative program of seminary education in theology, allowing students to substitute for the normal curriculum a period of residence in a popular colony.[77]

The new approach to seminary education caused great concern, especially among the clergy of the Archdiocese of Chihuahua. Daniel was accused of politicizing the Church, creating new Rodolfo Aguilars, and neglecting the spiritual dimension of seminary education.[78] René Blanco, a member of the Ciudad Juárez presbytery and Daniel's assistant, found himself socially rejected by most priests in Chihuahua and was criticized for being "too Latin American" in his thinking and favoring the poor over other social groups in his ministry.[79] In spite of fierce opposition, the expansion of the new program was so rapid that it appeared that the seminary would soon be emptied of all its remaining students. In 1981, the priests of the Archdiocese of Chihuahua, with the support of the prelate of Nuevo Casas Grandes, Hilario Chávez Joya, threatened to appeal to Rome in order to secure the termination of the program on the ground that it violated the basic Vatican rules concerning seminary education, including the one requiring that all such education occur within the confines of a building in order to "guard the seriousness and profundity of theological purpose."[80] Faced with a major revolt and rising doubts, Almeida, Talamás, and José

Llaguno withdrew their support of the program, and Daniel was obliged to resign.

During the 1970s, Almeida and Talamás, inspired by Medellín and Latin American liberation theology, placed great emphasis on the issue of social justice. In doing so they succeeded in alienating the bulk of Chihuahua's middle classes, resulting in a virtual divorce between the bishops and the most active segment of the laity. In the Archdiocese of Chihuahua, the clergy, caught between the competing claims of their parishioners and the bishop and extremely suspicious of Latin American liberation theology, turned decisively against Almeida. The result was a series of humiliating defeats for the bishops. Nor did the actions of Almeida and Talamás win much support from bishops outside their dioceses. The murder of Aguilar was completely ignored by the Mexican hierarchy, partly out of a desire not to upset the delicate equilibrium of Church-State relations, and partly because of the hostility that most Mexican bishops felt towards liberation theology.[81] By the end of the 1970s, the Chihuahua Church was divided and demoralized. During the 1980s, however, these wounds would disappear in a remarkably short span of time and the Chihuahua Church would achieve an unprecedented unity.

The 1980s: The Issue of Electoral Democracy

The first major Church initiative to address the question of electoral democracy in Chihuahua occurred in May, 1983, when Almeida issued a document entitled "Vote with Responsibility: A Christian Orientation." The document was published during the final stages of an unusually heated campaign for Chihuahua's municipal presidencies during which the PAN, fueled by widespread disenchantment with the disastrous economic mismanagement, corruption, and populism of the López Portillo *sexenio*, had acquired considerable momentum.

In the document, Almeida urged all voters to go to the polls in order to break the "traditional political apathy and indifference in which the average citizen has been maintained in Mexico."[82] Voters were exhorted not to slide back into political indifference after the elections but to continue monitoring the conduct of elected officials in order to assure good and honest government.[83] Public functionaries were warned that the combination of human sin and political power could lead not only to frequent abuses of the public trust but pave the way for a totalitarian system of government based on the absolutization and divinization of power.[84] Finally, the document deplored the use of threats and bribery to oblige citizens to vote in favor of a particular political party or candidate.

In issuing the document, Almeida asserted the Church's right to "evangelize the totality of human existence including the political dimension" and insisted that he was participating in politics only in "the broad sense" of orienting the public about the "fundamental values" that ought to govern the political sphere without endorsing a particular political party or candidate, which was an exclusively lay prerogative.[85] Yet indirectly, "Vote with Responsibility" almost certainly hurt the PRI and favored its main opponent, the PAN. In calling for an end to abstention at a time when most new voters would surely have turned against the PRI, the document may have helped the opposition win more votes than it might otherwise have received. Also, Almeida's references to corruption, lying, and demagoguery in public life, coupled with his warning concerning the dangers posed by power-hungry functionaries, in effect, amounted to an indictment of the PRI and its monopoly of government that spanned almost six decades. Finally, the document was issued in the midst of an intensely competitive campaign in which the PRI was clearly on the defensive and therefore had a greater impact than would otherwise have been the case.

The results of the 1983 municipal elections in Chihuahua were disastrous for the PRI. The PAN swept to victory in all of Chihuahua's major cities including Parral, Chihuahua City, and Ciudad Juárez, and found itself in the position of governing 70 percent of the state's population. The elections were marked by a significant decline in the level of abstention as compared to the municipal elections held three years earlier, and most of these new votes were captured by the PAN.[86] The PRI in Chihuahua, which had mostly ignored "Vote with Responsibility" during the campaign, now bitterly blamed the Church under Almeida for the loss of the elections.[87] The rising tension quickly erupted into a vicious battle of words, quite unprecedented in recent Mexican political history. On September 11, 1983, an article, virulently critical of the Church—"Of Conservatives, Church, and State"—appeared in all of Chihuahua City's major newspapers published under the auspices of the PRI's Directive Committee in Chihuahua. The article provided a summary of the main events in the history of Church-State conflict and then concluded that the Church had always been aligned with the forces of reaction and obscurantism against the Mexican state. The article accused the Church of harboring a constant desire for power and viewed the Church's recent intervention in the electoral process as a sinister attempt to restore its old privileges.[88] Two weeks later, on September 24, Almeida responded in a public letter entitled "Catholics and Civic Duty." He criticized the PRI for possessing a simplistic and self-serving vision of Mexican history as a contest between good and evil and portraying itself as the exclusive heir and guardian of Mexican nationalism and identity.[89] For Almeida, the PRI's claim to a monopoly on patriotism was not only open to question but extremely dangerous:

> According to this mentality, it would seem that the love of country is present only among those who belong to the PRI the others [being] a bunch of villains and traitors. This vision, in addition to being unjust, ingenuous, and arrogant, inevitably leads to an absolutist conception of power, with the consequent destruction of democracy.[90]

The prophetic nature of the archbishop's words would become apparent three years later, when many PRI members justified the rigging of the 1986 elections in Chihuahua as an act of "patriotic fraud." Finally, Almeida accused the PRI, by virtue of its attacks on the Church, of making its members choose between their faith and party affiliation, leading to a severe crisis of conscience.[91]

The PRI's ill-considered attack on the Church backfired. It drew attention to the fact that the PRI was an ungracious loser, placed Catholics in the PRI in a highly awkward situation, and, by its sheer hysteria, may have generated sympathy for the Church. Also, without denying the Church's role in adding to the general ferment of dissatisfaction prior to the elections, one can dismiss the hypothesis that it was the main cause of the PRI's electoral debacle. "Vote with Responsibility" reflected the mood of the electorate in Chihuahua far more than it influenced it. The rate of abstention would probably have declined anyway as more individuals turned to the ballot box to protest against the regime. And the criticisms that the document made of the PRI repeated in an oblique fashion what most

Chihuahuenses were already saying in even stronger terms. By blaming the Church for the 1983 results, the PRI revealed a misunderstanding of the forces shaping politics in the state, which encompassed virtually all sectors of society.

After the skirmish between the Church and the PRI in September, 1983, the Church maintained an aloof stance until the onset of the electoral campaign of 1986. The 1986 campaign was far more intense than the one in 1983, partly because the stakes were much higher, involving not only all of Chihuahua's municipal presidencies but the governorship as well. Also, the PAN was far better organized than it had been in 1983, and, by virtue of its successful administration of Chihuahua's major cities, the party had acquired new credibility and respect. Indeed, many believed that the PAN stood an excellent chance of becoming the first opposition party in postrevolutionary electoral history to win a gubernatorial race.

On March 19, 1986, less than four months before the elections were to be held, the Church broke its two-and-a-half year silence on political questions and issued a document entitled "Christian Coherence in Politics." Unlike "Vote with Responsibility," which was issued only in Almeida's name, "Christian Coherence in Politics" was written by all of Chihuahua's bishops, including Almeida, Talamás, Llaguno, and Chávez Joya, as well as Fernando Romo, bishop of Torreón in the neighboring state of Coahuila. The fact that it was supported by a broad coalition of bishops gave it far more authority and attention than it would otherwise have enjoyed. It was also far more critical of Mexico's political system than "Vote with Responsibility" had been. After declaring that the Church was against the "intolerance and absolutism of one man or one political party" and supporting the right of citizens to participate freely in public affairs, the bishops launched an unusually penetrating analysis of the problem of corruption. The pervasiveness of corruption was a structural phenomenon, stemming from the lack of accountability endemic to authoritarian regimes:

> The corruption that has taken over [our] institutions for some time now is primarily due to the unwillingness [of the political system] to open itself up to a sincere and authentic democracy. The lack of democracy in a party [i.e., the PRI] reveals a determined desire to ex-

ercise power in an absolute and uninterrupted fashion. And absolute power in necessarily limited human hands leads inexorably to corruption.[92]

The bishops warned that a government whose hold on power was not dependent on the wishes of the voters was effectively freed from the constant pressures, inherent in any democracy, to justify its actions and respond to public expectations.[93] For the bishops, corruption reflected the lack of democracy, which, in turn, reflected election fraud. They described the ways used to commit fraud and then concluded:

> These depravations and many others, to which we have all been witnesses, should not be tolerated by any Christian conscience, because they constitute a grave sin against various commandments of the law of God.[94]

The decision of the bishops to denounce electoral fraud vigorously in "Christian Coherence in Politics" was almost certainly made with a view to discouraging the regime from rigging the upcoming elections. There had been widespread speculation that this was exactly what the regime had in mind in order to avoid losing the governorship of a strategic border state to an allegedly "pro-Yankee" PAN. As if to undermine the PRI's habitual justifications for monopolizing power as well as the idea of a "patriotic fraud," the document also advised Catholics to be wary of the many rationalizations often advanced to support the continued existence of an undemocratic government, including the "fear that without it Mexico would be incapable of governing itself or fall into the hands of a party that would endanger the independence and security of the country."[95] The document criticized "totalitarian regimes" for claiming that people were not sufficiently mature to govern themselves while, at the same time, actively conspiring to maintain them in a state of "political immaturity," thereby creating a vicious cycle highly unfavorable to the achievement of democracy.[96]

"Christian Coherence in Politics" also urged all Catholics, especially those in the regime, not to be ashamed of their faith and to seek actively the implantation of the Kingdom of God in the temporal realm. In a sharp rebuke to Catholics active in the PRI, the bishops declared:

We can have every right to ask ourselves, whether political activity
in Mexico, whose exercise has become a synonym for corruption in
the eyes of many, would be the same if lay people holding public
offices, many of whom come from highly Christian families and were
trained in Catholic schools and apostolic groups, were coherent in
their Christian vocation.[97]

The bishops also chose to use the document as an occasion to give
voice to their dissatisfaction with the nature of Church-State relations in Mexico on two counts: the failure to grant the Church legal
personality and the excessive and "improper interference of the state
in the internal affairs of the Church."

As the elections neared, the fear that the regime was planning
to resort to fraud acquired even more credence. On July 2, four
days before the elections, Talamás declared that a decision had already been taken at the highest levels of the political system to
declare the PRI the winner even at the expense of the popular will.[98]
For his part, Almeida stated that he was deeply worried "because
there are serious indications that there will be fraud in the elections
on Sunday."[99] Meanwhile, on July 4, the press quoted Almeida as
saying that Fernando Baeza, the PRI's candidate for governor and a
professing Catholic, could be excommunicated if he won the governorship fraudulently.[100] A few days later, shortly after the elections, Almeida denied having "excommunicated anybody" but added
that "if a candidate for a public office professes to be a Catholic and
knows that he has been elected by fraud, it is his duty not to accept
power because it would be illegitimate."[101] Then, as people recovered from their initial shock at the extent of the fraud perpetrated
by the regime, which had exceeded even their wildest expectations,
huge protests began to erupt across the state.

On Sunday, July 13, in an extraordinary sermon revolving
around the parable of the Good Samaritan and delivered in all of
the parishes in the Archdiocese of Chihuahua, Almeida and his
presbytery condemned the elections as fraudulent:

> Last Sunday, the sixth of July, there was someone who fell into the
> hands of some highway robbers. Someone who suffered all manner
> of vexations, ill treatment, mockery, and scorn. Someone whose dig-
> nity was violated, who was threatened and lied to, and whose human
> rights were not respected. That someone was the people of Chihuahua.

> The people of Chihuahua, the victims of the prepotence of those who enjoy power have been left half dead on the highway.... We therefore energetically denounce the shameful events of the election day, Sunday, July 6. We denounce the falsehood, fraud, the slow pace of balloting, the highhandedness of the public forces ... the blackmail, the threats, and arbitrary acts of all kinds that occurred on that day.[102]

The sermon then made the dramatic announcement that all parishes in the archdiocese would remain closed on Sunday, July 20, as an act of protest and in solidarity with the people of Chihuahua.[103]

The decision to close the parishes was highly symbolic, since the last time the Church suspended services, in 1926, signaled the beginning of the *Cristero* war. The prospect of a suspension of religious services in Chihuahua naturally aroused extreme concern at the highest levels of both the regime and the Church. The regime viewed the suspension of religious services as a highly provocative intervention of the local Church in political matters that was sure to inflame passions further in Chihuahua.

The main objective of the Apostolic Delegate, Girolamo Prigione, was to avert a full-blown crisis in Church-State relations. Prigione, an Italian, and one of the Vatican's most skillful diplomats, took up his assignment in Mexico in 1978. Because there were no formal diplomatic ties between the Vatican and Mexico between 1926 and 1992, Prigione was officially considered the pope's representative to the Mexican hierarchy rather than the Mexican government, and he was therefore invested with the title of apostolic delegate instead of papal nuncio. His real function, however, was to be a liaison to the regime on an unofficial basis, with a view to winning diplomatic recognition of the Vatican and improving the status of the Church in Mexico. Prigione was well insulated from pressure by Mexican bishops, clergy, or laity because his authority derived directly from the pope and not the Mexican Church.

Manuel Bartlett Díaz, Secretary of the Interior, warned Prigione, a personal friend, that Almeida's decision to close the parishes would lead to a major confrontation between Church and state and unleash violence. Bartlett then asked the apostolic delegate to intervene.[104] Bartlett could have chosen to bypass the apostolic delegate and intervene directly, but that might have transformed Almeida into a rallying figure of the protest movement in Chihuahua and alienated the vast majority of the Mexican episcopate. He therefore chose the more prudent course of achieving his purposes through the apostolic delegate. While the apostolic delegate may not directly overrule a bishop acting autonomously in his own diocese, he can use his powers to ensure that the Vatican does so. At first, Prigione sought to resolve the matter without going to the Vatican. He convened a special meeting of the six-member presidency of the permanent council of the Mexican episcopate with Interior Secretary Bartlett.[105] Bartlett used the meeting to warn the bishops that "if next Sunday the Churches are closed, blood will run in Chihuahua. Who will be responsible? Think about it carefully."[106] The presidency immediately asked Almeida to reconsider his decision to suspend services, but Almeida refused, saying "I would do it only if the Holy Father orders me."[107] Prigione interpreted this statement as Almeida's way of suggesting a solution to the crisis and informed the Vatican of the situation in Chihuahua, presumably with the support of the presidency of the Mexican Episcopate.[108] Cardinal Achille Silvestrini, an official of the Vatican secretariat of state, immediately reacted: "Tell monsignor Almeida that he cannot do this, that it is not permitted by the canon law code. The Eucharist cannot serve as an instrument of political repression. Other means exist."[109] This was followed by an official letter from the Secretary of State of the Vatican, Agostino Casaroli, who reports directly to the pope, ordering Almeida "not to suspend worship ceremonies on Sunday, July 20, so that the people do not remain without the Eucharist."[110] Prigione then communicated the Vatican's order to Almeida personally, explaining that under canon law "the Eucharist could never be used as an instrument of political pressure."[111]

For Almeida, however, the proposed suspension of mass could still be justified on the purely theological basis of Jesus' exhortation that Christians first seek reconciliation with one another before presenting any offering to God, which had not yet occurred in Chihuahua and could not unless the elections were annulled.[112] Nevertheless, Almeida and his presbytery decided to obey the papal order and hold Mass after all. The overruling of Almeida was a clear example of the triumph of historical context over the universal claims of doctrinal renewal. For Almeida himself, the threat to close the parishes had already served much of its purpose:

> We felt that what we ought to do was obey the pope and truly give testimony of our obedience to the Holy Father. Firstly, because we had already achieved the objective desired by some of us, which was to denounce the fraud and attract attention [to it] inside and outside the country. It [the news] had already reached Canada, Spain, France. What had been published had been incredible. The denunciation, the denunciation of the fraud. There were more than two hundred reporters here.[113]

In Ciudad Juárez, Talamás and his presbytery also strongly condemned the elections as fraudulent. In a sermon read aloud in all of the parishes of the diocese on the Sunday after the elections, they declared: "We denounce the fraud, falsehood, manipulation, [and] mockery ... as an extremely grave social sin that Heaven cries out for."[114] Simultaneously, Talamás and his presbytery also issued a public message, which appeared in all major newspapers in Ciudad Juárez on July 13, 1986. The message accused the regime of having conspired to steal the election from the very start of the campaign and made note of the kinds of irregularities committed by the PRI on election day, including, among other things, the exclusion of opposition representatives from polling stations, the stuffing of ballot boxes before the polls even opened, denying people with credentials the right to vote after having removed their names from the electoral rolls, and allowing groups tightly controlled by the regime, such as soldiers, to vote more than once.[115] The message also reminded the regime that it could not expect to command obedience if its authority was illegitimate in origin, being based on the deliberate frustration of the will of the majority. It considered the protests sweeping Chihuahua as an entirely justified reaction to the imposition of a government of dubious legality. Finally, as if to support even stronger measures to defend the vote, the message declared:

> We exhort the people to acquire consciousness of their inalienable right to freely elect their rulers and work to create independent popular organizations that will make respect for their rights possible.[116]

Talamás and his presbytery, however, refrained from calling

for the suspension of religious services in their diocese. They felt that the Church was already protesting the fraud in a sufficiently vigorous manner to render a suspension of religious worship unnecessary.[117] Many viewed the measure as extremely imprudent and argued that the fact that Almeida was obliged to reverse his own initial decision to close the parishes proved them right.[118] There was also some concern that ordinary churchgoers might not be able to comprehend the rationale behind the suspension of religious services.[119] Indeed, one prominent priest argued that far from closing the parishes, it was imperative that they be kept open in order to provide a setting for religious reflection, prayer, forgiveness, reconciliation, and orientation at a critical moment of great crisis.[120] It must also be remembered that the Diocese of Ciudad Juárez had a relatively large number of priests directly involved in pastoral work with the urban poor. While almost all such priests strongly supported the stand taken by Talamás against electoral fraud, they were nonetheless afraid that the emphasis on electoral democracy might cloud the need for social justice.[121] They were also concerned that their actions could indirectly be helping the PAN, which they viewed as a party unfavorable to the cause of social justice.[122] As a result, Talamás's denunciations of the fraud, while unusually vigorous and forthright, did not reach the same heights as Almeida's did in the Archdiocese of Chihuahua. Nor would Talamás and his presbytery participate in the "democracy workshops" held in the Archdiocese of Chihuahua some months later.

Meanwhile, on August 7, 1986, with the protests showing no signs of abating and the regime continuing to defend the election results, Almeida, Talamás, and Llaguno issued another public statement, provocatively entitled "Moral Judgment on the Electoral Process," in which they demanded the annulment of the elections. The statement was published in the *Washington Post* the following week. In the statement, the bishops declared that the sheer scope and magnitude of the irregularities committed in the elections had seriously undermined their credibility.[123] The bishops warned that any official so elected would, for want of legitimacy, be unable to exercise meaningful authority without resorting to repression. They concluded that the only possible way to reestablish peace and tranquillity in Chihuahua was to hold new elections in which the will of the people would be fully respected. The bishops' call for the annulment of the elections was ignored by the regime, and Baeza was installed as governor in October.

After calling for the annulment of the elections, the bishops seemed to retreat for a time. This hiatus lasted, however, only until December, 1986, when Almeida announced a series of "Workshops on Catholics and Democracy." The "democracy workshops," as they were popularly called, began in January, 1987, in almost all of the Archdiocese of Chihuahua's sixty-odd parishes. Additional workshops cutting across parish lines were also instituted for specialized groups such as the secular clergy and religious orders. One such workshop at Chihuahua City's prestigious and privately run Technological Institute of Monterrey attracted a mix of seminary students, political party activists, housewives, and urban professionals.[124] The main purpose of the workshops was to provide a forum for systematic reflection on the issue of democracy in light of the Gospel and the teachings of the Church. Almeida argued that the need for such a forum could hardly be disputed, given the growing desire for democracy in a society that had been deliberately kept ignorant of democratic ways for decades of one-party rule. Almeida also hoped that the workshops would enable Catholics to deepen their understanding of the relationship between Christian values and democracy, so that the faithful could make their own distinctive contribution to the development of a democratic order in Mexico.

The workshops met once a week for two hours over a period of three months under the guidance of an authorized moderator. The main teaching aid for the workshops was a booklet officially issued in the name of the Archdiocese of Chihuahua, with an introduction by Almeida. The text was by Dizán Vázquez, one of Almeida's closest collaborators, with significant contributions by Almeida himself.[125] It was divided into six chapters: (1) the situation and aspirations of our people; (2) the scope and limits of the intervention of the Church; (3) the diverse forms of government; (4) the Church and democracy; (5) towards an integral democracy; and (6) education for democracy. The booklet contained a number of pungent observations on the nature of Mexico's political, economic, and social ills, the special contribution of democracy to their resolution, and strategies to achieve democracy, including peaceful resistance and active nonviolence. For example, the first chapter declared:

> Unfortunately, the regime has not known how to respond to the democratic aspirations of the people. It has shown itself to be a party dictatorship, thereby revealing a marked contrast between the democratic image that it seeks to present abroad and the limitations that it imposes on its own citizens [at home]. The government, instead of opening itself to an actual and real pluralism, obstinately persists in its inflexible and primitive methods. By trampling underfoot citizen rights and devaluing the exercise of the vote, it has inhibited the healthy [process] of political reform.[126]

Some criticisms were deleted without explanation from the second edition of the booklet issued in July, 1987.[127] It is quite possible that Almeida and his presbytery chose to tone down their anti-PRI stance because they felt more vulnerable to government reprisals in light of the fact that, by then, the level of protest against Baeza had declined considerably.

In addition to providing another occasion for criticizing the regime, the workshops served other objectives. They helped strengthen the rapport between Almeida and society at large by establishing a two-way feedback mechanism between them. On the one hand, the workshops gave Almeida an opportunity to explain his positions on electoral democracy and related subjects in considerable detail and clarified misunderstandings. On the other hand, ordinary lay people attending the workshops were provided with a highly participatory setting in which to discuss those positions and express any points of agreement or disagreement. Almeida was not only able to use the workshops as a means to educate society on democracy, but he was also able to incorporate the many insights developed by the workshops into his own thinking. Indeed, the workshops probably fostered an even higher level of consensus and cohesion among the bishop, clergy, and laity.

While the "democracy workshops" were a major source of irritation to the PRI, no serious attempt was made to interfere with their functioning. Instead, the PRI contented itself with a purely verbal attack on the workshops. Baeza stated that the Church's decision to organize workshops on democracy was as strange as the PRI choosing to organize workshops on prayer.[128] He declared that the Church was hardly the most qualified institution to preach democracy given its own "monarchical" structure of governance.[129] Baeza reminded Almeida of Jesus' exhortation to Christians "to render to Caesar the things that are Caesar's and to God the things that are God's" and added that the "participation of ministers of religious cults in politics was undesirable."[130]

The actions of Chihuahua's bishops on behalf of electoral democracy in the 1980s were well received by both the laity and clergy. In August, 1986, the president of the Lay Commission of the Archdiocese of Chihuahua, José García Rivas, declared that he had succeeded in obtaining the signatures of over 20,000 ordinary Catholics supporting Almeida's protests against electoral fraud.[131] In addition, the bishops' actions in favor of electoral democracy were applauded by virtually all factions of the priesthood.[132] Traditional pastors, who had viewed their mission mainly as the effective administration of the Holy Sacraments and who had vigorously opposed the Church's leftward shift in the 1970s, now openly proclaimed their love of democracy. Another strong source of support for the bishops' stand on clean elections came from priests belonging to the increasingly powerful and vocal Charismatic movement;[133] the Charismatic movement had been a relatively weak force in Chihuahua during most of the 1970s but had blossomed in the 1980s. Finally, both these groups were joined by most radical priests who, like Camilo Daniel, understood that far from there being a contradiction between electoral democracy and social justice, electoral democracy could actually be a means to achieve greater social justice. The decision of Chihuahua's bishops to support electoral democracy thus united the Church in a way that would have been impossible to envision in the 1970s. Both lay society and all factions of the clergy were now firmly arrayed behind the bishops. The painful wounds left by the conflicts of the 1970s were finally allowed to heal in the new atmosphere of ecclesiastical good will.[134] It would, however, be both wrong and unfair to suggest that the bishops seized on the issue of electoral democracy merely as a means to restore harmony to the Church, even though this was clearly one of its outcomes. Insofar as the bishops knew that they were acting with the full approval of their presbyteries and lay public opinion, they were able to develop confidence, and a willingness to persist.

Critical Factors in the Successes
and Failures of Chihuahua's Bishops:
Comparing the 1970s and 1980s

Why did the bishops' defense of electoral democracy in the 1980s succeed so well and their defense of social justice in the 1970s fail so utterly? In the 1970s, the bishops' call for social justice angered the bulk of Chihuahua's middle classes without eliciting a significant and sustained response from the groups that theoretically should have derived the most benefit from it, such as urban workers. Chihuahua's middle classes were able to launch an effective counterattack in the press and elsewhere in order to turn the tide of public opinion against the bishops. The middle classes also constituted the Church's main clientele. They were therefore able to directly pressure priests to disavow the positions on social justice expressed by their own bishops. The bishops were thus isolated both inside and outside the Church and were forced to retreat. In the 1980s, however, the bishops' call for electoral democracy was strongly supported by all social sectors, including the middle classes. Middle class parishioners now urged their pastors to support the bishop's defense of electoral democracy. Pastors who failed to do so ran the risk of having their credibility severely damaged. The weight of public opinion also inclined decisively in favor of the bishops' interventions as individuals from all walks of life condemned the fraud and approved of the actions taken by their bishops in protest. The bishops were thus able to make pronouncements concerning the elections from a position of growing strength and authority. Middle class support or the lack of it thus was a critical factor in determining both the Church's successes in the 1980s and its failures in the 1970s.

Another related factor explaining the divergent outcomes of the Church's two phases of activism was the bishops' sensitivity to the changing expectations of society. In 1972, the bishops' declarations ran completely counter to such expectations and therefore generated a storm of opposition. Indeed, the apocalyptic tone of the bishops' 1972 declarations seems quite unwarranted on the basis of the bank assaults alone. The tone becomes comprehensible only if one takes into account the impact of the Medellín conference and events at the national level such as the student revolt of 1968; the conference and the student revolt led the bishops to overreact to the bank assaults and read into them "signs of the times" that were at best only weakly present. The decisive causes of the bishops' declarations, for which the bank assaults were simply a convenient pretext, really lay far beyond society in Chihuahua. The inability of the bishops to adjust their doctrinally based prescriptions for the transformation of society in the abstract to the complex dynamics of social reality in Chihuahua led almost inevitably to disaster during the 1970s. By the 1980s, however, the bishops had clearly learned from past mistakes and began to display far greater sensitivity to the particular rhythms of society in Chihuahua. Unlike the 1970s, when the issue of social justice was artificially imposed on society by the Church and a relatively narrow group of social activists, the issue of electoral democracy had already taken on considerable importance in virtually all social sectors before the Church intervened. Instead of attempting to promote its own goals, the Church in the 1980s chose to respond to society's autonomously determined agenda.

Indeed, the bishops' actions in the 1980s were almost perfectly calibrated to respond to the precise expectations of society at different junctures. In 1983, the growing public dissatisfaction with the regime and unexpected momentum acquired by the PAN in the electoral campaign furnished Almeida with the perfect occasion to issue the document, "Vote with Responsibility." In comparison to later statements, the document was relatively mild in its criticism of the PRI, reflecting the novelty, uncertainty, and hesitancy that both society and the Church felt in challenging the established order for the first time in decades. During the 1985 federal deputy elections, the Church intervened only minimally; it had been stung by earlier PRI criticism holding it responsible for the party's electoral debacle in 1983 and was mindful of the fact that such elections tend to arouse far less public interest than those for the governorship or municipal presidencies. This silence was broken in March, 1986, by the document, "Christian Coherence in Politics," which was far more critical of the PRI than any previous document. The bishops' decision to escalate their criticism of the PRI so sharply reflected the higher stakes of the 1986 elections, the widespread anxiety that the regime was planning to resort to fraud, and the fact that the campaign that had already begun to arouse new levels of political passion. The climax of the Church's defense of electoral democracy, however, occurred only after the elections, when Almeida decided to order the suspension of religious services. The decision to close the parishes coincided with the most intense phase of social protest against the fraud. Drastic as the move to close the parishes seems, it corresponded closely to the expectations of society at that moment. After that, the level of protest by both the Church and society gradually began to lessen in intensity until it finally tapered off. In June, 1988, with society in Chihuahua exhausted and not a little cynical, Almeida issued only one five-page pastoral orientation regarding the coming elections for federal deputies.[135]

Ideological factors also help explain why the bishops' defense of electoral democracy in the 1980s generated far greater enthusiasm than their call for social justice in the 1970s, particularly among their clergy. The actions of Chihuahua's bishops in favor of social justice in the 1970s were viewed by many as an application of liberation theology. The Mexican Church, including Chihuahua, was, however, extremely uncomfortable with playing an activist role linked to Latin American liberation theology.[136] The Mexican Church was the only Church in Latin America, outside Cuba, to have suffered sustained persecution at the hands of a revolutionary regime. As a result, the Church was profoundly hostile to liberation theology. A number of Mexican bishops and clergy would have liked to see the Church play a more active role in society—provided the activism was not inspired by liberation theology. In the absence of such an alternative, these bishops routinely allied themselves with other bishops who sought to subordinate any kind of activist role, whether inspired by liberation theology or not, to the compulsions of Church-State relations. The result was the creation of a formidable coalition of bishops against liberation theology. Not surprisingly, then, Almeida's and Talamás's increasingly radical positions in favor of social justice during the 1970s were viewed with suspicion by both their own clergy as well as other episcopal colleagues around the country.

The bishops' decision to support electoral democracy in the 1980s, however, did not arouse the same ideological suspicions. The new emphasis on elections as the preferred vehicle of change, rather than the direct transformation of social structures, distanced the bishops from the radical left. In addition, the main beneficiary of the bishops' defense of electoral democracy was clearly the PAN, not the leftist political parties, though this was incidental to the bishops' purposes. Talamás and Almeida had therefore succeeded in developing an activist role for the Church that could not be linked to liberation theology. This, in turn, helps explain the nearly unanimous support that their defense of electoral democracy received from their presbyteries and the unusually high level of solidarity expressed by their episcopal colleagues.

THE NATIONAL CHURCH, 1986-92

The impact of the Chihuahua Church on the Church nationally was profound. The actions of Chihuahua's bishops in favor of electoral democracy provided the necessary spark for the formation of a new activist coalition composed of the majority of Mexican bishops in support of democracy. The Chihuahua Church's stance against election fraud won support from the majority of mainstream bishops,[137] none of whom was known for friendliness towards liberation theology and few of whom had any activist credentials. Chihuahua's bishops also received the support of the handful of bishops identified with liberation theology.[138] Finally, on August 19, 1986, the Conference of Mexican Bishops (CEM) issued a declaration on behalf of the entire episcopate affirming the Church's right and duty to illuminate social reality with the light of faith and reiterating its solidarity with those bishops seeking to defend the right of the citizenry to elect its rulers.[139] The actions of Chihuahua's bishops thus galvanized the vast majority of Mexican bishops in virtually all regions of the country into the formation of a new activist coalition around the issue of clean elections. This new coalition was not only far more powerful than the earlier coalition of activist bishops linked to liberation theology, but also subsumed the earlier activists.

Traditionally, the Mexican hierarchy has resisted an activist profile, partly because of their hostility towards Latin American liberation theology and partly because of their reluctance to risk conflict with the state. The political awakening of society in Mexico confronted the national hierarchy with a new situation. Either the Church could enthusiastically support the struggle for democracy across the country, thereby winning the approval of large sectors of society but damaging the Church's relationship with the state; or the Church could turn its back on the struggle for democracy, jeopardizing its credibility in society. Most Mexican bishops chose to respond positively to the growing societal pressure to speak out in favor of clean elections and democracy. Mexican bishops were also ideologically more comfortable with a temporal role for the Church linked to the support of electoral democracy, which, unlike the issue of social justice, they did not associate with liberation theology.

The growing politicization of the Mexican hierarchy deeply worried the regime, which passed a new election law in 1987 that imposed heavy fines and four-to-seven-year prison sentences for priests urging the electorate to abstain or vote for a party or candidate. Clergy were also barred from engaging in political activity in places of worship or any other location. The law, encapsulated in article 343, was approved by the Chamber of Deputies without debate, and the episcopate was not informed of the proposed changes beforehand.[140] Article 343 worsened relations between Church and state. The episcopate officially condemned the new legislation. In addition, twenty bishops signed a letter accusing the regime of violating the 1981 United Nations Declaration of Human Rights, to which Mexico is a signatory. The bishops also claimed the Mexican regime was violating their freedom of expression and opinion and harming the prospects for democracy. In addition, the episcopate sought to file a writ before the Supreme Court to stop the new legislation from taking effect. The article proved counterproductive in that it mobilized the hierarchy against the regime and made it possible for the Church to cast itself as a victim of government persecution.

By 1988, the Mexican hierarchy as a whole became deeply involved in promoting the cause of clean elections. Shortly before the 1988 presidential elections, twenty-five bishops bluntly declared that the Church would not accept fraud. In the wake of the elections that the PRD and PAN claimed had been fraudulent, the Mexican episcopate issued another, more cautious, statement, declaring that Mexicans in the 1988 elections had demonstrated a clear preference for a democratic system, but the bishops stopped short of calling the elections fraudulent.[141] In the 1991 congressional elections, the bishops issued a landmark document "Free and Democratic Elections," which called on the government to guarantee free elections, respect the citizenry's vote, and offer equal opportunities to each party.[142] The bishops explicitly declared that committing fraud was a sin. The Cardinal of Guadalajara, Juan Jesús de Posadas, even suggested that the "winning" PRI candidate for governor of San Luis Potosí resign because his victory was viewed as fraudulent.

The frequency with which the bishops addressed political topics during the 1980s and 1990s is an important index of their growing preoccupation with the political situation. Between 1978 and 1988, Mexican bishops issued 260 pronouncements, of which 145 were devoted to political themes (56%).[143] This was followed by family and sexual issues (27%), economic problems (14%), and education (3%). Considered as a single body, the Mexican episcopate devoted 9 of 16 pronouncements in the same period to political subjects (56%).[144] This is in sharp contrast to the 1960s and most of the 1970s, when the bishops hardly ever addressed political topics. Between 1965 and 1975, the Mexican episcopate dedicated only 3 of 35 messages to political themes (8.6%).[145]

Public opinion research also captured the new activist mood of the Mexican Church. One survey of Mexican priests conducted between 1988 and 1991 reveals some striking conclusions.[146] Of the priests surveyed, 90 percent felt that the current economic and political situation could generate conflicts that might imperil social peace, and 52 percent felt that violent protest could be justified as a last resort against the abuse of power. Eighty-four percent believed that the Church was concerned by the problem of election fraud, 89 percent that the main cause of abstention was the perception that the vote would not be respected, and 67 percent that denunciations of election fraud would not prosper unless the Church acted against the problem. Sixty-six percent felt that there was a contradiction between the Church's social doctrine and existing government policy, 89 percent that the Church needed to do more to promote the values of the Church's social doctrine, and 79 percent that the government was afraid that the Church's social work would lead to conflict with the state. Ninety percent of the respondents also agreed that it did not suit the regime for priests to take a more critical stance. On the reform of the constitution's anticlerical provisions, 86 percent of those surveyed believed that the Church should be granted legal personality, and another 75 percent felt that legalization would facilitate the Church's social mission. The survey further

revealed that Mexico's priests were quite indifferent to party la-
bels. Fully 67 percent believed that no political party represented
the interests of the majority of the population while 14 percent
believed that the PAN did and 18 percent that the Left did. In Chihuahua, the state most likely to have a clergy predisposed to the
PAN, only 13 percent thought that the party represented the interests of the majority. Two-thirds of the clergy surveyed read *Proceso,*
Mexico's most important leftwing, independent weekly magazine,
while less than one-fourth read Mexico's two leading intellectual
magazines, *Vuelta* and *Nexos,* combined.

RAPPROCHEMENT AND ITS EFFECTS

In 1992, the Salinas administration eliminated all the anticlerical articles of the constitution and established full diplomatic
relations with the Vatican.[147] Churches were recognized as autonomous legal entities through the creation of religious associations.
They were also allowed to own property and impart religious education in private schools. The ban on open-air liturgical services
was lifted, and the existence of religious orders recognized. Priests
were finally given the right to vote. The regime hoped that the
recognition of the Church and the establishment of relations with
the Vatican would help contain the growing activism of the Mexican hierarchy. The considerable skill shown by Prigione in reigning
in activist bishops, together with the specter of the growing
politicization of the Mexican hierarchy, strengthened Prigione's
bargaining power with the regime and may thus have facilitated
his goal of improving the status of the Church in Mexico. In addition, the regime had been severely weakened in the wake of the
1988 presidential elections, whose results had been denounced as
fraudulent by both opposition parties. Salinas, who had been elected
president with the lowest percentage of votes in the history of the
PRI, was therefore in desperate need of legitimacy and hoped to
win support from the Church and lay Catholics for his reform initiatives. Salinas's initially tenuous hold on the presidency also ruled
out the alternative of repressing the Church in order to deal with
the increasingly outspoken hierarchy.

Surveys revealed that the recognition of the Church and the

establishment of ties with the Vatican were moderately popular moves that could be expected to increase electoral support for the regime. In a survey conducted by *Nexos*, 68.4 percent of respondents felt that priests should have the same obligations and rights as other citizens.[148] In the same survey, 46 percent felt that nominating a personal representative to the Vatican would benefit the country, 30 percent said that it would make no difference, and only 9 percent believed that it would do harm. A majority—55 percent—felt that religion should be taught in schools while 37 percent opposed the idea. There was similar division about whether the Church should be allowed to own property, with 35.4 percent in favor and 57 percent opposed.

The process of negotiating with the regime was spearheaded by Prigione. In November, 1988, Archbishop Sergio Obeso, the president of the Mexican episcopate, disclosed that secret meetings between Prigione and government officials had been taking place since April and had yielded "tangible results," and that the day was not far off when the government would move to legalize the Church.[149] On December 1, 1988, a small group of top Mexican prelates led by Prigione attended Salinas's inauguration. This marked the first time since the Revolution that Church leaders had been present at a presidential inauguration. A major breakthrough occurred in 1990, when Salinas nominated a personal representative to the Vatican. The pope reciprocated by naming Prigione his personal representative to the Mexican government.

The decision gradually to reestablish ties to the Vatican may have obeyed a slightly different logic from the reform of the constitution. Mexico was one of few remaining states in the world to have no ties to the Vatican. Naming a personal representative sent a powerful signal to the international community that Mexico was serious about its "modernization" drive and may also have been intended to deflect opposition to NAFTA from the Catholic Church in the United States by sending a signal that the reform of the Church's status in Mexico was the next step. Vatican officials had already insisted that the reform of the constitution was a prerequisite for the establishment of full diplomatic ties. In any case, the constitutional reforms were approved by the Chamber of Deputies on July 9, 1992, and diplomatic relations were reestablished on September 20, 1992.

The recognition of the Church was a positive development for democracy. First, it eliminated the existing gap between law and reality. For more than fifty years, the Church had lived in a state of legal limbo: anticlerical provisions were not enforced but they remained on the books. Church officials and many others argued that this anomaly encouraged a general lack of respect for the law. From this perspective, the legalization of the Church marked a return to the rule of law which is the foundation of democracy. Second, the recognition of the Church had a positive impact on human rights. Many priests argued that depriving them of the right to vote was an infringement of international human rights conventions to which Mexico had acceded. In addition, the constitution's anti-Church articles were clearly incompatible with standard liberal freedoms, particularly those of religion, expression, and assembly. Finally, Church leaders believed that the reforms would facilitate the Church's mission in the areas of education, evangelism, and social work.

At the time, a number of bishops feared that the reforms constituted a *quid-pro-quo* whereby the government would lift restrictions on the Church in the expectation that Mexican Church leaders would limit the Church's involvement in politically explosive issues, such as election fraud and social justice. Genaro Alamilla, the spokesman of the Mexican episcopate, voiced the concern that the regime was "attempting to control the Church by using more modern methods."[150] The suspicion that the reforms were actually a deal was reinforced by the fact that Prigione had made a systematic effort to replace activist bishops nearing their retirement age of seventy-five with more pliant clerics who were usually from other states. Such coadjutor bishops were appointed to succeed Talamás and Almeida in 1988 and 1991, respectively. In the south, relatively unknown bishops were named as coadjutors to bishops identified with liberation theology. In 1993, Prigione supported a move to file charges with the Vatican Congregation of Bishops against Bishop Samuel Ruíz of the diocese of Chiapas to seek his removal from office for deviating from Church doctrine.[151] In the end, however, the Church continued to remain active in sensitive areas even after recognition; the fears of a *quid-pro-quo* proved incorrect.

Church-State relations were shaken by the assassination of Cardinal Posadas at Guadalajara airport on May 24, 1993, ostensibly at the hands of drug traffickers. The failure of the government to adequately investigate Posadas's murder caused a serious deterioration in Church-State relations. On June 24, 1994, Archbishop Hector González of Oaxaca and four other bishops on the Episcopal Commission for Social Work issued a thinly veiled attack on the regime, charging that "the narcotics trafficking mafia ... in particular has bought off or has associated with a significant number of public and military officials."[152] This statement drew an angry protest from the military, resulting in an apology from the Mexican episcopate. The statement was later reissued without the offending passage. Meanwhile, the new cardinal of Guadalajara called on anyone who had information about the killing of his predecessor to contact Church officials, anonymously if necessary. He added that the Mexican government had informed him that 40 percent of federal judicial police were in league with drug traffickers.[153] The murder remains unsolved.

The second major thorn in Church-State relations was the Chiapas rebellion on New Year's Day, 1994. At first, the government and other anti-Church groups accused Bishop Samuel Ruíz of the Diocese of Chiapas of fomenting the rebellion, despite no real evidence to that effect.[154] Chiapas, far to the south, had been bypassed by the agrarian reforms of the Revolution. Indigenous peasants suffered from an extremely skewed pattern of land distribution, grinding poverty, and exclusion at the hands of the state's dominant mixed-race *(mestizo)* population. The focus of the bishop's pastoral work since his consecration in 1960 was to empower indigenous communities, but this is not to say that he was for the Zapatista rebellion. During the 1960s, the diocese focused on sending out catechists to raise the level of political consciousness in the region, generate unity among the diverse indigenous tribes of the region, and teach the faith. Chiapas was also one the few dioceses in Mexico to institute permanent lay deacons from the main indigenous communities who soon became respected leaders. Ruíz also invited Jesuit and Dominican priests to resume their activities in the state after a long hiatus. In 1974, at the request of the governor of Chiapas, Manuel Velasco, Ruíz agreed to organize the state's first indigenous congress, which proved to be a milestone in the organization of an indigenous movement in the state. The 1970s were marked by a sharp escalation in the level of politicization in the state.

During the 1980s, the situation in Chiapas worsened signifi-

cantly. The spread of cattle ranching by the landowning elite worsened land distribution, and the collapse of world coffee prices caused
wages to fall. Large-scale repression under governor Absalón
Castellanos (1982–88), an army general, and Patrocinio González
Garrido (1988–93) closed off political space to peaceful peasant
movements that had developed in the 1970s, such as the Independent Confederation of Agricultural Workers and Peasants (CIOAC),
the Emiliano Zapata Peasant Organization (OCEZ), and the Unión
de Uniónes, a federation of *ejidos*. In several cases, priests gave
moral support to such movements. In Simojovel, for example,
Father Joel Padrón, who had returned to Chiapas after a stint in
Nicaragua, found himself in the midst of a tense struggle between
indigenous landless agricultural workers and coffee plantation
owners. In 1991, Padrón was jailed for allegedly encouraging a
land takeover by CIOAC. He was released forty-nine days later,
after an international outcry. In addition, the diocese of Chiapas
formed the Fray Bartolomé de las Casas Center in 1989 to monitor
violations of human rights in the state. Chiapas's close proximity to
the Central American revolutionary cauldron contributed directly
to the militarization of the state, which in turn raised the likelihood of the use of repression against peasant organizations. The
presence of large numbers of Central American refugees added
an unpredictable element to the mix of social tensions in the state.
Finally, the 1980s were also marked by the arrival of a new breed
of activists from outside that state, who quietly integrated themselves into indigenous communities.[155] They may have been inspired by the revolutionary movements in Central America. Their
work is what probably culminated in the formation of the
Emiliano Zapata National Liberation Army (EZLN) and the resort to armed rebellion. In the wake of the rebellion, Ruíz quickly
emerged as an indispensable mediator between the EZLN and
the government. In June, 1998, with the two sides still bogged
down and his own credibility severely questioned by the government, Ruíz stepped down as mediator.

Drug trafficking and social justice concerns thus became central to the Church's mission in the 1990s. By contrast, major electoral reforms reduced the importance of the issue of fraud. On the
eve of the 1994 presidential elections, the bishops described the
voter registration list as "reliable" and limited themselves to calling

for unity and order. Some analysts claimed that the Church was trying to distance itself from the PRD which still felt the list had been manipulated.[156] The more likely explanation is that the bishops simply believed that the list was a good one. It had been audited by an international consortium, the PRD presented almost no evidence to support its claims of manipulation, and the other main opposition party, the PAN, considered the list acceptable.

The normalization of Church-State relations thus did not dampen the Church's involvement in major social and political questions for several reasons. First, the number of bishops and clergy ordained prior to Vatican II has gradually declined, resulting in a more modern clergy with fewer memories of past Church-State conflicts and more disposed towards a broader view of the Church's mission in society. Second, the doctrinal reforms of Vatican II and the Latin American Bishops' Conferences have also had plenty of time to reach all levels of the Church. Third, bishops remain subject to the influence of the wider society, particularly in their own dioceses; and social pressures can play a major role in triggering an ecclesiastical response. Fourth, bishops and clergy are canonically autonomous in their own dioceses and cannot easily be overruled. Major church leaders like Cardinal Sandoval and Archbishop González, whose careers were nurtured by Prigione, have thus often taken an independent stance at variance with the papal nuncio. Indeed, in November, 1994, the Mexican episcopate signaled its independence from the papal nuncio and its commitment to remaining involved in addressing the nation's social problems by electing Bishop Sergio Obeso Rivera of Xalapa as their new leader. As president of the episcopate in the 1980s, Obeso supported Chihuahua's bishops in their opposition to election fraud. He also encouraged the development of ecclesial base communities in his own diocese. It is worth noting that the episcopate elected an activist bishop like Obeso despite the fact that the appointments of 52 of the 88 bishops present had been overseen by Prigione. Finally, normalization deprived the government of a dual lever of control over the Church: the threat that anticlerical laws could be implemented if the Church became too critical of the regime, and the prospect of reform as a reward for good behavior.

Symptomatic of the new mood of the Mexican episcopate was its deteriorating relationship with Prigione. Prigione's support of the charges against Ruíz at the Vatican angered many Church activists. His decision to sponsor an urban priest as the successor to the late José Llaguno, the bishop of the Tarahumara, was also poorly received. In addition, Prigione was embarrassed by revelations in the press that he had met with drug lords Ramón and Benjamin Arrellano Félix, the two main suspects in the Posadas killing, on two occasions.[157] The meetings occurred with the knowledge of Interior Secretary González Garrido and Salinas, while law enforcement agencies were engaged in an intensive manhunt for them. In 1998, Prigione was succeeded by a new papal nuncio.

CONCLUSION

The Mexican Church underwent great change during the 1980s and the 1990s. The *modus vivendi* that had characterized Church-State relations since 1940 gave way in the 1980s and 1990s to a more activist Church intent on evangelizing all spheres of reality, including the political and social. The Chihuahua bishops' decision to rally against electoral fraud in the 1980s was a watershed in the rise of a more politically engaged Church in Mexico. The emergence of an increasingly activist Church in Chihuahua was partly the result of the long-term effects of doctrinal change on the state's clergy and bishops, which predated the political awakening of society in the 1980s and 1990s, and partly a response to the mounting societal pressures on the bishops to intervene in defense of democracy that marked the 1980s. Unlike their attempts in the 1970s to promote social justice, the bishops' stance in favor of free elections in the 1980s met with widespread approval in Chihuahua and nationally, reflecting the greater middle-class support for free elections rather than more radical initiatives to change society directly. The Chihuahua bishops' decision to support clean elections in turn provided a catalyst for the creation of a national coalition of bishops in favor of democracy. The growing willingness of the Church to speak out in favor of democracy also increased its credibility as an institution in society in Chihuahua and nationally. The decision of the state to reform the constitution and establish diplomatic relations with the Vatican was a direct response to the growing power of the Church to generate and channel opposition against the regime, first revealed by the events in Chihuahua, and a thinly disguised attempt to win the Church's support at a moment of weakness for the regime. Instead, the reforms actually gave the Church more room to pursue its mission and failed to arrest the trend towards the involvement of bishops and clergy in social and political matters. The growing strength of the Church helped check the power of the state, increased the pressure on the regime for democratic reforms, and provided a powerful channel for Mexicans to voice their discontent.

5

The Emergence of
Civic Associations

The 1980s and 1990s were marked by an explosion of activity by a wide variety of civic associations dedicated to the promotion of democracy, clean elections, and human rights.[1] A recent survey of 250 Non-Governmental Organizations (NGOs) active in the human rights arena (including political rights) showed that only a handful were created prior to the 1980s, 89 in the 1980s, and virtually all the rest in the 1990s.[2]

The growth of such NGOs thus escalated dramatically during the 1980s and 1990s, reflecting three major changes. First, the political awakening of society provided a powerful impetus from below for the creation of civic associations seeking democracy. The growing competitiveness of elections, the emergence of election fraud as the central fault line dividing society from the state, and the new willingness of citizens to join civic associations provided a favorable social environment for the formation of civic associations. Indeed, the social characteristics of the membership of civic associations mirrored the changing nature of Mexican society. Over 72 percent of the members of Mexican human rights organizations possessed a university education; for organizations active in the promotion of women's rights the figure rises to 81 percent, and 90 percent for environmental groups.[3] The civic associations were overwhelmingly young in their composition, with the majority of members between 21 and 39 years of age: for human rights organizations,

205

the number of members between 21 and 40 was 71 percent; women's organizations 72 percent; and environmental groups 76 percent.[4] The civic associations also relied on a large amount of voluntary work, ranging from 41.6 percent for human rights organizations, 54.7 percent for women's groups, to 74 percent for environmental groups.[5] Second, the involvement of social leaders, particularly businessmen, intellectuals, and clergy, increased the availability of institutional entrepreneurs with leadership skills, financial resources, and personal prestige to invest in the formation of new civic associations. Institutional entrepreneurs created a vast web of citizen groups by capitalizing on favorable social conditions, mobilizing international support, and innovating new forms of organization. Third, international actors facilitated the development of Mexican civic associations by providing vital technical and financial assistance and giving them international legitimacy.

Conjunctural factors undoubtedly played a significant role in the development of civic associations. The Central American conflicts of the 1980s sparked the creation of human rights organizations in Mexico, particularly the Mexican Academy for Human Rights (AMDH), to defend the rights of refugees entering Mexico and support human rights groups in Central America. The failure of the government to respond adequately to the tragedy of the Mexico City earthquake of 1985 contrasted sharply to the outpouring of assistance from ordinary citizens and voluntary associations, and many contemporary social movements, particularly in the federal district, can trace their origins to the earthquake. The attempt by the Salinas administration to end the tax-exempt status of NGOs in 1989 sparked the formation of a coalition of civic organizations, Convergence of Civil Organizations for Democracy (Convergencia), which later became an important player in election monitoring. Finally, the creation of the National Commission of Human Rights (CNDH) in 1990 as an official governmental agency constituted an open acknowledgment that Mexico had a human rights problem and made human rights a legitimate part of political discourse, thereby legitimizing the activity of both domestic and international NGOs operating in this field.

It would, however, be wrong to view the development of civic associations simply as the outgrowth of a series of fortuitous events. Institutional entrepreneurship was required to form organizations even in response to external events like the Central American crisis. The outpouring of support for the victims of the earthquake reflected an underlying capacity for social mobilization that already existed. The creation of the CNDH was a political response by the Salinas administration to respond to the growing domestic and international concern about human rights in Mexico in the context of the free trade debate. Indeed, the CNDH was formed on the eve of the publication of a highly critical report by Americas Watch on the human rights situation in Mexico. Deeper processes were at work that explain why these events had such a powerful impact on the development of civic associations.

The growth of civic associations has major implications for democratization. Putnam argues that civic associations are important for democracy because they create norms of reciprocity and trust, which are required for the smooth functioning of social, political, and economic life.[6] For Tocqueville, the importance of civic associations lies in the fact that they give society the capacity to counterbalance state power, articulate demands, provide arenas for participation and civic learning, generate frameworks of personal meaning, and check individualism.[7] Tocqueville also points out that associations can act as buffers to drain away excess participation, which threatens democratic stability. William Kornhauser views civic associations as a barrier to totalitarianism by preventing society from atomizing into an inert mass capable of being manipulated by nondemocratic elites.[8] Finally, numerous Catholic social theorists, including Pope Leo XIII and Pope Pius XI, stress the importance of intermediate organizations to provide a context for the development of the material and spiritual potential of the person, which occurs in association with others.[9]

This chapter assesses the contribution of civic associations to democratization in Chihuahua. It analyzes the emergence of the Civic Alliance as Mexico's most important domestic election-monitoring organization in the 1990s, shifting the focus to the national level. Finally, it probes the relationship between civic associations and other institutional actors, such as the Catholic Church and political parties.

CIVIC ASSOCIATIONS IN MEXICO'S REGIONS: THE CASE OF CHIHUAHUA

Agents of Further Politicization

The emergence of civic associations was the result of the politicization of society and social leaders; in turn, the civic associations became agents of further politicization. Cross-national research demonstrates that members of voluntary associations are more likely than the population as a whole to express opinions on a variety of political questions, to engage in political discussions, to feel that they can influence the political process, and to become directly involved in political activity.[10] These findings hold for all types of voluntary associations, whether their goals are political or nonpolitical in character.[11] While all voluntary associations in Chihuahua contributed in one way or another to further politicization, the Mexican Employers' Confederation (COPARMEX), the Integral Human Development and Citizen Action Organization (DHIAC), and the National Civic Feminine Association (ANCIFEM) were particularly important in this regard.

Unlike the business chambers, which were created by law in 1938, membership in COPARMEX is voluntary and covers the entire gamut of business activity rather than a specific sector only. COPARMEX was founded as a national organization in 1929 as an attempt to counter the growing radicalism of revolutionary leaders and ensure that the viewpoint of business would be taken into account in the government's handling of the delicate area of industrial relations. Between 1946, when Miguel Alemán took office as president, and 1970, COPARMEX lost much of its earlier *raison d'etre* by virtue of the political elite's pro-business policies; instead the Employer's Confederation dedicated itself to providing technical assistance to the private sector. Between 1970 and 1976, COPARMEX became more combative, reflecting the crisis in business-government relations provoked by Echeverría's inflammatory socialist rhetoric, his confrontation with the Monterrey industrial elite, and the expropriation near the end of his administration of vast tracts of Mexico's most productive farmland in the states of Sinaloa and Sonora. The nationalization of the banking system in 1982 and the eruption of Mexico's most serious economic crisis since the Great Depression strengthened COPARMEX's new role as Mexico's main defender of business ideology.

The shock of bank nationalization and the economic crisis produced a surge in the growth of COPARMEX, particularly among the owners of small and medium-sized businesses. By 1986, COPARMEX consisted of five regional federations, 51 Entrepreneurs' Centers in major cities, including Chihuahua City and Ciudad Juárez, and six delegations in Mexico City, yielding a grand total of 18,000 employers as its members.[12] COPARMEX does not address the practical concerns of particular businesses, like obtaining government licenses, but instead focuses on broad political and economic themes. Ideologically, COPARMEX supports the idea of "modernization" in both economic and political realms.[13] In the area of economic modernization, COPARMEX advocates the privatization of parastatal industries, a more flexible labor code, greater opportunities for foreign investment, lighter taxation, the privatization of the *ejido*, the elimination of subsidies, a smaller bureaucracy, and an export-oriented economic model.[14] Politically, it advocates drastic curbs on the power of the president, the separation of powers and checks and balances between the branches of government, the open participation of businessmen in party politics, and honest elections. COPARMEX argues that democracy constitutes a prerequisite for sustained economic growth because that system discourages public corruption, reduces society's vulnerability to arbitrary behavior by the government, and prevents the concentration of decision-making power in the hands of a few error-prone individuals.

DHIAC was established in 1976 by a group of young professionals, most of whom had recently graduated from the National Autonomous University of Mexico (UNAM).[15] Taking their cue from the fact that José López Portillo had been elected president in 1976 without any opposition, the main goal of the founders of DHIAC was to promote civic consciousness as the basis for the achievement of democracy.[16] The growth of the organization was slow until 1982, when middle-class professionals, worried by their declining economic prospects and angry at the government's handling of the economic crisis, began joining the organization in increasing numbers. By the late 1980s, DHIAC claimed approximately 25,000 members and has branches in several cities, including Mexico City.[17] DHIAC shares the ideology of COPARMEX, though DHIAC's focus is on political rather than economic questions. The president of DHIAC from 1987 to 1990, Jorge Sandoval, served as president of COPARMEX from 1984 to 1986 and on March 12, 1988, DHIAC endorsed Clouthier, the PAN's candidate for president and a past-president of both COPARMEX (1978–81) and Mexico's Business Coordinating Council (1981–83), as "the candidate of the citizenry." DHIAC was formally established in Chihuahua in 1983 at the initiative of a group of young professionals from Chihuahua City, who wanted to play a role in the political renewal that had just begun to sweep the state.[18]

ANCIFEM was founded as a national organization in 1972 by a group of middle-class women from León, Guanajuato, who were initially concerned about the spread of pornography.[19] The main goals of ANCIFEM are the promotion of civic consciousness among women, the strengthening of intermediate organizations to protect society from the state, the defense of the family as the basic unit of society, and the promotion of higher moral standards.[20] By the late 1980s, ANCIFEM had roughly 100,000 members and sympathizers and branches in forty-six cities.[21] ANCIFEM's presence was, however, strongest in the central states of Guanajuato, Jalisco, and Puebla, and the Mexico City metropolitan area. The majority of ANCIFEM's members are practicing Catholics, but ANCIFEM as an organization functions independently of the Church.[22] Its financing comes from membership dues and donations from the business community. ANCIFEM shares the ideological perspectives of COPARMEX and DHIAC, but draws explicitly on Catholic social doctrine as the source of its inspiration. While ANCIFEM's Chihuahua City branch was established in 1976 and closely tied to the agenda of ANCIFEM as a national organization, ANCIFEM's branch in Ciudad Juárez was formed in 1983 for the sole purpose of mobilizing support among women for Francisco Barrio's bid for mayor.[23]

COPARMEX, DHIAC, and ANCIFEM contributed to politicization in a number of ways. They helped train potential political leaders and served as a channel of leadership recruitment for political parties, particularly the PAN. This was especially true of COPARMEX and its Entrepreneurs' Centers around the country. The long list of former COPARMEX or Entrepreneur Center leaders who went on to become important PAN figures includes, among others, Clouthier, Fernando Canales, currently governor of Nuevo

León, Barrio, and Gustavo Elizondo, who was elected mayor of Ciudad Juárez in 1998. While DHIAC and ANCIFEM have produced a number of PAN leaders like Jaime Aviña, past president of DHIAC, and Cecilia Romero, past president of ANCIFEM, COPARMEX is far more important as a source of leadership recruitment for the PAN than any other civic association. By virtue of the fact that membership is voluntary, unlike membership in the business chambers, COPARMEX attracts the most leadership-oriented members of the business community. COPARMEX, and to a lesser extent DHIAC and ANCIFEM, also provided their members with a network of connections spanning the country, thus helping them become familiar with national-level problems and facilitating the exchange of information across regions.

COPARMEX, DHIAC, and ANCIFEM stimulated greater citizen involvement in public affairs by providing an arena for participation that is an alternative to political parties. Many Mexicans, particularly urban middle-class professionals and businessmen, were reluctant to participate in opposition parties because they feared becoming the target of government reprisals, associated political parties with endemic corruption and cynical horse trading, and did not believe that the regime would allow the opposition to win. The civic associations enabled individuals who were reluctant to become directly involved in opposition party politics to find a satisfactory outlet for their participatory energies.

The civic associations contributed to politicization by furnishing leaders to the PAN and creating an alternative arena to political parties for participation, in Chihuahua and nationally as well. The Chihuahua branches of the civic associations, however, particularly DHIAC and COPARMEX, also made their own contribution to politicization in the state. In June, 1983, DHIAC sponsored a televised debate between candidates for mayor of Chihuahua City, pitting the PRI's Luís Fuentes Molinar against the PAN's Alvarez.[24] The debate was moderated by the president of DHIAC in Chihuahua.[25] It marked the first time that the PRI had been willing to engage in a real debate with the opposition on television in any part of the country and gave the electorate an opportunity to judge the candidates and their proposals side by side. In the 1986 state elections, however, no debate was held, probably because the PRI feared it would lose. The civic associations were nevertheless active in keeping the

electorate informed. In 1984, DHIAC members in Chihuahua conducted an analysis of the platforms of the various political parties,
and each member in turn invited a group of friends to do the same.[26]
As the 1986 state elections approached, DHIAC and ANCIFEM
formed a committee to disseminate information about the electoral
process throughout the country and break the information blockade being imposed on Chihuahua by the government-controlled
media. The goal was to sensitize national opinion to the possibility
of fraud in Chihuahua, thereby making fraud in Chihuahua a national issue and raising the cost of committing fraud.[27]

As far as COPARMEX was concerned, the Entrepreneurs' Center of Chihuahua City, along with the local business chambers, issued a statement demanding that the elections be conducted in an
honest fashion and that the government respect the outcome.
Shortly after the elections, they condemned the elections as fraudulent and called on businessmen to close their businesses for twelve
hours in protest. The Entrepreneurs' Center and the business chambers also exhorted their members to paralyze the local banking system by withdrawing their money in the largest amounts possible
without prior notice and to declare their taxes using zeros only.
Finally, the Entrepreneurs' Centers of Chihuahua City and Ciudad
Juárez urged de la Madrid to annul the elections and mobilized
considerable support from Entrepreneurs' Centers around the
country. No other Entrepreneurs' Center in the country has ever
gone as far as the one in Chihuahua in protesting election fraud.
The branches of DHIAC and COPARMEX in Chihuahua had their
own independent dynamics that set them off from their national
federations.

Strengthening the PAN

Civic associations—especially the Civic Front for Citizen Participation (FCPC), the Coalition of Neighborhood Committees
(COCOVE), the Committee for the Democratic Struggle (COLUDE)
in Ciudad Juárez, and the Family Patrimony Committee (CPF) of
Parral—strengthened the PAN's candidates for mayoral office in
1983, gave them valuable political support during their terms in
office, and took over key party functions that the PAN found
itself unable to discharge. In January, 1983, PAN leaders in Ciudad

Juárez invited Barrio to seek the party's nomination for mayor. Barrio, however, was concerned that if he openly sought the PAN's nomination, he would lose support among middle-class professionals and businessmen, who were reluctant to identify themselves with the PAN, despite their disenchantment with the PRI.[28] He felt it would be wiser to first declare his intention to run as an independent candidate and mobilize support around that candidacy, then seek the PAN nomination.[29] Barrio established the FCPC to marshal financial, political, and moral support in the business community and the professional classes for his ostensibly independent bid for mayor. PAN and FCPC leaders knew that Barrio would eventually seek the PAN's nomination, but rank-and-file members were kept in the dark. The strategy worked, because when Barrio finally sought and won the PAN's nomination, the overwhelming majority of FCPC members agreed to continue supporting him and only a minority fell away.[30]

In Parral, the Family Patrimony Committee (CPF) strongly supported Gustavo Villarreal, the PAN's candidate for mayor in 1983. The CPF had been established in April, 1982, to protest the PRI mayor's disastrous project to resurface the city's pavements. The project, which was initiated by the mayor without consulting the population but with generous financial assistance from the state government, was characterized by massive corruption from its inception.[31] The workmanship was extremely shoddy, with new layers of pavement being merely dumped onto old ones, thus blocking household drains and creating severe sanitation problems. With corruption having eaten away most of the funds originally earmarked for the project, dismayed city residents were then asked to foot the entire bill. The CPF thus quickly gained massive popularity, and its decision to back Villarreal for mayor was an important element in his ultimate victory. As soon as he took office as mayor, Villarreal announced that city residents would only be expected to defray 25 percent of the cost of the project.

The civic associations also helped strengthen the PAN mayors while they were in office. In Ciudad Juárez and Chihuahua City, the PRI mayors had channeled a significant proportion of city services to popular colonies through the Popular Defense Committee (CDP), a powerful semi-co-opted organization. The CDP's strategy was to establish new settlements by seizing urban property and then pressuring the government for appropriate services in exchange for giving political support to the PRI. But the CDP was unwilling to secure property titles for the settlers because it feared that the settlers would desert the organization the moment they had tasted the security of legal ownership.[32] Armed with the power to evict the settlers living under its jurisdiction, the CDP was able to force them to perform physical labor, attend CDP rallies and demonstrations, and obey the rules imposed by the CDP's directive elite. The PAN mayors were reluctant to continue channeling municipal services through the CDP and formed representative neighborhood committees to act as the link between popular colonies and the municipal authorities. Meanwhile, the state government in the hands of the PRI encouraged the CDP to destabilize Ciudad Juárez and Chihuahua City and thus furnish the PRI-controlled state legislature with a pretext to invoke its constitutional power to dissolve the PAN municipal administrations. Barrio's response was to appeal to the neighborhood committees to join hands under the banner of COCOVE to confront the CDP and show the extent of the PAN's popular support in the city.[33] COCOVE, FCPC, and other organizations held a rally on June 20, 1984, to ratify the citizenry's support for Barrio. The rally was attended by roughly 10,000 people from all social classes, though the majority were clearly from popular colonies. This visible demonstration of Barrio's strength was enough to make the regime and CDP back off, though the CDP would avenge itself in the 1986 state elections by prohibiting political parties from campaigning in its colonies, refusing to allow PAN representatives access to voting precincts located in CDP "territory," and not condemning election fraud.

The civic associations, particularly COLUDE, took over key party functions that the PAN was unable to discharge because of its weakness. COLUDE, founded in 1985, was an umbrella group of the major civic associations in Ciudad Juárez. COLUDE, as well as its constituent civic associations, were financed by three wealthy businessmen, Alfonso Murgia, treasurer of the municipal administration of Francisco Barrio and the owner of a chain of music and laundry businesses; Federico Barrio, the head of a *maquiladora* construction company and Francisco Barrio's brother; and Francisco Villareal, a man of highly independent views who sold most of his businesses in order to be less vulnerable to government pressures (he participated in a forty-one day hunger strike against election fraud in the 1986 state elections—see chapter 3).

COLUDE helped raise money for PAN candidates, particularly Francisco Barrio's bid for the governorship in 1986. COLUDE also took over the task of defending the vote in the 1986 state elections in Ciudad Juárez, because the PAN was too divided and disorganized to develop, let aside implement, a coherent plan for defending the vote.[34] COLUDE's strategy to defend the vote failed, and rebuilding the PAN's organizational strength during Elizondo's term as president of the party's municipal committee (1986–88) paved the way for the PAN in Ciudad Juárez to mount a highly successful defense of the vote in the 1988 federal elections completely on its own. COLUDE nonetheless played an important role in gathering evidence of election fraud, including video tapes of fraud in progress, and in publicizing election fraud in Chihuahua at the national level, by inviting 100 observers from other parts of the country to witness the 1986 state elections.

Connecting the Agendas of Peripheral Groups to the Wider Society

The civic associations, especially the Democratic Peasant Movement (MDC), helped connect the agendas of peripheral groups to the wider society. The MDC, which was founded in the fall of 1985, was the outgrowth of a series of fortuitous events. In 1981, Camilo Daniel resigned as rector of the Catholic Church's seminary in Chihuahua City and was appointed a parish priest in the rural town of Anáhuac, about seventy miles northwest of Chihuahua City. Struck by the level of rural marginalization in the area and strongly committed to the biblical call for social justice, Daniel began to orient the community towards collective action by using his sermons to develop a sense of shared grievance.[35] In 1983, Humberto Ramos, a PRI dissident running as the candidate of the Socialist Workers' Party (PST), was elected mayor of the municipality of Cuauhtémoc, where Anáhuac is located. A close alliance quickly developed between Ramos and Daniel.[36] Ramos offered Daniel political protection and development assistance, while Daniel offered Ramos the chance to strengthen his rural following in the municipality. In March, 1985, Ramos and Daniel founded the Union for the Progress of the

Campesinos of the Bustillos Lagoon (UPCALA), which brought together *campesinos* drawn from thirteen communities in the region.
A few months later, Daniel and Ramos formed the MDC to fight for
higher grain prices from the government's rural procurement agency,
CONASUPO. The nucleus of the MDC consisted of Daniel, Ramos,
UPCALA, the Alliance of the *Campesinos* of the Northwest (ACN),
and Antonio Becerra Gaytán, the leader of the Unified Socialist Party
of Mexico (PSUM) in Chihuahua and its candidate for governor in
1986, the ACN and Gaytán joining the MDC by invitation. The PAN
also strongly supported the MDC without being a formal member.

In December, 1985, the MDC seized a large number of
CONASUPO warehouses around the state to secure an increase in
the "guaranteed" price of maize. By January, 1986, approximately
20,000 *campesinos* were participating in the MDC, and sixty-nine
warehouses in ten municipalities, mainly in the northwestern part
of the state, had already been taken over.[37] The timing was perfect.
The government, fearing the spread of anti-regime sentiment from
urban to rural areas in a critical election year, agreed to a significant
hike in the "guaranteed" maize price.

In January, 1988, with elections approaching once more, the
MDC, now renamed the Democratic Front of Peasant Organizations of Chihuahua (FEDOCH), again seized CONASUPO warehouses and successfully obtained an increase in the "guaranteed"
price for maize. In December, 1987, FEDOCH held a "Peasant Forum" and demanded that maize prices be indexed to gasoline prices.
When the government failed to respond, FEDOCH seized warehouses around the state and initiated a march of *campesinos* from
Cuauhtémoc to Chihuahua City, a distance of about 100 kilometers.
As the marchers neared Chihuahua City, they were greeted by
crowds of urban supporters. The rural visitors then proceeded to
take over the *plaza* in front of the statehouse and held a foot-wash-
ing ceremony.[38] During their one-month long occupation of the
plaza, FEDOCH joined hands with the urban Consumers' Front
(FEDECO) consisting of the PAN, PSUM, and various civic associations, to hold an open-air trial of the Economic Solidarity Pact (PSE),
a package of economic stabilization measures recently introduced
by the de la Madrid regime. FEDOCH toured newspaper offices in
the city to demand fair coverage of their movement and held a full-
fledged rural festival in the *plaza*. Daniel, Ramos, and Javier

Benavides, the president of the PAN in Chihuahua City, went on a hunger strike to pressure the regime, and sympathy hunger strikes occurred in other cities around the state as well. Support for the *campesinos* poured in from the Church, the business community, political parties, and civic associations. In February, 1988, the governor finally relented and granted an increase in maize prices.

The *campesino* movement led by the MDC and FEDOCH was highly successful. In January, 1986, the government swiftly authorized a hefty increase in maize procurement prices for Chihuahua. In February, 1988, the government, after a long standoff, agreed to raise maize prices in Chihuahua, even though this violated the strict price controls in effect throughout the nation as a result of the PSE. The success of the *campesino* movement is best explained by its ability to connect the struggle for higher procurement prices to the wider society, which prevented the *campesino* movement in Chihuahua from becoming isolated and thus more vulnerable to government repression.

Indeed, the *campesino* movement was timed to coincide with key political events in Chihuahua. In December, 1985, Baeza had just been named the PRI's candidate for governor in Chihuahua, and the regime was desperately seeking to improve its image in the state. In December, 1987, Chihuahua was in turmoil over the drastic subsidy cuts and price freezes decreed by the PSE, and was gearing up for the 1988 federal elections. In the hope of extracting greater concessions, the movement was thus timed to coincide with the regime's weakest political moments.

The fact that the movement was supported by both the Church and opposition parties made it impossible for the government to repress the MDC / FEDOCH without provoking a major political crisis in the process. At the same time, the movement would probably not have enjoyed the protective mantle of the Church and opposition parties had it been led by simple *campesinos* rather than the triad of Daniel, Ramos, and Becerra. Daniel's involvement in the movement was supported by Bishop Almeida, who emphatically stated that the priest's activities were consistent with his mission and in no way constituted a form of political leadership.[39] Almeida's support was decisive; without it, Daniel would have been deprived of the Church's legitimation and would probably have had to suspend his activities. Daniel also won the enthusiastic support of his fellow priests, in contrast to their attitude towards his earlier attempts to restructure seminary education during the 1970s (see chapter 4). In July, 1986, fifteen priests representing virtually all the major factions of the clergy in the Archdiocese of Chihuahua publicly expressed their solidarity with Daniel "in his struggle for the defense of the fundamental rights of man."[40] They also declared that any act of violence directed against him would be interpreted as an attack on the entire presbytery itself. In January, 1988, thirty-one priests signed a similar declaration supporting the MDC's fresh demands for higher maize prices.[41]

Daniel acknowledged that in the 1980s it had become possible for him to say and do things, without causing any flutter in the Church, that in the 1970s would have generated a wall of opposition and misunderstanding.[42] Why were the same priests who angrily opposed the Church's incipient commitment to greater social justice in the 1970s willing to support a much more widespread movement for social justice, the MDC / FEDOCH, in the 1980s? Significantly, the MDC / FEDOCH fight for higher maize prices was directed entirely against the government rather than any particular social class. It was thus able to feed into the wider struggle of organized society against the regime that was already occurring in the electoral arena and that cut across class lines. The MDC's desire for social justice and the rest of Chihuahua's desire for clean elections reinforced each other at the expense of a common enemy, the Mexican state. Also, the MDC avoided using the kind of radical rhetoric that had characterized the Church's earlier attempts to achieve social justice in the 1970s and generated so much resistance, particularly among the clergy. The struggle for electoral democracy thus created new and unsuspected opportunities for movements seeking social justice not through a redistribution of wealth from one segment of society to another but directly from the state itself.

The movement also deliberately sought to develop an urban dimension by forming alliances with groups, like the Consumer's Front, and shifting the locus of its activities to Chihuahua City, where it could stir up urban public opinion in its favor and gain publicity. Many of the movement's tactics—such as relay hunger strikes by prominent priests and politicians, long marches by *campesinos,* the symbolic act of foot washing, and the staging of festivals—were tailored to attract the attention of the urban media and win the hearts of urban Chihuahua. In April, 1986, Daniel, Ramos, and Becerra sought to give formal expression to the symbiosis between the MDC / FEDOCH's struggle for higher grain prices and the wider society's struggle for clean elections in Chihuahua by forming the Movement for Electoral Democracy (MDE). While many of the *campesinos* in the MDC shied away from the MDE, fearing repression if they opposed the regime in the electoral arena,[43] the MDE significantly increased support for the MDC / FEDOCH in the larger society. The MDC / FEDOCH was a rare success story in the world of peasant organizing in Mexico, reflecting its excellent sense of timing, the links of its leaders to powerful institutions, its cultivation of a strong urban dimension, and the symbiotic interaction between the goals of the MDC / FEDOCH and those of the larger society.

Election Monitoring

Election monitoring by citizens' groups became a staple feature of Mexican elections only in the 1990s. The Movement for Electoral Democracy(MDE) in Chihuahua furnishes a rare example of a civic organization in the 1980s that not only mobilized the population against fraud but also made a serious effort to investigate accusations of fraud and pressed for electoral reform. The MDE acted as an umbrella organization for opposition political parties like the PAN, PSUM, and the Mexican Workers Party (PMT), as well as for non-party organizations like Chihuahua's ecclesial base communities, the Democratic Teachers' Movement, the MDC, and all the major urban middle-class civic associations, particularly DHIAC, ANCIFEM, COCOVE, and FCPC.

On July 9, 1986, the MDE held a massive rally attended by approximately 8,000 people in Chihuahua City's main *plaza,* where it condemned the elections of July 6 as fraudulent and demanded their annulment.[44] On July 20, 1986, the MDE held a second rally attended by about 5,000 people, where it again censured the elections and threatened to paralyze communications in the state as a means of protest.[45] The sheer number of organizations comprising the MDE and their ideological heterogeneity gave the MDE's denunciation of fraud considerable weight.

To conduct an independent evaluation of the electoral process, the MDE also established a "popular jury" of eight individuals known for their moral uprightness in the community and unconnected to any political party. On August 9, 1986, after almost a month of analyzing election data and gathering testimony from opposition political parties (the PRI refused to participate in the process) and ordinary citizens, the "popular jury" issued its verdict. After detailing numerous electoral irregularities, criticizing the PRI and the PAN for their ostentatious campaigns, and rejecting the intervention of the United States government and the Catholic Church in Mexican politics, the "popular jury" demanded the abrogation of Chihuahua's election code, the adoption of democratic election laws, and the annulment of the 1986 elections.[46] The criticisms of the PAN and the Church probably reflected the leftist orientation of the members of the "popular jury" and may also have been a strategy to enhance the credibility of their verdict. While the verdict of the "popular jury" had no legal force and could therefore not be implemented, it further eroded the credibility of the PRI's official election victories.

The MDE provided an important precedent for the development of a full-blown election-monitoring exercise by citizens' groups during the 1992 gubernatorial elections. Early in 1991, a coalition of left-leaning organizations joined hands to provide a citizen presence in the 1992 state elections. The Wave for Democracy, as the coalition came to be known, consisted of the state's ecclesial base communities, the state PRD outfit, rural groups like FEDOCH, and the Solidarity and Human Rights Defense Commission (COSYDDHAC). The Wave for Democracy developed strong ties to national civic organizations such as the Citizens' Movement for Democracy (MCD), the National Accord for Democracy (ACUDE), Convergence of Civil Organizations for Democracy (Convergencia), and the Council for Democracy. These national organizations had emerged in the early 1990s to promote clean elections and democracy. The presence of national civic organizations in Chihuahua ensured that the work of Wave for Democracy would receive considerable national publicity and benefit from their international connections. The Council for Democracy conducted a highly accurate quick count of the results of the 1992 state elections, with technical help from the National Democratic Institute (NDI). National civic organizations also invited the Carter Center to be present for the state elections of Michoacán and Chihuahua. The Carter Center's presence signaled the international community's interest in a clean election.

Shortly before the elections, the Wave for Democracy issued a widely circulated report that criticized the regime for diverting public resources into the PRI's campaign and for failing to furnish proper legal channels for appeals against decisions of the state electoral tribunal. On election day itself, the Wave for Democracy mobilized 450 observers armed with cellular telephones and citizens band radios to monitor voting in the state's eighteen electoral districts. The results of the quick count became available only a few hours after the polls closed; the PAN was the winner of the gubernatorial election, with 52 percent of the vote as against 41 percent for the PRI. The quick count virtually mirrored the official results released later after the vote tabulation was completed.

Promoting Human Rights

The mounting human rights abuses stemming from the government's war on drugs in Chihuahua led directly to the formation of the Solidarity and Human Rights Defense Commission (COSYDDHAC) in 1988. It was initially composed almost entirely of women and presided over by Bishop José Llaguno until his death in 1992. Llaguno's diocese, located in the remote, sparsely populated mountains of the indigenous Tarahumara people, had emerged as one of the most important zones of drug trafficking in the country. The organization experienced considerable success. In October, 1989, COSYDDHAC led a campaign against the routine practice of torturing defendants in police custody to extract confessions and persuaded the PRI-dominated state congress to adopt a law criminalizing the use of torture; this was the first time any such law had made it onto the statute books of a Mexican state.[47] COSYDDHAC also coordinated a movement to compel the governor of Chihuahua to remove a close friend, Elías Ramírez, as chief of the federal judicial police in Chihuahua and his son, Raul Ramírez, as chief of the state judicial police after both father and son were implicated in numerous incidents of torture and murder in the state.[48] COSYDDHAC was also active in fighting for the fair investigation of crimes suspected of having been politically motivated, such as the murder of the well-known political columnist Victor Manuel Oropeza in July, 1991. In 1992, the organization participated in the Wave for Democracy to monitor state elections. Since then, COSYDDHAC has focused on improving prison conditions in Chihuahua, denouncing human rights abuses against the Tarahumara by the army, advising *campesinos* involved in land disputes, and demanding investigations of corruption in the state. A recent attempt to assassinate its current president, Camilo Daniel, mobilized the Mexican human rights community and drew international condemnation.[49] COSYDDHAC's ties to the Church and the larger human rights network give the organization a margin of protection—and access to highly motivated and experienced leaders—that kept the organization alive, despite such risks.

Facilitating Opposition Unity

Civic associations played an important role in fostering opposition unity across the ideological spectrum. In Chihuahua, the MDE brought together organizations of very different political persuasions in a common struggle for clean elections. In addition, COLUDE, inspired by the support of opposition political parties, civic associations, and intellectuals at the national level for the movement against electoral fraud in Chihuahua, held a conference of all opposition forces, irrespective of ideology, in Ciudad Juárez on August 9, 1986. The conference was attended by the national leaders of the PAN and several leftist parties; civic associations, such as the MDE and the Pro-Business and Society group of Guadalajara; and prominent individuals like Clouthier and Rogelio Sada Zambrano, a former business executive of the Monterrey Business Group.[50] The conference concluded with the extraordinary announcement that the participants had agreed to form a National Democratic Movement (MDN) and hold a National Forum for Effective Suffrage.[51] Meanwhile, Alvarez, Villareal, and Oropeza ended their forty-one-day hunger strike in protest of electoral fraud (see chapter 2) and announced that they would continue their struggle for clean elections in Mexico through the MDN.

The National Forum for Effective Suffrage was inaugurated on September 6, 1986, in Mexico City. It was attended by all major opposition political parties, a host of civic associations, and pro-democracy activists.[52] The participants agreed to hold a series of regional forums to mobilize the country around the issue of clean elections, condemned electoral fraud in Chihuahua, Oaxaca, and Durango in the 1986 elections, and promised to support actions being taken in repudiation of "the imposition of spurious rulers."[53] The National Forum for Effective Suffrage was, however, marred by unseemly turf battles, and the experiment in opposition unity represented by the MDN proved to be short lived. Yet the fact that it occurred at all was a breakthrough that helped lay the foundations for future alliances among the ideologically heterogeneous and politically competing sectors of the Mexican opposition in order to promote democracy.

CIVIC ASSOCIATIONS AT THE NATIONAL LEVEL: THE CIVIC ALLIANCE AND THE PRESIDENTIAL ELECTIONS OF 1994

Mexican NGOs became interested in election monitoring as part of their work on human rights only in the early 1990s. The most professional and important of these groups, the Civic Alliance, fielded over 12,000 observers on election day and countless more participated in its quick count. The origins of the Civic Alliance can be traced to the early 1990s, when a group of leading intellectuals and social activists became concerned with the issue of clean elections. This marked a turning point in the history of Mexican intellectuals, particularly on the left of the political spectrum, who had previously neglected the role of elections as a means of confronting authoritarianism. The legalization of the communist party and other leftist groups in 1977, the growing competitiveness of elections during the 1980s and 1990s, and the rise of election fraud as a central issue between society and the state in the wake of the 1988 presidential elections produced a new awareness of the importance of electoral democracy among intellectuals and social leaders. The tremendous success of the FDN in 1988 and the creation of the PRD in 1989 also reinforced interest in the role of elections among them.

The nucleus of the Civic Alliance consisted of seven NGOs, all of which were established in the 1980s and 1990s:[54] (1) The Mexican

Academy for Human Rights (AMDH) was formed in 1984 but initially focused more on Central America; (2) the Convergence of Civil Organizations for Democracy emerged in 1989 as an umbrella organization to preserve the tax-exempt status of Mexican NGOs; (3) the Higher Institute for Democratic Culture (ISCD) was established in 1988 to promote public debate and human rights; (4) the Citizens' Movement for Democracy (MCD) emerged in 1991 as a network of organizations to promote democracy in Mexico, centered around the late Salvador Nava, the opposition unity candidate for governor of San Luis Potosí in 1991; (5) the Council for Democracy also emerged in the early 1990s to foster impartial elections and was headed by a distinguished former member of the ruling party; (6) the National Accord for Democracy (ACUDE) was created in 1991 to promote conditions for a dialogue among the three major parties for a transition to democracy and contained a number of leading intellectuals, such as Jorge Castañeda, Miguel Basáñez, and Adolfo Aguilar; (7) and the Rosenblueth Foundation provided valuable technical expertise and enjoyed considerable prestige among Mexico's scientific community. In turn, roughly 450 NGOs around the country were affiliated with the Civic Alliance directly or through the umbrella organizations that constituted its core.

All of these groups were on the center left of the political spectrum, with the exception of the more conservative ISCD, which had strong ties to the business community, the PAN, and the International Republican Institute (IRI). They had all had prior experience in electoral monitoring and had developed significant international connections. The AMDH mounted the first formal observation of a Mexican election in the state elections of 1991 in San Luis Potosí while the Council for Democracy and the Rosenblueth Foundation conducted a quick count of the 1991 federal elections in Mexico City in cooperation with NDI. Between 1991 and 1993, these and other organizations observed fifteen local elections, conducted four quick counts, and even organized a plebiscite on whether Mexico City should have a democratic form of government.

The spectacular growth of the Civic Alliance can be attributed to three factors. First, fair elections had already become a major societal issue, thus providing a reservoir of public support for the organization. Second, the seven founding groups were all closely identified with highly respected figures who served as political entrepreneurs by harnessing growing domestic and international concern for transparent elections to facilitate the growth of the Civic Alliance. Third, the organizational structure of the Civic Alliance was highly decentralized, with the apex organization serving as an umbrella for over 400 NGOs around the country. This loose structure gave the Civic Alliance extraordinary range and flexibility and made it immune to government repression. Cohesion was also assured by the prestige of its leadership, overlapping membership among its constituent organizations, and a clearly defined mission.

The importance of the Civic Alliance lies not only in its contribution to fair elections but its institutional capacity to provide a voice for the citizenry and check the power of the state. Indeed, the crucial role played by domestic observers in the 1994 elections provided evidence of the emergence of a more participatory political culture in Mexico. Over 89,000 Mexicans signed up to participate in the process of monitoring the presidential elections throughout the country.[55] The sheer number of domestic observers was without precedent in Mexican history and paralleled the massive effort mounted by the National Movement for Free Elections (NAMFREL) in the Philippines in 1986 that led to the downfall of the dictator Ferdinand Marcos.

Nor is the Civic Alliance's contribution to the organizational development of the NGO movement to be underestimated. Networking among NGOs in Mexico has become an efficient way of generating economies of scale, sharing information, raising the cost of state repression even in isolated regions, developing international alliances, and maximizing effectiveness in a political system that has systematically sought to fragment independent movements. Networking also reflects the vast improvement in communications that has occurred in Mexico, particularly with the advent of fax machines and electronic mail, which not only reduce transaction costs but also make it possible to create a sense of shared identity among highly disparate NGOs.

Networking played an important role in the recent conflict in Chiapas. NGOs reacted with extreme swiftness to the outbreak of hostilities between the government and the Emiliano Zapata National Liberation Army (EZLN) on January 1, 1994. Within two days, the first representatives of Mexican NGOs arrived in Chiapas, to be followed three days later by an international human rights delegation invited by Mexican NGOs.[56] In the first three months of the conflict, 400 Mexican NGOs in 11 networks and 100 international NGOs conducted diverse missions in Chiapas.[57] Mexican NGOs active in Chiapas quickly created two major networks: the NGO Coordination of San Cristobál for Peace (CONPAZ), which consisted of NGOs based in Chiapas; and the Civil Space for Peace (ESPAZ), which consisted of NGOs from the rest of the country.[58] The first priority of NGO networks in Chiapas was to pressure for a cessation of hostilities. A march for peace in Mexico City organized by Mexican NGOs was attended by approximately 100,000 people. Shortly thereafter, the government declared a truce and initiated peace talks with the rebels.

Mexican NGOs have continued to play a crucial role in Chiapas by diffusing information about the conflict in the rest of Mexico and abroad and by challenging official versions of the conflict in the electronic media and elsewhere. They have also constituted a powerful pressure group in favor of peace, a conciliatory approach towards the EZLN, and steps to improve the welfare of the indigenous peoples in the state, which ranks perennially at the bottom of all of Mexico's leading social indicators. The Civic Alliance also organized a referendum at the request of the EZLN on August 27, 1995, to ask Mexican citizens their opinion about the future role of the EZLN. Approximately 1.1 million people across the country participated in the referendum run by 40,000 volunteers.[59]

By the mid-1990s, the traditional distinction between those working for social and economic rights and those working for political rights had thus broken down completely. Both sets of rights were seen to be mutually interdependent, and close institutional ties now existed between NGOs active in both areas. Even the EZLN leader, Sub-Commander Marcos, attributed the poverty of the indigenous peoples in Chiapas to the lack of democracy, which had deprived them of the representation necessary to press for their rights within the political system. Electoral democracy thus seems to have been a central plank of his agenda not just for tactical reasons but ideological ones as well.

The United Nations Electoral Assistance Program (UNEAP) played an important role in supporting the Civic Alliance.[60] The UNEAP was formally invited by the Mexican government to provide technical and financial assistance to Mexico's domestic election monitoring organizations, which the government recognized were a crucial ingredient of a credible election.[61] The government could have financed the domestic observer groups directly but this would have been seen as a transparent attempt to co-opt them and would have undermined their credibility. The government also hoped that the involvement of the UNEAP in training and financing domestic observer groups would make them more professional and objective in their work. The government was particularly worried about the Civic Alliance, an umbrella group of independent NGOs which the government felt was biased towards the leftist Democratic Revolutionary Party (PRD) and which had quickly emerged as the country's most credible election-monitoring group. The government obviously hoped that the UNEAP would finance a variety of domestic observer groups from across the political spectrum to ensure that no one civic organization acquired a monopoly on judging the elections, especially not the Civic Alliance. Indeed, while the UNEAP earmarked $1.5 million to the Civic Alliance, or three-quarters of the Civic Alliance's $2 million budget for 1994, the UNEAP also insisted on promoting the observation efforts of the mammoth National Teachers' Union (SNTE), which has powerful ties to the PRI, as well as the Mexican Employers' Confederation (COPARMEX).

Relations between the Civic Alliance and UNEAP were often tense. The Civic Alliance bitterly resented the UNEAP's determination to finance election-monitoring groups that were linked to the government and the Alliance hinted that the Mexican government and the UNEAP were complicit. There were also clashes over spending priorities. The Civic Alliance, for example, wanted to conduct its own audit of the *padrón* but was vetoed by the UNEAP, which felt that this was a poor use of its funds given the audits already underway by IFE and McKinsey. The Civic Alliance leadership chafed at the UNEAP's interference, but its heavy reliance on UNEAP funds prevented an open rupture. Nor was it in the UNEAP's interest to allow a breakdown in its relationship with Mexico's most important domestic election observer group because this would jeopardize the UNEAP's own credibility as an objective international organization above the fray of Mexican politics.

The Civic Alliance also received $150,000 from the National Endowment for Democracy (NED) and $50,000 from the National

Democratic Institute (NDI). While the amount of money that the NED and the NDI provided to the Civic Alliance was small, these two organizations nonetheless made a significant contribution to the democratization of the electoral process. The fact that the Civic Alliance was supported by the NED, with its bipartisan congressional support and distinguished board of directors, set the Civic Alliance apart from all the other domestic observer groups by giving it international legitimacy, particularly among U.S. opinion makers. The Civic Alliance's ability to influence international opinion may in turn have worked to enhance its bargaining power vis-à-vis the Mexican government. On the other hand, Civic Alliance leaders fretted about the dangers of accepting U.S. congressional support through the NED, which could lead to the Civic Alliance being tarred as an instrument of U.S. interventionism. NED's decision to award its prestigious 1995 Democracy Award to Sergio Aguayo, one of the founding members of the Civic Alliance, represented a public endorsement of the Civic Alliance's work by the international community that further enhanced its credibility, and facilitated the organization's work as it adapted to the new challenges of the Zedillo *sexenio*.

The NDI's involvement in designing the quick count, conducted by the Civic Alliance in the wake of the closing of the polls, significantly improved both its technical soundness and believability. The NDI also supported regional forums on the Civic Alliance electoral observation efforts in the cities of San Luis Potosí, Guadalajara, and Veracruz which brought together 200 local civic leaders in each city, the national coordinators of the Civic Alliance, and international civic leaders from Chile, Paraguay, and the Philippines.[62] In addition, NDI sponsored a Civic Alliance seminar in Mexico City to train election observers that brought together 120 community leaders from all of Mexico's thirty-one states and the Federal District.[63] These conferences helped to win over regional elites for the Civic Alliance's electoral monitoring efforts and facilitated its development as a nationwide organization.

International actors have played an increasingly important role in Mexico's civic movement in large part because Mexican NGOs typically lack stable sources of domestic financing. This is partly due to the fact that contributions to NGOs that are not directly involved in development assistance are not tax-deductible. Business leaders have also been reluctant to finance NGOs identified with human rights issues because they are perceived as too left wing in their orientation and presumably hostile to business interests. Mexican NGOs have thus been compelled to depend on either government or international financing. Many NGOs have been reluctant to accept government financing for fear of compromising their independence. As a result, they have become disproportionately dependent on external sources of funding. Human rights organizations, including those active in the promotion of democracy, received 43.3 percent of their financing from foreign sources; civic organizations focusing on issues viewed as salient in developed countries were significantly more dependent on foreign support, with women's groups receiving 57.4 percent of their budget from foreign sources, and environmental groups a whopping 87.5 percent.[64] The consequences of this financial dependence are not necessarily negative. Most external funders have opted to work within the parameters set by domestic NGOs and have refrained from acting as agenda-setters themselves. In addition, Mexican NGOs, in order to attract foreign financing, have had to develop a high level of professionalism, accountability, and transparency in their workings.

The Civic Alliance played a pivotal role in democratization by nudging the regime further down the path of reform, acting as a deterrent to election fraud, and creating "civil society." The Civic Alliance also conducted several studies of the electronic media to track coverage of the presidential race that revealed a pattern of serious bias in favor of the PRI, and the Alliance placed pressure on the government to address structural inequities between political parties. By conducting a highly credible quick count, the Civic Alliance also made fraud much more difficult at the counting stage.

CIVIC ASSOCIATIONS, POLITICAL PARTIES, AND THE CATHOLIC CHURCH: DYNAMICS OF INTERACTION

The National Level

By the 1990s, civic associations defending democracy had expanded to the point that real tensions began to occur between them and political parties. The PRI regarded the Civic Alliance as biased towards opposition parties generally, and claimed that many of its leaders were PRD sympathizers. Civic Alliance leaders responded that it was only natural for a civic organization seeking the democratization of a country to attract a significant number of opposition supporters; this had also occurred in both the Philippines and Chile under similar circumstances. In addition, the Civic Alliance prohibits those holding leadership positions in the organization from being political party leaders or candidates for elective office. The PAN feared that the Civic Alliance favored the PRD but acknowledged that the organization had grown more professional over time. Paradoxically, the party that was probably most threatened by the resurgence of the Civic Alliance was the PRD. Initially, the Civic Alliance had planned to disband after its task was over but this decision was reversed after the 1994 presidential elections. The success of the Civic Alliance and the third-place finish by the PRD's Cárdenas in the 1994 elections led to a debate within the Civic Alliance about whether to turn it into a center-left political party that would replace a supposedly inept and moribund PRD. In the end, it was decided that it was better to remain a civic organization rather than risk the organization's prestige as an impartial body of citizens.

The Civic Alliance and the Mexican civic movement thus came into their own by the mid-1990s and could no longer be seen as appendages of opposition political parties. The Civic Alliance's organizational reach, political visibility, and international connections rivaled, and in some cases even surpassed, those of political parties. In addition, by mobilizing thousands of citizens to defend clean elections rather than the victories of a given political party, the Civic Alliance developed a higher moral standing than any political party; it performed a crucial task of which political parties were incapable except in rare circumstances.

A significant proportion of the Civic Alliance's members and leaders were drawn from the Catholic Church. Of the individuals involved in the creation of Mexican human rights NGOs (including many affiliated with the Civic Alliance), 17 percent came from Christian groups, 20 percent from academia, and 35 percent from a history of social and political activism.[65] According to Rogelio Gómez Hermosillo, a well-know ecclesial base community (CEB) adviser, almost one-quarter of the 21,000 Civic Alliance volunteers came from the CEBs, religious orders, and Catholic youth organizations.[66] Gómez himself served on the national coordinating commission of the Civic Alliance. In addition, ten of the thirty-two Civic Alliance state coordinators were CEB activists, and two of them were ordained priests.[67] Only 4 percent of those active in the foundation of these NGOs identified themselves as members of a political party.[68]

The Regional Level

The relationship between Chihuahua's civic associations and the PAN was surprisingly conflictual, given the fact that they shared similar goals. Some *panistas* claimed that the civic associations were diverting participation away from the PAN, while the civic associations argued that they were increasing the total level of participation by giving people who would never have participated in a political party an alternative channel to become active in public affairs. The relationship between the civic associations and the PAN was especially difficult in Ciudad Juárez, where the civic associations had come into existence for the sole purpose of getting Francisco Barrio elected as mayor in the 1983 elections. Their loyalty was to Barrio as an individual and not the PAN as an organization. Barrio's reluctance to identify himself with the PAN and his appointment of only a token number of *panistas* to his new administration provoked a major conflict with the generation of *panistas* who had controlled the party from the 1970s to 1984 and led to an immediate deterioration in the relationship between the PAN in Ciudad Juárez and the civic associations arrayed behind Barrio. The leaders of the civic associations, particularly the Civic Front for Citizen Participation (FCPC) and the Committee for the Democratic Struggle (COLUDE), had an extremely low opinion of the PAN, which they regarded as hopelessly disorganized, full of "losers" willing to keep on butting their heads against the wall of electoral fraud, and prone to excruciatingly slow decision-making processes marked by endless discussions and fruitless debates.[69] For their part, the *panistas* accused the civic associations and their wealthy sponsors of attempting to take over the party to further their own interests.

No major conflicts occurred between the civic associations and the PAN in Chihuahua City, however. This reflected the fact that the PAN's candidate for mayor of Chihuahua City in 1983, Luís H.

Alvarez, was a veteran *panista* who was willing to cooperate with the party. The PAN state committee in Chihuahua City was also much stronger than the PAN municipal committee in Ciudad Juárez and did not need the civic associations. Finally, the business community in Chihuahua City decided to support the PAN directly rather than act through the civic associations.

The conflict between the civic associations and the PAN in Ciudad Juárez became less intense over time. This was partly the result of the decline of the prestige of the civic associations in the wake of their failure to defend the vote successfully in the 1986 state elections. The decrease in tensions also reflected the decision of many rank-and-file civic association members to support the PAN when Gustavo Elizondo, a past president of COPARMEX and former member of FCPC, was elected party president in 1986. Elizondo greatly strengthened the PAN's organizational structure, completely eliminating its dependence on the civic associations and enabling the PAN to mount a highly successful defense of the vote in the 1988 federal elections, when the party won all three federal deputy seats corresponding to Ciudad Juárez. Finally, Barrio, aware of the growing institutional strength of the PAN and the fact that his public image was totally caught up with the PAN whether he liked it or not, chose to reduce his own support of the civic associations.

In general, where the PAN was weak and dependent on civic associations, conflict occurred; where the PAN possessed a well-developed institutional identity, conflict was less frequent. As the PAN grew stronger over time, the relationship with civic associations improved correspondingly. To the extent that civic associations engaged in activities best performed by ordinary citizens rather than political parties, such as election monitoring, the potential for conflict was also significantly reduced. Opposition parties thus collaborated well with the Wave for Democracy in the 1992 state elections.

The civic associations, particularly some of the larger umbrella groups, became the scene of open skirmishes between rival political parties. The PAN became convinced that Antonio Becerra of the leftist PSUM, who had won less than 1 percent of the vote in the 1986 gubernatorial race, was using the Movement for Electoral Democracy (MDE) to speak to crowds that he could never have assembled on his own and thereby increase his standing and that of his party at the expense of the PAN.[70] The PAN was furious when

Becerra spoke last and overran his allotted time by thirty minutes at a major rally sponsored by the MDE.[71] The PAN argued that, because most of the crowds attending MDE rallies were *panistas,* the PAN and not Becerra should have been allowed to speak last and for the longest time. Ramos's reply was that the majority were discontented individuals, not necessarily *panistas.*[72] The PAN was also afraid that its own events could become confused with those of the MDE, felt that it was not being treated as a full partner in the MDE, and believed that Camilo Daniel and Humberto Ramos had been seduced by the charismatic Becerra.[73] While the PAN never formally withdrew from the MDE, it ceased all support for the organization, which eventually fizzled out. One lesson from this episode is that umbrella organizations that include rival political parties are more likely to be torn asunder than those that exclude them.

The relationship between the middle-class civic associations and the Church were smoother. Most of these associations, like COPARMEX, DHIAC, ANCIFEM, FCPC, and COLUDE, based their ideology on traditional Catholic social doctrine as enunciated in papal encyclicals like *Rerum Novarum* (1891), *Quadragesimo Anno* (1931), *Mater et Magistra* (1961), and *Pacem in Terris* (1963). In general, the ideology of the urban middle-class civic associations stressed broad principles, such as: the inherent dignity of the person, the pursuit of the common good as an alternative to class conflict, the importance of intermediate organizations to give society the organizational capacity to resist the tyranny of the state and develop human potential, the right of all persons to own private property to ensure their rights subject to the common good, and the principle of subsidiarity, which legitimizes and limits state intervention to only those functions that cannot be performed by lower instances. These groups were nourished by the Church's social teachings, and were overwhelmingly Catholic in membership, but they possessed no formal ties to it.

The more left-wing Christian groups, particularly the Democratic Peasant Movement (MDC), the Movement for Electoral Democracy (MDE), and COSYDDHAC, drew their inspiration mostly from the Latin American Bishops' Conferences at Medellín (1968) and supported the call of the Puebla Conference (1979) for a "preferential option for the poor" by the Church.[74] Many of these groups possessed direct links to the Church, with clergy and occasionally bishops participating in their foundation and leadership, thereby reducing their vulnerability to repression by the state.

CONCLUSION

The growth of civic associations in the 1980s and 1990s reflected three major trends: First, the political awakening of society and the large increase in the number of ordinary Mexicans seeking democracy created extremely fertile conditions for the sprouting of new civic associations with clean elections, respect for human rights, and democracy as their central aims. Second, social leaders emerged as institutional entrepreneurs, who provided the leadership necessary to form new NGOs. Third, international actors served as important sources of finance and technical assistance for Mexican NGOs involved in the promotion of democracy, and enhanced their international visibility and credibility.

Civic associations played a critical role in generating a more open political environment in Chihuahua. They acted as agents of further politicization by training potential political leaders, transforming ordinary citizens into political activists, and engaging in high profile actions that stimulated greater citizen involvement in politics. They strengthened the PAN by supporting its candidates and taking over key functions that the party felt unable to perform itself; gave credibility to opposition charges of fraud; acted as catalysts for unprecedented displays of opposition unity at the regional and national levels; and monitored elections at the state level. Finally, civic associations helped connect the concerns of marginalized groups, particularly *campesinos,* to the wider movement for democracy in Chihuahua, enabling one to feed off the other. At the national level, civic associations, particularly the Civic Alliance, helped ensure a fairer electoral process in 1994. As Putnam, Tocqueville, Kornhauser, and several Catholic theorists point out, the growth of civic associations is likely to have a significant effect on democratization by promoting institutional pluralism, checking the state, and structuring society.[75] The emergence of civic associations seeking democracy, along with growing activism by opposition parties and the Catholic Church, made it increasingly difficult for the regime to resist calls for change.

6

The Response of the Mexican State: Political Reform in the 1980s and 1990s

The Mexican regime showed considerable political flexibility in responding to growing pressures for democratization. By the late 1990s, the regime had initiated wide-ranging electoral reforms and recognized opposition victories in gubernatorial elections in several major states, the capital, Mexico City, and a host of municipalities around the country. The PRI successfully democratized the procedures for selecting candidates for public office first in Chihuahua, then in several other states, and finally by choosing the party's candidate for president in an open primary. At the same time, sweeping economic reforms had the effect of weakening state control over society and encouraging pluralism. The Mexican case of one-party adaptation to democratic change is interesting for three reasons: First, it provides a test case of whether an official political party like the PRI is capable of transforming itself into a democratic party. Second, it highlights the possible connections between the dual processes of economic and political reform. Third, the Mexican case affords an opportunity to think about the causes of reformist policies, deepening our understanding of reform processes generally.

Three factors might explain the regime's reformist impulse. First, one might argue, as this book does, that reform was primarily the product of growing pressure for democracy from society and institutional actors, such as opposition parties, the Catholic Church, and civic associations. Second, one might claim that reform was the product of elite choices. Reforms required the acquiescence of the

235

regime, which was more than simply a passive actor responding to pressures for change. The regime could have sought to repress the movement for democracy, as occurred in China in 1989, although this would have had high political and economic costs. Third, one could argue that reform was the outcome of growing international pressures for democratization fueled by Mexico's decision to open up its economy to the outside world. These three factors interacted with each other in intriguing ways, but the analysis of this topic is best left to the conclusion of the book.

THE RECOGNITION OF OPPOSITION PARTY VICTORIES

In the world of Mexican politics under de la Madrid and Salinas, a clear distinction existed between opposition victories *per se* and those recognized by the regime. The 1980s and 1990s were marked by a trend towards both more opposition victories and more governmental acceptance of them. The motives for recognizing opposition victories varied significantly across time. In 1983, de la Madrid recognized the PAN's victories in major cities around the country as a defensive move to provide a safety valve at a time of crisis. By the time of the Salinas administration, opposition parties, particularly the PAN, had grown much stronger and for the first time possessed the organizational capacity both to deter fraud by monitoring the polls and to protest fraud after the fact through civil disobedience. At the same time, the regime was anxious to mollify critics of NAFTA in the U.S. Congress who argued that the U.S. should not enter a free trade agreement with a country as undemocratic as Mexico. The regime knew that the opposition could put up a bitter fight in the event of fraud, which would give ammunition to NAFTA critics.

The price of election fraud rose dramatically during the Salinas administration and led directly to the decision to recognize the PAN's victory in the gubernatorial races in Baja California Norte (1989), and Chihuahua (1992). In both states, the PAN possessed an extremely strong organizational structure capable of monitoring elections and paralyzing normal life if fraud occurred. Within hours of the polls closing in Baja California Norte, the PAN released individual tallies from the state's precincts showing that it had won the governor's race. The regime also knew that political chaos in these two border states would do irreparable damage to its image in the United States and imperil NAFTA. The PAN's decision to enter into a dialogue with the regime also made it psychologically easier for the Salinas administration to recognize its victories and took the pressure off to recognize those of the PRD. The ability of the opposition to mount protests against fraud and the desire to head off international criticism was so strong that the Salinas administration was willing to dismiss the official PRI winner and allow an interim PAN governor to take office in Guanajuato in 1991, even though the PAN failed to present strong evidence to prove its victory.

The politics of election recognition under Salinas revealed a profound fissure between the national leadership and state level PRI leaders, with the president imposing the recognition of opposition victories on recalcitrant state PRI outfits and countermanding state-level victories by PRI candidates. Indeed, Salinas clearly deployed presidential power to sweep away state-level obstructions to democratization. Under Zedillo, the regime moved towards a policy of routinely recognizing opposition victories at the local and state levels. The number of Mexicans governed by the PAN rose from 13.2 million to 24.7 million between January and November, 1995, during which time the PAN won gubernatorial races in three major states and mayoral elections in several major cities. In 1997, the PRI lost its majority in the lower house of Congress, the PAN captured the states of Nuevo León and Querétaro, and Cárdenas was elected mayor of Mexico City; in 1998, the PRD won control of the state of Zacatecas.

ELECTORAL REFORMS

The Salinas and Zedillo administrations adopted important electoral reforms in 1993, 1994, and 1996 as a sequel to the modest reforms of 1989 and 1990. The main motivating force for reform in 1993 and 1994 was the government's search for a credible victory in the 1994 presidential elections. The low credibility of elections in the wake of the fiasco of the 1988 elections, as well as the growing ability of opposition parties and civic associations to make fraud a potent domestic and international issue, compelled the government to follow a reformist policy. Foreign investors also clearly wanted a credible election in order to avoid political instability. The sensitivity of foreign investors was underlined by the large amount of foreign capital that was withdrawn from Mexico in the wake of the Chiapas rebellion and the Colosio assassination. The government's need for credibility in effect gave Mexico's two main opposition parties, the PAN and the PRD, a potential veto over electoral reform initiatives. The opposition's main bargaining leverage lay in their ability to reject the results of the elections, a card the PRD and the PAN could play only if they refused to participate in the electoral reform process, thus undermining the legitimacy of the election verdicts themselves.

The domestic and international environment in 1993 and 1994 was thus quite propitious for serious electoral reforms that might push Mexico further down the path toward democracy. The government wanted to ensure a credible result, which required that it satisfy the expectations of the main suppliers of credibility: opposition political parties, domestic election-monitoring associations, and international actors such as the U.S. Congress, the international media, and the foreign investor community. The political price of credibility for the regime depended on the relative bargaining power of the regime vis-à-vis potential opponents, domestic and foreign. Through 1993, the position of the regime in relation to the opposition and outside actors was strong. Mexico was perceived to be a stable and prosperous country on the way to democracy. Salinas enjoyed considerable prestige at home and abroad as a reforming statesman and was a serious candidate to head the new World Trade Organization. The regime thus had an incentive to negotiate with the opposition parties, but not to give up too much in its quest for credibility.

The September, 1993, electoral reforms were thus restricted in scope. They involved changes in both the Constitution and the country's election code (COFIPE).[1] With regard to the constitutional changes, the size of the Senate was doubled to 128 seats, with four senators, instead of two, being elected from each state. The party in first place would win three senate seats, with the fourth seat going to the party in second place. This opened up the Senate to the opposition but also guaranteed the overrepresentation of the majority party. In addition, the "governability clause"—this gave the party in first place an automatic absolute majority of seats in the Chamber of Deputies—was eliminated and the maximum number of seats that any single party could hold in the Chamber was reduced to 63 percent, ensuring that no single party could secure the two-thirds majority required to amend the Constitution on its own. The Federal Election Institute (IFE) was charged with certifying the results of senate and congressional elections, eliminating the old system whereby incoming senators and congressmen ruled on the validity of their own elections. A new Federal Elections Tribunal (TFE) was set up, consisting of the Chief Justice and four members of the judiciary chosen by a two-thirds vote of the Chamber of Deputies; the TFE examined disputes relating to the certification of senate and congressional races. The creation of the TFE was a positive step towards a more objective system of electoral justice.

With regard to the reform of the election code, the September, 1993, reforms introduced the concept of campaign spending limits for the first time, but the formula and criteria for setting limits, and the limits themselves, went unspecified. In order to promote transparency in party finances, parties were required to submit a public report to the IFE detailing campaign revenues and expenditures. Individual contributions to political parties were set at 1 percent of public election financing, which translated into U.S. $666,667 per contributor. Anonymous donations were legalized for the first time, but they were limited to 10 percent of the amount of public election financing, or approximately U.S. $6.6 million; labor unions could donate up to 5 percent of public financing, or U.S. $3.3 million. Contributions from businesses, churches, and foreign organizations were prohibited. The government also issued a new fraud-proof identity card for voters and improved the quality of the voter registration list.

The 1993 reforms were severely criticized by the PRD. The reforms left intact the regime's control of the IFE, the organization charged with running Mexican elections. The General Council, the apex body of the IFE, consisted at the time of twenty-one seats, including the president of the General Council, who also served as the Minister of the Interior, political party representatives, and six magistrate councilors, who were supposed to be independent but in practice voted with the PRI on all major decisions and had been selected by Salinas with the approval of two-thirds of the Chamber

of Deputies. The PRI / government controlled seven seats directly
and at least fourteen seats if one took into account the votes of the
magistrate councilors and the three smaller political parties who
also tended to vote with the PRI. The PRI / government could thus
control potentially two-thirds of the seats on the General Council
of the IFE, thereby damaging the IFE's credibility as an independent and unbiased agency. The 1993 reforms also said nothing about
the role of international observers, who remained technically illegal under Mexican law. Nor did the reforms address the fundamental problems of ensuring media access to all political parties and
balanced news coverage of the electoral process by Mexico's television barons, who enjoyed close ties with the ruling party. Although
the reforms made an initial stab at the issue of campaign finance,
the limit on individual contributions was very high and no formal
spending ceilings were set for the campaign. The basic issues of ensuring a level playing field and the objectivity of the IFE thus went
unresolved.

The eruption of a major peasant uprising in the southern state of
Chiapas, on New Year's Day, 1994, galvanized the regime into con-
templating more serious reforms. The Chiapas rebellion was timed
to take maximum advantage of the political opportunity afforded
to the guerrillas by the presidential elections. The willingness of
the Zapatista National Liberation Army leader, Sub-Commander
Marcos, to make clean elections a central plank of his agenda, along
with the rights of indigenous peoples, allowed the movement in
Chiapas to link up with the wider movement for democracy in
Mexico and added to the fear that violence might erupt if the election results were generally disbelieved. In addition, Marcos's
highly sophisticated use of the domestic and international media
to publicize his message increased the pressure felt by the government to take serious steps to open up the electoral process. The
assassination of the PRI's presidential candidate Luís Donaldo
Colosio in the border city of Tijuana on March 23, 1994, gave further
momentum to the reform process by raising the specter of generalized chaos in the wake of a disputed election outcome.

Both the Chiapas uprising and the killing of Colosio suggested
that the consequences of an election that lacked credibility might
be far more serious than originally envisaged in 1993—and not easily
contained by the regime. The PRI's nightmare was a scenario in

which the PRI candidate won a highly contested race by a narrow margin with the opposition crying fraud. PRI leaders feared that this would unleash civil violence and prolonged political instability that would tear the country asunder, drive away foreign investors, and jeopardize the country's crucial relationship with the United States. Public opinion data suggest that this scenario may not have been all that far off the mark, with approximately 30 percent of all respondents in one poll conducted by the Civic Alliance on June 30, 1994, expecting violence with ungovernability, 35 percent expecting violence and repression, and only 17 percent expecting no violence in the event of election fraud.[2] In short, the Chiapas rebellion and the assassination of Colosio increased the regime's perception of what might happen if the PRI candidate failed to win credibly, gave opposition parties more leverage in their dealings with the regime, and encouraged the government to make significant concessions to ensure a reasonably transparent process.

As a result, the government agreed to further reforms in 1994.[3] It agreed to reform the IFE to allow it greater room to function as an autonomous body. The IFE's magistrate councilors were replaced by six citizen councilors chosen by consensus between all three main political parties, rather than at the behest of the president, and appointed by a two-thirds vote of the Chamber of Deputies. Political parties were denied the right to vote, but could continue to participate in IFE debates. The president of the IFE was replaced by the new Minister of the Interior, Jorge Carpizo, who had enjoyed a reputation for impartiality and personal integrity as Mexico's first president of the National Human Rights Commission. The voter registration list was subject to two rigorous audits, one by the IFE in conjunction with political parties, except the PRD, which declined to participate, and the other by a consortium of private consulting firms, including the well-known international group, McKinsey. International "visitors" were invited to officially observe all phases of the electoral process for the first time in Mexican electoral history, domestic observers were given greater flexibility and authority to monitor the election process, stiff criminal penalties were imposed on those committing various forms of election fraud, and a special prosecutor's office was created to investigate and prosecute charges of election fraud. These new changes provided three crucial ingredients necessary for a free election that had been missing from the 1993 set of reforms: a reliable voter registration list, more autonomous election authorities, and international observers.

Although Zedillo was elected by a landslide victory, his authority was severely weakened by the lack of support from within his own party for his stand in candidacy, the eruption of a major economic crisis at the outset of his *sexenio* followed by severe austerity measures, and the president's own desire to decentralize power. Presidential vulnerability combined with opposition pressure led to a new round of path-breaking electoral reforms in 1996.[4] These reforms resulted from long, drawn-out negotiations among the three major parties, with Zedillo playing a less visible role in the process than his predecessor, Salinas.

The reforms continued the process of bolstering the independence of the IFE from both executive and legislative control. The IFE would no longer be headed by the Interior Minister but by a citizen chosen by consensus and approved by a two-thirds vote of the Chamber of Deputies. The right to vote in IFE decisions would now be limited to eight electoral councilors (the successors of citizen councilors) and the president of IFE; legislative councilors would no longer be eligible to vote but, like political party representatives, could participate in discussions. Electoral councilors were barred from involvement in party politics or government for three years prior to their designation and were chosen by consensus, subject to a two-thirds vote in the Chamber. They were to serve six-year terms. The reforms also reduced the overrepresentation of the majority party in the Senate by allocating 32 of its 128 seats on the basis of proportional representation; in the Chamber, the majority party was limited to no more than 300 seats, with its share of seats not to exceed its share of the vote by more than 8 percent. Significantly, the reforms provided for the first direct election of the mayor of Mexico City since the 1920s and theoretically opened the door for Mexicans living abroad to vote in the presidential elections of 2000, although they did not in fact do so due to technical constraints. Both these reforms were expected to benefit the opposition: the PRD and PAN enjoyed strong support in Mexico City, and Mexicans abroad were considered supportive of the opposition.

For the first time, the 1996 reforms established the Supreme Court as the final arbiter of Mexican election results. The Federal Election Tribunal was made an integral part of the Supreme Court and staffed by judges appointed by the Chief Justice with the approval of two-thirds of the Chamber of Deputies. The Supreme Court was also given the right to review the constitutionality of election laws and decisions at both the federal and state levels. This reform allows the Supreme Court to exercise judicial review in a system traditionally dominated by the executive branch, and to use federal power against regional bosses—who attempt to rig elections, particularly in southern Mexico.

In the area of campaign and party finances, the new reforms obliged political parties to submit detailed reports on income and expenditure flows, not just during the campaign, as under the 1994 reforms, but on an annual basis as well. The 1996 reforms accepted the principle that political parties would draw the bulk of their financing from public rather than private sources but failed to agree on the amount of public financing. The PRI wanted to set public financing at much higher levels than the PAN and the PRD. In the end, PRI deputies voted alone to approve an unprecedented $278 million in public financing for all political parties, with 30 percent being allocated equally among all parties and 70 percent according to their share of the vote in the last election. Accordingly, the PRI stood to receive about U.S. $111.5 million, the PAN $66 million, and the PRD $49 million for the 1997 campaign. The limit on the size of individual contributions was lowered from 1 percent to .05 percent of public financing (roughly U.S. $139,000 for 1997).

While campaign spending limits were set at very high levels, the shift towards public financing meant that opposition parties would find it easier to reach those spending limits; in the past, only the PRI could spend its allotment. In addition, by expanding the level of public financing, the new campaign finance regime raised the amount of money available for all three parties, not only the PRI. Finally, the shift towards public financing and stringent monitoring of political party finances should have a dampening effect on political corruption.

The Mexican electronic media, traditionally closed to the opposition, has shown signs of opening in recent years. In 1994, the three presidential candidates agreed to hold an unprecedented televised debate that brought the campaign to life and was widely perceived to have been won by the PAN candidate. The 1996 electoral reforms sought to improve media access by allowing the IFE to spend the equivalent of 12 percent of public financing to buy time slots for political party advertising. In addition, the IFE was charged with the task of monitoring the electronic media for signs of bias, issuing reports on media coverage every fifteen days during a campaign, and pressuring for a more open media climate.

THE CHALLENGE OF INTERNAL PARTY REFORM

The growing electoral competitiveness of the opposition, the trend towards the recognition of opposition victories, and electoral reforms that made it harder for the official party to win by unfair means placed the PRI under enormous pressure to reform itself in order to survive. Skeptics like Lorenzo Meyer have argued that reforming the PRI is a virtual impossibility.[5] John Bailey, while agreeing that the prospects for party reform are not bright, leaves open the possibility, in view of the existence of "significant reform currents" inside the PRI, and he hopes that "the rhythm of Mexican politics will provide opportunities for renewal."[6] Skeptics point out that the PRI was created, not as a democratic political party, but as an instrument of presidential power to control both the revolutionary elite and society. The party has no tradition of internal elections, individual membership, and independence from executive authority. Seventy years in power have dulled its ability to compete in the electoral marketplace without government support, and disentangling the dense network of ties that bind the PRI and the state may not be possible without sacrificing the PRI altogether.

Others, like Delal Baer, claim that the PRI could evolve into a democratic party.[7] Baer argues that economic reforms have forced the PRI to restructure its alliances by building bridges to the business community and middle classes, the groups most likely to support party reform.[8] She points out that the PRI never took on the economic and bureaucratic functions of the Soviet Communist Party (CPSU) and remained pragmatic in flavor and tone, thus making the Mexican ruling party more reformable than the CPSU.[9] Luís Rubio also makes the case that the economic reforms undermined the corporatist system of labor control, thus facilitating internal party democratization by weakening the CTM.[10]

The PRI in Chihuahua
during the Baeza Administration:
The PRI Begins to Reform Itself

Baeza's Economic Programs

On the whole, the experience of the PRI in Chihuahua confirms the view that the party is capable of reforming itself. The political awakening of society and social leaders in Chihuahua placed enormous pressure on the government to enact democratizing reforms in the state. The main problem facing the Baeza administration when it took office in Chihuahua in October, 1986, was its crippling lack of legitimacy. Baeza was almost universally regarded as a *de facto* governor; he had been brutally imposed on Chihuahua in a fraudulent election orchestrated by the central government. Desperate to acquire legitimacy and redeem his personal reputation, the new governor immediately adopted a strategy of social conciliation. He invited opposition parties to submit proposals for the reform of the state's controversial election code, and a series of public forums were held to discuss the matter. He openly proclaimed his Catholic convictions, assured the archbishop that future elections in Chihuahua would be beyond reproach, extended financial assistance for the restoration of dilapidated parishes, and personally accompanied the archbishop on tours of public works initiated by his government. He wooed the business community by staffing his cabinet with an overwhelming majority of businessmen and technocrats, much to the dismay of traditional PRI *políticos*. Finally, the governor set a tone of openness for his administration by his own accessibility and cordiality.

Baeza also embarked on a massive program of road construction, with generous financial assistance from the central government which was anxious to mollify Chihuahua. The rapid industrialization of the state in recent years had placed the state's always-deficient communications network under considerable stress, and it seemed only a matter of time before transportation bottlenecks would choke off further economic growth. In the first three years of the Baeza administration, a new road was built from Chihuahua City to Parral, the state's third largest city, significantly cutting travel time and opening up a vast swath of rural hinterland for development. A project was launched in cooperation with the private sector to widen the two-lane road connecting Ciudad Juárez and Chihuahua City to four lanes, thus surmounting a major obstacle to the state's economic growth. The road between Chihuahua City and Delicias, the state's most important center of agricultural production and the governor's hometown, was also widened to four lanes. New roads were built in the Tarahumara mountains, making it harder for drug traffickers to hide out and facilitating the development of the lumber industry. And the construction of highway bypasses and new access routes alleviated traffic congestion in the state's larger cities.

Baeza's program of road construction helped the business community by improving the state's economic prospects and generating lucrative construction contracts. It helped workers by expanding employment. More importantly, bigger and better roads symbolized Chihuahua's new prosperity and raised the morale of the population. That Baeza's program of road construction was well received in Chihuahua did not, however, necessarily translate into greater support for the PRI. Indeed, many *Chihuahuenses* saw the government's decision to invest heavily in Chihuahua, despite a severe budgetary crunch, as a direct result of the strength of the opposition in the state and concluded that the best way to get the government to loosen its purse strings was not to vote for the PRI.

Towards PRI Reforms in Chihuahua

Far more important than social conciliation or lavish public investment was the regime's decision to restructure the PRI in Chihuahua completely by democratizing the selection of the party's candidates for elective office in 1989. Traditionally, PRI candidates for elective office in Chihuahua, as in other parts of the country, were simply designated from above, without much regard to local conditions; various party luminaries, including the president, leading members of his cabinet, the national and state leadership of the National Peasants' Confederation (CNC) and the Mexican Workers' Confederation (CTM), state governors, and local *caciques* selected the candidates. Many of these candidates were unknown or unpopular in their prospective constituencies and sometimes even within the local PRI organization. PRI candidates were at a major disadvantage when running against PAN candidates, who had been democratically elected by a convention of rank-and-file PAN members and often acted as lightening rods of regional resentment against the central government. As a result, the PRI machine often had to rig elections so that its candidates would win.

In Chihuahua, the PAN's electoral victories in 1983, 1985, and 1988 seemed to indicate that the PRI candidates would not win unless they enjoyed clear local popularity. Also, the political cost of committing election fraud in Chihuahua had risen dramatically in the wake of the disputed elections of 1986. Both the fear that PRI candidates designated from above would lose and the growing unacceptability of election fraud convinced Baeza and national PRI leaders to permit the democratization of the party in Chihuahua.

Internal democratization would enable the PRI in Chihuahua to field more electable candidates because rank-and-file party members were by definition more representative of the state's population than distant party elites. Further, internal democratization would rekindle the enthusiasm of PRI members and leaders in Chihuahua, who had grown demoralized as a result of the constant imposition of candidates by Mexico City. Democratically elected candidates would also be able to mount more powerful campaigns because they would enjoy greater legitimacy inside and outside the party.

Before primary elections could be held, however, the PRI in Chihuahua had to develop an accurate list of party members. This was not as easy as it might seem at first glance. Traditionally, the members of the PRI (and its predecessors the PNR and the PRM) were affiliated organizations, and only rarely individual citizens. Individual PRI membership occurred indirectly through collective organizations, particularly the party's three sectors—the Mexican Workers' Confederation (CTM), the National Peasants' Confederation (CNC), and the National Confederation of Popular Organizations (CNOP). Most such indirect membership was obligatory, with members of official trade unions being automatically enrolled in the PRI as a condition of their union membership. Thus, while the PRI officially had several million members at any given time, only a tiny fraction felt any personal commitment to the party.[11] In order to develop an authentic membership list, the PRI in Chihuahua was compelled to conduct a door-to-door campaign designed to identify PRI supporters in their homes and enroll them directly as individual members of the party.

Another related challenge facing the PRI in Chihuahua was to revive its moribund territorial structure in order to create an appropriate organizational framework for electing the PRI's candidates for public office. Traditionally, the three sectors—the CTM, the CNC, and the CNOP—had served as the party's main link with society. The growing complexity of Mexican society as a result of rapid economic development, the ossification of the sectors at the hands of unrepresentative leaders, and the paucity of financial resources in the 1980s to prevent rank-and-file members of the CTM and CNC from deserting the official party meant that the sectors had long ceased to serve as links between society and the PRI. If the party was to staunch the erosion of its support, it would be necessary to bypass the sectors and reach out directly to society by rejuvenating the PRI's territorial structure. A strong territorial structure would help the party recruit new members directly and give them an organizational context in which to participate actively in the party as individuals, including participating in internal elections. In Chihuahua, the PRI greatly strengthened its territorial structure by reactivating party committees in 1,611 electoral sections throughout the state and opting for the election of the presidents of the PRI's municipal committees.

Finally, PRI reformers had to come to an agreement with the national leadership of the party's sectors before primary elections could be held in Chihuahua. The sectors were not inclined to surrender their access to a secure quota of elected offices. The CTM was particularly worried that its candidates would be defeated in primary contests because rank-and-file PRI members in the country's increasingly heterogeneous urban areas were more likely to be drawn from a diverse spectrum of groups and could not be relied on to endorse candidates put forward by organized labor.

The issue of internal democratization in Chihuahua was taken up directly with Fidel Velázquez by the PRI's National Executive Committee (CEN).[12] Velázquez, probably because he knew that the project of internal democratization had the support of President Salinas, acquiesced to holding primary elections in Chihuahua.[13] It is highly unlikely that Velázquez would have agreed to Baeza's plan to democratize the PRI without active pressure from the party's CEN led by PRI national president, Luís Donaldo Colosio, and possibly even Salinas himself. For his part, Baeza declared that he had no preferred candidates and promised that no government functionaries would be allowed to impose any candidates of their own.

The Election of PRI Mayoral Candidates in Chihuahua

The PRI's mayoral candidates in Chihuahua were elected by two processes. In the state's largest eight cities, including Chihuahua City, Ciudad Juárez, Delicias, Camargo, Parral, Cuauhtémoc, Nuevo Casas Grandes, and Jiménez, candidates were elected by delegates from the party's territorial and sectoral wings. These cities were too big for the direct election of candidates without generating chaos in the process. Territorial delegates were elected by the PRI's sectional committees, and sectoral delegates were elected by their respective sectors. Nonsectoral organizations, like the Revolutionary Youth Front (FJR) and the Council for Women's Integration (CIM), were also allowed to elect a small share of delegates to the conventions. A total of 2,050 assemblies were held by the PRI's sectional committees, sectors, and organizations to elect 11,796 delegates to the conventions.[14] The number of delegates that each assembly could elect was not fixed; it varied according to attendance, so as to reflect real as opposed to nominal membership strength. All assemblies were conducted under the close observation of a representative of the PRI state committee.

The three sectors held 1,029 assemblies and elected 5,625 delegates, or an average of 5.5 delegates per assembly; the PRI's sectional committees held 956 assemblies and elected 5,045 delegates or 5.3 delegates per assembly; and the FJR and CIM held 65 assemblies and elected 1,126 delegates or 17.3 delegates per assembly.[15] Rough parity thus existed between the sectoral and territorial delegates, with the former outnumbering the latter by a modest 580 delegates. When, however, one takes into account the fact that the delegates from the youth and women's organizations were more likely to vote with the territorial delegates, then the sectoral delegates were outnumbered by 546 delegates. Also, given the fact that the three different sectors were unlikely to vote as a single bloc, the formula of rough parity between the territorial and sectoral delegates was more than sufficient to tip the balance of power in the primary conventions in favor of delegates from the PRI's territorial

structure and prevent the CTM and CNC from foisting poor candidates on the party.

Twenty-two individuals registered themselves as pre-candidates for the party's mayoral ticket in the eight cities,[16] yielding an
average of 2.75 pre-candidates per city. The barriers to entry were
deliberately kept low—only the endorsement of one of the three
sectors, or one nonsectoral organization, or one sectional committee, or a small number of party members in the municipality was
needed to register as a pre-candidate. The elections were orderly;
delegates cast their ballots in transparent ballot boxes and the counting followed thereafter. The competitiveness of the election was
underlined by the results: some candidates won by relatively narrow margins, and labor fared poorly except in Cuauhtémoc, where
the CTM candidate won by 95 votes.

In the remaining 59 smaller municipalities, PRI candidates for
mayor were elected directly by all those eligible to vote in the general elections, whether they were PRI members or not. Opening
these elections to all voters, regardless of party affiliation, made it
even more likely that the aspirant who was most acceptable locally
would actually win the PRI ticket. Also, smaller towns in Mexico,
more so than big towns, tend to be dominated by only one or two
organizations. If the PRI had opted for indirect election of party
candidates in small towns, then the lion's share of delegates would
have gone to these dominant organizations at the expense of the
party's sections and organizations that were not part of the local
power structure. Entering the race for mayoral nominations in the
59 municipalities were 221 individuals, an average of 3.7 aspirants
per municipality.[17] The direct primaries in the smaller municipalities were thus more competitive than the indirect primaries in the
larger municipalities, which yielded an average of 2.75 aspirants
per city. Like the mayoral candidates in the larger cities, the PRI's
candidates for the 18 seats in the state legislature in 1989 were
chosen indirectly by delegates from the party's sectoral and territorial structures; the CNC and CTM won three nominations apiece.

New Election Code in Chihuahua

The PRI has always functioned as "the party of the state" rather
than "the party in power." The systematic bias of election laws and

procedures in favor of the PRI was one clear manifestation of its privileged position as the "party of the state." Baeza's decision to sponsor a new state election code, which incorporated key opposition demands and made fraud much harder to commit, was thus a significant step towards separating the PRI from the state in Chihuahua. The democratization of candidate selection and the adoption of a fairer election code were mutually reinforcing processes: internal democratization allowed the PRI to field better candidates who were less dependent on fraud to win, while the greater difficulty of committing fraud as a result of the new election code provided a powerful incentive for the PRI to strengthen the electoral competitiveness of its candidates for public office by democratizing internally. A fairer election code would improve the government's relations with society, deprive opposition political parties of a major weapon with which to attack the PRI, and bestow credibility on any future PRI election victories. As one PRI leader wryly observed: "The PRI has to win elections twice, once in the ballot boxes and once in the battle of credibility."[18]

Adopted by the state legislature in December, 1988, Chihuahua's new election code contained sweeping reforms:

1. Each political party would be allowed two representatives per voting precinct or *casilla* instead of just one.
2. Transparent ballot boxes would be used for the first time in the history of Mexican elections.
3. The use of indelible ink would be obligatory.
4. The president and secretaries of *casillas* would be selected by a majority of the Municipal Election Commission (CME) rather than only its president, thus implying consultation with the opposition.
5. Those responsible for counting the votes in each *casilla* would be designated by lottery.
6. Ballot boxes would be placed in a spot visible to party representatives.
7. The time limit for filing charges of misconduct against election officials would be extended.
8. Electoral organizations would have to accept and respond rapidly to queries made by political parties or citizens.

9. Auxiliary personnel in the *casillas* would have to be authorized by a majority of the CME rather than its president, and their names, and functions released to political parties in a timely fashion.
10. Votes would be counted afresh if a difference existed between the *casilla* election return in the hands of the CME and the copies in the hands of political parties.
11. *Casilla* presidents would have to surrender election packets to the CME immediately and could be accompanied by party representatives.
12. Candidacies could no longer be canceled for conducting propaganda on the day of the election, though fines would be applied.
13. *Casillas* would no longer be subdivided without consulting political parties.[19]

Election reform in Chihuahua was deepened in 1992, when the regime permitted and financed a full-fledged review of the state voter registration list conducted by the PAN. A number of problems detected by the audit were also quickly rectified prior to the elections.

Effect of the Internal Democratization of the PRI in Chihuahua on the PRI Nationally

The impact of the internal democratization of the PRI in Chihuahua on the PRI nationally was significant. Chihuahua marked the first time in the history of the PRI that the party had succeeded in democratizing the selection of its candidates for elective office. The last attempt to democratize the party internally had occurred in 1965, when Carlos Madrazo was PRI national president, but the experiment was quickly abandoned in the face of massive resistance from party bosses. Madrazo was forced to resign and was later killed in a suspicious plane crash.[20] The 1989 electoral victories of the PRI in Chihuahua sent a healthy message to the PRI nationally that the party could democratize candidate selection and conduct a clean election without self-destructing in the process, even though the PRI's triumphs in 1989 were probably due more to the low voter turnout than the reforms. The PRI in Chihuahua was held up as a model for the party to follow throughout the nation. PRI national president Colosio in his statement conceding defeat to the PAN in the race for governor of Baja California Norte in 1989, where the party had failed to introduce reforms, simultaneously lauded the PRI's election triumphs in Chihuahua as a shining example of what the PRI could achieve by internal democratization.[21] PRI leaders from other states quickly descended on Chihuahua to learn from the party's experience there.[22]

The democratization of the PRI in Chihuahua was a dress rehearsal for the wide-ranging reforms approved at the party's fourteenth national assembly held in September, 1990.[23] The PRI's statutes were amended to provide for the democratic election of all candidates for mayor, governor, state deputy, federal deputy, and senator. The barriers for entering the race for the party ticket were set at low levels: 5 percent of the support of individual party members in the municipality for mayor and 20 percent of individual party members in the state for senator and governor. The party's next candidate for president would no longer be chosen directly by the president but by a majority vote of the National Political Council, a collection of party luminaries. The PRI's territories and sectors would enjoy a parity of delegates at conventions to elect party candidates and on the National Political Council. Individual affiliation to the party would take place directly through the party's sectional or municipal committees, membership in a sector or organization would not be required to become a party member, and a new category for party sympathizers was created. Instead of retaining the old definition of the PRI as a party of sectors and citizens, the assembly redefined the PRI as a party of citizens, organizations, and sectors, reversing the order to give citizens pride of place. Finally, so as to encourage the decentralization of the party, the assembly stripped the National Executive Committee (CEN) of its power to remove state-level PRI leaders and appoint delegates to oversee the activities of PRI state committees. The basic idea behind all the reforms was to make the PRI more permeable as an organization to society.

PRI Reforms Stymied by Vested Interest

Yet, these changes were not implemented and served mostly as a masquerade to legitimize candidates already chosen beforehand. The national assembly gave PRI leaders enough discretionary power to delay and stymie the reforms. The National Political Council was vested with the power to alter resolutions approved by the national assembly, even though the latter was a more representative body. The provision that all candidates for elective office at the local, state, and congressional levels be selected by democratic procedures was diluted by the ability of the National Political Council to grant "exceptions" when necessary. The National Political Council was also supposed to provide a more democratic mechanism for the selection of the party's candidate for president by taking it out of the hands of the president. The new statutes were notably silent, however, about how members would be selected, and in the end they were simply appointed by Salinas.[24]

In the 1991 primary elections in the state of Nuevo León, Sócrates Rizzo, a long-time friend of Carlos Salinas, was elected as the PRI's candidate for governor from a field of six aspirants; the two most serious contenders for the governorship, aside from Rizzo himself, were persuaded not to register themselves as aspirants and were not among the six official pre-candidates.[25] In the state of Colima, however, the PRI's attempt to manipulate the primary election for governor backfired. To clear the way for Socorro Díaz, the editor of the Mexico City daily, *El Día*, and the preferred candidate of Salinas, the PRI forced the two most serious contenders, Carlos Vázquez and Roberto Anzar, not to put their names forward and registered a relatively weak politician, Carlos De la Madrid Virgen, as her main opponent.[26] Angry at their exclusion, Vázquez and Anzar threw their considerable local support behind De la Madrid, who quickly became a champion of regionalist resistance against the imposition of Díaz by Mexico City.[27] The campaign sparked an upsurge of citizen interest and grew increasingly acrimonious, with both sides trading accusations of fraud. In the end, De la Madrid was declared the winner of the party's ticket for governor with 57.7 percent of the vote as against 42.3 percent for Díaz.[28] Unfortunately for the PRI, Socorro Díaz refused to accept her defeat gracefully and publicly accused the PRI in her newspaper of rigging the election.[29] The lesson of Colima is instructive because it shows that once formal mechanisms of internal democracy are in place, they can easily slip out of the control of party leaders and become hard to manipulate.

Even in Chihuahua, the experiment with internal primaries ran into serious difficulties. In the 1992 state elections, the PRI's candidate for governor was imposed on the state party, despite accusations of possible links with the state's drug mafia. Baeza later claimed that he had nothing to do with the decision, which he attributed to Salinas.[30] Candidates for municipal office were also chosen by undemocratic means, although the institutional form of doing so through conventions was preserved.[31] In 1994, PRI candidates for federal deputy races were chosen by *auscultación,* a shadowy process of choosing candidates on the basis of consulation among the main "factors" of power rather than by competitive elections. Conventions did occur but, with only one candidate in most districts, they functioned mostly as rubber-stamps.[32]

In other states between 1988 and 1994—such as Michoacán, San Luis Potosí, Guanajuato, Yucatán, Tabasco, and Chiapas— candidates for governor were also chosen by *auscultación* with the approval of the president rather than democratic means. Nor was the process for choosing the PRI's nominee for president in 1994 any different from 1988. After floating the names of six pre-candidates and ostensibly consulting with leaders of the PRI and domestic interest groups, the president selected Colosio as his successor,[33] and the National Political Council then ratified him as the PRI's nominee. In the wake of the Colosio assassination, Salinas retained control of the selection process by nominating Zedillo, despite opposition from party conservatives.

The failure of internal democratization experiments to prosper in Chihuahua and nationally reflected the difficulty of coaxing vested interests to give up their control over candidate selection except under extraordinary circumstances. The pace of internal democratization was also held up by often justified concerns that primary elections might get out of hand, provoke divisions in the party, and push losing candidates into the arms of the opposition. And the government itself was more than a shade reluctant to surrender such a powerful instrument of control over party leaders as the divvying up of candidacies, or to dilute the president's own faculty to designate candidates for major offices.

Federal election reforms under Salinas made fraud more difficult to commit and have theoretically furnished a spur to internal democratization. But these new laws did not affect state election practices, which remained vulnerable to fraud—with the exception of PAN-ruled states, which put state election reform at the top of their agenda. Given the slow pace of internal democratization, despite the reform of federal election codes, one could conclude that

PRI leaders believed that the costs of internal democratization, such as loss of control and heightened party divisions, outweighed whatever benefits might accrue to the party in terms of greater appeal in an intensely competitive electoral arena.

Although the model of competitive internal primaries did not take root inside the PRI during the Salinas *sexenio*, the kinds of candidates fielded by the party changed significantly. One of the pillars of PRI electoral strategy was to lure away from the opposition the business support that had contributed to the growth of the PAN by fielding candidates from the business community. This task was made much easier by the open economic policies followed by de la Madrid and Salinas, which restored business confidence in the Mexican regime. PRI candidates across the country were increasingly young, business-oriented professionals who gave the party a new face and provided stiff competition to the PAN. As the PRI found it more difficult to siphon off state funds into party coffers and the PRI became more attractive to business, its financial dependence on big business grew accordingly.

New Wave of Reform

Party reform accelerated under Zedillo, with Chihuahua once again in the vanguard. In 1998, the PRI in Chihuahua opted to hold internal primaries to determine its candidates for party office at both the state and municipal levels. The decision to hold primaries in Chihuahua was the result of several factors: Chihuahua was an important state in the hands of the opposition, and the gubernatorial election represented the last hope for the PRI to take back a state ruled by the PAN before the presidential elections of 2000. The party in Chihuahua contained a number of democratizers, associated with former governor Baeza, who exerted pressure for a more open process. The party in Chihuahua was also well prepared to carry out internal primaries, unlike several other parts of the republic. Zedillo was also enthusiastically behind holding an open primary in Chihuahua, and there was little opposition to him on that score especially with the passing of Velázquez, the old CTM boss.

The gubernatorial primary pitted three of Chihuahua's best-known politicians against each other: Patricio Martínez García, Mario De la Torre, and Artemio Iglesias. Both Iglesias and De la Torre were identified with the PRI's old guard in Chihuahua, unlike Martínez, who had developed a close relationship with Barrio as mayor of Chihuahua City and came to politics relatively late after a career as a real estate salesman. Procedurally, the primaries were open to all registered voters: 233, 280 people voted in the gubernatorial primary, with 125,565 votes cast for Martínez, 83,226 for Iglesias, and 14,553 for De la Torre.[34] The primaries were conducted by Heladio Ramírez, a former governor of Oaxaca, known for his reformist views. Municipal primaries also went well, with the exception of Ciudad Juárez, where the losing PRI candidate apparently instructed his followers to vote for the PRD, resulting in an extremely close victory for the PAN.

Internal PRI Conflict over Reform

The holding of open primaries in 1998 in Chihuahua, followed by the PRI's victory in the gubernatorial elections, had a major impact on democratization of the PRI nationally. The Chihuahua model was associated with success in a new period of open elections. Zedillo himself came out in favor of open primaries in which the general public could vote as a way of determining the PRI's next presidential candidate.[35] Open primaries were initially opposed, however, by the traditional wing of the party led by Manuel Bartlett, the governor of Puebla, who argues that "it must be the party that picks its candidate, rather than the public that elects a candidate for the party."[36] Arturo Nuñez, the PRI's leader in Congress, stated that the party's old strategy of picking of unity candidates "has worked splendidly" and warned of the divisive effects of primaries.[37] Open primaries thus emerged as a highly contentious issue within the PRI, dividing modernizers from traditionalists. In the end, the PRI decided that implementing democratic procedures for the selection of party candidates was clearly the right way to improve the PRI's electoral performance. After experimenting with open primaries in a dozen states, beginning with Chihuahua in 1998, the party's national assembly meeting in May, 1999, revamped the PRI's statutes to allow its next presidential candidate to be selected by means of an open primary.[38] The November primary pitted Francisco Labastida, the Interior Minister, widely considered the choice of Zedillo, against party conservatives Manuel Bartlett, Roberto

Madrazo, and Humberto de la Roque Villanueva.[39] Labastida won the primary by a huge margin, with the presidential favorite bagging 273 electoral districts and 55 percent of the vote. The turnout rate in the primary was 18 percent with four out of five voters identifying themselves as PRI supporters; only 5 percent supported opposition parties. While Labastida enjoyed a clear advantage over his rivals because of the logistical support that several PRI governors extended to him during the campaign, the process was basically a very open one marked by a fair candidate registration process, intense competition among the four candidates (initially five), and the right to vote being extended to all registered voters. The open primary in November thus represented a fundamental break with the *dedazo* tradition, despite the flaws in the process, and all of the losing candidates accepted the outcome.

The dynamics of the conflict between PRI reformers and conservatives were extremely complex. Part of the complexity stemmed from the ambivalent role of the presidency. Neither de la Madrid nor Salinas was a committed democratizer: Salinas gave priority to economic reform over political, while de la Madrid aborted his short-lived political opening in 1983 in deference to objections from the party's sectors. In general, conservatives seemed to be encrusted in the PRI's sectors, particularly the CTM and the CNC, as well as state party organizations, particularly in the more backward south, where the PRI was captured by local elites.

The conflict between conservatives and reformers under Salinas was relatively muted, partly because the Salinas reform project was more economic than political, and partly because the presidency was strong enough to override opposition from conservatives when it did choose to engage in political reform. Salinas was thus able to compel the state PRI in Baja California Norte to accept his decision to recognize the PAN victory in 1989, despite protests from local PRI leaders. In Chihuahua, the local PRI does not appear to have had a hand in the choice of Macias as its candidate for governor in 1992, and some speculated that Salinas picked a "loser" to solve the Chihuahua problem by handing the state over to the PAN. Nor was the conservative wing of the PRI able to prevent the extensive electoral reforms of 1994 once Salinas decided to improve the credibility of the electoral process, or to oblige Salinas to pick a successor to the slain Colosio more to their liking than

Zedillo. During his term, Salinas also intervened in several state elections in response to protests against fraud by the PAN and other groups, replacing elected PRI governors with interim ones from the PAN in Guanajuato and the PRI in San Luis Potosí. It is also worth pointing out that the interim governorship in San Luis Potosí was initially offered to Salvador Nava, the state's most important civic leader, who declined to accept. In the 1992 Michoacán elections, an interim PRI governor replaced the official winner, also from the PRI, after protests by the PRD, which claimed victory. This outcome was, however, more the result of a presidential decision that involved larger calculations about how to treat Cárdenas than an effect of pressure from state party leaders to keep the state in PRI hands.

Only toward the end of the Salinas *sexenio* and during the Zedillo administration did the clash between conservatives and reformers become more explicit. Some claim that the assassination of PRI candidate Colosio was the result of a conspiracy by PRI "dinosaurs" who were troubled by his reformist views.[40] Conservatives became more vocal in their opposition to reform under Zedillo, partly because the pace of political reform quickened as well. In Tabasco, state party leaders, taking a cue from the opposition, staged protests against Zedillo's call for new elections after mounting evidence that the governor, Roberto Madrazo, had been fraudulently elected in 1994. Zedillo backed off and Madrazo remained in power. In the 1996 national assembly, PRI delegates were able to force a change in the statutes, requiring the next PRI candidate for president to be a "militant, and party leader, and have held an elected position," disqualifying most of Zedillo's cabinet and making it possible for party old guard to contend for the nomination.[41] On the other hand, the president won most of his battles with party conservatives, who were unable to prevent the deepening of electoral reform in 1996, the election of Cárdenas as mayor of Mexico City, and open primaries in Chihuahua in 1998, then several other states, and finally at the national level to choose the party's 2000 presidential nominee.

THE DEMOCRATIZING IMPACT OF ECONOMIC REFORM

The shift towards real economic restructuring—rather than simple stabilization—near the end of the de la Madrid *sexenio* and the aggressive pursuit of an export-oriented model of development under Salinas undermined the PRI's traditional power bases. The 1992 decision to permit the dismantling of the Mexican *ejido* allowed peasants for the first time since the 1930s to buy and sell land, pledge their land as collateral for bank loans, and enter into contracts with foreign investors to modernize the agricultural sector.[42] But it also dealt a potentially lethal blow to the state's control structure in rural areas. Since the 1930s, the PRI had relied on the *ejido* to keep peasants on the land in subjection to the state. *Campesinos* who failed to support the system ran the risk of being expelled from the *ejido,* deprived of their land, denied bank loans from the official National Rural Credit Bank, or violently repressed. The National Peasants' Confederation (CNC) could be relied upon to mobilize rural votes on election day—it is no accident that the PRI racked up some of its largest majorities in the federal elections of 1991 in those districts of Chiapas that are today under the control of Sub-Commander Marcos's Emiliano Zapata National Liberation Army (EZLN). Salinas, the modernizer, fared poorly in urban areas in the disputed 1988 elections, obtaining his margin of victory from the impoverished countryside; only during the 1990s did opposition parties, particularly the PRD, begin to make real inroads in the PRI's rural vote bank. The main motivation for permitting the disbanding of the *ejido* was economic—the Salinas administration decided that this was the best way to boost rural productivity and open the agricultural sector to external investment. But the phasing out of the *ejido* will lead to the decay of the official party structure in rural Mexico just as de-collectivization has undermined the power of the Chinese communist party in rural areas.[43] This need not translate into a loss of voter support for the PRI if *campesinos* successfully turn themselves into modern capitalist farmers, prosper under the new market regime, and hence vote PRI; this prospect is unlikely to materialize, however, particularly as cheaper corn imports become liberalized over the next fifteen years as a consequence of the North American Free Trade Agreement (NAFTA).

Real wage rates in Mexico during the 1980s fell by more than 50 percent, the sharpest decline in all of Latin America. Analysts have attributed the regime's ability to manage this calamitous drop in purchasing power successfully, without major violence, to Mexico's corporatist system of labor control, rooted in the Mexican

Workers' Confederation (CTM) and other organizations.[44] On the other hand, official unions were unable to prevent their members from voting for opposition parties in growing numbers. In the presidential elections of 1988, important official labor union leaders were defeated, and the PAN made gains among the working classes throughout the 1980s and 1990s. The fact that the regime was unable to maintain political control over labor while managing to enforce painful cuts in real wages reflected two new realities: First, official labor leaders, recognizing that the maintenance of political control over labor was no longer viable in urban areas, concentrated increasingly on wage management as their primary task. Mechanisms such as the refusal to register an opposition union, the exclusion of troublesome workers from the union, the co-optation of labor bosses, and the declaring of strikes as illegal by the authorities were now employed to achieve economic ends, not political ones. Second, the balance of power shifted away from organized labor in the 1980s as a result of high rates of unemployment, the opening of the economy to international competition, and persistent pressure from the unorganized sector, thus making it difficult for organized labor to press their demands successfully.

The combination of a crisis-driven resource crunch coupled with an ideological preference for privatization led to the sale of state-owned enterprises under de la Madrid and Salinas, reversing the trend towards state ownership in the 1970s. Privatization shifted economic resources—and power—away from the state to domestic and foreign investors. The sale of state-owned enterprises also eliminated the regime's control over the employees of these institutions and prevented the regime from penalizing private businesses that might support the opposition by canceling purchasing contracts or refusing to supply critical inputs. The need for the regime to obtain legitimacy for its privatization initiatives enhanced the bargaining power of the PAN, which supported the regime in exchange for concessions on electoral reform and the recognition of opposition party victories.

The decision of the Salinas administration to seek greater economic integration with the United States through NAFTA as a solution to the fundamental problems of the Mexican economy heightened the regime's vulnerability to international pressures for democratization.[45] The Mexican government chose to open up its economy to the world at exactly the same time as international pressures for democratization were growing because of a global trend towards democratization and the promotion of democracy was emerging as the central theme of post–Cold War U.S. foreign policy. These changes have resulted in the internationalization of Mexican politics. Economic interdependence increased the payoffs to domestic opposition groups for mobilizing international actors to exert external pressure for democratization. Consequently, the U.S. Congress, the media, and international non-governmental actors began to pay greater attention to Mexican issues generally; cross-border coalitions on issues such as human rights, labor laws, and environmental regulation were also facilitated, strengthening such groups within Mexico. Economic integration implied a loss of sovereign control over economic policy with respect to Mexico's trading partners, international investors, and market forces, thereby further constraining the state.

SOCIAL PROGRAMS: AN OBSTACLE
TO DEMOCRATIZATION?

The Salinas administration fed vast amounts of money into social programs for Mexico's rural and urban poor, particularly through the National Solidarity Program (PRONASOL) and Programa del Campo (PROCAMPO), a program designed to subsidize farmers' production. Between 1988 and 1993, approximately $11 billion were spent on social programs, partly funded from the proceeds received from the sale of state-owned enterprises to furnish a social safety net at a time of unprecedented economic restructuring. One of the most innovative aspects of PRONASOL was its decentralized administrative structure. Solidarity committees were set up at the local level to involve local community leaders in the design and implementation of social programs. PRONASOL had profound political consequences. It created a new territorial organization directly controlled by the president that completely bypassed the PRI's sectoral structure, thereby giving Salinas an alternative mechanism to mobilize grassroots support that could have potentially replaced the official party. Since recipients of PRONASOL funds were not required to be members of the PRI, the program allowed the president to carve out a new relationship with independent social movements around the country that blunted their radicalism in exchange for enhancing their efficacy. Finally, there is evidence that PRONASOL funding may have been used to improve the electoral performance of the PRI. Regression analysis reveals that regions that voted in favor of the PRD in the 1988 presidential elections were more likely to receive PRONASOL funds.[46] Curiously, states where the PAN had done well in 1988 were likely to receive less PRONASOL funding during state elections.[47] This may reflect the fact that the PAN has done better in the more advanced regions of the country, particularly the north, that were less susceptible to being influenced by pork-barrel politics, thereby discouraging the regime from investing more PRONASOL money. PRONASOL made its relationship with the PRI explicit by using party symbols and signs. The pro-regime bias of PRONASOL was highlighted by the fact that states that received less PRONASOL funding were more likely to support the PAN in gubernatorial elections held in 1991.[48] In addition, PRONASOL funding increased when state and local elections were in progress in different regions, and then dropped off after the elections. PRONASOL spending was probably at least one factor in the significant recuperation experienced by the PRI in the 1991 congressional elections, when the party won 61 percent of the vote, an eleven-point improvement over its performance in 1988.

Opposition parties were deeply concerned that the money used for government social programs would to used to buy votes for the official party in the 1994 presidential elections, especially in rural Mexico. The PAN claimed that the government was planning to spend roughly $4 billion in the two months preceding the elections through PRONASOL and PROCAMPO. The government, responding that it could not halt investment in public programs merely because of the elections, also argued that the mere fact that it was channeling funds into poverty-stricken areas was a sign of its democratic responsiveness and that all democratic governments used social programs to garner public support. Government supporters claimed that just because a citizen happened to benefit from a public program did not automatically oblige her or him to vote for the official party as long as the secrecy of the ballot was not violated. This sidestepped the difficulty of maintaining ballot secrecy in remote rural areas where intimidation is a fact of life and where, until recently, opposition parties found it difficult to post a representative to monitor voting.

PRONASOL probably had negative effects on democratization but positive effects on the alleviation of poverty in Mexico's rural zones. It enhanced the personal power of the president, strengthened the PRI's electoral prospects, and placed opposition parties at a competitive disadvantage with the official party. Further, no serious attempt was made to turn the program into the nucleus of a democratic alternative to the PRI or even to use it as a bargaining chip to force PRI leaders to accept party reform.

CONCLUSION

The Mexican regime changed significantly between 1988 and 1999. Opposition parties were allowed to win a greater share of power, particularly at the local and state levels. Electoral reforms greatly reduced the danger of fraud in federal elections. The most serious efforts to democratize the selection of ruling party candidates was made in Chihuahua, where an open primary produced a PRI candidate capable of taking the state back from the PAN. The example of a successful and democratic PRI in Chihuahua clearly inspired national party leaders, particularly Zedillo, who became the first president in Mexican history to apply the Chihuahua model of open primaries to the selection of the party's presidential nominee for 2000, effectively doing away with the old *dedazo* system. Economic reform undermined the corporatist foundations of the ruling party, transferred power from the state to society, and led to the growth of transnational linkages that also facilitated democratization. By 1999, the Mexican regime was thus far more democratic than it had been in 1982, setting the stage for a transfer of power to an opposition party in 2000.

7

Conclusion

This book's argument about democratiza-
tion in Chihuahua and Mexico as a whole focuses on the role of
institutional change. The 1980s and 1990s were marked by what I
have characterized as the political awakening of society. This awakening was marked by growing electoral competitiveness, more opposition political party victories, protests against election fraud and
a generalized demand for democracy, higher rates of electoral participation, rapidly shifting voter preferences and growing independence
from party machines, and a surge in membership for opposition
parties and civic associations. The political awakening of society
encouraged social leaders to challenge the one-party state more
aggressively. Social leaders saw the growth of popular discontent
with the regime as an opportunity to press for democracy because
it gave them a larger reservoir of support on which to draw in their
contest with the one-party state.

Social leaders had sought to democratize the system long before the civic upsurge of the 1980s and 1990s. In the case of the National Action Party (PAN), party leaders since the 1940s had tried to
test the limits of opposition within the one-party state and contributed meaningfully to an expansion of political space as a result. The
same was true of clergy, who sought to deepen the role of the Church
without undermining the *modus vivendi* of the postrevolutionary
period. Social leaders fought serious institutional battles to make
their organizations more saleable to society: PAN leaders, for example,

spent almost the entire 1970s feuding over whether the party should give priority to electoral participation or to raising civic consciousness. Social leaders served as transmitters of new ideas to their institutions; doctrinal change in the Catholic Church, for example, encouraged the Church to be open to a greater temporal mission in society. In the case of businessmen, social leaders became politicized partly because of the nationalization of the banking system in 1982 and partly because of the effects of the economic crisis. Finally, social leaders harnessed the civic upsurge of the 1980s and 1990s for the growth of their own organizations and used their new-found strength to pressure the state for concrete political reforms ranging from the recognition of the Church as a legal entity in 1992 to major electoral reforms in 1993, 1994, and 1996.

The combination of "crafting" by social leaders and the groundswell of popular support beginning in the 1980s resulted in a major transformation of institutions in ways that were highly conducive to democratization.[1] Opposition parties became stronger, as did the Church; civic associations proliferated; and the Institutional Revolutionary Party (PRI) came under great pressure to adopt democratizing reforms. The growth of opposition parties contributed to decentralization of the state and municipal levels, and to the emergence of a system of checks and balances at the federal and state levels. The growth of institutional pluralism was one of the most important features of Mexican democratization in the 1980s and 1990s.

WHY THE POLITICAL AWAKENING OF SOCIETY?

Political Space

One precondition for the political awakening of society in Chihuahua and Mexico was the availability of political space. The Mexican regime provided a significant level of political space for groups outside the regime to operate. Three factors were important in explaining the availability of political space in Mexico: First, as a way of garnering democratic legitimacy, the regime itself found it convenient to allow opposition groups to exist, elections to occur, and the press to function. The search for legitimacy in a one-party dominant regime led to significant electoral reforms in 1963, 1973, and 1977 that broadened opposition participation in the political system. Second, both PAN and Church leaders throughout the 1940–80 period sought to wrest political space from the regime. The Church took full advantage of the *modus vivendi* to expand its social influence, although it avoided serious conflicts with the state in order to keep Church-State relations on an even keel, and to encourage the reform of the anticlerical provisions of the 1917 constitution. The PAN for its part gradually sought to build up a presence, beginning with the election of three PAN deputies to the national legislature in 1946 followed by attempts to build up the party's standing in Mexico's municipalities and states in the 1950s and 1960s. The PAN also pressured the regime to introduce the party deputy system in 1963, thereby augmenting its seats in the Chamber of Deputies. More difficult to quantify is the party's role in forcing debate on important public policy issues, influencing public opinion, and instilling democratic values. Finally, the growth of industry after 1940 created a large middle class and business community, which over time reduced the power of the state. Echeverría's deteriorating relationship with the business community, for example, was met by growing capital flight, which helped provoke the devaluation of 1976. López Portillo's attempt to stem the onset of the economic crisis of the 1980s by nationalization of the banking system also generated rampant capital flight and the abandonment of his strategy to defend the *peso*.

Social and Economic Development

Rapid social and economic development between 1940 and 1980 resulted in the emergence of an increasingly urban, literate, and middle-class society with a high level of social complexity and pluralism that was not easily compatible with one-party dominance.

The creation of a large business community, as we have seen, led to a decline in the policy-making autonomy of the Mexican state.[2] The growth of the middle classes and business community gave opposition parties and civic associations a new reservoir on which to draw leadership skills and financial support. The middle classes also possessed a stronger sense of political efficacy, a greater capacity to make demands on the state, and higher standards for ethical behavior in government. As Riding points out, the emergence of corruption in the 1970s as a major issue reflected changing norms about what was permissible in the eyes of middle-class Mexicans, who "began to identify corruption as a principal cause of bad government."[3]

Unlike labor and the peasantry, the middle classes were not well integrated into the corporatist structure of the PRI. This was even more true of the middle classes in Chihuahua: the small presence of state-owned enterprises, the dependence of the economy on exports, and the growing importance of the *maquiladora* industry meant that Chihuahua's middle classes were less tied to the regime than in central Mexico. Middle-class support for the PRI thus had a soft underbelly: as long as economic times were good, the middle classes supported the system; when the economy sputtered, as it did in the 1980s, the system lacked the power to keep the middle classes loyal.

The Economic Crisis of the 1980s

The economic crisis of the 1980s mobilized a society that already possessed a variety of prerequisites for democracy, including a reasonable level of wealth, education, and urbanization, as well as a large and diverse middle class and business community.[4] In addition, the crisis occurred in a political environment where at least some space existed in which to protest the effects on society. These initial conditions explain in turn why the crisis contributed to a political awakening of society rather than some other outcome. One of the first effects of the crisis was to detach the middle classes from the PRI; the middle classes emerged as the backbone of the Catholic Church's attempts to promote democracy as well as strong supporters of opposition political parties and many civic associations. The crisis also undermined the relationship between the state and labor unions, as was demonstrated in the 1988 elections, when important labor leaders were defeated in their constituencies. And opposition parties, especially the Democratic Revolutionary Party (PRD), began to make significant inroads into the PRI's rural base in the late 1980s and 1990s.

The impact of the crisis was at first most severe in Chihuahua and other northern border states. Devaluation undermined the capacity of northerners to purchase U.S. goods, dramatically reduced exports, and produced glaring contrasts between life on the Mexican side of the border and on the U.S. side. Not surprisingly, anger at the regime fed on deep-rooted resentment of the central government, which most Chihuahuans blamed for the crisis. As Williams notes, the crisis in the north also coincided with several incidents of racial bias against immigrants from central and southern Mexico.[5]

One of the most salient features of the political awakening of society produced by the crisis was its electoral dimension. Mexico, as Joseph Klesner points out, offers an example of an electoral path to democratization.[6] As we have seen, the regime allowed elections to take place regularly, even if they served as rituals to ratify official candidates. The fact that such an electoral channel existed at all made it possible for individual citizens to voice their anger with the regime's economic policies through the ballot box. The regime encouraged citizens to do so by recognizing local level PAN victories in Chihuahua and elsewhere in 1983; the subsequent decision to close off the electoral channel by resorting to fraud in the latter half of the de la Madrid *sexenio* sparked a widespread demand for democracy.

INSTITUTIONAL CHANGE:
CHIHUAHUA AND THE NATIONAL LEVEL

The political awakening of society was first most apparent in the Mexican north, particularly in Chihuahua, where it took three main forms: (1) an electoral rebellion against the PRI marked by the PAN's sweep in the 1983 municipal elections (when the party won control over 70% of the state's population), massive protests against election fraud in the 1986 state elections, and a PAN victory in the governor's race in 1992; (2) the influx of new members into the PAN and civic associations; and (3) the development of a two-party system in the state characterized by stiff competition between the PRI and the PAN, with the PRI winning some important triumphs, including several federal deputy seats in 1989, 1994, and 1997, major municipalities like Chihuahua City in 1995, and finally the governorship in 1998.

Social leaders, especially clergy and businessmen, also played

a major role in the movement for democracy in Chihuahua, funding the PAN and running as its candidates, denouncing fraud, forming civic associations to promote democracy, and feeding reform
politics within the PRI. The political awakening of society and the
actions of social leaders in Chihuahua in the 1980s and 1990s transformed the state's institutional map: The PAN emerged as a real
counterweight to the PRI; the Church became a strong supporter of
democracy, enhancing its institutional prestige; civic associations
emerged to promote clean elections; and the PRI was successfully
democratized.

Regional-level institutional change in Chihuahua had a major
impact on Mexican politics as a whole. All the major institutions
active in Chihuahua—the PAN, the PRI, and the Catholic Church—
were national in scope. The state-level institutional transformations
initiated by the political awakening of society in Chihuahua and its
social leaders traveled upwards to the national layers of these same
organizations and laterally to their branches in other states. This
process was made easier by the fact that Chihuahua has always
been considered one of Mexico's most important states because of
its economic and historical significance, geographical size, and location on the U.S. border.

While the impact of politics in Chihuahua on the national level
in the 1980s and 1990s was considerable, it must be stressed that
the process was also reciprocal. The regime, by engaging in fraud,
deepened the movement for democracy in Chihuahua and its national significance. In the period before 1980, the efforts of national
PAN and Church leaders to expand political space enhanced the
prospects for a political awakening generally, including Chihuahua.
Doctrinal change in the Church globally made the Church in Chihuahua more open to the aspirations of society. Strategic and ideological shifts in the national PAN in the 1970s also made it easier for the
party in Chihuahua to emerge as society's main vehicle for mobilization against the regime. Thus the political awakening of society
in Chihuahua was itself the result of factors that were operating
nationally as well.

For much of its history, the PAN had been oriented fundamentally towards the promotion of civic consciousness rather than
towards winning political power. This reflected the weakness of the
party in a context in which popular support was lacking to chal-

lenge one-party dominance. At this stage, the actions of PAN leaders were crucial in preserving and strengthening the party as an
institution under adverse conditions. PAN leaders devoted much of
the period to expanding political space by wresting concessions from
the regime. The party succeeded in winning a number of municipalities, gaining a presence in the Chamber of Deputies, sparking
debate over government policies, and nudging the regime to adopt
electoral reforms in 1964 and 1973. During the 1970s party leaders
engaged in a wrenching debate about the future direction of the
party: the resulting strategic redefinition produced a party far more
oriented towards winning power through elections than before, and
more sensitive to the concerns of the business community.

The transformation of the national PAN in turn made it possible for the party to become a channel for societal discontent with
the regime in Chihuahua and elsewhere, beginning in the early
1980s. The combination of growing mass support for the PAN in
Chihuahua coupled with political entrepreneurship by state party
leaders, enabled the Chihuahua PAN to create a new party capable
of winning power, putting into practice what had already occurred
in theory at the level of the national PAN. PAN leaders in Chihuahua created a party that went beyond its traditional middle-class
base to embrace the urban and rural poor; campaigns were geared
towards winning rather than educating; new strategies were put
into place to "defend the vote," including improved party organization, civil disobedience, and appeals to international public opinion; and the party's preoccupation with doctrinal purity gave way
to a more pragmatic approach as it found itself in a governing position in the state.

The changes in the PAN in Chihuahua had a profound impact
on the PAN nationally. First, the model was associated with success: the party had swept municipal elections in 1983, performed
well in federal deputy elections in 1985, and would probably have
won the governorship in 1986 had those elections been clean. This
was therefore a model worth copying. The fact that the model had
developed in Chihuahua, an important state where the PAN has
deep roots, may have added to its appeal to the party as a whole.
Second, rising voter disenchantment with the regime nationally
seemed to indicate that the conditions that existed in Chihuahua to
build a more victory-conscious party were prevalent at the national

level as well. Although the FDN (National Democratic Front) was the main opposition party to benefit from the 1988 presidential elections, the dramatic increase in support for both opposition parties indicated that the political awakening of society was not simply a regional phenomenon, limited to the north, but a national one as well. Third, the protests against fraud in the 1986 state elections, including Alvarez's hunger strike, had attracted national attention and sympathy from PAN rank and file. Combined with the high level of internal democracy within the PAN, the protests made it possible for Alvarez to win the PAN national presidency in 1987, thus unleashing a transformation of the party nationally along the lines of the party in Chihuahua. Under Alvarez and his successor, Carlos Castillo, the party focused on introducing sweeping organizational and other changes to place the party in a position to win offices at all levels, including the presidency. One important change was the opening of a dialogue with the regime in the wake of the 1988 elections. This policy led to positive results in the areas of electoral reform and the recognition of PAN victories. By engaging in a constructive dialogue with the regime, PAN leaders played a vital role in converting the opposition's new electoral strength into democratic reforms.

The respite from Church-State conflict after 1940 provided by the *modus vivendi* led to a dramatic recovery of the Catholic Church as a religious and social actor, which translated into a *de facto* expansion of political space. Church leaders fearful of provoking renewed conflict with the State sought to avoid politicizing the Church's deepening role in society. As a result, the Church remained largely aloof from politics during the 1940–80 period. The decision of Chihuahua's bishops and clergy to become involved in protesting election fraud marked a watershed in the history of Church-State relations after 1940. The involvement of Chihuahua's bishops and clergy in electoral questions was partly due to exogenous factors, such as the process of doctrinal renewal within the global Church, which had a strong effect on the state's bishops, and partly as a response to social pressure from below. In Chihuahua, the Church emerged from its defense of fair elections a much stronger institution. After a series of humiliating defeats in the 1970s when the bishops' call for social justice had alienated many priests, and frightened the state's middle classes, the bishops' defense of democracy now received almost unanimous support from their presbyteries, the lay middle classes, and society as a whole. The lesson was clear: middle-class support was a vital ingredient in the success of Church initiatives, particularly in a more developed state like Chihuahua. The Church's new rapport with society in Chihuahua in the 1980s in turn strengthened its institutional credibility and prestige, and its capacity to check the power of the regime.

The Chihuahua Church's support of democracy had profound effects on the Mexican Church. Mexican Church leaders rallied in support of Chihuahua's bishops both individually and collectively. Why did the Chihuahua Church's defense of clean elections have so much national resonance? First, Chihuahua's bishops, by defending electoral democracy, in effect carved out a temporal role for the Church not linked to liberation theology; this in turn helps explain why they received overwhelming support from the relatively conservative Mexican hierarchy. Second, the fact that bishops around the country were subject to similar societal pressures for fair elections made them more sympathetic to Chihuahua's bishops. Third, the dramatic outcry over fraud in the 1986 Chihuahua elections made it difficult for the hierarchy to remain silent in the face of such a serious abuse of power. Finally, Church leaders may have been perturbed by the apostolic delegate's resort to the Vatican to compel Almeida to abandon his plan to protest fraud by suspending Mass, and chose to signal their independence by supporting him. The Chihuahua Church's defense of clean elections sparked the mobilization of a new majoritarian coalition of Mexican bishops seeking greater democracy.

The growing politicization of the Church's hierarchy frightened the regime. At first, the government reacted by passing draconian electoral legislation in 1987 that stiffened the penalties for priests seen to be interfering in politics, further alienating the hierarchy. The following year, with the election of Salinas, the government chose a softer approach, reaching out to the Church by inviting several bishops to attend his inauguration. This was followed by talks to consider normalizing Church-State relations. The government undoubtedly hoped to defuse the politicization of the hierarchy and strengthen the political system that had been badly shaken by the cloud surrounding Salinas's election. The establishment of diplomatic relations in 1991 and the reform of the anticlerical constitutional articles in 1992 did little, however, to arrest the growing involvement of the Church in overtly political questions from social justice in Chiapas to condemning links between drug traffickers and the army. Chihuahua thus set the Mexican Church on a new course of political involvement that in turn furnished a powerful, if twisted, incentive for the state to proceed with the normalization of national Church-State relations. There was little doubt that by the end of the 1990s the Church was significantly more powerful relative to the State than at any time in the post-1940 period, although this "power" had to be balanced against the growing independence of the laity in a period of rapid secularization.

The 1980s and 1990s in Chihuahua were also characterized by a significant expansion in the role of civic associations. The growth of civic associations was propelled by political entrepreneurs from above and by the influx of new members from below. Civic associations, such as the Integral Human Development and Citizen Action Organization (DHIAC), the National Civic Feminine Association (ANCIFEM), the Civic Fronts of Ciudad Juárez and Parral, and the Mexican Employers' Confederation (COPARMEX) provided an alternative channel of participation to political parties, compensated for the initial organizational weakness of the PAN in many parts of the state, and nourished leadership skills tapped by the PAN. Civic associations, such as the Movement for Electoral Democracy (MDE), that functioned like umbrella groups for different political tendencies enhanced the credibility of opposition party claims of fraud, organized to defend society's right to free elections, and made it possible for the electorally weak left to influence politics in the state. While most of the urban civic groups were middle class in orientation, the state also witnessed the rise of an important peasant movement, the Democratic Peasant Movement (MDC), which developed links to the wider struggle for democracy in Chihuahua to increase the relevance of the MDC and its success. The MDC's leadership went on to create the Democratic Electoral Movement (MDE), but many *campesinos* stayed away from the MDE for fear of retaliation by the government. As a *campesino* organization, the MDC was successful at extracting two increases in the "guaranteed" grain price from the state administration.

The fact that some of Chihuahua's civic organizations, like COPARMEX, DHIAC, and ANCIFEM, were active nationally meant that their branches in Chihuahua had access to a national network of ties, information, and support. Groups like COPARMEX had also made their contribution to the expansion of political space before 1980 by fostering the voluntary organization of business. The fact that such national civic organizations existed meant that, in most cases, there were regional institutional structures available to harness the benefits of the political awakening of society and to furnish arenas for leadership. Unlike the PAN and the Church, however, Chihuahua's civic associations had less of an impact on the national stage. They played a less visible part in Chihuahuan politics than the PAN and Church, with whom they developed close relations tinged by rivalry. This may explain why they had less effect on their own national organizations, where these existed, or in national politics more generally. On the other hand, fraud in Chihuahua—and the role of the state's civic associations in publicizing it—generated a national outcry for clean elections, thus indirectly contributing to the growth of election-monitoring organizations, like the Civic Alliance, at the national level. Some Chihuahua associations, like the MDC, also furnished particular examples of tactical success that could successfully be applied to other regions.

The evolution of the PRI is one of the great success stories of Chihuahua. Initially, in the early 1980s, the PRI in Chihuahua was not very different from the PRI nationally. It was marked by a strong symbiosis with the state, dependence on its traditional sectors for mobilizing votes, particularly the National Peasants' Confederation (CNC) and the Mexican Workers' Confederation (CTM), the designation of candidates for party and public office by highly undemocratic means, and a reputation for using fraud to "win" elections. Today, the PRI in Chihuahua is as internally democratic as the PAN. Indeed, the PRI's victory in the 1998 gubernatorial elections was largely the product of an unprecedented opening of the party's procedures to select its candidate for governor by an open primary in which all registered voters could participate. The result was the selection of a candidate who had far more in common with the outgoing PAN governor, Francisco Barrio, than with his own party. Patricio Martínez, a former real estate salesman and mayor of Chihuahua City, when he developed a close relationship with Barrio, easily defeated two candidates linked to the old party machine. This probably could not have occurred without an open primary.

The shift in the PRI's strategy occurred in stages. The protests against fraud in 1986 raised the cost of stealing elections, while electoral reforms made it more difficult for PRI candidates who were designated from above to win fairly: If the PRI wanted to win, it had to democratize the selection of its candidates. In 1989, a limited experiment, whereby PRI candidates for Chihuahua's major cities were chosen by a complex delegate system with significant representation for the territorial wing of the PRI, resulted in the PRI winning in several municipalities, including Chihuahua City. The 1989 experiment had the support of both Chihuahua's governor, Baeza, and Salinas, who persuaded the CTM's then leader, Fidel Velázquez, to go along with the plan. The experiment was abandoned in 1992 when the PRI's candidate for governor, Chuy Macias, a gray figure suspected of links to drug traffickers, was handpicked by Salinas. The result was a clear victory for the PAN, fielding Barrio for the second time. If the PRI opted for an open primary in 1998, it was because PRI leaders concluded that the only way they could win was to choose a candidate that was popular in Chihuahua. The intensely competitive nature of Chihuahua politics, with the PRI winning control of the state legislature in 1995, showed that the party could take back the governorship with a good candidate. Zedillo seems to have favored an open primary as a way to recapture power in the last election in an opposition-ruled state before 2000, sideline other candidates identified with the traditional party apparatus, and set the stage for a more a democratic procedure to select the PRI's next presidential candidate.

The national implications of the PRI's transformation in Chihuahua are profoundly significant. The party's transformation in Chihuahua showed that the PRI could be democratized, despite its past as an electoral instrument of state elites, and that a democratic PRI may be more competitive than an undemocratic one. When the PRI in Chihuahua chose candidates by democratic means in 1989 and 1998, the party prospered; when the party resorted to authoritarian methods of candidate designation, as in 1992, it was defeated. The Chihuahua PRI's transformation also provided evidence that the PRI could democratize candidate selection without provoking serious factional conflict in the process; on the contrary, democratic selection procedures, by conferring legitimacy on party nominees, encouraged losers to accept their defeats. With elections growing more competitive nationally, electoral reforms making fraud difficult, and opposition parties ruling several states and major cities, such as Mexico City and Monterrey, the conditions that drove the Chihuahua PRI to democratize candidate selection became present nationally, making it easier for the Chihuahua model of a self-confident, democratic, and successful PRI to be transmitted to the PRI as a whole. This is precisely what happened: In the wake of the success of the Chihuahua gubernatorial primary in 1998, the model of open primaries was adopted in several other states as well, and then extended to the process of selecting the PRI's presidential nominee for the 2000 elections in November, 1999, after the reform of the party's statutes earlier that year. The movement for democracy in Chihuahua thus had a powerful and important effect on three critical national institutions: the PAN, the Church, and the PRI and furnishes a vital example of how regional politics can in turn influence national-level politics.

INSTITUTIONAL CHANGE: THE CASE OF THE DEMOCRATIC REVOLUTIONARY PARTY (PRD)

This book has focused primarily on institutions that were affected by regional politics in Chihuahua. It has not concentrated much on Mexico's left-of-center opposition party, the Democratic Revolutionary Party (PRD). This is not to deny that the PRD, like the PAN, Catholic Church, and civic associations, has played an important role in Mexican democratization.[7] The theoretical framework of institutional change that I developed in this book also applies to the PRD. This book argues that the growth of stronger institutions to counterbalance state power was the result of two factors: the political awakening of society and the role of leadership. In the case of the PRD, both these elements played an important role in the growth of the party.

Frustrated PRI dissident elites led by Cuauhtémoc Cárdenas abandoned the official party in 1987 after the nomination of Salinas as the PRI's official candidate for president; they objected to the impending continuation of de la Madrid's "neo-liberal" policies by Salinas, the lack of a democratic process to select PRI presidential candidates, and the betrayal of the promises of the Mexican revolution by the new technocratic elite. Cárdenas also saw a new opportunity in the growing societal alienation from the regime to mount the first serious challenge to the regime in decades.[8] Initially, Cárdenas's main allies came from three parastatal parties allied with the regime—the Authentic Party of the Mexican Revolution (PARM), the Popular Socialist Party (PPS), and the Cardenista Front for National Reconstruction (PFCRN), previously known as the Socialist Workers Party (PST); these parties supported him in hopes of raising their own low voter support and of doing a deal with the regime after the election. Formally, Cárdenas ran as the PFCRN candidate. As the campaign heated up, with Cárdenas drawing unprecedented popular support, the *cardenista* coalition, the National Democratic Front (FDN), expanded to include the independent Mexican Socialist Party (PMS) with its presidential candidate, Herberto Castillo, standing down in favor of Cárdenas.

The PMS was the product of several changes in the independent left going back to the 1970s.[9] In 1977, the Mexican Communist Party and several other leftist parties were legalized and began participating in elections for the first time since the 1930s. Like PAN elites, the left engaged in intense internal debates in the 1970s that resulted in a new emphasis both on the importance of elections as a path to political power and on the intrinsic value of democracy.[10] As if to signal their commitment to elections, the communists, along with several left groups, reorganized as the Unified Socialist Party of Mexico (PSUM) in 1981. The PMS, founded to unify the independent left in 1987, was largely the product of a merger between the PSUM and the Mexican Workers Party (PMT).

The phenomenal success of the FDN at the polls in the 1988 elections (see chapter 2) surprised virtually all political analysts. The 1988 presidential elections showed that the political awakening of society was no longer limited to northern Mexico but had become truly national in scope. According to Domínguez and McCann, voters engaged in a "two-step" process before deciding for which party to cast their ballots.[11] In the first step, voters decided whether to vote for the opposition on the basis of two factors: (a) their perception of the opposition's capacity to beat the PRI and (b) whether the economy and social peace would suffer if an opposition candidate were elected. Opposition voters were those who felt that the PRI was becoming weaker and that social harmony and the economy would not be hurt in the event of a party other than the PRI coming to power. In the second step, opposition voters chose between the PAN and the PRD on the basis of factors such as class, level of religiosity, union membership, and economic policy preferences. A large number of opposition voters also engaged in strategic voting by supporting the opposition party most likely to defeat the PRI, whether or not they disagreed with its policy stances on particular issues.

As a result of the growth of opposition voter support in 1988, the FDN emerged as the strongest opposition party, even though the PAN also improved its performance. In the wake of the FDN success, the parastatal parties fell away and returned to their traditional stance of favoring the PRI, while Cárdenas floated the idea of forming a new left-of-center political party to capitalize on his showing in the 1988 elections. The formation of the PRD in 1989 consolidated both the traditional left and the former PRI-left into one umbrella. The Salinas *sexenio* was a difficult one for the PRD, marked by growing repression of the PRD leaders, election fraud against the party in Michoacán and elsewhere, and vilification of the party in the official media. During this time, PRD leaders were able to create reasonably democratic procedures to select candidates for party and public office, extended the party's presence to several states and municipalities around the country, and successfully prevented factional conflicts from undermining the consolidation of the party in a repressive context.

On the whole, the PRD leadership, unlike the PAN, avoided dialogue with the Salinas regime.[12] This was understandable given the embittered personal relationship between Salinas and Cárdenas, and Cárdenas's fear that he might lose credibility if he negotiated with Salinas. But the decision not to dialogue had costs: It produced divisions within the PRD with a few major leaders, like Porfirio Muñoz Ledo, favoring a softer approach; gave the party a reputation for intransigence and confrontation that played straight into the hands of the government's propaganda machine; and meant that the PAN was forced to go it alone in negotiations over electoral reforms, although the PRD remained important to the process insofar as the party could undermine the credibility of any reform package by refusing to vote for it. The 1989 / 90 reforms negotiated principally between the PAN and the PRI were bitterly attacked by the PRD as the result of collusion. The PRD also refused to support the 1993 reforms, which the party felt did not do enough to assure an independent election commission, a level playing field between the PRI and the opposition, and an accurate voter registration list. The 1994 reforms, which only partly addressed these concerns, were supported by a part of the PRD's parliamentary delegation, giving them broader legitimacy. The division of the PRD over the 1994 reforms reveals two different impulses that guided party decision making: On the one hand, the PRD wanted to keep its image of independence as well as the option of denouncing the 1994 elections as fraudulent by not supporting the reforms; on the other hand, voting for the reforms provided an incentive for the PRI, which wanted to assure a credible victory for Zedillo, to allow the reforms in the first place and improved the PRD's image as a responsible party.

Internal divisions, the fraying of popular support due to repression, haphazard organization, and the party's reputation for confrontation cost the PRD heavily. In the 1991 federal elections, the PRD's share of the vote dropped to just 9 percent. In 1994, the PRD's share of the vote recovered to 17 percent, but strategic voting by left wing voters, who had supported Cárdenas in 1988, favored the PAN, which won 26 percent of the vote, the party's best showing in a presidential race ever. The PRD also seems to have been hurt in the 1994 elections by Cárdenas's poor performance in the presidential debate and the damage to the party's image after Cárdenas held a highly publicized meeting with the Zapatista National Liberation Army Sub-Commander Marcos in the Chiapas jungle. Conversely, the PRI may have gained from a wave of sympathy and voter fears of instability after the assassination of its presidential candidate, Luís Donaldo Colosio, on March 28, 1993, in Tijuana.

In the wake of the 1994 debacle, PRD leaders, including Cárdenas, pursued a new course of dialogue with the regime. The removal of Salinas as a factor in Mexican politics, the failure of confrontation to produce concrete gains for the PRD, and the institutional weakness of Zedillo, who had come to power as a stand-in candidate and now needed social legitimacy to apply the harsh adjustment measures that followed the devaluation of the *peso* in December, 1994, created favorable conditions for a dialogue between the PRI and PRD. At first the dialogue seemed to come unstuck over the failure of the regime to comply with its commitment to remove the fraudulently elected PRI governor of the state of Tabasco.[13] But continued efforts involving all three parties eventually led to the adoption of far-reaching electoral reforms in 1996. This, along with the Zedillo government's policy of routinely recognizing opposition victories by the PAN and the PRD, produced a measure of normalcy in Mexican electoral politics that was truly exceptional. The new electoral context created by the reforms and popular discontent with the regime fueled by the latest economic crisis led to the loss of the PRI's majority in the Chamber of Deputies, Cárdenas's victory in the race for mayor of Mexico City, and the fall of two important states to the PAN.

The emergence of the PRD was the product of the interplay of leadership and the political awakening of society. Leadership choices produced the FDN, which furnished society with a credible instrument to challenge one-party hegemony in 1988 for the first time in decades. But the perception that society was ripe for such a challenge was one reason why Cárdenas and his supporters abandoned the PRI in the first place. In the barren years of the Salinas *sexenio*, leadership was particularly important in sustaining the newly created party under very harsh conditions. One criticism of the PRD is that it has been overly identified with the personality of its main founder, Cárdenas, stunting its institutional development. This line of reasoning, however, misses the advantages of such a central figure to give the PRD coherence, stability, and electoral visibility in its infancy. Nor was the PRD unique in this regard: the PAN depended much on its founders in its early years. This is not to say that the PRD's leadership was uniformly wise: clearly, confrontation with the regime cost the party and contributed to its poor showing in 1991 and 1994. On the other hand, the decision of the PRD leadership to dialogue with the regime over electoral reform and take advantage of the government's perception that the social effects of the latest crisis could only be peacefully contained by "institutional" solutions led to the breakthrough reforms of 1996. The success of the PRD in the mayoral elections in Mexico City was the result of the expansion of political space that resulted from the new electoral reforms, the high level of politicization characterizing Mexico City voters, and diminishing support for the PRI due to the corrosive effects of the crisis and measures taken to stabilize the economy.

THE CONSEQUENCES FOR DEMOCRACY

The growing strength of opposition political parties, the Catholic Church, and civic associations in Chihuahua and nationally created far more powerful counterweights to the previously dominant one-party state, thereby promoting greater institutional pluralism; improved society's capacity to articulate demands; generated new arenas for the development of civic skills and social trust; and placed the regime under intense pressure to adopt crucial electoral reforms and democratize the PRI. There is also evidence that the spate of opposition victories at the state level is having a profound impact on regional-level democratization by opening up space for democratic political practices and by obliging the central government to accept some decentralization of power in the states.[14]

The growing strength of the opposition in the federal Chamber of Deputies as a result of the 1988 presidential elections also compelled the government during the 1988–91 period to negotiate actively with the opposition to win the two-thirds approval necessary to pass crucial initiatives in the areas of electoral reform and privatization. The recovery of the PRI in the 1991 legislative elections made consensus less necessary from a strictly legal point view because the party recovered its two-thirds majority, but the opposition was strong enough in the Chamber to make it necessary for the government to consult with the PAN and the PRD to ensure legitimacy for its initiatives. The Salinas administration thus actively continued to court opposition party support for constitutional reform initiatives affecting the status of the Church, the *ejido*, and elections. The need for the regime to obtain legitimacy for its privatization initiatives may have enhanced the bargaining power of the PAN, which promised to support privatization in exchange for concessions on crucial issues such as electoral reform and the recognition of opposition party victories. The loss of the PRI's majority in the Chamber of Deputies in the wake of the 1997 Congressional elections produced the most assertive Congress ever and helped further redress the imbalance between the executive and legislative branches.

INTERNATIONAL EXPLANATIONS
FOR DEMOCRATIZATION

One alternative explanation to the domestically-focused analysis of institutional change in Chihuahua and Mexico presented here is, of course, the role of international pressures. The main transmission belts of international pressures for democratization on the Mexican government were the U.S. government, U.S. Congress, international media, and international organizations, governmental or non-governmental. Systemic approaches would lead us to believe that international pressures for democratization were the result of broad changes in the international system that have little to do with Mexican politics, such as the global trend towards democratization and the emphasis on the promotion of democracy as a unifying principle of U.S. foreign policy in the post–Cold War era.[15] The decision of the Salinas administration to seek greater economic integration with the United States through NAFTA as a solution to the fundamental problems of the Mexican economy heightened the regime's vulnerability to international pressures for democratization.[16]

The problem with the systemic approach is that it fails to focus on the process by which international pressures come into play. In particular, the systemic approach leaves out the role of domestic actors in mobilizing international ones to pressure the regime for democratization. The political awakening of society and the efforts of social leaders strengthened social institutions, including their ability to influence international actors. The PAN, for example, filed formal accusations before the Inter-American Human Rights Commission (IAHRC) of the Organization of American States (OAS) protesting fraud in regional elections in 1986 (Chihuahua) and 1995 (Yucatán). The Civic Alliance actively cooperated with international actors in the 1994 presidential elections and received financial and technical assistance from the National Democratic Institute (NDI), the National Endowment for Democracy (NED), and the United Nations. More informally, opposition party leaders from the PAN and the PRD cultivated connections in U.S. academia, Congress, the media, and non-governmental organizations. During the Salinas administration, the regime developed a sophisticated international public relations strategy to counter opposition criticisms abroad, win approval of NAFTA, and assure U.S. opinion makers that Mexico was on the right track politically and economically.

In short, international pressures would likely not have been very significant had domestic groups not first made a concerted effort to exploit Mexico's vulnerability to systemic pressures for democracy by raising the issue of election fraud with international actors. International pressures also came into play only after the lack of democracy had became a major domestic issue in Mexico. In other words, domestic actors had to make fraud a serious issue domestically before international actors would pay attention. International actors did not set the agenda for democratization in Mexico but were in a far more reactive position. International pressures were thus an intervening variable mediating the effect of a politically awakened society—and hence stronger societal institutions—on democratization in Mexico.

If international pressures for democratization were largely the outcome of domestic pressures, this does not mean that they were trivial in their impact. Salinas's desire to secure approval of NAFTA may have induced him to recognize PAN victories at the state level. But international censure would not have been much of a possibility had the PAN not possessed the institutional capacity to make fraud a potent issue through civil disobedience and appeals to domestic and international opinion. In addition, the ability of the PAN and civic associations to mount increasingly effective election-monitoring efforts discouraged the regime from attempting to rig elections in the first place. In the 1989 gubernatorial race in Baja California Norte, won by the PAN, the party was able to provide the tally of the results of voting within a few hours of the closure of the polls, thereby making it extremely difficult for the regime to manipulate the official count. One reason that the government wanted to bolster the credibility of the electoral process by enacting electoral reforms was to reassure its international partners that it was serious about democracy, yet the 1994 electoral reforms were much more wide-ranging in scope than the 1993 reforms. What changed was not the level of international pressure but the domestic politi-

cal situation. The Chiapas rebellion and the assassination of the
PRI's presidential candidate made a social explosion in the wake of
a disputed election outcome seem increasingly likely, thereby forcing the hand of the regime. The existence of stronger opposition
parties and civic associations—as a result of the political awakening
of society and the actions of social leaders—also meant that these
events would be rapidly translated into greater pressure on the regime to negotiate more serious reforms. It is also worth noting that
the 1996 electoral reforms were approved when international
pressures on Mexico were at a relatively low ebb, with the NAFTA
debate over and Chiapas no longer receiving as much foreign media coverage.

TOP-DOWN EXPLANATIONS OF
DEMOCRATIZATION

Mexico is a centralized political system with power historically concentrated in the hands of the president. It is therefore easy
to assume that democratization in such a system must inevitably
flow from the top downwards. This study finds the top-down explanation of democratization in Mexico unpersuasive. The president did not make decisions in a vacuum but reacted to pressures
for democratization. This study shows that the primary source of
democratization stemmed from pressures by the citizenry, opposition political parties, the Church, and civic associations. These pressures in turn explain why the regime chose to follow a course of
political opening.

During the Salinas administration, the president intervened
repeatedly in state elections—San Luis Potosí, Guanajuato, and
Michoacán being the most prominent examples—to replace PRI
governors elected in tainted processes with interim governors from
the PRI or the PAN. These moves responded to pressures placed on
the presidency by the PAN and other groups through civil disobedience and other tactics. With regard to Baja California Norte and
Chihuahua, where PAN victories were recognized in 1989 and 1992,
the president was aware that failing to do so could produce a major
confrontation similar to the one in Chihuahua in 1986 that would
do considerable damage to the regime's domestic and international

reputation. Nor does a decision to recognize an opposition victory explain the opposition victory itself. People may cast more ballots for the opposition if they feel that their votes will be respected, but this does not by itself account for why they would want to do so.

Going further back to the de la Madrid *sexenio,* it has been argued that his decision to recognize a host of opposition victories in the 1983 municipal elections was an example of top-down democratization. Yet, de la Madrid's main reason for recognizing the PAN's 1983 victories was to provide a safety valve to release social pressure that had accumulated as a result of the crisis. Even his ill-advised decision to commit fraud in the 1986 state elections in Chihuahua and the 1988 presidential elections was a direct response to the growing popularity of the opposition.

Electoral reforms under Salinas also represented a clear response to growing social pressures for democracy. For the first time, electoral reforms in 1994 were the joint product of negotiations between the government and opposition parties, particularly the PAN and the PRD. The fact that the 1994 reforms went deeper than the ones in 1993 was a direct reflection of the escalation of social pressures for democracy during Mexico's most troubled presidential campaign in decades. The 1996 reforms, negotiated between all three major parties, represented an attempt by Zedillo to increase political legitimacy and provide an institutional solution to the potential for social upheaval generated by the 1994–95 crisis.

A different case in point is the Ley Federal de Organizaciones Politícas y Procesos Electorales (Federal Law of Political Organizations and Electoral Processes, LOPPE), enacted in 1977, when there were fewer apparent pressures on the regime to democratize. The LOPPE expanded the number of seats reserved for the opposition in the Chamber of Deputies and legalized leftist parties, including the former Communist party. Yet, the LOPPE was not introduced to further democracy but to improve the regime's legitimacy, which had been undermined by the fact that López Portillo had been elected without opposition in 1976. In addition, the regime sought to bring Mexico's leftist parties into the political system in order to discourage violent attempts to change the system that had begun to manifest themselves since the early 1970s. The fact that the regime was concerned about legitimacy and the growth of guerrilla violence indicates that, even then, its perception of societal pressures was an important factor in the decision to approve the LOPPE. In any event, the weakness of the opposition was such that opposition parties were unable to take advantage of the expanded access to the Chamber until much later. Nor did the LOPPE as a federal initiative address the issue of electoral reform at the state level, where opposition parties were to become particularly strong in the 1980s and 1990s.

There were also crucial aspects of the democratization process that lay outside the president's control, particularly the growth of civic consciousness fueled by long-term social and economic change. The president's control over important societal institutions also eroded in the 1980s and 1990s with the Catholic Church, opposition parties, and civic associations—partly in response to the growth of civic involvement—all becoming increasingly assertive. This in turn circumscribed his influence over the process of democratization.

Conclusion

During the 1980s and 1990s, Chihuahua emerged as Mexico's most important laboratory for democratic change. A state that had been largely dominated by the PRI for the entire postrevolutionary period witnessed dramatic changes, including the rapid rise of the PAN as a major force in Chihuahua politics, the emergence of the Catholic Church as a crucial player in promoting democracy, the mushrooming of civic associations, pioneering and ultimately successful attempts to democratize the PRI, and the growth of a competitive two-party system by the end of the 1990s. These changes in Mexico's largest state in turn left a major mark on national politics, with the national PAN being reshaped largely in the image of the PAN in Chihuahua, the Mexican Church as a whole becoming more involved in political issues ranging from the defense of democracy to the promotion of social justice, and the PRI adopting the open primary system first used in Chihuahua to choose gubernatorial candidates in several states and then its presidential candidate in 2000.

Chihuahua was also a harbinger for changes that were occurring more generally throughout Mexico. The political awakening of society that was most apparent in the Mexican north in the early to mid-1980s had by 1988 become a national phenomenon, propelling, along with the actions of social leaders, the same sorts of institutional changes on the national stage that had already begun to occur in Chihuahua. Elections, which had been mostly noncompetitive rituals, became fiercely contested in the 1980s and 1990s. Opposition parties, which at the beginning of the 1980s had been weak and disorganized, emerged as powerful organizations increasingly capable of challenging the hegemony of the ruling party at the national level. Civic associations that had been nonexistent only fifteen years earlier blossomed in the late 1980s and 1990s to play a vital role in bringing democracy to Mexico, particularly through their electoral observation efforts. The Catholic Church, which had remained under the shadow of the state for much of the post-revolutionary period, emerged as an increasingly important actor on a range of social issues. Electoral reforms in the 1990s made fraud in federal elections much less likely than at any time in the history of Mexican elections. By 1999, Mexico was a far more institutionally plural country than in 1982, offering a better balance between societal institutions, on the one hand, and the state, on the other, more conducive to democracy as envisaged by Tocqueville. In 2000, an opposition party, the PAN, won the presidency, completing Mexico's transition to democracy. The epilogue discusses the Mexican 2000 elections in detail.

Epilogue

The July 2, 2000, Mexican Presidential Elections

In a real sense, the revolt against the dominance of the one-party regime in Mexico began with the uproar
over election fraud in 1986 in Chihuahua. There had always been
protests against election fraud in the past, but these had rarely had
consequences for system-wide change. The 1986 election in Chihuahua marked the first time that fraud did have consequences,
hurting the regime's image domestically and abroad, vastly strengthening the PAN in Chihuahua and nationally, and building a movement against election fraud that in the space of a few years engulfed
the entire nation. The process of change ignited by Chihuahua saw
its logical culmination in the presidential elections in 2000, which
signaled a sea change in Mexican politics and effectively completed
the country's long-awaited transition to democracy.

For those who questioned the view that a political awakening
of society had occurred in Mexico during the 1980s and 1990s, the
results of the presidential elections provided conclusive evidence to
the contrary. The PAN's candidate, Vicente Fox Quesada, swept the
presidential elections by a margin of almost 7 percent, with Fox
winning 43.5 percent of the vote, the PRI's Francisco Labastida 36.8
percent, and the PRD's Cuauhtémoc Cárdenas just 17 percent.[1] The
voter turn-out was a healthy 64 percent, less than the 78 percent
peak reached during the crisis-laden 1994 elections but much greater
than the 50 percent recorded in 1988, although data for 1988 are
highly suspect. In PRI-controlled Chihuahua, Fox carried the state—

with 49.6 percent of the vote compared to Labastida's 41.6 percent and Cárdenas's 7 percent—consolidating the emerging two-party system there. In the Federal Chamber of Deputies, no single party emerged with an absolute majority, but the Alliance for Change, consisting of the PAN and the Mexican Ecological Green Party (PVEM) won about 45 percent of the Chamber's 500 seats, the PRI 41.4 percent, and the Alliance for Mexico, consisting of the PRD and several small left-oriented parties, just 13.6 percent. In the Senate, a similar picture emerged, with no party winning an absolute majority. The PAN and its ally, the Greens, won about 41.4 percent of the Senate's 128 seats, the PRI 46 percent, and the PRD and its allies 12.5 percent. The PAN also won the state of Morelos by a huge majority, garnering 54.3 percent of the vote, while the PRI mustered only 26.9 percent. The party also retained control over Guanajuato, with 56.7 percent of the vote over the PRI's 33.8 percent. In Mexico City, the PRI was virtually wiped out, with the PRD winning the post of Head of Government with 39.9 percent of the votes, the PAN 33.6 percent, and the PRI just 22.8 percent; the PRI also failed to win any of the city's sixteen *delegaciones* or subdivisions, captured in their totality by the PAN and PRD.

This decisive rejection of a party associated with decades of authoritarian practices said much about the transformation of the Mexican electorate underlying the political awakening of society. But the 2000 elections provided other evidence that pointed to a political awakening of society. It is true that the number of domestic observers declined from 89,000 in 1994 to 36,781 in 2000, but these observers were far better trained than in 1994, with about 90 percent being drawn from some 410 civic organizations and only 10 percent participating as individuals.[2] Their work was aided by a more thorough identification of problem *casillas*, voting sites, or of problem geographical zones by both the major civic groups and the political parties. The PAN prepared and circulated a list of some 30,000 *casillas* where fraud might be expected to occur, which observer groups could target for special attention. In addition, a technical committee set up by the Federal Election Institute (IFE), consisting of a small group of distinguished Mexicans, was made responsible for allocating UN-provided funds to finance the activities of domestic observer groups on the basis of a strict competitive process to improve their efficacy at observation. Several major groups like the

Civic Alliance, Citizen Presence, Citizens' Movement for Democracy, COPARMEX, and the Teachers' Union all received a significant portion of the funds to conduct their quick counts and observation efforts from this source.

Another reason why domestic observers became less important in 2000 is that that the political parties themselves got better at managing the task of electoral observation. For the first time, both the PAN and the PRD were able to post representatives in most of the country's approximately 114,000 *casillas,* a major achievement given the logistical and other challenges involved. By June 30, three days before the elections, the IFE had accredited 106,278 people as party representatives from the PAN, representing 93.7 percent of the voting booths, 101,711 from the PRD, with 89.7 percent coverage, and 110,074 from the PRI, with 97 percent coverage.[3] Both the PAN and PRD claimed that they had actually posted far more representatives than the official figures indicated and taken steps to prevent the no-shows that had bedeviled previous elections by choosing party representatives more carefully, in order to improve motivation, and by giving them more training. Finally, the decline in civic "non-party" observers also reflected the growing credibility of Mexican elections in the wake of 1996 electoral reforms.

In addition, the most important pillar of the 2000 elections was the citizen-run Federal Election Institute (IFE), which ran the elections from start to finish. The IFE, which was reformed in 1996 to exclude political party representatives from all decision making, was controlled by nine citizen councilors nominated and approved by the three major political parties. The IFE was the only electoral organization trusted by the opposition: Both Fox and Cárdenas expressed their confidence in the IFE. They had less trust in the Electoral Tribunal—which was part of the relatively unreformed judiciary and responsible for adjudicating electoral disputes—and virtually no trust in the Fiscalia Para Delitos Electorales (FEPADE), a government agency charged with prosecuting electoral crimes.[4] The fact that Mexico possessed an independent authority supervising the elections made the transition to democracy far easier and bolstered confidence in the process. In order to prevent and detect fraud in the country's *casillas,* the IFE designed a highly sophisticated system: Some 18,000 roving *asistentes,* or monitors, were trained and commissioned to observe voting in every seven *casillas* and then report back on any problems, such as whether the *casillas* opened on time, *casilla* officials appeared for duty, or irregularities that may have taken place. This information was then immediately sent via the internet from the country's three hundred districts to IFE headquarters for continuous monitoring by political parties and the IFE itself during election day. Roving monitors were also expected to raise questions about incidents with the district councils for immediate action and gather evidence to prosecute fraud later, thus fulfilling an important deterrent function as well. The combination of the IFE's roving monitors, civic observers, and party representatives testified to the vigor of Mexican society and played an important role in deterring fraud by raising the chances that it would be detected quickly.

The IFE also took extraordinary steps to ensure a credible count: The Program of Preliminary Results (PREP), based on the results recorded in each *casilla* at the close of voting and transmitted immediately to IFE headquarters in Mexico City, would be released through the night of July 2 with 90 to 95 percent of the PREP being reported by the morning of July 3. In addition, the IFE commissioned three quick counts based on a carefully stratified random sample of the country's *casillas;* three independent polling organizations would carry out the quick counts, which would be released between 10 and 11 P.M. on election night to calm speculation about the results. The official count would begin on Wednesday, July 5, three days after the elections, in the country's 300 districts, to be later certified by the Electoral Tribunal. In the end, the results of the PREP, the two quick counts conducted by Gallup and Berumen (the third by Alduncin was released later due to "technical difficulties"), and the official count were basically the same, with only small variations among them.

The extent to which the elections were citizen-run is vividly captured by the fact that all the approximately 800,000 officials responsible for manning the voting booths on polling day were chosen from the voter registration list by lottery, including *casilla* presidents, secretaries, ballot counting staff, and their stand-by replacements. This was a long way from the old days when *casilla* officials were simply nominated by the government and imposed on the citizenry. The elections themselves were marked by an extraordinary degree of civility and only a small number of reported irregularities, most of which were resolved fairly quickly during the day. The most important indicator of civility was, of course, the fact that national power passed peacefully from an official party, the PRI, to an opposition party, the PAN, for the first time.

Several factors explained the success of the transition that took place in the 2000 elections. The fact that Fox won by a margin of seven points made it very difficult to derail the transition; his victory was just too clear and decisive for it to be questioned seriously by anyone. Based on several pre-election polls, many feared that the presidential race would be extremely close and plunge the country into a potential political crisis. Fox himself stated that he would not accept the results of the elections in a very close race, partly because of the negative effects on the PAN caused by vote buying by the official party. Both Cárdenas and Fox were deeply concerned that government social programs were being used to gain votes for the PRI, especially Progresa, a program targeted at 2.6 million poor women in rural areas, who received financial assistance in return for enrolling their children in schools and taking them for regular visits to government health clinics.[5] The opposition charged the government with favoring PRI supporters in allocating program benefits, spreading fear that the program would end if the PRI lost power, allowing the list of beneficiaries to fall into the hands of the PRI campaign, and pressuring beneficiaries to commit to voting PRI on election day.[6] So serious were the concerns about the misuse of government programs that a special congressional commission under the leadership of PAN federal deputy, Elodia Gutiérrez, was set up over the objections of the PRI to investigate charges of vote buying, but the commission received little cooperation from the government.[7] Government officials claimed that if Progresa beneficiaries voted PRI, this was not because of coercion but simply because they were happy with the program.[8] The government also pointed out that very few complaints had been filed against officials for misusing Progresa funds for political ends, but the opposition insisted this was because of a well-grounded fear of retaliation, the complexity of seeking judicial recourse in Mexico, and the low sense of political efficacy among those who typically receive government benefits. In the end, however, the wide margin of victory for Fox indicated that government programs like Progresa had not had the effect of swaying votes in favor the PRI that the opposition had feared. More likely, rural women and other groups availed themselves of government assistance without feeling any obligation to vote PRI, and, because the vote was secret (due to the long process of electoral reforms that had preceded the elections), the government could do nothing to enforce loyalty to the PRI among the constituents of such programs. This validated the view of some international observers that as long as the balloting and count were clean, vote buying before the elections could not seriously alter the final outcome.

The role played by both Fox and Zedillo facilitated a smooth transition to democracy. Prior to the elections, Fox stated that he had had no contact with Zedillo during the campaign to discuss the transition. One source of worry for the opposition was that Zedillo had failed to suspend government publicity for government programs thirty days before the election, which even Carlos Salinas had done during the 1994 campaign. One PAN leader predicted that Zedillo would support the PRI's Labastida until the elections because of the relentless pressure from the party's "dinosaurs" but would support the PAN afterwards if it won fair and square.[9] While Zedillo was under pressure from the PRI's dinosaurs, he was also the president who had agreed to the electoral reforms of 1996, which opened the door to a potential opposition victory in 2000, recognized the PRD's victory in the election for Head of Government of Mexico City in 1997, and supported an open primary to choose the PRI's presidential candidate for 2000. Zedillo, who had come to power as a result of a tragic historical event, the assassination of Colosio, owed nothing to the PRI's dinosaurs, who opposed both his political and economic program. He had far more in common with the PAN than with his opponents in the PRI. His entire legacy would depend on how he handled the outcome of the 2000 presidential elections. Botched and he would go down in history as a weak and temporizing villain; handled with dignity and he would enter the history books as Mexico's greatest democratizing president. In the end, Zedillo chose wisely: At about 11:00 P.M., he appeared on Mexican television to concede Fox's victory, congratulating him warmly and promising the government's full support to the new president-elect. It was no accident that it was Zedillo who first acknowledged Fox's victory, only then followed by Labastida, who stated tersely that the tendency of the voting did not favor his candidacy.

Fox also deserves considerable credit in creating the underlying conditions that allowed Zedillo to recognize his triumph. Fox was the only one of the three major candidates who consistently exuded the aura of a winner. He succeeded in building a consensus around him as the only candidate who could bring democracy to Mexico by creating a coalition of unlikely allies, including traditional PAN leaders; reform-minded intellectuals associated with the left, such as Jorge Castañeda and Adolfo Aguilar Zinser; former PRD and PRI president, Porfirio Muñoz Ledo; a section of the Catholic laity and even a few of its hierarchy; and a significant portion of the business community, which trusted the former Coca-Cola route manager who had risen to lead Coke in Mexico before plunging into politics. Fox generated an air of confidence and momentum that was infectious and quickly translated into a popular wave in his favor. Cárdenas, himself a great figure in the story of Mexican democratization, was in 2000 largely a spent force, running for the presidency for the third consecutive time. For Labastida, the main problem was defending a party that had simply been in power for too long—and all its accumulated sins—to a largely unsympathetic electorate. As Fox pointed out, the PAN's key constituency consisted of voters identified with the future, primarily younger, more educated, largely urban, and better-off voters, while the PRI's voters tended to be more rural, less educated, and often from the poorer segments of Mexican society.[10] By 2000, the electoral arithmetic favored the PAN, not the PRI, which was basically faced with the problem of hanging on to a shrinking share of the electorate in the face of massive social and economic change unleashed in part by the PRI's own efforts to transform Mexico. Finally, behind Fox lay the power of an awakened society with strong institutions, including the PAN itself but also the PRD, the Church, and an assortment of increasingly vocal civic associations as well as the citizen-run IFE, which could no longer be relied upon to cover-up fraud. Not to recognize an opposition victory would surely have plunged the country into a massive political and economic crisis: Zedillo therefore did not simply choose to do the right thing. He was obliged to do so by the growing power of Mexican society that supported democracy as an alternative to the continuance of one-party rule at the national level.

Finally, the smooth transition was aided by the presence of

approximately 860 international observers, including President Carter himself, although their importance was reduced by the large margin by which the PAN won. The strategy of Carter's delegation was to support the IFE's version of the results, because the delegation's small size made it impossible to come to any independent judgment about the process; the delegation instead focused on observing the behavior of the political parties themselves, as well as the IFE and the main domestic election monitoring groups, rather than the actual voting in the *casillas*. But there was a sound logic in supporting the IFE as well: As an independent organization charged with supervising the elections, the IFE could be trusted to release reliable and accurate results. Backing it would bolster the IFE in relation to other groups, such as political parties, that might have a vested interest in challenging the official results. If the results were extremely close and questioned by one or more of three major parties, then the strategy would be to pressure and monitor the Electoral Tribunal to adjudicate all electoral disputes fairly and try to calm the situation. In the end, however, this strategy never had to be implemented, for the large margin of victory meant that the IFE's results, confirmed by several exit polls and quick counts conducted by other organizations, were accepted by all the players within a few hours of the closing of the polls. While it is virtually impossible to quantify the effects of international observers on the electoral process in 2000, they probably helped deter fraud before and during the elections by placing the government under heavy international scrutiny and may also have had a positive effect on voter turnout insofar as their presence encouraged voters to think that their votes would be respected. But again because of the large margin of the PAN's victory, the international observers were much less important than might have been the case had the result been closer.

Election night at PAN campaign headquarters was a predictably happy affair. At around 4:00 P.M., President Carter and his small entourage, including this author, arrived to meet with Fox: Fox immediately produced the results of the latest exit polls, all of which showed the PAN significantly ahead of the PRI, and said, "Mr. President, we're winning!" At around 5:00 P.M., 30 minutes after Carter had left, Fox came out of his study, gave the author a victory sign, and then blurted out "we're seven points ahead!" before darting back in. The exit polls, which could not be disclosed officially until 8:00 P.M. under the law, continued to show a significant lead for Fox. By about 7:00 P.M., the atmosphere in the war room on the upper floor of the PAN's campaign headquarters, where the author had been posted for most of the evening, had visibly lightened, with smiles abounding and lots of guarded talk of victory. Shortly thereafter at 7:30 P.M., Luís Felipe Bravo Mena, the PAN president, and most of Fox's team rapidly descended to hold a press conference downstairs. To a packed hall, Bravo Mena declared victory in the state races for governor in Guanajuato and Morelos and a deadheat between the PAN and PRD in the race for Head of Government of Mexico City, but refrained from proclaiming victory in the presidential elections except to say that it had been a historic day and asked the press to wait until 8:00 P.M. when exit poll data could formally be released. By 8:00 P.M., all eyes were glued to the large television monitors installed in the PAN's special hall for party invitees: first came the exit polls, all showing Fox ahead by significant margins.[11] Close to 9:00 P.M., Fox declared cautiously that the voting had placed him ahead of the other two candidates. Then came the results of the ten or so quick counts conducted by the IFE, the three political parties, the two major television channels, and major civic associations, all of which again showed Fox in the lead by a fairly wide margin.[12] The sheer number of quick counts, and their accuracy, was itself a powerful sign of the vitality of Mexican society. This was followed by Cárdenas, who at 10:30 P.M. publicly accepted that the results showed a clear preference for Fox. And at around 11:00 P.M., Zedillo in a speech to the nation declared that "the next president of Mexico will be Vicente Fox Quesada." Soon after, Francisco Labastida became the first presidential candidate from the official party in history to concede defeat to an opposition party.

Notes

1. INTRODUCTION

1. Robert D. Putnam, with Robert Leonardi and Rafaella Y. Nanetti, *Making Democracy Work: Civic Traditions in Modern Italy* (Princeton: Princeton University Press, 1993).

2. Ibid., p. 98.

3. Ibid., p. 153.

4. Ibid., pp. 149–51.

5. Ibid., pp. 121–37.

6. See Samuel P. Huntington, *Political Order in Changing Societies* (New Haven: Yale University Press, 1968), ch. 1. See also Michel Crozier, Samuel P. Huntington, and Joji Watanuki, *The Crisis of Democracy: Report on the Governability of Democracies to the Trilateral Commission* (New York: New York University Press, 1975), ch. 2, "The United States," by Samuel Huntington.

7. Gabriel Almond and Sidney Verba, *The Civic Culture: Political Attitudes and Democracy in Five Nations* (Princeton: Princeton University Press, 1963).

8. Ibid., ch. 1.

9. Gabriel Almond, "The Intellectual History of the Civic Culture Concept," in Gabriel Almond and Sidney Verba, *The Civic Culture Revisited* (Boston: Little, Brown, and Company, 1980), pp. 16–17.

10. Resource mobilization theorists stress the role of strategic choice and institutional entrepreneurship in the growth of social movements from a rational choice perspective. A good example of this genre of scholarship as applied to Vietnam is Samuel Popkin, *The Rational Peasant: The Political Economy of Rural Society in Vietnam* (Berkeley: University of California Press). See also Mayer N. Zald and John D. McCarthy, eds., *Social Movements in an*

Organizational Society: Collected Essays (New Brunswick: Transaction Books, 1987); and Frontiers of Sociology Symposium, Vanderbilt University, *The Dyanamics of Social Movements: Resource Mobilization, Social Control, and Tactics* (Cambridge, Mass.: Winthrop Publishers, 1979). See also Mancur Olson, *Logic of Collective Action* (Cambridge: Harvard University Press, 1965).

11. On mores and religion, see Alexis de Tocqueville, *Democracy in America*, vol. 1, part 2, ch. 9; vol. 2, part 1, ch. 5; part 2, ch. 8 and 9.

12. Ibid., vol. 1, part 2, ch. 9, pp. 305–8.

13. For examples of the top-down view, see works by Miguel Centeno, *Democracy within Reason* (University Park: Pennsylvania State University Press, 1994); and George Philip, *The Presidency in Mexican Politics* (New York: St. Martin's Press, 1992), especially ch. 6.

14. The neglect of regional politics reflected the tendency of scholars, particularly political scientists, to concentrate on the centralized Mexican state. Relatively little emphasis was given to Mexico's regions. This has now begun to change: Examples of regional-level scholarship include Jeffrey W. Rubin, *Decentering the Regime: Ethnicity, Radicalism, and Democracy in Juchitán, Mexico* (Durham: Duke University Press, 1997); and Gilbert M. Joseph and Daniel Nugent, eds., *Everyday Forms of State Formation* (Durham: Duke University Press, 1994).

15. This study has benefitted from the rich methodological insights of Gary King, Robert Keohane, and Sidney Verba, *Designing Social Inquiry: Scientific Inference in Qualitative Research* (Princeton: Princeton University Press, 1994), especially ch. 1, 3, 4, 5, and 6.

16. See, for example, Victor Perez-Diaz, *The Return of Civil Society: The Emergence of Democratic Spain* (Cambridge: Harvard University Press, 1993); and John Keane, ed., *Civil Society and the State: New European Perspectives* (New York: Verso Books, 1988).

17. Representative examples of this literature on political participation include Lester Milbrath, *Political Participation: How and Why Do People Get Involved in Politics?* (Chicago: Rand McNally, 1965); Karl Deutsch, "Social Mobilization and Political Development," *American Political Science Review* 55, no. 4 (December 1969), pp. 493–515; Norman H. Nie and Sidney Verba, "Political Participation," in Fred Greenstein and Nelson Polsby, eds., *Handbook of Political Science: Nongovernmental Politics* (Reading, Mass.: Addison-Wesley, 1975); Sidney Verba, Norman H. Nie, and Jae-On Kim, *Participation and Political Equality: A Seven-Nation Comparison* (Cambridge: Cambridge University Press, 1978); Samuel P. Huntington and Joan Nelson, *No Easy Choice: Political Participation in Developing Countries* (Cambridge: Harvard University Press, 1976); Douglas A. Hibbs, Jr., *Mass Political Violence: A Cross-National Causal Analysis* (New York: Wiley, 1973); Albert Hirschmann, *Exit, Voice, and Loyalty* (Cambridge: Harvard University Press, 1970); and Albert Hirschman, *Shifting Loyalties: Private Interest and Public Action* (Princeton: Princeton University Press, 1982).

18. Jonathan Fox argues that associational autonomy is as necessary for democratization as electoral competition. See Jonathan Fox, "The

Difficult Transition from Clientelism to Citizenship: Lessons From Mexico,"
World Politics 46, no. 2 (January, 1994), pp. 151–84.

2. THE POLITICAL AWAKENING
OF MEXICAN SOCIETY

1. Guillermo O'Donnell and Philippe Schmitter, *Transitions from Authoritarian Rule: Tentative Conclusions about Uncertain Democracies* (Baltimore: Johns Hopkins University Press, 1993).

2. On the effects of economic crises on democratization, see, for example, Stephan Haggard and Robert Kaufman, *The Political Economy of Democratic Transitions* (Princeton: Princeton University Press, 1995); Jeffrey Frieden, *Debt, Development, and Democracy: Modern Political Economy and Latin America, 1965–1985* (Princeton: Princeton University Press, 1991); and Voytek Zubek and Judith Gentleman, "Economic Crisis and the Movement toward Pluralism in Poland and Mexico," *Political Science Quarterly* 109, no. 2 (Summer, 1994), pp. 335–60.

3. On the link between socioeconomic development and democracy, see Robert Dahl, *Polyarchy* (New Haven: Yale University Press, 1971), pp. 62–80; Samuel Huntington, *The Third Wave: Democratization in the Late Twentieth Century* (Norman: University of Oklahoma Press, 1989), pp. 59–72; and Seymour Martin Lipset, *Political Man: The Social Bases of Politics* (New York: Doubleday, 1960), pp. 45–76.

4. For a study on the importance of social mobilization profiles in influencing political outcomes of regime transitions in China and Russia, see Minxin Pei, *From Reform to Revolution: The Demise of Communism in China and the Soviet Union* (Cambridge: Harvard University Press, 1994), pp. 58–62.

5. On the evolution of the Mexican electoral system, see Juan Molinar Horcasitas, *El tiempo de la legitimidad: Elecciones, autoritarismo, y democracia en México* (Mexico City: Cal y Arena, 1991); see also Guadalupe Pacheco Méndez, *El PRI en los procesos electorales de 1961 a 1985* (Mexico City: Universidad Autónoma de México, 1986).

6. Miguel Basáñez, *La lucha por la hegemonía* (Mexico City: Siglo Veintiuno Editores, 1982).

7. On the importance of marketization for democratization, see Pei, *From Reform to Revolution*, ch. 1, 2, and 6 (pp. 1–84, 179–210).

8. On the relationship between the PAN and the business community, see Vikram K. Chand, "Politicization, Institutions, and Democratization in Mexico," Ph.D. dissertation (Cambridge: Harvard University, 1991), ch. 3.

9. An excellent study of the Terrazas-Creel empire is Mark Wasserman, *Capitalists, Caciques, and Revolution: The Native Elite and Foreign Enterprise in Chihuahua, Mexico 1854–1911* (Chapel Hill: University of North Carolina Press, 1984).

10. For an excellent analysis of the origin and history of the

Monterrey industrial elite, see Alex M. Saragoza, *The Monterrey Elite and the Mexican State* (Austin: University of Texas Press, 1988).

11. For a detailed analysis of these transactions, see François Lartigue, *Indios y Bosques: Políticas forestales y comunales en la Sierra Tarahumara* (Mexico: Ediciones de Casa Chata, 1983), pp. 41– 66.

12. Author's interview with Eloy Vallina, Jr., president of the Chihuahua Group (September 26, 1988, Chihuahua City).

13. Author's interview with Jaime Bermúdez, creator of the multinational assembly industry in Mexico, founder and head of the Bermúdez Group, and municipal president of Ciudad Juárez 1986–89 (August 26, 1988, Ciudad Juárez).

14. Ibid.

15. For a more detailed account of the Border Industrialization Program, see Oscar J. Martínez, *Ciudad Juárez: El auge de una ciudad fronteriza a partir de 1848* (Mexico: Fondo de Cultura Económica, 1982), pp. 177–87.

16. Ibid., p. 179.

17. Harley Shaiken, *Mexico in the Global Economy: High Technology and Work Organization in Export Industries* (San Diego: Center for U.S.-Mexican Studies, University of California, San Diego, 1990), p. 38.

18. For a detailed analysis of the factors leading to Ford's decision to invest in an engine-producing facility, see Harley Shaiken, with Stephen Herzenberg, *Automation and Global Production: Automobile Engine Production in Mexico, the United States, and Canada* (San Diego: Center for U.S.-Mexican Studies, University of California, 1987), pp. 41–53. For an analysis of the changing automobile industry in Mexico, see Kevin Middlebrook, "The Politics of Industrial Restructuring: Transnational Firms' Search for Flexible Production in the Mexican Automobile Industry," *Comparative Politics* (April, 1991).

19. This statistic is from Jorge G. Castañeda, *México: El futuro en juego* (Mexico: Joaquín Mortiz Planeta, 1987), p. 124.

20. Wayne A. Cornelius et al., "Overview: The Dynamics of Political Change in Mexico," in Wayne A. Cornelius, Judith Gentleman, and Peter Smith, eds., *Mexico's Alternative Political Futures* (La Jolla: Center for U.S.-Mexican Studies, University of California, San Diego, 1989), p. 7.

21. On the relationship between socioeconomic status and political participation, see Norman H. Nie and Sidney Verba, "Political Participation," in Fred Greenstein and Nelson Polsby, eds., *Nongovernmental Politics* (Reading, Mass.: Addison-Wesley, 1975), pp. 40–46; see also Samuel P. Huntington and Joan Nelson, *No Easy Choice: Political Participation in Developing Countries* (Cambridge: Harvard University Press, 1976), pp. 80–89.

22. Nie and Verba, "Political Participation," pp. 32–38.

23. Joseph L. Klesner, "Modernization, Economic Crisis, and Electoral Alignment in Mexico," *Mexican Studies / Estudios Mexicanos* 9, no. 2 (Summer, 1993), pp. 187–224.

24. René Villarreal, "The Policy of Import-Substituting Industrialization," in José Luís Reyna and Richard S. Weinert, eds., *Authoritarianism*

in Mexico (Philadelphia: Institute for the Study of Human Issues, 1977), pp. 67–107.

25. Alan Riding, *Distant Neighbors: A Portrait of the Mexicans* (New York: Vintage Books, 1986), pp. 215–19.

26. Shaiken, *Mexico in the Global Economy*, p. 11.

27. I am indebted for much of my understanding of Chihuahua's pattern of historical development to Zacarias Márquez Terrazas, one of Chihuahua's most distinguished historians and the chronicler of Chihuahua City. See author's interviews with Zacarias Márquez Terrazas (September 19, 1988, and September 20, 1988, Chihuahua City).

28. For a summary of the Apache wars, see Filiberto Terrazas Sánchez, *La guerra Apache en México* (Mexico: Costa Amic editores, 1977).

29. This perception was confirmed by the delegate to Chihuahua of the federal government's Budget and Planning Ministry (SPP). Author's interview with Jacinto Segura, SPP Delegate to Chihuahua (January 30, 1987, Chihuahua City).

30. Enrique Alduncin, *Los valores de los Méxicanos: México: Entre la tradición y la modernidad* (Mexico: Fomento Cultural Banamex, 1986), pp. 89–91.

31. Wayne A. Cornelius, "Political Liberalization and the 1985 Elections in Mexico," in Paul W. Drake and Eduardo Silva, eds., *Elections and Democratization in Latin America, 1980–85* (San Diego: Center for Iberian and Latin American Studies, University of California, 1986), p. 124.

32. Ibid.

33. The PAN won in Districts 3 in 1955, 6 in 1961, 2 in 1964, and 1 in 1967. Data taken from Franz A. Von Sauer, *The Alienated "Loyal" Opposition: Mexico's National Action Party* (Albuquerque: University of New Mexico Press, 1974), pp. 178–80.

34. Riding, *Distant Neighbors*, p. 116.

35. Alberto Aziz Nassif, *Prácticas electorales y democracia en Chihuahua* (Mexico: Cuadernos de la Casa Chata, no. 151, 1987), p. 74.

36. Author's interview with Oscar Ornelas, governor of Chihuahua, 1980–85 (March 26, 1987, Chihuahua City).

37. Aziz, *Prácticas electorales y democracia en Chihuahua*, p. 79; and "Licencia al gobernador de Chihuahua," in *Las razones y las obras: Gobierno de Miguel de la Madrid, tercer año* (Mexico: Presidencia de la República, Fondo de Cultura Económica, 1986), p. 493.

38. For a good analysis of these changes, see Francisco Ortíz Pinchetti, "El PRI ganará en Chihuahua y la única verdad será la suya," *Proceso* 10,503 (June 23, 1986), pp. 17–18. For the code itself, see Gobierno del Estado de Chihuahua, part 3 of *Código administrativo*, book 4 of *Los partido políticos y procesos electorales* (Chihuahua: Dirección de Gobernación, 1986), especially pp. 3–6, 31–32, and 40–48.

39. Alberto Aziz Nassif, "Los límites de la democracia electoral," *Revista Mexicana de Sociologia* 49, 4 (October–December, 1987), p. 197.

40. Ortíz Pinchetti, "El PRI ganará en Chihuahua," p. 19.

41. Ibid. See also Ortíz Pinchetti, "Gobernación previó hasta la anulación de la elección en Chihuahua," *Proceso* 10,505 (July 7, 1986), pp. 6–10.

42. Aziz, "Los límites de la democracia electoral," p. 198.

43. Ibid.

44. The most reliable accounts of fraud in the 1986 state elections in Chihuahua are Ortíz Pinchetti, "Gobernación previó hasta la anulación de la elección en Chihuahua," pp. 6–10; Francisco Ortíz Pinchetti, "También la indignación se previó en Chihuahua y se le inutiliza," *Proceso* 10,506 (July 14, 1986), pp. 6–14; Aziz, "Los límites de la democracia electoral," pp. 196–201; Juan Miguel de Mora, *Elecciones en México: Se repetirá el ejemplo de Chihuahua* (Mexico: EDAMEX, 1988), pp. 68–114; "Información político y social," in *Información procesada de Chihuahua* (July, 1986), pp. 34–40; "Dictámen del jurado popular al pueblo de Chihuahua," *Diario de Chihuahua* (August 8, 1986), p. 12; and Armando Revueltas, *Así fue: Ciudad Juárez, Chihuahua, 1986: Una historia digna de contarse* (please note that *Armando Revueltas*, "Arming Revolts," is a clever pseudonym). This account of election-day fraud is based on all these sources as well as the author's interviews with political actors in Chihuahua.

45. Juan Molinar Horcasitas, "Regreso a Chihuahua," *Nexos* 10,111 (March, 1987), p. 29. All the data presented here concerning Chihuahua's list of registered voters or *padrón* are from this article.

46. Gobierno del Estado de Chihuahua, *Chihuahua, proceso electoral 1986* (Chihuahua: Dirección de Gobernación, 1987), p. 249.

47. Ibid., pp. 245, 291.

48. Author's interview with Fernando Baeza, governor of Chihuahua, 1986–92 (September 15, 1988, Chihuahua City).

49. Gobierno del Estado de Chihuahua, *Chihuahua, proceso electoral 1986*, pp. 183–209, 251–57, and 271–75.

50. Hector Aguilar Camín et al., "El caso Chihuahua," *Proceso* 10,508 (July 28, 1986), p. 4.

51. Inter-American Commission on Human Rights, "1990: Resolution No. 01 / 90, Cases 9768, 9780, 9828 of Mexico, May 17, 1990, Final Report" (Washington, D.C.: Organization of American States, 1990), p. 122.

52. For a detailed summary of the 1992 results, see Victor Orozco, "Los resultados electorales: Posibles tendencias objectivas," *Cuadernos del Norte*, special edition, December, 1992; see also Alberto Aziz Nassif, *Chihuahua: Historia de una alternativa* (Mexico City: Ediciones La Jornada, 1994), especially pp. 136–45.

53. Orozco, "Los Resultados Electorales," p. 36.

54. For an detailed analysis of this audit, see Instituto Federal Electoral, Registro Federal de Electores, *Actividades del Registro Federal de Electores en el Estado de Chihuahua* (Mexico City: July, 1992).

55. Aziz Nassif, *Chihuahua*, p. 140.

56. Under the new election code, the PRI as the winner of the sen-

ate race received two of the state's three seats and Alvarez as the runner-up received the third.

57. Author's interview with Raul García Acosta, president of the PAN in Ciudad Juárez (October 8, 1994, Ciudad Juárez).

58. Author's interview with Antonio Badia and Mauricio Ostos, PAN municipal government functionaries (October 6, 1994, Ciudad Juárez).

59. Carter Center / National Democratic Institute delegation interviews with Artemio Iglesias, president of the PRI in Chihuahua (August 20, 1994, and August 21, 1994, Chihuahua City). The author was a member of the delegation.

60. Instituto Federal Electoral, *Resultados de elecciones federales de 1997 en Chihuahua* (Mexico City: IFE, 1997; available on-line at http://www.ife.org.mx/wwworge/chih.htm).

61. Enrique Rodriguez Vazquez, "El PRI obtuvo mayoría en elección de diputados y PAN en la de Senadores," *Diario de Chihuahua* (July 11, 1997).

62. Alejandro Gutiérrez, "Con mi triunfo se demuestra que el PRI no estaba muerto; tampoco puede hablarse del principio del fin del PAN: Patricio Martínez," *Proceso* 1,132 (July 12, 1998), internet version.

63. See Olga Aragón, "PRI gana 45 municipios, entre ellos Chihuahua; PAN 19, incluido Juárez," *Diario de Chihuahua* (July 7, 1998); and Gamaliel Linares, "Retiene PRI mayoría en el congreso local," *Diario de Chihuahua* (July 7, 1998).

64. This calculation does not include the municipal elections of 1971, for which no data is available.

65. Author's interview with Cuauhtémoc Cárdenas, candidate for the Mexican presidency in 1988 for the National Democratic Front (FDN) (April 11, 1988, Mexico City).

66. Cornelius et al., "Overview," p. 20.

67. Elías Chávez, "Jornadas de titubeos del secretario de gobernación," *Proceso* 11,610 (July 11, 1988), p. 22.

68. Ibid.

69. Interview with Clouthier in José Agustín Ortiz Pinchetti, *La democracia que viene: Ejercicios de imaginación política* (Mexico: Editorial Grijalbo, 1990), p. 332.

70. Ibid.

71. Cornelius et al., "Overview," p. 19.

72. Arturo Alvarado, "Los resultados de la elección para senadores," in Germán Pérez del Castillo et al., *La voz de los votos: Un análisis crítico de las elecciones de 1994* (Mexico City: Miguel Angel Porrua, 1995), p. 281.

73. Arturo Sánchez Gutiérrez, "La elección de la Cámara de Diputados," in Pérez del Castillo et al., *La voz de los votos,* p. 267.

74. Instituto Federal Electoral, *Resultados definitivos de los computos distritales de la elección de presidente de los Estados Unidos Mexicanos* (Mexico City: Instituto Federal Electoral, 1994).

75. For a summary of the results of the various quick counts, see

Arturo Alvarado, "La jornada electoral de 1994: Una larga y circular travesía," in Pérez del Castillo et al., *La voz de los votos*, p. 197.

76. Two surveys of likely voters by international polling organizations showed Zedillo receiving 46 percent of the vote (Belden and Russonello / Ciencia Aplicada poll, July 23–August 1, 1994) and 54.7 percent (Indermerc–Louis Harris poll, July 30–August 6, 1994). Surveys by domestic polling organizations also projected Zedillo as the winner with 46 percent (*El Norte / Reforma* poll, July 23–29); only the MORI de México poll, which relied on street interviews for half its respondents, was significantly off—it projected Zedillo as the winnter with just 38 percent of the vote (MORI de México poll, July 25–August 1, 1994).

77. On the 1997 midterm elections, see Joseph Klesner, "Democratic Transition? The 1997 Mexican Elections," *Political Science and Politics* 30, no. 4 (December, 1997), pp. 703–11; and the Carter Center of Emory University, *The Carter Center Delegation to Observe the July 6, 1997, Elections in Mexico* (Atlanta: Emory University, 1997).

78. Instituto Federal Electoral, *Código Federal de Instituciones y Procedimientos Electorales* (Mexico City: Instituto Federal Electoral, 1994), article 24(b), p. 15.

79. Cynthia Anderson-Barker, *Election Fraud in Mexico: A Case Study of Elections in Michoacán State on July 12, 1992* (Los Angeles: Loyola Law School, 1993), p. 9.

80. The PAN, for example, won the municipal presidency of Quiroga, Michoacán in 1946, Zamora in 1947, and Uruapan in 1967. Data taken from Von Sauer, *The Alienated "Loyal" Opposition*, p. 179.

81. Anderson-Barker, *Election Fraud in Mexico*, p. 10.

82. For the PRD's accusations and the PRI's reply, see the statement issued by the PRI state committee, "Michoacán: Balance del proceso electoral," *La Jornada* (July 15, 1992).

83. Anderson-Barker, *Election Fraud in Mexico*, p. 21.

84. The Carter Center of Emory University, *Report of the Team Sent by the Council of Freely Elected Heads of Government to Witness the Observation of the Elections in Michoacán and Chihuahua, Mexico* (Atlanta: Carter Center of Emory University, July 13, 1992).

85. For an analysis of the state elections in San Luis Potosí and Guanajuato, see Silvia Gómez Tagle, ed., *Las elecciones de 1991: La recuperación official* (Mexico City: Ediciones La Jornada, 1993), pp. 189–218, 373–422.

86. The PAN elected one federal deputy from Yucatán in 1958 and 1964, respectively (Von Sauer, *The Alienated "Loyal" Opposition*, pp. 178–79).

87. For a study of the history of anti-centralism in Yucatán, see Nelson Reed, *The Caste War of Yucatán* (Stanford: Stanford University Press, 1964).

88. Tim Golden, "Vote Fraud Fight Flaring in Mexico," *New York Times* (December 6, 1993).

89. Frente Cívico Familiar et al., *The Elections in Yucatán, Mexico:*

Summary and Conclusions of Citizen Observers (Merida: November 28, 1993), p. 5.

90. Results of Jalisco state elections of 1995 are taken from Partido de Acción Nacional, Secretariado de Relaciones, *Acción Internaciónal* no. 19 (February 30, 1995), p. 2.

91. Von Sauer, *The Alienated "Loyal" Opposition*, p. 181.

92. Ibid., pp. 178–79.

93. Instituto Federal Electoral, *Memorias del proceso electoral federal de 1991*, tome 6, vol. 4 (part 1a), pp. 95–111.

94. Instituto Federal Electoral, *Resultados definitivos de los computos distritales de la elección de presidente de los Estados Unidos Mexicanos.*

95. Results of Guanajuato state elections of 1995 are taken from Partido de Acción Nacional, Secretariado de Relaciones, *Acción Internaciónal* no. 23 (June 30, 1995), p. 3.

96. Tim Golden, "Opposition in Mexico Calls Vote Fraudulent," *New York Times* (May 31, 1995), p. A12.

97. These irregularities are catalogued in National Action Party, *The Democratic Plea of PAN in Yucatán* (Mexico City: PAN, June 27, 1995).

98. Andrés Manuel López Obrador, *Tabasco, víctima del fraude electoral* (Mexico City: Editorial Nuestro Tiempo, 1990), p. 109.

99. Ibid.

100. Tim Golden, "Mexico Is Shown Paper Trail of Illicit Campaign Spending," *New York Times* (June 13, 1995), p. A3.

101. Ibid.

102. See Alduncin, *Los valores de los Mexicanos;* Miguel Basáñez, *El pulso de los sexenios: 20 años de crisis en México* (Mexico: Siglo Veintiuno Editores, 1990); and the Gallup Organization, Inc., *Eco / Gallup Mexico Pre-election Survey, Press Release #1* (New York: June 19, 1988); Gallup Organization, Inc., *Eco / Gallup Mexico Pre-election Survey, Press Release #2* (New York: June 26, 1988).

103. Jorge I. Domínguez and James McCann, *Democratizing Mexico: Public Opinion and Electoral Choice* (Baltimore: Johns Hopkins University Press, 1996).

104. Alduncin, *Los valores de los Méxicanos*, pp. 77–81.

105. Ibid., p. 110.

106. Ibid., p. 177.

107. Basáñez, *El pulso de los sexenios*, p. 218.

108. Ibid., p. 249.

109. Ibid., p. 277.

110. Ibid., p. 278–79.

111. Miguel Basáñez, "Encuesta Electoral 1991," *Este País* no. 5 (August, 1991), pp. 3–6.

112. Gallup Organization, Inc., *Eco / Gallup Mexico Pre-election Survey, Press Release #2*, pp. 2–3.

113. Ibid., pp. 3–4.

114. Domínguez and McCann, *Democratizing Mexico*, pp. 32–41.

115. Ibid., p. 47.

116. See, for example, Adalberto Almeida y Merino et al., "Coherencia cristiana en la política: A los católicos que militan en los partidos políticos" (Chihuahua City: Archdiocese of Chihuahua, March, 1986), pp. 6–7.

117. Partido de Acción Nacional, *Plataforma, 1986–1992* (Chihuahua: March, 1986), p. 9.

118. On this, see Robert Putnam, *Making Democracy Work: Civic Traditions in Modern Italy* (Princeton: Princeton University Press, 1993), especially ch. 5, pp. 121–62.

119. Only on rare occasions was this hegemony ever challenged: examples include the 1956 and 1959 gubernatorial elections in Chihuahua and Baja California Norte respectively and the 1967 and 1969 municipal elections in Sonora and Baja California Norte respectively, where PAN candidates ran strongly against winning PRI candidates in fraud-tainted elections.

120. O'Donnell and Schmitter, *Transitions from Authoritarian Rule,* p. 19.

3. THE TRANSFORMATION OF MEXICO'S NATIONAL ACTION PARTY (PAN): FROM CIVIC EXAMPLE TO POLITICAL POWER

1. Data from Partido de Acción Nacional, *Acción Internacional,* no. 28 (November 30, 1995); PAN Research Secretariat, *Basic Information about the Party* (Mexico City: January, 1994). See also the PAN website at http://www.pan.org.mx for 1999 data.

2. Data adapted from Soledad Loaeza, *El Partido Acción Nacional: La large marcha, 1939–1994: Oposición leal y partido de protesta* (Mexico: Fondo de Cultura Económica, 1999), p. 33.

3. Donald Mabry, *Mexico's Acción Nacional: A Catholic Alternative to Revolution* (Syracuse: Syracuse University Press, 1973); and Abraham Nuncio, *El PAN: Alternativa de poder or instrumento de la oligarquía empresarial* (Mexico: Editorial Nuevo Imagen, 1986), p. 21.

4. Franz A. Von Sauer, *The Alienated "Loyal" Opposition: Mexico's Partido Acción Nacional* (Albuquerque: University of New Mexico Press, 1974).

5. See Loaeza, *El Partido Acción Nacional,* especially pp. 17–104, 329–98, and 553–68. See also Soledad Loaeza, "El PAN: De la oposición leal a la impaciencia electoral," in Loaeza, *El llamda de las urnas* (Mexico: Cal y Arena, 1989), pp. 241–71.

6. James W. Wilkie and Edna Monzon de Wilkie, *México visto en el siglo XX: Entrevistas con Manuel Gómez Morin* (Mexico: Editorial JUS, 1978), pp. 110–12; also from author's interview with Juan Landerreche Obregón, son-in-law of Gómez Morin and a founding member of the PAN (October 3, 1989, Mexico City).

7. Author's interview with Juan Landerreche Obregón.

8. The best analysis of the "seven sages" is Enrique Krauze's *Caudillos culturales en la revolución mexicana* (Mexico: Siglo Veintiuno Editores, 1985).

9. A detailed analysis of Gómez Morin's contributions during this period appears in Krauze, *Caudillos culturales en la revolución*, pp. 104–18 and 228–39.

10. For Gómez Morin's critique of the revolution, see Krauze, *Caudillos culturales en la revolución*, pp. 193–99.

11. Manuel Gómez Morin, "Informe a la Asamblea Constituyente de Acción Nacional, rendido el 14 de Septiembre de 1939," in *Diez años de México: Informes del jefe de Acción Nacional* (Mexico: Ediciones PAN, 1983), pp. 6–7.

12. Krauze, *Caudillos culturales en la revolución*, p. 241.

13. Ibid., p. 242.

14. See his remarkable letter to José Vasconcelos dated November 3, 1928, reproduced in Krauze, *Caudillos culturales en la revolución*, pp. 273–78.

15. Krauze, *Caudillos culturales en la revolución*, pp. 276–77.

16. See his essays "La Universidad de México—Su naturaleza jurídica" and "La Universidad de México—Su función y la razón de ser de su autonomía," in Manuel Gómez Morin, *"1915" y otros ensayos* (Mexico: Editorial JUS, 1973), pp. 79–128.

17. Author's interview with Juan Landerreche Obregón.

18. Gómez Morin, *"1915" y otros ensayos*, pp. 93–95.

19. Author's interview with Carlos Castillo Peraza, editor of *Palabra*, the PAN's doctrinal and ideological journal (Santes Católicos, "Convocatoria y conclusiones de la Convención Iberoamericana de Estudiantes Católicos," September 19, 1989, Mexico City).

20. Convención Iberoamericana de Estudiantes Católicos, "Convocatoria y conclusiones de la Convención Iberoamericana de Estudiantes Católicos, 12 al 22 de Diciembre de 1931," in Luís Calderón Vega, *Cuba 88: Memorias de la UNEC* (Mexico: 1959), Appendix, p. 23.

21. Ibid., pp. 19–20.

22. Author's interview with Juan Landerreche Obregón.

23. "Convención Iberoamericana de Estudiantes Católicos," in Calderón Vega, *Cuba 88*, pp. 39–41.

24. For some interesting observations on the organizational culture of the UNEC, see Calderón Vega, *Cuba 88*, pp. 50–51, 96–98.

25. Ibid., p. 135.

26. Ibid., pp. 185–92.

27. Luís Calderón Vega, *Memorias del PAN: I* (Mexico: Editorial JUS, 1978), p. 25.

28. Ibid.

29. Ibid.

30. Author's interview with Carlos Castillo Peraza.

31. Author's interview with Juan Manuel Gómez Morin, PAN mem-

ber and son of Manuel Gómez Morin (September 18, 1989, Mexico City); also, author's interview with Juan Landerreche Obregón.

32. This summary of Efraín González Luna's political and social ideas is derived from the following of his writings: "La persona, el bien común, y la cultura," in González Luna, *Humanismo político*, vol. 1 (Mexico: Ediciones PAN, 1984), pp. 133–52; "El hombre y el estado," in *Humanismo político*, vol. 1, pp. 97–108; "El hombre y el estado (continuación)," in *Humanismo político*, vol. 1, pp. 109–16; "Deber cívico y política orgánica," in *Humanismo político*, vol. 1, pp. 117–33; "Democracia, vínculo de unidad nacional," in González Luna, Christlieb Ibarrola, Preciado Hernández, Gómez Morin, and González Torres, *La democracia en México* (Mexico: Editorial JUS, 1962), pp. 9–34; and González Luna, *Los católicos y la política en México* (Mexico: Editorial JUS, 1988).

33. For a fuller summary of Efraín González Luna's economic and social ideas, see the following of his writings: "La dignidad del trabajo," in *Humanismo político*, vol. 2 (Mexico: Ediciones PAN, 1984), pp. 91–104; "La economía contra el hombre," in *Humanismo político*, vol. 2, pp. 105–11; "Clases sociales y lucha de clases," in *"Clases sociales y lucha de clases" y otros temas*, vol. 8 (Mexico: Editorial JUS, 1977), pp. 53–71.

34. Krauze, *Caudillos culturales en la revolución*, p. 287.

35. Author's interview with Juan Landerreche Obregón.

36. See Nuncio, *El PAN;* and Kathleen Bruhn, *Taking on Goliath: The Emergence of a New Left Party and the Struggle for Democracy in Mexico* (University Park: Pennsylvania State Press, 1997), p. 45.

37. Juan Landerreche Obregón has an old exam from Gómez Morin's student years in which he advocates the formation of a political party as the solution to Mexico's ills.

38. Manuel Gómez Morin, "1915," in *"1915" y otros ensayos*, pp. 30–31.

39. Wilkie and Monzon de Wilkie, *México visto en el siglo XX*, pp. 39–41; Manuel Gómez Morin, "Informe a la nación (respuesta al discurso pronunciado en Chilpancingo por el presidente de la república Gral. Lázaro Cárdenas, el día 20 de Febrero de 1940)," in *Diez años de México*, pp. 23–40.

40. Gómez Morin, "1915," pp. 31–38.

41. Wilkie and Monzon de Wilkie, *México visto en el siglo XX*, p. 120.

42. Author's interview with Carlos Castillo Peraza.

43. Manuel Gómez Morin, "Informe a la Asamblea Constituyente de Acción Nacional, rendido el 14 de Septiembre de 1939," in *Diez años de México*, pp. 12–14; Efraín González Luna, "Técnica de salvación," in *Humanismo político*, vol. 1, pp. 20–22, 24.

44. Efraín González Luna, "Neurosis de la escaramuza," in *Humanismo político*, vol. 1, pp. 29, 32, 34.

45. Franz A. Von Sauer, *The Alienated "Loyal" Opposition*, p. 102.

46. Ibid., pp. 133–34.

47. Author's interview with Luís H. Alvarez, national president of the PAN (September 19, 1989, Mexico City).

48. Ibid.

49. Ibid.

50. Mabry, *Mexico's Acción Nacional*, p. 53.

51. Ibid., pp. 53–54.

52. Author's interview with Luís H. Alvarez.

53. Asamblea Constituyente del Partido Acción Nacional, "Proyección de los principios de doctrina aprobados por la XVIII Convención Nacional, Mayo de 1965," in *Principios de doctrina* (Mexico: EPESSA, 1985), pp. 58–61.

54. Ibid., pp. 62–63.

55. Acción Nacional, *Cambio democrático de estructuras: Memoria de la XX Convención Nacional celebrada del 7 al 9 de febrero de 1969 en la Ciudad de México, D.F.* (Mexico: Ediciones de Acción Nacional, 1969), pp. 7–8.

56. Ibid., p. 20.

57. Efraín González Morfín, *Solidarismo* (Mexico: Ediciones de Acción Nacional, 1974), pp. 9–15.

58. Efraín González Morfín, "Concentración o distribución de la propiedad," in *Justicia y reforma social* (Mexico: Ediciones de Acción Nacional, 1967), pp. 34–48.

59. Author's interview with José Angel Conchello, PAN national president 1972–75 and president of the PAN in Mexico City 1987 to 1990 (April 6, 1988, Mexico City).

60. José Angel Conchello, "Discurso del Lic. José Angel Conchello D., presidente de Acción Nacional," in *8a Asamblea XXIV Convención: Documentos* (Mexico: Ediciones de Acción Nacional, 1975), pp. 14–18.

61. Ibid., pp. 18–22.

62. Ibid., pp. 23–25.

63. Elías Chávez, "Conchello se defiende: Hay prominentes panistas que sirven al Grupo Monterrey," *Proceso* 2,76 (April 17, 1978), pp. 6–8.

64. Author's interview with José Angel Conchello.

65. Author's interview with Bernardo Bátiz, PAN secretary general 1972–75 and 1984–87 (October 4, 1989, Mexico City).

66. Elías Chávez, "Conchello se defiende," p. 7.

67. Author's interview with José Angel Conchello, PAN national president 1972–75 and president of the PAN in Mexico City 1987 to 1990 (April 13, 1989, Mexico City).

68. Comisión Editorial del Partido Acción Nacional, "Plataforma política y social 1976–1982," in *El México de la oposición: 7 plataformas presidenciales* (Mexico: EPESSA, 1986), pp. 140, 145, 154.

69. See his speech to PAN national councillors on February 25, 1978: "González Morfín: La reforma política fortalece el control sobre los partidos," *Proceso* 2,75 (April 10, 1978), pp. 10–13.

70. Efraín González Morfín, "El significado de Acción Nacional," in *8a Asamblea XXIV Convención: Documentos* (Mexico: Ediciones de Acción Nacional, 1975), pp. 118–132; also "La doctrina de Acción Nacional," in

Efraín González Morfín, José González Torres, and Adolfo Christlieb Ibarrola, *Tres esquemas* (Mexico: Ediciones de Acción Nacional, 1969), p. 3.

71. "González Morfín: La reforma política fortalece el control sobre los partidos," *Proceso* 2,75 (April 10, 1978), pp. 10–13.

72. Author's interview with José Angel Conchello (April 6, 1988).

73. Author's interview with Carlos Castillo Peraza, editor of *Palabra*, the PAN's doctrinal and ideological journal (September 20, 1989, Mexico City).

74. Author's interview with Manuel González Hinojosa, PAN national president 1969–72 and 1976–78 (September 25, 1989, Mexico State).

75. Author's interview with José Angel Conchello.

76. Author's interview with Manuel González Hinojosa.

77. Author's interview with José Angel Conchello (April 13, 1988).

78. Author's interview with Bernardo Bátiz.

79. Ibid.

80. Efraín González Morfín, "En AN, un partido dentro de otro partido," *Proceso* 2,76 (April 17, 1978), pp. 8–9.

81. Author's interview with Manuel González Hinojosa.

82. Carlos Arriola, "La crisis del Partido Acción Nacional (1975–1976)," *Foro Internacional* 17,4 (April–June, 1977), p. 552.

83. "González Morfín: La reforma política fortalece el control sobre los partidos," *Proceso* 2,75 (April 10, 1978), p. 12.

84. Fernando Estrada Samano has since returned to the party at the invitation of Luís H. Alvarez. For the motives of those who resigned, see Elías Chávez, "La desintegración del PAN: Muchos dirigentes son simples oportunistas," *Proceso* 2,75 (April 10, 1978), pp. 13–16. Also see Elías Chávez, "Acusan tres renunciantes: Conchello dió subsidios para dividir al PAN," *Proceso* 2,76 (April 17, 1978), pp. 10–11.

85. Author's interview with José Angel Conchello (April 6, 1988).

86. PAN statutes make a distinction between party members and adherents; adherents should seek to promote the objectives of the party but do not have to subscribe to the party's doctrine or statutes. See articles 8 and 9, PAN statutes, 1999, http://www.pan.org./frames/inbas/htm.

87. Author's interview with Luís H. Alvarez. For a summary of this conflict, see Armando Chávez, *Sesenta años de gobierno municipal: Jefes políticos del distrito bravos y presidentes del municipio de Juárez 1897–1960* (Mexico: 1959), pp. 369–89.

88. Von Sauer, *The Alienated "Loyal" Opposition*, p. 131.

89. Author's interview with Guillermo Prieto Luján, president of PAN State Committee of Chihuahua (February 2, 1987, Chihuahua City).

90. Author's interview with Luís H. Alvarez.

91. Author's interview with Manuel González Hinojosa.

92. Author's interview with Guillermo Prieto Luján.

93. Author's interview with Luís H. Alvarez.

94. Author's interview with Guillermo Prieto Luján, president of PAN State Committee of Chihuahua (September 16, 1988, Chihuahua City).

95. These figures are derived from official federal election data from 1961 to 1985 presented in Silvia Gómez Tagle, "Los adjetivos de la democracia en Chihuahua," *Argumentos: Estudios críticos de la sociedad* (June, 1987), p. 96.

96. Miguel Basáñez, *El pulso de los sexenios: 20 años de crisis en México* (Mexico: Siglo Ventiuno Editores, 1990), pp. 248–75.

97. Ibid.

98. Ibid., pp. 276–308.

99. Ibid.

100. Roderic Ai Camp, "The PAN's Social Base," in Victoria E. Rodriguez and Peter M. Ward, eds., *Opposition Government in Mexico* (Albuquerque: University of New Mexico Press, 1995), p. 72.

101. Alberto Aziz Nassif, "La coyuntura de las elecciones en Chihuahua," in Carlos Martínez Assad, ed., *Municipios en conflicto* (Mexico: Instituto de Investigaciones Sociales / UNAM with G.V. Editores, 1985), p. 122.

102. Ibid.

103. Camp, "The PAN's Social Base," p. 68.

104. Author's interview with Antonio Morales Mendoza, secretary general of the PAN State Committee of Chihuahua (February 2, 1987, Chihuahua City).

105. Ibid.

106. That *maquiladoras* may politicize women does not necessarily imply that they enhance the status of women. For an interesting discussion of the impact of *maquiladoras* on the status of women, see Susan Tiano, "Maquiladoras in Mexicali: Integration or Exploitation?" in Vicki Ruiz and Susan Tiano, eds., *Women on the U.S.-Mexico Border: Response to Change* (Boston: Allen and Unwin, 1987), pp. 77–101.

107. Mabry, *Mexico's Acción Nacional,* pp. 109–10.

108. Author's interview with Cecilia Ostos, Maria Luz Pazos, and Elva Lafon de la O, leaders of the National Civic Feminine Association (ANCIFEM), in Ciudad Juárez (August 25, 1988); also author's interview with Victoria Chavira, former Secretary of Organization of the PAN's 1988 Senate Campaign Committee for Blanca Magrassy de Alvarez and Gustavo Elizondo (September 14, 1988, Chihuahua City).

109. Author's interview with Silvia Luján Peña, secretary of Feminine Action, PAN State Committee of Chihuahua (September 20, 1988, Chihuahua City).

110. On this topic, see Kathleen Staudt and Carlota Aguilar, "Political Parties, Women Activists' Agendas, and Household Relations: Elections on Mexico's Northern Frontier," *Mexican Studies / Estudios Mexicanos* 8, no. 1 (Winter, 1992), pp. 87–106; and Lilia Venegas, "Women in the Border: The *Panista* Militants of Tijuana and Ciudad Juarez," in Victoria E. Rodriguez, ed., *Women's Participation in Mexican Political Life* (Boulder: Westview Press, 1998).

111. The account that follows is based on my interview with Gustavo Villarreal, municipal president of Parral from 1983–86 (May 11, 1987, Parral).

112. Author's interview with Sergio Conde Varela, secretary of municipal government for Ciudad Juárez from 1983–86 (September 23, 1987, Ciudad Juárez).

113. Author's interview with Alfonso Murgía, treasurer in the municipal administration of Francisco Barrio in Ciudad Juárez 1983–86 (September 25, 1987, Ciudad Juárez). Also author's interview with Carlos Aguilar, municipal president of Camargo 1983–86 (July 7, 1987, Camargo).

114. Author's interview with Raymundo López López, co-founder of the Comité Defensa Popular of Ciudad Juárez (October 22, 1987, Ciudad Juárez).

115. Author's interview with María Jesús Solís and José Martínez Bejarano, activists from the low-income Colonia Abraham González in Camargo (July 8, 1987, Camargo).

116. Author's interview with Antonio Badía, secretary general of the Municipal Committee of the PAN in Ciudad Juárez (September 18, 1987, Ciudad Juárez).

117. Author's interview with Francisco Barrio, PAN candidate for governor of Chihuahua State in 1986 and former Municipal President of Ciudad Juárez, 1983–86 (September 30, 1987, Ciudad Juárez).

118. On this, see Yemile Mizrahi, "Rebels without a Cause? The Politics of Entrepreneurs in Chihuahua," *Journal of Latin American Studies* 26 (1994), pp. 137–58; and Mizrahi, "Entrepreneurs in the Opposition: Modes of Political Participation in Chihuahua," in Victoria E. Rodriguez and Peter M. Ward, eds., *Opposition Government in Mexico* (Albuquerque: University of New Mexico Press, 1995).

119. Author's interview with Eloy Vallina, president of the Grupo Chihuahua (September 26, 1988, Chihuahua City).

120. Cited in Alberto Aziz Nassif, *Prácticas electorales y democracia en Chihuahua* (Mexico: Centro de Investigaciones y Estudios Superiores en Antropología Social, Cuadernos de la Casa Chata #151, 1987), p. 92. See also Marco A. Rascón and Patricia Ruiz, "Chihuahua: La disputa por la dependencia," *Cuadernos Políticos* 47 (July–September, 1986), p. 30.

121. Author's interview with Silvia Luján Peña.

122. "Panorama económico," in *Información Procesada de Chihuahua* (May, 1986), p. 14.

123. Author's interview with Jaime Bermúdez Cuaron, municipal president of Ciudad Juárez (August 26, 1988, Ciudad Juárez).

124. ITESM has also produced reform-minded PRI leaders like Luís Donaldo Colosio.

125. "Panorama económico," in *Información Procesada de Chihuahua* (July, 1986), p. 9.

126. Ibid., p. 11.

127. Ibid., pp. 8, 13.

128. "Panorama económico," in *Información Procesada de Chihuahua* (August, 1986), p. 13.

129. Author's interview with Guillermo Luján Peña, owner of Materiales Tarahumara and member of PAN's State Committee of Chihuahua (February 23, 1987, Chihuahua City).

130. Francisco Barrio Terrazas, "A pesar de todo lo que tiene preparado el sistema, en Chihuahua ganaremos 2 a 1," *La Nación* 44,1707 (May 15, 1986), p. 10.

131. Ibid.

132. Author's interview with Francisco Barrio.

133. Ibid.

134. "Información política y social," in *Información Procesada de Chihuahua* (May, 1986), p. 17.

135. Ibid.

136. See their joint statement, "Por la verdad en Chihuahua," *Proceso* 10,508 (July 28, 1986), p. 3.

137. Ibid.

138. See Alvarez's statement to this effect, reproduced in Juan Miguel de Mora, *Elecciones en México: ¿Se repetirá el ejemplo de Chihuahua?* (Mexico: EDAMEX, 1988), p. 52.

139. Francisco Ortiz Pinchetti, "De consumarse el fraude, Baeza tendrá que gobernar sobre tres cadaveres, dicen los ayunantes," *Proceso* 10,509 (August 4, 1986), pp. 10–11. Also Francisco Ortiz Pinchetti, "Luís H. Alvarez, tres semanas en huelga de hambre: 'Quiero vivir, vero como hombre libre,'" *Proceso* 10,507 (July 21, 1986), p. 12.

140. Francisco Ortiz Pinchetti, "A los 112 kilos de peso Clouthier inicia su ayuno: 'Lo único que pido, y por eso estoy sin tragar, es que Salinas cumpla sus promesas," *Proceso* 12,633 (December 19, 1988), p. 14.

141. Heberto Castillo, "Caminar, no morir," *Proceso* 10,510 (August 11, 1986), p. 20.

142. Ibid.

143. Francisco Ortiz Pinchetti, "En Chihuahua parece gestarse una alianza pluripartidista de oposición, por la democracia," *Proceso* 10,510 (August 11, 1986), pp. 18–19.

144. Francisco Ortiz Pinchetti, "Incipiente organización opositora, respuesta a la política de arrasamiento," *Proceso* 10,511 (August 18, 1986), p. 15.

145. Ibid., p. 18.

146. Ibid., p. 19.

147. Armando Revueltas, *Así fué, Cd. Juárez, Chihuahua 1986: Una historia digna de contarse*, pp. 98–99 (the pseudonym *Armando Revueltas* means "Arming Revolts"). According to Antonio Badía, PAN secretary general in Ciudad Juárez, the book was written by Federico Barrio, the brother of Francisco Barrio, who is involved in the *maquiladora* industry.

148. Author's interview with Alejandro Paz Facio, director, Association of *Maquiladoras* (December 9, 1986, Chihuahua City).

149. Revueltas, *Así fué*, p. 111.

150. Author's interview with Antonio Badía, secretary general of the

Municipal Committee of the PAN in Ciudad Juárez (September 2, 1988, Ciudad Juárez).

151. Author's interview with Antonio Badía (September 18, 1987).

152. Author's interview with Antonio Badía (September 2, 1988).

153. Ibid.

154. Author's interview with Jaime González Bernal, PAN coordinator of Active and Pacific Civil Resistance (RECAP) in Ciudad Juárez (August 22, 1988, Ciudad Juárez).

155. Author's interview with Carlos Angulo, secretary of Electoral Action, PAN Municipal Committee of Ciudad Juárez (August 28, 1988, Ciudad Juárez).

156. Author's interview with Antonio Badía.

157. Ibid.

158. Author's interview with Jaime González Bernal.

159. This account of the impact of computerization on the PAN in Ciudad Juárez is based on my interview with Antonio Badía.

160. Oscar Hinojosa, "Naufragaron las promesas de elecciones límpias," *Proceso* 11,610 (July, 1988), p. 10.

161. "Apresurado, el PRI se autoproclamó triunfador," *Ahora* 2,82 (July 8–15, 1988), p. 4.

162. For a summary of foreign press coverage of the 1986 elections in Chihuahua, see Suzanne Bilello, "La prensa extranjera y las elecciones en Chihuahua, Julio de 1986," in Gerardo Bueno, ed., *México—Estados Unidos, 1986* (Mexico: El Colegio de México, 1987), pp. 157–69. On de la Madrid's visit to Washington, see Manuel Robles, "Furibunda reacción contra el PAN, por llevar sus protestas a Washington," *Proceso* 10,511 (August 18, 1986), pp. 12–13.

163. The charges against the regime filed by the three PAN candidates for public office are summarized in Javier Corral Jurado, "La OEA revisa el caso Chihuahua," *La Nación* 45,1734 (July 10, 1987), pp. 3–5. See also Inter-American Commission on Human Rights, "1990: Resolution no. 01 / 90 Cases 9768, 9780, and 9828 of Mexico, May 17, 1990: Final Report" (Washington, D.C.: Organization of American States, 1990), pp. 98–102.

164. Inter-American Commission on Human Rights, "1990," pp. 103–5.

165. Ibid., pp. 104, 118.

166. Ibid., p. 105.

167. Ibid., p. 122.

168. Ibid., p. 123.

169. Carlos Puig, "Informe de la Comisión de Derechos Humanos de la OEA, ante denuncias del PAN," *Proceso* 13,694 (February 19, 1990), p. 21.

170. "Analizará la asamblea de la OEA el informe sobre México," *La Jornada* (May 25, 1990), p. 1.

171. Pascal Beltrán del Río, "Dió entrada a denuncias del PRD el Centro de Derechos Humanos, de le ONU," *Proceso* 13,707 (May 21, 1990),

p. 26. Ironically, one of the sharpest critics of the PAN's decision to appeal to the OAS was Heberto Castillo, who is now a distinguished leader of the PRD. See Heberto Castillo, "Izquierda-derecha, discrepancias de fondo," *Proceso* 10,517 (September 29, 1986), p. 37.

172. Author's interview with Francisco Barrio, PAN candidate for governor of Chihuahua State in 1986 and former municipal president of Ciudad Juárez, 1983–86, (August 24, 1988, Ciudad Juárez).

173. Author's interview with Luís H. Alvarez, municipal president of Chihuahua City, 1983–86, and PAN national president, 1987–93 (February 18, 1987, Chihuahua City).

174. Author's interview with Luís H. Alvarez (September 19, 1989).

175. Pérez Mendoza, "Luís H. Alvarez no ve motivo para desistir; 'Yo creo que va a morir pronto,' dice su sacerdote," *Proceso* 10,510 (August 11, 1986), p. 14.

176. Author's interview with Guillermo Prieto Luján.

177. Author's interview with Carlos Castillo Peraza.

178. Ibid.

179. Author's interview with Abel Vicencio Tovar, PAN national president 1978–84, PAN secretary general 1987 to present, and PAN parliamentary coordinator 1988 to present (March 17, 1988, Mexico City).

180. Author's interview with Juan Landerreche Obregón.

181. Author's interview with Luís H. Alvarez.

182. An excellent analysis of this issue in historical perspective has been done by Gerardo Medina, "Las prerogativas de los partidos políticos," *La Nación* (March 1, 1987), pp. 3–5, 31.

183. Ibid., p. 4.

184. The figure of 23 billion *pesos* is quoted in Rodrigo Vera, "La aceptación del subsidio convierte el PAN en partido multimillionario," *Proceso* 12,629 (November 21, 1988), p. 21.

185. Author's interview with Luís H. Alvarez.

186. Ibid.

187. Ibid. See also Vera, "La aceptación del subsidio."

188. Salvador Corro, "Clouthier lanza huevos y el PRI se muestra cauto: Con pintoresquismo y abstención se afronta el drama de sinaloa," *Proceso* 11,522 (November 3, 1986), pp. 12–17.

189. Francisco Ortiz Pinchetti, "'Vamos por todo, las condiciones están dadas,' Asegura Clouthier," *Proceso* 11,578 (November 30, 1987), pp. 10–14.

190. See his speech to the National Citizen Assembly sponsored by Integral Human Development and Citizen Action (DHIAC) on March 12, 1988, in Manuel J. Clouthier, "Poder ciudadano y resistencia civil," *Diálogos con el pueblo*, vol. 2, *A la mitad del camino* (Mexico: EPESSA, 1988), pp. 11–18. Clouthier was proclaimed "Candidate of the Citizenry" for the Mexican presidency by DHIAC at this function, which I had the opportunity to attend.

191. Manuel Robles, "Barrio, Clouthier, Bátiz, estrategia y lenguaje

nuevos: Que la gente aprenda que puede devolver los golpes," *Proceso* 11,532 (January 12, 1987), pp. 13–15.

192. See his interview with Ricardo Rocha in Manuel J. Clouthier, "Entrevista del periodista Ricardo Rocha al Ing. Manuel J. Clouthier, candidato del PAN a la presidencia de la república," *Diálogos con el pueblo*, vol. 1, *Los primeros cien días de campaña* (Mexico: EPESSA, 1988), pp. 19–24.

193. See, for example, his speech at the closing event of his campaign, in Manuel J. Clouthier, "Mitin. cierre de campaña nacional. Zócalo de la Ciudad de México," *Diálogos con el pueblo*, vol. 3, *La recta final* (Mexico: EPESSA, 1988), pp. 193–205.

194. I accompanied Clouthier to several campaign events in June, 1988.

195. Manuel J. Clouthier, "Tarea de articulación de una lucha popular: Eso debe ser la campaña," *Diálogos con el pueblo*, vol. 1, p. 9.

196. Author's interview with Norberto Corella, secretary of National Relations for the PAN's National Executive Committee (March 17, 1988, Mexico City). Also see Leticia Castillo, "En secreto, obispo filipino pregona aquí ante disidentes," *Ahora* 1,44 (October 16–23, 1987), p. 3.

197. Author's interview with Jaime González Bernal; also author's interview with Norberto Corella. Jaime González Bernal's summary of Eugene Sharp's three-volume book was published as *La lucha política noviolenta: Criterios y técnicas* (1988).

198. I attended as an observer a two-day course on civil disobedience at the PAN's Mexico City headquarters on February 26 and 27, 1988. The comments that follow are based on this experience.

199. Author's interview with Luís H. Alvarez.

200. Ibid.

201. Elías Chávez, "Jornadas de titubeos del Secretario de Gobernación," *Proceso* 11,610 (July 11, 1988), p. 22.

202. Ibid.

203. Luís Felipe Bravo Mena, "La lección de las elecciones," *Palabra* 2,7 (January–March, 1989), p. 36.

204. Author's interview with Luís H. Alvarez.

205. Luís H. Alvarez, "Un solo renglón," *Memoria y esperanza: Discursos de Luís H. Alvarez* (Mexico: EPESSA, 1988), pp. 225–28.

206. Author's interview with Luís H. Alvarez.

207. The PAN's call to dialogue was formally issued on November 16, 1988, two weeks before the inauguration of Salinas as president. See Luís H. Alvarez and Abel Vicencio Tovar, "Compromiso nacional por la legitimidad y la democracia," *Palabra* 2,7 (January–March, 1989), pp. 62–70.

208. For a summary of his inaugural address, see Enrique Maza, "Y Salinas de Gortari empezó a desgranar promesas de un México con todo resuelto," *Proceso* 12,631 (December 5, 1988), pp. 12–15.

209. Alvarez, "Proponer el futuro, crear la esperanza," *Memoria y esperanza*, pp. 304–6.

210. Author's interview with Luís H. Alvarez.

211. Alvarez acknowledged that the role of neutral arbiter of democracy might "not be a bad one" for Salinas to follow (author's interview with Luís H. Alvarez).

212. On the role of the president and the negotiating process in general, see Gerardo Galarza, "Un debate prueba que la reforma electoral dividió a los panistas," *Proceso* 13,689 (January 15, 1990), pp. 20–25; Galarza, "Admite Luís H. Alvarez las discrepancias en su partido y se congratula de ellas," *Proceso* 13,690 (January 22, 1990), pp. 6–11; Galarza, "La dirigencia del PRI niega que hubo compromiso con el PAN sobre reforma política," *Proceso* 13,692 (February 5, 1990), pp. 24–28; Galarza, "Salinas 'ha respetado su palabra'; y el PAN sacó adelante la reforma electoral oficial," *Proceso* 12,677 (October 23, 1989), pp. 11–15.

213. See, for example, the following articles by an important PRD expert on electoral questions: Jorge Alcocer V., "Desvarío panista," *Proceso* 12,677 (October 23, 1989), pp. 30–34; and Alcocer V., "No al PRD," *Proceso* 13,715 (July 16, 1990), pp. 36–37.

214. Author's interview with Alberto Torres, former president of the PAN Municipal Committee of Ciudad Juárez (September 25, 1987, Ciudad Juárez). Also, author's interview with Juan Saldaña Rodríguez, PAN leader (August 29, 1988, Ciudad Juárez).

215. Author's interview with Antonio Badía.

216. Ibid. Also, Author's interview with Antonio Badía (September 18, 1987).

217. Author's interview with Alberto Torres.

218. Author's interview with Juan Saldaña Rodríguez.

219. Author's interview with Felix Bueno, PAN candidate for municipal president of Parral in 1986 and former president of the PAN district committee in Parral (May 15, 1987, Parral). Also author's interview with Juan Saldaña Rodríguez.

220. Author's interview with Alberto Torres.

221. Author's interview with Francisco Barrio (September 30, 1987).

222. Ibid.

223. Ibid.

224. Ibid.

225. This account of the CEN's reaction is based on the author's interview with Bernardo Bátiz, PAN secretary general 1972–75 and 1984–87 (May 19, 1988, Mexico City).

226. The quotation is from my interview with José Angel Conchello (April 13, 1988).

227. Author's interview with Bernardo Bátiz (October 4, 1989).

228. Author's interview with José Angel Conchello; author's interview with José González Torres, PAN national president 1959–62 and PAN candidate for the Mexican presidency in 1964 (September 29, 1989, Mexico City).

229. Ibid.

230. "Our Withdrawal from the National Action Party," *The Other Side of Mexico*, no. 28 (September–October, 1992), pp. 7–8.

231. See, for example, Peter Ward, "Policy Making and Policy Implementation among Non-PRI Governments: The PAN in Ciudad Juárez and
in Chihuahua"; and Victoria Rodríguez, "Municipal Autonomy and the
Politics of Intergovernmental Finance: Is It Different for the Opposition?"
in Rodríguez and Ward, *Opposition Government in Mexico*, pp. 135–52 (Ward)
and pp. 153–72 (Rodríguez).

232. For an assessment of the changes introduced in the PAN-ruled
state of Baja California Norte, see Victoria E. Rodríguez and Peter M. Ward,
Political Change in Baja California: Democracy in the Making? (La Jolla: Center
for U.S.-Mexican Studies, University of California, San Diego, 1994). See
also Yemile Mizrahi, "Dilemmas of the Opposition in Government: Chihuahua and Baja California," *Mexican Studies / Estudios Mexicanos* 14, no. 1
(Winter, 1998), pp. 151–89.

233. On the PAN's role in electoral reforms under Salinas, see Jorge
Alcocer "Recent Electoral Reforms in Mexico: Prospects for a Real Multiparty Democracy," in Riordan Roett, ed., *The Challenge of Institutional Reform in Mexico* (Boulder: Lynne Rienner Publishers, 1995), pp. 57–76.

234. Luís Rubio, "Economic Reform and Political Change in Mexico,"
in Riordan Roett, ed., *Political and Economic Liberalization in Mexico: At a
Critical Juncture* (Boulder: Lynne Rienner, 1993), p. 48.

4. THE CATHOLIC CHURCH AND
DEMOCRATIZATION IN MEXICO

1. Daniel H. Levine, *Popular Voices in Latin American Catholicism*
(Princeton: Princeton University Press, 1992), especially ch. 1 and 9.

2. Ibid., pp. 344–50.

3. See Jean Meyer, *El catolicismo social en México hasta 1913* (Mexico:
Instituto Mexicano de Doctrina Social Cristiana, 1985).

4. Bailey, *Viva Cristo Rey! The Cristero Rebellion and the Church-State
Conflict in Mexico* (Austin: University of Texas Press, 1974), p. 82.

5. Jean Meyer, *La Cristiada*, vol. 3, *Los Cristeros* (Mexico: Siglo
Veintiuno Editores, 1987), pp. 290–97.

6. José Gutiérrez Casillas, *Historia de la Iglesia en México* (Mexico:
Editorial Porrúa, 1984), p. 567.

7. Otto Granados Roldán, *La Iglesia católica mexicana como grupo
de presión* (Mexico: Universidad Nacional Autónoma de México, 1981),
pp. 40–41.

8. Gutiérrez Casillas, *Historia de la Iglesia en México*, p. 600.

9. Ibid., p. 568.

10. Granados Roldán, *La Iglesia católica mexicana como grupo de presión*, p. 40.

11. For an excellent analysis of these particular conflicts over education, see Soledad Loaeza, *Clases medias y política en México: La querella escolar, 1959–63* (Mexico: El Colegio de México, 1988), part 2. See also Patricia

Arias, Alfonso Castillo, and Cecilia López, *Radiografía de la Iglesia en México, 1970–1978* (Mexico: Universidad Nacional Autónoma de México, 1988), pp. 63–68.

12. For a summary of the pope's visit and its implications, see Soledad Loaeza, "La Iglesia católica mexicana y el reformismo autoritario," *Foro Internacional* 25,2 (October–December, 1984), pp. 159–65.

13. Eduardo Sota García and Enrique Luengo González, *Entre la conciencia y la obediencia: La opinión del clero sobre la política en México* (Mexico City: Universidad Iberoamericana, 1994), p. 64.

14. Author's interview with Zacarías Márquez Terrazas, historian of Chihuahua (September 19, 1988, Chihuahua City).

15. Ibid.

16. Ibid.

17. Ibid.

18. Ibid.

19. Jean Meyer, *La Cristiada*, vol. 1, *La guerra de los Cristeros*, (Mexico: Siglo Veintiuno Editores, 1987), p. 25.

20. Author's interview with Zacarías Márquez Terrazas.

21. Wifredo Guinea, ed., "Constitución pastoral sobre la Iglesia en el mundo actual *(Gaudium et Spes),*" *Los documentos del Vaticano II* (Mexico: Editorial "El," 1966), no. 40, p. 233.

22. Ibid., no. 25, p. 218.

23. Margaret E. Crahan, "Church and State in Latin America: Assassinating Some Old and New Stereotypes," *Daedalus* 120, no. 3 (Summer, 1991).

24. Guinea, ed., "Constitución pastoral sobre la Iglesia en el mundo actual *(Gaudium et Spes),*" no. 36, p. 228.

25. Daniel H. Levine, "Religion and Politics, Politics and Religion: An Introduction," in Daniel H. Levine, ed., *Churches and Politics in Latin America* (Beverly Hills: Sage Publications, 1979), p. 23.

26. Wifredo Guinea, ed., "Constitución dogmática sobre la Iglesia *(Lumen Gentium),*" *Los documentos del Vaticano II* (Mexico: Editorial "El," 1966), no. 9, pp. 16–17.

27. Levine, "Religion and Politics, Politics and Religion," p. 21.

28. Guinea, ed., "Constitución pastoral sobre la Iglesia en el mundo actual *(Gaudium et Spes),*" no. 43, p. 239.

29. Ibid., no. 43, p. 238.

30. Guinea, ed., "Constitución dogmática sobre la Iglesia *(Lumen Gentium),*" no. 22, p. 35.

31. Final Document of Commission 1, Sub-Commission A of the Medellín Conference, "Justicia," in *Christus* 33,396 (November, 1968), p. 1027.

32. Conferencia del Episcopado Mexicano, *La evangelización en el presente y en el futuro de América Latina: Documento aprobado de la III Conferencia General del Episcopado Latinoamericano, Puebla* (Mexico: Librería Parroquial de Clavería, 1984), pp. 4–5.

33. Ibid., no. 486, p. 127.

34. Ibid., nos. 531 and 532, pp. 134–35.

35. Ibid., nos. 1134–52, pp. 227–30.

36. Ibid., nos. 521–23, pp. 132–33.

37. Ibid., no. 541, p. 136.

38. Final Document of Commission 1, Subcommission B of the Medellín Conference, "Paz," in *Christus* 33,396 (November, 1968), pp. 1042–43.

39. Sota García and González, *Entre la conciencia y la obediencia*, p. 48.

40. Michael Tangeman, *Mexico at the Crossroads: Politics, the Church, and the Poor* (Maryknoll, N.Y.: Orbis Books, 1955) p. 47.

41. J. Gutiérrez Casillas, *Historia de la Iglesia en México* (Mexico City: Editorial Porrua, 1984), pp. 494–96.

42. Enrique D. Dussel, *De Medellín a Puebla: Una década de sangre y esperanza 1968–1979* (Mexico: Editorial Edicol, 1979), p. 160.

43. "Carta Pastoral del Episcopado Mexicano sobre el desarrollo e integración de nuestra patria en el primer aniversario de la encíclica *'Populorum Progresio,'* 26 marzo 1968," in Conferencia del Episcopado Mexicano, *Documentos colectivos del Episcopado Mexicano* (Mexico: Comisión Episcopal de Medios de Comunicación Social, 1985), see especially pp. 131, 132, 155–88.

44. Jaime Pérez Mendoza, "Por petición de Bartlett el Vaticano ordenó que hubiera misas en Chihuahua," *Proceso* 10,509 (August 4, 1986), p. 8.

45. Dussel, *De Medellín a Puebla*, p. 81.

46. "Panorama religioso," *Información procesada de Chihuahua* (June, 1986), p. 81.

47. Dussel, *De Medellín a Puebla*, p. 523.

48. For an understanding of the bishop's pastoral orientation, see Adalberto Almeida y Merino, *El proceso evangelizador y su organización: Tercera Carta Pastoral* (Chihuahua: Editorial Camino, 1985), pp. 57–62; and Manuel Talamás Camandari, *¿Cuál es su excusa?* (Mexico: Ediciones Paulinas, 1986), pp. 141–62, 187–97.

49. Author's interview with Adalberto Almeida y Merino, Archbishop of Chihuahua (December 16, 1986, Chihuahua City).

50. Author's interview with Dizán Vásquez, director of the Diocesan Center of Communication (September 8, 1988, Chihuahua City).

51. Almeida y Merino, *El proceso evangelizador y su Organización*, p. 10.

52. Author's interview with José Solis, parish priest (October 20, 1987, Ciudad Juárez).

53. Author's interview with Félix Martínez, seminary professor and expert on the history of the Catholic Church in Chihuahua (September 30, 1988, Chihuahua City).

54. Arias, Castillo, and López, *Radiografía de la Iglesia en México*, p. 41.

55. Almeida y Merino, *El proceso evangelizador y su organización*, p. 79.

56. For the events leading up to the formation of the CDP, see Victor Orozco, "Las luchas populares en Chihuahua," *Cuadernos Políticos* 9 (July–September, 1976), especially pp. 50–55.

57. Arzobispado de Chihuahua, "Declaración del arzobispo y sacerdotes de Chihuahua sobre los sucesos violentos ocurridos allá," (Chihuahua: January 28, 1972).

58. Ibid.

59. Ibid.

60. Ibid.

61. Ibid.

62. "Declaración del arzobispo y sacerdotes de Ciudad Juárez sobre la situación nacional," *Christus* 37,437 (April, 1972), p. 45.

63. Ibid., p. 46.

64. Ibid.

65. Author's interview with José García Arribas, president of the Diocesan Lay Commission in Chihuahua City (March 5, 1987, Chihuahua City).

66. Ibid.

67. Ibid.

68. Ibid.

69. Orozco, "Las Luchas Populares en Chihuahua," pp. 55–63; author's interview with René Blanco, parish priest (October 16, 1987, Ciudad Juárez).

70. Author's interview with Hugo Blanco, parish priest (October 14, 1987, Ciudad Juárez).

71. Author's interview with Augustin Becerra, parish priest (March 16, 1987, Chihuahua City).

72. Ibid.

73. Ibid.

74. Equipo de Reflexión de Pastoral, "La muerte del P. Aguilar: Reto a nuestra conciencia cristiana," *Christus* 42,498 (May, 1977), p. 61.

75. For a justification of Camilo's decision to restructure seminary education, see the document, *La formación sacerdotal y el Seminario Regional del Norte*, 1981, which, while officially without an author, was written mostly by Camilo when he was rector of the seminary.

76. Ibid., p. 76.

77. For a summary of these events, see Félix Martínez, *Historia del seminario de Chihuahua* (Chihuahua: Editorial Camino, 1986), pp. 170–74.

78. Author's interview with René Blanco.

79. Ibid.

80. Ibid.

81. Arias, Castillo, and López, *Radiografía de la Iglesia en México*, p. 59.

82. Adalberto Almeida y Merino, *Votar con responsibilidad: Una orientación cristiana* (Chihuahua: Editorial Camino, 1983), p. 6.

83. Ibid., p. 7.

84. Ibid., p. 11.

85. Ibid., pp. 3–5.

86. For an excellent analysis of the new voting patterns revealed in 1983 in Chihuahua, see Alberto Aziz Nassif, "La coyuntura de las elecciones

en Chihuahua 1983," in Carlos Martínez Assad, ed., *Municipios en conflicto* (Mexico: Instituto de Investigaciones Sociales–Universidad Nacional Autónoma de México, 1985), especially pp. 111–23.

87. Ibid., p. 95.

88. Ibid., p. 124.

89. Adalberto Almeida y Merino, "Los católicos y el deber cívico," *Norte* (September 24, 1983), p. 2.

90. Ibid., p. 5.

91. Ibid., pp. 5–6.

92. Adalberto Almeida y Merino et al., "Coherencia cristiana en la política: A los católicos que militan en los partidos políticos" (March, 1986), pp. 6–7.

93. Ibid.

94. Ibid., p. 8.

95. Ibid., p. 9.

96. Ibid.

97. Ibid., pp. 12–13.

98. "Panorama religioso," *Información procesada de Chihuahua* (July, 1986), p. 118.

99. Ibid., p. 119.

100. Ibid.

101. Ibid., p. 122.

102. Adalberto Almeida y Merino, homily for Sunday, July 13, 1986, in Partido Acción Nacional, *Sin más armas que la vida misma* (Mexico: EPESSA, 1986), p. 251.

103. Ibid., p. 253.

104. Jaime Pérez Mendoza, "Por petición de Bartlett el Vaticano ordenó que hubiera misas en Chihuahua," p. 7.

105. Oscar Hinojosa, "Prigione, enlace de Bartlett para reprender a obispos críticos," *Proceso* 10,511 (August, 1986).

106. Roderic Ai Camp, *Crossing Swords: Politics and Religion in Mexico* (Oxford University Press, 1997), p. 65.

107. Raul Monje, "Prigone se contradice," *Proceso* 510 (August 11, 1986), p. 17.

108. Ibid.

109. Camp, *Crossing Swords*, p. 65.

110. Jaime Pérez Mendoza, "Por petición de Bartlett el Vaticano ordenó que hubiera misas en Chihuahua," p. 6.

111. "Panorama religioso," *Información procesada de Chihuahua* (July, 1986), p. 123.

112. Author's interview with Adalberto Almeida y Merino.

113. Quoted in Alfonso Sahagún, "Talleres de la democracia: Una iniciativa de cambio político pacífico. Dimensión social de la fe," *La Nación* 45,1733 (June 15, 1987), p. 22.

114. This homily is reprinted in *La Nación* 44,1712–13 (August, 1986), p. 20.

115. "Mensaje del Obispo y Presbiterio de Ciudad Juárez, a todo el pueblo," ibid., p. 21.

116. Ibid.

117. Author's interview with Oscar Enríquez, parish priest (October 14, 1987, Ciudad Juárez).

118. Author's interview with Hugo Blanco.

119. Author's interview with Oscar Enríquez.

120. Author's interview with Vicente Machado, parish priest (October 14, 1987, Ciudad Juárez).

121. Author's interview with Oscar Enríquez.

122. Ibid.

123. Adalberto Almeida y Merino et al., "Juicio moral sobre el proceso electoral," in Partido Acción Nacional, *Sin más armas que la vida misma*, p. 257.

124. This workshop, held on February 19, 1987, was attended by the author.

125. Sahagún, "Talleres de la democracia," p. 22.

126. Miguel A. Granados Chapa, "Talleres de la democracia: Opiniones del clero en Chihuahua," *Norte* (February 17, 1987), p. 3A.

127. *Taller sobre los católicos y la democracia: Segundo documento de trabajo* (Chihuahua: Arquidiocesis de Chihuahua, 1987).

128. Eduardo Fernández Armendariz, "Dimes y diretes sobre los talleres," *Norte* (January 30, 1987), p. 3E.

129. Ibid.

130. Ibid.

131. "Panorama religioso," *Información procesada de Chihuahua* (August, 1986), p. 83.

132. Author's interview with Dizán Vásquez.

133. Ibid.

134. Author's interview with Tomás Ortiz, parish priest (March 18, 1987, Chihuahua City); author's interview with René Blanco.

135. Adalberto Almeida y Merino, "Los aspectos éticos de las próximas elecciones: Orientación pastoral" (Chihuahua: Arzobispado de Chihuahua, 1988).

136. The hostility of the Mexican bishops to liberation theology is well known. For an excellent analysis of their efforts to control its spread in Mexico, see Arias, Castillo, and López, *Radiografía de la Iglesia en México*.

137. "Panorama religioso," *Información procesada de Chihuahua* (July, 1986), p. 124; ibid. (August, 1986), p. 80; ibid. (September, 1986), p. 69–70.

138. Carlos Fazio, "El episcopado contra 'la desinformación' oficial sobre sus actividades," *Proceso* 10,513 (September 1, 1986), pp. 13–15; "Panorama religioso," *Información procesada de Chihuahua* (August, 1986), p. 80.

139. Conferencia Episocopal Mexicano, "Declaración de los obispos mexicanos" (August 19, 1986), in *La Iglesia habla: Orientaciones pastorales de los obispos de México sobre el tema cívico-político* (Monterrey: USEM, 1987), pp. 217–19.

140. Camp, *Crossing Swords*, p. 67.

141. Ibid., p. 63.

142. Ibid., pp. 63–64.

143. Victor M. Ramos Cortés, *Poder, representación, y pluralidad en la Iglesia* (Guadalajara: Universidad de Guadalajara, 1992), p. 38.

144. This number is derived from data in Ramos Cortés, *Poder, representación, y pluralidad en la Iglesia.*

145. This number is derived from data on episcopal statements in Conferencia del Episcopado Mexicano, *Documentos colectivos del Episcopado Mexicano: A diez años del Concilio Vaticano.*

146. Sota García and González, *Entre la conciencia y la obediencia*, ch. 4, 5, 6.

147. For an analysis of the process of rapprochement, see Allan Metz, "Mexican Church-State Relations under President Carlos Salinas de Gortari," *Journal of Church and State* 34, no. 1 (Winter, 1992); and Roberto Blancarte, "Recent Changes in Church-State Relations in Mexico: An Historical Approach," *Journal of Church and State* 35, no. 4 (Autumn 1993).

148. "Encuestalía: Quien quiere un Papa?" *Nexos* 148 (April, 1990).

149. Tangeman, *Mexico at the Crossroads*, p. 71.

150. Carlos Fazio, *Samuel Ruiz: El caminante* (Mexico City: Espasa Calpe Mexicana, 1994), p. 194.

151. Sonia Morales and Rodrigo Vera, "Samuel Ruiz ha resistido, desde 1960, hostigamientos, acusaciones, condenas, agresiones, injurias," *Proceso* 956 (February 27, 1995), pp. 12–17.

152. Tangeman, *Mexico at the Crossroads*, p. 86.

153. Ibid., p. 104.

154. On the role of the Church, see Fazio, *Samuel Ruiz*. On the rebellion itself, see, Neil Harvey, *Rebellion in Chiapas: Rural Reforms, Campesino Radicalism, and the Limits of Salinism* (La Jolla: Center for U.S.-Mexican Studies, University of California, San Diego, 1994).

155. Tangeman, *Mexico at the Crossroads*, p. 11.

156. Ibid., p. 106.

157. Ibid., pp. 105–6.

5. THE EMERGENCE OF CIVIC ASSOCIATIONS

1. The term *human rights* as used in this chapter includes political, legal, and electoral rights as a central component of the concept of human rights.

2. Sergio Aguayo Quezada and Luz Paula Parra Rosales, *Los organismos no gubernamentales de derechos humanos en México: Entre la democracia participativa y la electoral* (Mexico: Academia Mexicana de Derechos Humanos, 1997), pp. 24–27.

3. Ibid., Appendix B, Table 6, p. 55.

4. Ibid., Appendix B, Table 4, p. 54.

5. Ibid., Appendix B, Table 3, p. 54.

6. Robert Putnam, *Making Democracy Work: Civic Traditions in Modern Italy* (Princeton: Princeton University Press, 1993), especially ch. 6, pp. 163–85.

7. Alexis de Tocqueville, *Democracy in America*, ed. J. P. Mayer (Garden City: Anchor Books, 1969), vol. 1, pp. 62–84, 174–95, 287–301; and vol. 2, pp. 442–49 and 509–30.

8. William Kornhauser, *The Politics of Mass Society* (New York: The Free Press, 1959), pp. 21–113.

9. Leo XIII, "Rerum Novarum," in *Ocho grandes mensajes*, ed. Jesús Iribarren and José Luis Gutiérrez (Madrid: Biblioteca de Autores Cristianos, 1971), pp. 19–56; Pius XI, "Quadragesimo Anno," in *Ocho grandes mensajes*, pp. 63–120; and Michel Creuzet, *Los cuerpos intermedios* (Madrid: Speiro, S.A., 1977), pp. 51–127, 173–232.

10. Gabriel A. Almond and Sidney Verba, *The Civic Culture: Political Attitudes and Democracy in Five Nations* (Princeton: Princeton University Press, 1963), pp. 300–22.

11. Ibid., p. 309.

12. Luís Felipe Bravo Mena, "COPARMEX and Mexican Politics," in Sylvia Maxfield and Ricardo Anzaldúa Montoya, *Government and Private Sector in Contemporary Mexico* (San Diego: Center for U.S.-Mexican Studies, University of California, 1987) p. 92.

13. For COPARMEX's vision of modernization, see XLVII Asamblea Nacional Ordinaria, *Participar para modernizar a México* (Mexico: COPARMEX, 1986), especially pp. 15–24, 28–36, 39–40; and XLIX Asamblea Nacional Ordinaria, *Modernización o crisis y autoritarismo* (Mexico: COPARMEX, 1986), especially pp. 3–11, 17–21, 28–30.

14. Centro Empresarial de Chihuahua, *Proposiciones de COPARMEX para resolver algunos de los problemas de México* (Chihuahua: COPARMEX, [n.d.]).

15. Author's interview with Ramón Hernandez Flores, national president of the Integrated Human Development and Citizen Action organization (DHIAC) 1979–82 (April 20, 1988, Mexico City).

16. Author's interview with Jaime Aviña, national president of DHIAC 1982–87 (April 22, 1988, Mexico City).

17. The membership figure is from the author's interview with Marcos Enrique Herrera González, director of DHIAC's newsletter *Poder Ciudadano* (March 16, 1988, Mexico City). The distribution of DHIAC's branches is from Marcos Enrique Herrera González, "1988, Nueva versión de 1910: Clouthier," *Poder Ciudadano* 4 (April, 1988), p. 5.

18. Author's interview with Salvador Cortés, president of DHIAC in Chihuahua 1983–88 (September 6, 1988, Chihuahua City).

19. Author's interview with Gabriela Romero, vice-president of the National Civic Feminine Association (ANCIFEM) (April 27, 1988, Mexico City).

20. Asociación Nacional Civica Femenina, *La ANCIFEM* (México: ANCIFEM, [n.d.]).

21. Author's interview with Gabriela Romero.

22. Ibid.

23. Author's interview with Cecilia Ostos, Elva Lafon de la O., and Luz María Pazos, leaders of ANCIFEM in Ciudad Juárez (August 25, 1988, Ciudad Juárez).

24. Author's interview with Salvador Cortés.

25. Ibid.

26. Ibid.

27. Ibid.

28. Author's interview with Francisco Barrio, mayor of Ciudad Juárez, 1983–86, and PAN governor of Chihuahua, 1992–96 (August 24, 1988, Ciudad Juárez).

29. Ibid.

30. Ibid.

31. Author's interview with Francisco Maldonaldo, president of the Family Patrimony Committee (CPF) (May 18, 1987, Parral).

32. Author's interview with Raymundo López López, co-founder of the Popular Defense Committee (CDP) of Ciudad Juárez (October 22, 1987, Ciudad Juárez).

33. Author's interview with Sergio Conde Varela, secretary of the municipal government of Ciudad Juárez, 1983–86 (September 23, 1987, Ciudad Juárez).

34. Author's interview with Carlos Angulo, secretary of Electoral Action for the PAN Municipal Committee of Ciudad Juárez, 1986–89 (August 27, 1988, Ciudad Juárez).

35. Author's interview with Camilo Daniel, parish priest (May 5, 1987, Sisoguichi).

36. Author's interview with Humberto Ramos Molina, mayor of Cuauhtémoc, 1983–86 (April, 27, 1987, Cuauhtémoc).

37. Camilo Daniel and Victor Quintana, *Sembrando entre la nieve: El movimiento campesino democrático … su lucha* (Zapopan: EDOC-PRAXIS, 1987), p. 16.

38. Author's interview with Camilo Daniel, parish priest (September 27, 1988, Anáhuac).

39. Author's interview with Adalberto Almeida y Merino.

40. José Dolores Cano et al., "A la opinión pública," *La Nación* 44,1712–13 (August, 1986).

41. *Información procesada* (January, 1988), p. 32.

42. Author's interview with Camilo Daniel Pérez, parish priest (September 27, 1988, Ciudad Anáhuac).

43. Author's interview with Camilo Daniel, parish priest (April 25, 1987, Anáhuac).

44. Francisco Ortiz Pinchetti, "Tambien la indignación se previó en Chihuahua y se le inutiliza," *Proceso* 10, 506 (July 14, 1986), p. 14.

45. "Información política y social," *Información procesada de Chihuahua* (July, 1986), p. 69.

46. "Dictamen del Jurado Popular al Pueblo de Chihuahua," *Diario de Chihuahua* (August 8, 1986), p. 12.

47. Victor M. Quintana Silveyra, "La protesta social en Chihuahua en los ochentas," in Rubén Lau and Victor M. Quintana, *Movimientos populares en Chihuahua* (Ciudad Juárez: Universidad Autónoma de Chihuahua, 1991), p. 106.

48. Francisco Ortiz Pinchetti, "Inseguridad y violencia signos del gobierno de Fernando Baeza," *Proceso* 14,769 (July 29, 1991), p. 27.

49. Daniel García, "Piden a gobierno celeridad en el caso del atentado al Padre Camilo," *Diario de Juárez* (June 4, 1998).

50. Francisco Ortiz Pinchetti, "Incipiente organización opositora, respuesta a la política de arrasamiento," *Proceso* 10,511 (August, 18, 1986), pp. 15–16.

51. Ibid., p. 18.

52. Juan Miguel de Mora, *Elecciones en México: Se repetirá el ejemplo de Chihuahua?* (México: EDAMEX, 1988), pp. 238–40.

53. "Declaración del Foro por el Sufragio Efectivo," in de Mora, *Elecciones en México*, pp. 233–41.

54. On the origins of the Civic Alliance, see Sergio Aguayo, "A Mexican Milestone," *Journal of Democracy* 6, no. 2, pp. 159–61.

55. It should be noted that approximately half of these domestic observers came from organizations linked to the PRI, such as the Movimiento para la Certidumbre (MOCE) and the National Teachers Union (SNTE).

56. Aguayo Quezada and Parra Rosales, *Los organismos no gubernamentales de derechos humanos en México*, p. 36.

57. Ibid.

58. Ibid.

59. Ibid., p. 39.

60. See Vikram K. Chand, "Democratisation from the Outside In: NGO and International Efforts to Promote Open Elections," *Third World Quarterly* 18, no. 3 (1997), pp. 543–61.

61. For a statement of the goals of the UN mission, see Unidad de Asistencia Electoral, *Posibilidades de apoyo a organizaciones no gubernamentales de observadores electorales en México* (Mexico City: UN Mission, May 23, 1994).

62. "Briefing Paper for the National Democratic Institute for International Affairs and the International Republican Institute's Joint International Delegation to the 1994 Mexican Elections" (August, 1994), p. 14.

63. Ibid.

64. Aguayo Quezada and Parra Rosales, *Los organismos no gubernamentales de derechos humanos en México*, Appendix B, Table 7, p. 56.

65. Aguayo Quezada and Parra Rosales, *Los organismos no gubernamentales de derechos humanos en México*, p. 13.

66. Rogelio Gómez Hermosillo, cited in Michael Tangeman, *Mexico at the Crossroads: Politics, the Church, and Poor* (Maryknoll, N.Y.: Orbis Books, 1995), p. 104.

67. Ibid.

68. Aguayo Quezada and Parra Rosales, *Los organismos no gubernamentales de derechos humanos en México*, p. 12.

69. Author's interview with Federico Barrio, resident, Constructora Intel (October 19, 1987, Ciudad Juárez).

70. Author's interview with Victor Rodríguez Guajardo, president of the PAN Municipal Committee in Cuauhtémoc (April 26, 1987, Cuauhtémoc).

71. Ibid.

72. Author's interview with Humberto Ramos.

73. Author's interview with Victor Rodríguez.

74. Author's interview with Camilo Daniel (April 5, 1987).

75. Putnam, *Making Democracy Work*; Tocqueville, *Democracy in America*; and Kornhauser, *The Politics of Mass Society*.

6. THE RESPONSE OF THE MEXICAN STATE: POLITICAL REFORM IN THE 1980s AND 1990s

1. For a detailed study of the September, 1993, reforms, see the Carter Center of Emory University, the Council of Freely-Elected Heads of Government, *Electoral Reform in Mexico* (Atlanta: Carter Center of Emory University, 1993).

2. These results are from a poll conducted by the domestic election monitoring group, Civic Alliance, dated June 30, 1994.

3. For an analysis of the 1994 set of reforms, see the Council of Freely Elected Heads of Government, *Elections in Mexico: Third Report* (Atlanta: The Carter Center of Emory University, 1994).

4. For an analysis of the 1996 reforms, see The Carter Center of Emory University, *The Carter Center Delegation to Observe the July 6, 1997, Elections in Mexico* (Atlanta: Carter Center, 1997). For a historical perspective on reforms, see Joseph Klesner, "Electoral Reform in Mexico's Hegemonic Party System: Perpetuation of Privilege or Democratic Advance?" Paper presented at the 1997 meeting of the American Political Science Association, Washington, D.C., August 28–31.

5. For the skeptical view, see Lorenzo Meyer, "Democratization of the PRI: Mission Impossible?" in Wayne A. Cornelius et al., *Mexico's Alternative Political Futures* (La Jolla: Center for U.S.-Mexican Studies, University of California, San Diego, 1989).

6. John Bailey, *Governing Mexico: The Statecraft of Crisis Management* (New York: St. Martins Press, 1988), p. 120.

7. M. Delal Baer, "Mexico's Second Revolution: Pathways to Liberalization," in Riordan Roett, ed., *Political and Economic Liberalization in Mexico: At a Critical Juncture?* (Boulder: Lynne Rienner Publishers, 1993), pp. 51–68.

8. Ibid., p. 57.

9. Ibid., p. 65.

10. Luis Rubio, "Economic Reform and Political Change in Mexico," in Roett, *Political and Economic Liberalization in Mexico*, pp. 39–41.

11. For a good analysis of the PRI's approach towards affiliation, see Luís Javier Garrido, "Un partido sin militantes," in Soledad Loaeza and Rafael Segovia, eds., *La vida política mexicana en crisis* (Mexico: El Colegio de México, 1987), pp. 61–76.

12. Author's interview with Rafael Oceguera Ramos, member of the PRI's National Executive Committee (CEN) and former delegate of the CEN to the PRI in Chihuahua in 1989 (September 5, 1990, Mexico City).

13. Ibid. On Salinas's support for the democratization of the PRI, see his speech at Puebla as PRI presidential candidate on April 22, 1988, entitled "Los retos de la democracia," reprinted in Carlos Salinas de Gortari, *El reto* (Mexico: Editorial Diana, 1988), pp. 37–58; see also Salinas's speech at Querétaro to the PRI on March 4, 1989, "La precisión del cambio," reprinted in *Nexos* 136 (April, 1989).

14. Manuel Villa, "Democratizar en Chihuahua," *Cuadernos de Nexos* 11 and 12, pp. xiv, xv, in *Nexos* 138 (June, 1989).

15. Ibid. Calculation of averages mine.

16. Ignacio Sachman, *Operación Chihuahua: Vanguardia de la modernización política nacional* (Mexico: El Nacional, 1989), p. 55.

17. Ibid., p. 77.

18. Author's interview with Rafael Oceguera.

19. Miguel Angel Romero, "Chihuahua: laboratorio político," *El cotidiano* 6,30 (Julio–Agosto, 1989), p. 18.

20. Raul Cruz Zapata, *Carlos A. Madrazo: Biografía política* (Mexico: Editorial Diana, 1988), pp. 17–19.

21. The complete text of his statement appears in Georgina Saldierna, "Reconocimiento oficial del PRI al triunfo de Ruffo," *La Jornada* (July 5, 1989), p. 12.

22. Author's interview with Rafael Oceguera.

23. For the text of these reforms, see XIV Asamblea Nacional, "Dictamen de la comisión de estatutos," in *Participación viva* (Mexico: Partido Revolucionario Institucional, 1990), pp. 56–69.

24. Elías Chávez, "Historias que a los priístas distinguidos les gustaría olvidar," *Proceso* 14,749 (March 11, 1991), p. 12.

25. Luis Angel Garza, "Olvidadas las ilegalidades en su encumbramiento, Sócrates Rizzo avanza hacia la gubernatura de Nuevo León," *Proceso* 14,747 (February 25, 1991), pp. 5–17.

26. Francisco Ortíz Pinchetti, "Los Colimenses lo tomaron en serio e hicieron de de la Madrid un auténtico rival de Socorro Diaz," *Proceso* 14,751 (March 25, 1991), p. 25.

27. Ibid., pp. 24–25.

28. Francisco Ortíz Pinchetti, "En Colima, el PRI se mostró en toda su intimidad," *Proceso* 14,752 (April 1, 1991), p. 10.

29. Carlos Marín, "Vehículo de la frustración de su directora, 'El Día' le reprocha al PRI todo lo que le encubrió," *Proceso* 14,752 (April 1, 1991), pp. 8–9.

30. Jeanette Becerra Acosta, "Cuando fui gobernador no pude apoyar los cambios en el PRI, reconoce Fernando Baeza," *El Excelsior* (February 10, 1998).

31. Carter Center / National Democratic Institute delegation interview with Artemio Iglesias, president of the PRI in the State of Chihuahua (August 20, 1994, Chihuahua City). The author was a member of the delegation.

32. Author's interview with Hector González Mocken, President of the PRI in Ciudad Juárez (October 8, 1994, Ciudad Juárez).

33. George Grayson, *A Guide to the 1994 Mexican Presidential Election* (Washington, D.C.: Center for Strategic and International Studies, 1994), p. 27.

34. E. Rodríguez and A. Gutiérrez, "Entregan constancia de mayoria a Patricio," *Diario de Chihuahua* (March 11, 1998).

35. Sam Dillon, "Mexico's New Radical Politics: Primary Elections," *New York Times* (July 22, 1998), p. A 1.

36. Ibid.

37. Antonio Arrellano Caracas, "Cuestiona Nuñez la viabilidad de la Consulta interna para elegir candidatos," *La Crónica* (July 27, 1998).

38. For the new rules, see Partido Revolucionario Institucional, Consejo Político Nacional, *Acuerdo general para la postulación del candidato a la presidencia de la república para el período, 2000–2006* (May 17, 1999) (http://www.pri.org).

39. For an excellent discussion of the significance of the November primary, see Wayne A. Cornelius, "Mexico's Presidential Succession: Implications of the PRI Primary Election," paper presented at the Seminar on Mexican Electoral Politics, 1999–2000, Princeton University, December 10, 1999.

40. Wayne A. Cornelius, *Mexican Politics in Transition: The Breakdown of a One-Party Dominant Regime* (La Jolla: Center for U.S.-Mexican Studies, University of California, San Diego), p. 3.

41. Joy Langston, "Why Rules Matter: The Formal Rules of Candidate Selection and Leadership Selection in the PRI, 1978–1996," Working Paper no. 58 (Mexico City: Centro de Investigación y Docencia Económicas, 1996), pp. 26–27.

42. On Salinas's land reforms, see Merilee Grindle, "Reforming Land Tenure in Mexico: Peasants, the Market, and the State," in Riordan Roett, ed., *The Challenge of Institutional Reform* (Boulder: Lynne Reinner Publishers, 1995), pp. 39–56. See also, Alain De Janvry, Gustavo Gordillo, and Elisabeth Sadoulet, *Mexico's Second Agrarian Reform: Household and Community Responses, 1990–1994* (La Jolla: Center for U.S.-Mexican Studies, University of California, San Diego, 1997).

43. On the political effects of Chinese decollectivization, see Minxin Pei, "Creeping Democratization in China," *Journal of Democracy* 6, no. 4 (October, 1995), pp. 73–76.

44. Laurence Whitehead, "Mexico's Economic Prospects: Implications for State-Labor Relations," in Kevin Middlebrook, ed., *Unions, Workers, and the State in Mexico* (La Jolla: Center for U.S.-Mexican Studies, University of California, San Diego, 1991), pp. 57–83.

45. Robert A. Pastor, *Integration with Mexico: Options for U.S. Policy* (New York: Twentieth Century Fund, 1993), especially pp. 27–28 and 65–67.

46. Juan Molinar Horcasitas and Jeffrey A. Weldon, "Electoral Determinants and the Consequences of National Solidarity," in Wayne A. Cornelius, Ann L. Craig, and Jonathan Fox, eds., *Transforming State-Society Relations in Mexico: The National Solidarity Strategy* (La Jolla: Center for U.S.-Mexican Studies, University of California, San Diego, 1994), p. 133.

47. Ibid., p. 137.

48. Ibid., p. 141.

7. CONCLUSION

1. On "crafting," see Giuseppe Di Palma, *To Craft Democracies: An Essay on Democratic Transitions* (Berkeley: University of California Press, 1990).

2. See George Philip, *The Presidency in Mexican Politics* (New York: St. Martins Press, 1992), pp. 167–83.

3. Alan Riding, *Distant Neighbors: A Portrait of the Mexicans* (New York: Vintage Books, 1984), p. 183. Another study of corruption is Stephen D. Morris, *Corruption and Politics in Contemporary Mexico* (Tuscaloosa: The University of Alabama Press, 1991), especially pp. 1–20 and 115–42.

4. On the link between socioeconomic development and democracy, see Robert Dahl, *Polyarchy* (New Haven: Yale University Press, 1971), pp. 62–80; Samuel Huntington, *The Third Wave: Democratization in the Late Twentieth Century* (Norman: University of Oklahoma Press, 1989), pp. 59–72; and Seymour Martin Lipset, *Political Man: The Social Bases of Politics* (New York: Doubleday, 1960), pp. 45–76.

5. Edward J. Williams, "The Resurgent North and Contemporary Mexican Regionalism,' *Mexican Studies / Estudios Mexicanos* (Summer, 1990), especially pp. 313–16.

6. See Joseph L. Klesner, "An Electoral Route to Democracy? Mexico's Transition in Comparative Perspective," review essay, *Comparative Politics* 30, no. 4 (July, 1998).

7. Recent works on the PRD include Kathleen Bruhn, *Taking on Goliath: The Emergence of a New Left Party and the Struggle for Democracy in Mexico* (University Park: Pennsylvania State University Press, 1997); and Adolfo Aguilar Zinser, *¡Vamos a ganar! La pugna de Cuauhtémoc Cárdenas por el poder* (Mexico City: Editorial Oceano de México, 1995). See also Jorge G. Castañeda, *Utopia Unarmed: The Latin American Left after the Cold War* (New York: Vintage Books, 1994).

8. Author's interview with Cuauhtémoc Cárdenas (April 11, 1988, Mexico City).

9. On the evolution of the Mexican Left since late 1960s, see Barry Carr, *Mexican Communism, 1968–1983: Eurocommunism in the Americas?* (La Jolla: Center for U.S.-Mexican Studies, University of California, San Diego, 1985).

10. On these changes, see Castañeda, *Utopia Unarmed*, especially chapters 11 and 12.

11. See Jorge I. Domínguez and James McCann, *Democratizing Mexico: Public Opinion and Electoral Choice* (Baltimore: Johns Hopkins University Press, 1996), pp. 110–15, 145–48.

12. On the issue of dialogue, see Bruhn, *Taking on Goliath*, especially pp. 150–59.

13. Aguilar Zinser, *¡Vamos a Ganar¡* p. 457.

14. A good study of the effects of opposition governments on democratic practices at the regional level is Victoria E. Rodríguez and Peter M. Ward, eds., *Opposition Government in Mexico* (Albuquerque: University of New Mexico Press, 1995).

15. Anthony Lake, "From Containment to Enlargement," speech at Johns Hopkins University (SAIS), September 21, 1993.

16. Robert A. Pastor, *Integration with Mexico: Options for U.S. Policy* (New York: Twentieth-Century Fund, 1993), especially pp. 27–28, 65–67.

EPILOGUE: THE JULY 2, 2000, MEXICAN PRESIDENTIAL ELECTIONS

1. These figures are based on the Program of Preliminary Results (PREP) run by the Federal Election Institute (IFE), which may vary slightly from the final count.

2. Data on 2000 provided by Juan Molinar, citizen councillor, Federal Election Institute (IFE).

3. Data provided by Juan Molinar, citizen councillor, IFE.

4. Carter Center delegation interview with Cuauhtémoc Cárdenas, presidential candidate for the Alliance for Mexico (June 13, 2000, Mexico City); Carter Center delegation interview with Vicente Fox Quesada, presidential candidate for the Alliance for Change (June 13, 2000, Mexico City). The author was a member of the delegation.

5. Carter Center delegation interview with Cuauhtémoc Cárdenas; Carter Center delegation interview with Vicente Fox Quesada (June 30, 2000, Mexico City). The author was a member of the delegation.

6. For more on this, see the Carter Center of Emory University, *The July 2, 2000, Elections in Mexico: A Pre-Electoral Assessment* (Atlanta: Carter Center, 2000).

7. Author's interview with Elodia Gutiérrez, president of the Commission, 2000 (June 16, 2000, Mexico City). Conducted for the Carter Center.

8. Author's interview with Carlos Jarque, minister of social development (June 16, 2000, Mexico City); author's interview with Romarico

Arroyo, minister of agriculture (June 19, 2000, Mexico City). Conducted for the Carter Center.

9. Author's interview with Jose González Morfín, secretary general of the PAN (June 16, 2000, Mexico City). Conducted for the Carter Center.

10. Carter Center delegation interview with Vicente Fox Quesada (June 13, 2000, Mexico City).

11. The results of five of the major exit polls were as follows: (1) Mori (Democracy Watch): 42% (Fox), 32% (Labastida), and 19% (Cárdenas); (2) Redes Consultores (PAN); 41.57% (Fox), 38.61% (Labastida), and 17% (Cárdenas); (3) TV-Azteca (Covarrubias-Sofres)—Adjusted Result: 43.9% (Fox), 34.6% (Labastida), and 17.8% (Cárdenas); (4) Televisa (Mitovsky): 44% (Fox), 38% (Labastida), and 16% (Cárdenas); and (5) Chamber of Radio and Television: 43% (Fox), 34% (Labastida), and 16% (Cárdenas). Sources: Juan Molinar, citizen councillor, IFE; TV-Azteca results reported in *Milenio* (July 5, 2000), p. 7; and the author's personal notes of results as reported on television on election night.

12. The results of the ten major quick counts are as follows: (1) Citizen Presence: 41.9% (Fox), 36% (Labastida), and 17% (Cárdenas); (2) Berumen (IFE): 42.30% (Fox), 35.30% (Labastida), 16.60% (Cárdenas); (3) Applied Statistics: 42.60% (Fox); 37.80% (Labastida), and 16.90% (Cárdenas); (4) AC Nielsen (Chamber of Radio and Television); 42.92% (Fox), 37.06% (Labastida), and 17.13% (Cárdenas); (5) Alduncin (IFE): 43.50% (Fox), 34.60% (Labastida), and 16.70% (Cárdenas); (6) Gallup (IFE): 42.50% (Fox), 36.30% (Labastida), and 16.30% (Cárdenas); (7) Gauss (PAN): 43.75% (Fox), 36.42% (Labastida), and 17.30% (Cárdenas); (8) Pearson (PRI): 43.23% (Fox), 36.24% (Labastida), and 17.21% (Cárdenas); (9) ONOEM (Teachers Union): 44.12% (Fox), 37.21% (Labastida), and 16.16% (Cárdenas); and (10) TV-Azteca (Covarrubias-Sofres)—Adjusted Result: 42.65% (Fox), 34.85% (Labastida), and 17.15% (Cárdenas). Sources: Juan Molinar, citizen councillor, IFE; TV-Azteca results reported in *Milenio* (July 5, 2000), p. 7.

Author's Interviews

Most of these interviews were conducted by the author on his own initiative. The author was also a member of several delegations sent by the Carter Center to assess the electoral process in Mexico in 1993, 1994, 1997, and 2000. In addition to being a member of these delegations, the author served as the principal consultant to the Carter Center's Mexican Elections Project for most of the 1990s, and the field representative of the Carter Center during the 2000 electoral process. Interviews where the author participated as a member of a Carter Center delegation, or where he conducted an interview for the Carter Center, are marked with an asterisk; the others were conducted by the author on his own initiative. In those interviews where more than one person may have been present, usually only the primary person is listed, with all references to that interview citing only that person.

Aceves, Florencio. Director, *Revista Scorpio.* January 29, 1987; February 3, 1987; March 25, 1987; September 7, 1988; Chihuahua City.

Acosta, Magdalena Guadiana de. President, Municipal Committee of the PAN of Jiménez. With Jesús José Acosta, Luís Alberto Lightbourne, and Romana Camacho. July 13, 1987; Jiménez.

Acosta, Roberto. Former president of the PAN Municipal Committee of Delicias. July 1, 1987; Delicias.

Acosta, Soledad. Popular colony leader and PAN sympathizer in Parral. May 20, 1987; Parral.

Aguayo, Sergio. President, Civic Alliance. July 9, 1997*; Mexico City.

Aguilar, Carlos. PAN municipal president of Camargo 1983-86. July 7, 1987; Camargo.

Aguilar Coronado, Humberto. National secretary of Electoral Affairs, PAN. June 16, 2000*; Mexico City.

Aguilar Zinser, Adolfo. Mexican intellectual. September 7, 1993*; Mexico City.

Alamilla Arteaga, Genaro. President of the Social Communication Com-

337

mission of the Mexican Bishops' Conference (CEM) and Bishop of Atzacapotzalco. May 25, 1988; Mexico City.

Alarcón, César. Director, *Maquiladora* Association of Ciudad Juárez. October 9, 1987; Ciudad Juárez.

Alcocer Patina, Fernando. President, Impregnadora López Mateos. December 10, 1986; Chihuahua City.

Alderete, Manuel. Director, Economic Development of the State of Chihuahua. September 7, 1988; Chihuahua City.

Almada, Carlos. Director of the Federal Registry of Voters. September 9, 1993*; June 16,1994*; Mexico City.

Almeida, Genaro. Vice-president, Human Rights Rescue Organization. December 10, 1986; Chihuahua City.

Almeida y Merino, Adalberto. Archbishop of Chihuahua. December 16, 1986; Chihuahua City.

Alvarez, Adolfo. Baptist minister. October 21, 1987; Ciudad Juárez.

Alvarez, Luís H. Municipal president of Chihuahua City, 1983–86 and PAN national president, 1987–93. February 18, 1987; September 19, 1989; August 20, 1994*; Chihuahua City and Mexico City.

Américo Lastra, Sergio. President, Committee for the Democratic Struggle (COLUDE). September 21, 1987; Ciudad Juárez.

Angulo, Carlos. Secretary of electoral action in the PAN Municipal Committee of Ciudad Juárez, 1986–89; partner in law firm of Angulo, Calvo, Enríquez y González, S.C. August 27, 1988; Ciudad Juárez.

Arias, Ramiro. Manager of Shelter Projects, American Industries International. March 23, 1987; Chihuahua City.

Armendariz Delgado, Arturo. Director of the interior, state government of Chihuahua. February 3, 1987; Chihuahua City.

Arreola, Reginaldo. Director, forestry division, Ponderosa Industrial. January 30, 1987; Chihuahua City.

Arrieta, Guillermo. President, Municipal Committee of the PAN, Camargo. With Luís Méndez Meléndez, Silerio Reyes, and Horacio Romero. July 10, 1987; July 11, 1987; Camargo.

Arronte, Alfonso. Ex-president of the Entrepreneurs' Center of Ciudad Juárez; founding member of the Civic Front of Ciudad Juárez. September 23, 1987; Ciudad Juárez.

Arroyave Ramírez, Manuel. President, National Federation of Private Schools (CNEP) A.C. May 20, 1988; Mexico City.

Arroyo, Romarico. Secretary of agriculture, government of Mexico. June 19, 2000*; Mexico City.

Arrubarena, José Antonio. President, Institute for Judicial Studies. April 19, 1988; Puebla.

Aviña, Jaime. President of Integral Human Development and Citizen Action (DHIAC), 1982–87. April 22, 1988; Mexico City.

Ayala, Miguel. Analyst, Mexican Employers' Confederation (COPARMEX). March 8, 1988; Mexico City.

Ayala, Rafael. Vice-president, National Parents Union (UNPF). June 8, 1988; Mexico City.

Badía, Antonio. President of the PAN in Ciudad Juárez; member of PAN municipal government, 1993–96. September 18, 1987; September 2, 1988; October 6, 1994; Ciudad Juárez.

Baeza López, Alonso. President, Entrepreneurs' Center of Chihuahua City. December 15, 1986; Chihuahua City.

Baeza Meléndez, Fernando. Governor of the State of Chihuahua 1986–92. September 15, 1988; Chihuahua City.

Barajas Martínez, Fernando. Owner, Manzaneros Unidos. May 7, 1987; Cuauhtémoc.

Barbosa, Porfirio. Comptroller, government of Mexico City. June 27, 2000; Mexico City.

Barrio, Federico. President, Constructora Intel. October 29, 1987; Ciudad Juárez.

Barrio, Francisco. PAN candidate for governor of Chihuahua State in 1986; municipal president of Ciudad Juárez, 1983–86. September 30, 1987; August 24, 1988; Ciudad Juárez.

Barros Horcasitas, José Luís. Coordinator of advisors for internal and external policy, the Mexican presidency. June 13, 2000*; Mexico City.

Basave, Agustín. President of the Border Commission, Mexican Chamber of Deputies. September 8, 1993*.

Bátiz, Bernardo. Secretary general of the national PAN, 1972–75, 1984–87. May 19, 1988; October 4, 1989; Mexico City.

Becerra, Augustín. Parish priest. March 16, 1987; Chihuahua City.

Becerra Gaytán, Antonio. Candidate of the Unified Socialist Party of Mexico (PSUM) for governor of Chihuahua, 1986. December 16, 1986; September 22, 1988; Chihuahua City.

Becerril Straffron, Rodolfo. President of the Foreign Relations Commission, Federal Chamber of Deputies. September 8, 1993*; June 15, 1994*; Mexico City.

Beltran, Ulises. Technical adviser to the Mexican president. September 9, 1993*; June 17, 1994*; July 9, 1997*; Mexico City.

Benavides, Javier. President, PAN Municipal Committee, Chihuahua City. September 12, 1988; Chihuahua City.

Bermúdez Cuaron, Jaime. PRI municipal president of Ciudad Juárez, 1986–89; head of the Bermúdez Group. August 26, 1988; October 7, 1994; Ciudad Juárez.

Blanco, Hugo. Parish priest. October 14, 1987; Ciudad Juárez.

Blanco, René. Parish priest and vicar general of the diocese of Ciudad Juárez. October 16, 1987; October 8, 1994; Ciudad Juárez.

Bueno, Felix. Former president of the PAN District Committee in Parral; PAN candidate for municipal president of Parral, 1986. With José Luís Castruita and Zeferino Cisneros, May 13, 1987. Alone, May 15, 1987; Parral.

Burrolla Flores, Luís. Parish priest. March 20, 1987; Chihuahua City.

Bustamante, Guillermo. President, UNPF. April 13, 1988; Mexico City.

Calderón, Enrique. President, Rosenblueth Foundation. September 7, 1993*; Mexico City.

Calderón, Felipe. Secretary general of the PAN, 1993–96; president, 1996–present. September 7, 1993*; June 14, 1994*; July 8, 1997*; Mexico City.

Camacho Solis, Manuel. Presidential candidate of the Party of the Democratic Center in 2000. June 28, 2000*; July 2, 2000*; Mexico City.

Cárdenas, Cuauhtémoc. Candidate for the Mexican presidency for the National Democratic Front (FDN), 1988; presidential candidate of the PRD, 2000. April 11, 1988; June 13, 2000*; Mexico City.

Castillo Peraza, Carlos. President of the PAN, 1993–96. September 19, 1989; September 20, 1989; August 26, 1994*; Mexico City.

Chacón Rojo, Ramón. President, Entrepreneurs' Center of Ciudad Juárez. October 8, 1987; Ciudad Juárez.

Chávez Barrón, Hector. Director, Monterrey Technological Institute for Higher Studies (ITESM), Chihuahua campus. March 17, 1987; September 30, 1988; Chihuahua City.

Chavira, Hector. PAN activist. September 28, 1988; Chihuahua City.

Chavira, Victoria. Secretary of organization of the PAN's State Campaign Committee in 1988. September 14, 1988; Chihuahua City.

Conchello, José Angel. President of the PAN in Mexico City 1987–present; national president of the PAN, 1972–75. April 6, 1988; April 13, 1988; Mexico City.

Conde Varela, Sergio. Secretary of municipal government of Ciudad Juárez, 1983–86. September 23, 1987; Ciudad Juárez.

Corrella, Norberto. Secretary of national relations for the PAN's National Executive Committee. March 17, 1988; Mexico City.

Cortés, Salvador. President of Integral Human Development and Citizen Action (DHIAC) in Chihuahua, 1983–88. November 11, 1986; September 6, 1988; Chihuahua City.

Creel, Santiago. Citizen councillor. September 18, 1994*; Mexico City.

Daniel Pérez, Camilo. Parish priest; co-founder of the Democratic Peasant Movement (MDC) and the Democratic Electoral Movement (MDE). April 25, 1987; May 4, 1987; September 27, 1988; Anáhuac and Sisoguichi.

De Avila, Carmen. PAN federal deputy. May 21, 1987; Parral.

De la Peza, José Luís. President of the Electoral Tribunal of the Judicial Power of the Federation. July 7, 1997*; June 14, 2000*; Mexico City.

Delgado, Marta. President, Citizen Presence. June 21, 2000*; Mexico City.

Duarte Aldaz, José Andrés. Businessman in the wood industry. May 23, 1987; Parral.

Elizondo, Gustavo. President of PAN in Ciudad Juárez, 1986–88. September 28, 1987; Ciudad Juárez.

Enríquez, Oscar. Parish priest. October 14, 1987; Ciudad Juárez.

Erives Erives, Eloisa. PAN candidate for municipal president of Cuauhtémoc in 1983; owner, Papelería América. March 14, 1987; Cuauhtémoc.

Espino B., Annelena. Marketing manager, Economic Development of the State of Chihuahua. December 5, 1986; Chihuahua City.

Faesler, Julio. Civic Alliance leader. September 7, 1993*; September 10, 1993*; June 18, 1994*. President of the International Affairs Commission of the Chamber of Deputies. June 13, 2000*; Mexico City.

Félix Muñoz, Javier. Ex-secretary of organization, PAN Municipal Committee. September 22, 1988; Chihuahua City.

Fernández, Miguel. Treasurer of the PAN National Executive Committee (CEN); PAN candidate for municipal president of Chihuahua City in 1986. March 18, 1987; Chihuahua City.

Fox Quesada, Vicente. PAN candidate for the presidency in 2000. June 13, 2000*; June 30, 2000*; and July 2, 2000*; Mexico City.

Franco Guzman, Ricardo. Special prosecutor for electoral crimes. August 26, 1994*; Mexico City.

Fuentes, Sandra. Secretary of international affairs, PRI. June 14, 2000*; Mexico City.

García, Amalia. PRD Secretary of international relations. September 7, 1993*; June 14, 1994*; August 24, 1994*; Mexico City. National president of the PRD. June 13, 2000*; Mexico City.

García Acosta, Raul. President of the PAN in Ciudad Juárez. October 8, 1994; Ciudad Juárez.

García Arribas, José. President of the Diocesan Lay Commission of Chihuahua. March 5, 1987; Chihuahua City.

Gaytán Zuverza, Juan. President, Barillero Group. March 12, 1988; Chihuahua City.

Gómez Morin, Juan Manuel. Secretary general of the national PAN 1969–72; son of PAN founder Manuel Gómez Morin. September 18, 1989; Mexico City.

Gongora, Mario. Former PAN Activist. September 13, 1988; September 14, 1988; Chihuahua City.

González, Beatriz. PAN Candidate for federal deputy in 1988 from Cuauhtémoc; PAN leader in a popular colony. April 30, 1987; Cuauhtémoc.

González, Mario. President of the Chihuahua Branch of the UNPF. December 12, 1986; Chihuahua City.

González Bernal, Jaime. PAN Coordinator of Active and Pacific Civil Resistance (RECAP) in Ciudad Juárez. August 22, 1988; Ciudad Juárez.

González de la Rosa, Lorenzo. President of the Union for the Progress of the Peasants of the Bustillos Lake (UPCALA). May 5, 1987; Anáhuac.

González de las Casas, Horacio. PAN municipal president of Delicias, 1983–86. June 29, 1987; July 1, 1987; Delicias.

González Hinojosa, Manuel. National president of PAN, 1969–72, 1976–79. September 25, 1989; State of Mexico.

González Mocken, Hector. President of the PRI in Ciudad Juárez. October 8, 1994; Ciudad Juárez.

González Morfín, José. Secretary general (adjunct), PAN National Executive Committee. June 16, 2000*; Mexico City.

González Múzquiz, Mario. Director general, Duraplay of Parral, S.A.; president, Economic Development of the State of Chihuahua. March 6, 1987; Chihuahua City.

González Schmal, Jesús. PAN candidate for senator from Mexico City, 1988; former parliamentary coordinator of the PAN in the Chamber of Deputies. March 15, 1988; Mexico City.

González Torres, José. National president of PAN, 1959–62; PAN candidate for the Mexican presidency, 1964. September 29, 1989; Mexico City.

Grajeda, Guillermo. Former general manager, Mining Association of Chihuahua City. December 9, 1986; Chihuahua City.

Guerrero, Rafael. PAN candidate for municipal president of Saucillo, 1983. July 5, 1987; Saucillo.

Gutiérrez Estrada, Elodia. President of the Special Commission to Prevent the Misuse of Federal Public Resources in the 2000 Electoral Process, Chamber of Deputies. June 16, 2000*; Mexico City.

Hernández, Juan Pablo. Secretary general of the PAN Municipal Committee in Parral. May 26, 1987; Parral.

Hernández Flores, Ramón. National president of Integral Human Development and Citizen Action (DHIAC) 1979–82. April 20, 1988; Mexico City.

Hernández Hernández, Jesús. PAN leader in Ciudad Juárez. September 18, 1987; Ciudad Juárez.

Herrera González, Enrique. Director of *Poder Ciudadano*, a newsletter published by Integral Human Development and Citizen Action (DHIAC). March 16, 1988; Mexico City.

Herrera Martínez, Eloy. Owner of a small mining company. May 24, 1987; Parral.

Iglesias, Artemio. Senator and president of the PRI in Chihuahua State. March 6, 1987; Cuauhtémoc. August 21, 1994; Chihuahua City.

Jarque, Carlos. Minister of social development, government of Mexico. June 16, 2000*; Mexico City.

Labra, Armando. Sub-secretary of the Ministry of the Interior, government of Mexico. June 19, 2000*; Mexico City.

Lajous, Roberta. Secretary of international relations of the PRI. September 8, 1993*; Mexico City.

Landerreche Obregón, Juan. Founding member of PAN and son-in-law of Manuel Gómez Morin; director of publishing company Jus. October 3, 1989; Mexico City.

Ledon, Luís. Director, Serfín Bank, Northwestern Region. February 20, 1987; Chihuahua City.

Leiva Martínez, José Dolores. PAN leader in popular colony Francisco Villa, Delicias. July 1, 1987; Delicias.

Leos Flores, Mauro. Owner, Miniatura Pharmacy. With Dr. Mauro Leos López. March 18, 1987; Chihuahua City.

Limas Frescas, Soledad. President, National Civic Feminine Association (ANCIFEM), Chihuahua City. September 29, 1988; Chihuahua City.

López López, Raymundo. Co-founder of the Popular Defense Committee (CDP) of Ciudad Juárez. October 22, 1987; Ciudad Juárez.

Lózano, Antonio. PAN representative to the Federal Election Institute (IFE); attorney general of Mexico, Dec., 1994–Dec., 1996. September 7, 1993*; June 14, 1994*.

Luege, José Luís. PAN representative to the Federal Election Institute (IFE). September 7, 1993*; June 14, 1994*; Mexico City.

Lujambio, Alonso. Citizen councillor, the Federal Election Institute (IFE). July 6, 2000*; Mexico City.

Luján Peña, Guillermo. Member of PAN State Committee, Chihuahua State; owner of Materiales Tarahumara. February 23, 1987; Chihuahua City.

Luján Peña, Silvia. Secretary of feminine action, PAN State Committee. September 20, 1988; Chihuahua City.

Machado, Vicente. Parish priest. October 14, 1987; Ciudad Juárez.

Maldonaldo, Francisco. President of the Family Patrimony Committee (CPF). May 18, 1987; Parral.

Mares Paredes, Leopoldo. Owner, Futurama chain; owner, Mercados del Real. March 12, 1987; Chihuahua City.

Mariscal, Guillermo. Apple grower. May 7, 1987; Cuauhtémoc.

Márquez Chávez, Rafael. President of the New Wine Cultural Center. October 20, 1987; Ciudad Juárez.

Márquez Terrazas, Zacarías. Historian and chronicler of Chihuahua City. March 28, 1987; September 19, 1988; September 20, 1988; August 20, 1994; Chihuahua City.

Martínez, Diego. Jesuit priest. December 10, 1986; Chihuahua City.

Martínez, Enrique. Parish deacon. February 24, 1987; Chihuahua City.

Martínez, Félix. Seminary professor and expert on the history of the Catholic Church in Chihuahua. February 16, 1987; September 30, 1988; Chihuahua City.

Martínez, Ifigenia. Economist and candidate for senator for the FDN in 1988. April 14, 1988; Mexico City.

Mendoza, Eduardo. Director general, Higher Institute for Democratic Culture. September 7, 1993*; June 14, 1994*; Mexico City.

Muñoz Ledo, Porfirio. President of the PRD. September 7, 1993*; June 14, 1994*; Mexico City.

Molinar Horcasitas, Juan. Citizen councillor, the Federal Election Institute (IFE). July 5, 1997*; July 9, 1997*; June 21, 2000*; Mexico City.

Morales Mendoza, Antonio. Secretary general of the PAN State Committee in Chihuahua. November 4, 1986; December 16, 1986; January 29, 1987; February 2, 1987; September 30, 1988; Chihuahua City.

Murgia, Alfonso. Treasurer in the municipal administration of Francisco Barrio, 1983–86; leader of the civic group movement in Ciudad Juárez; important businessman. September 25, 1987; Ciudad Juárez.

Nguyen, Dong. Representative of the United Elections Assistance Program in Mexico. June 14, 1994*; June 18, 1994; July 5, 1997*; Mexico City.

Nuñez, Arturo. Director general of the Federal Election Institute (IFE). September 9, 1993*; June 14, 1994*; Mexico City.

Oceguera Ramos, Rafael. Member of the PRI's National Executive Committee (CEN); Delegate of the CEN to the PRI in Chihuahua in the 1989 elections. September 5, 1990; Mexico City.

Ocejo, Jorge. Secretary of relations, PAN Executive National Committee. June 16, 2000*; Mexico City.

Ochoa, Carlos. Public relations manager, Chihuahua motor plant, Ford Motor Company. December 9, 1986; Chihuahua City.

Ordóñez, Raul. President, Human Rights Rescue Organization. December 11, 1986; Chihuahua City.

Ornelas Kuchle, Oscar. Governor of the State of Chihuahua, 1980–85. March 26, 1987; Chihuahua City.

Ortiz, Tomás. Jesuit priest in a popular colony. March 18, 1987; Chihuahua City.

Ostos, Cecilia. President of the National Civic Feminine Association (ANCIFEM), Ciudad Juárez. With María Luz Pazos and Elva Lafon de la O. August 25, 1988; Ciudad Juárez.

Pacheco, Guadalupe. Assistant secretary of International Relations of the PRI. September 3, 1993*; Mexico City.

Paredes, Beatriz. Assistant secretary of the Interior Ministry. June 17, 1994*; Mexico City.

Pascoe, Ricardo. Representative of PRD presidential candidate Cuauhtémoc Cárdenas. June 17, 1994*; Mexico City. Spokesperson for the PRD. July 8, 1997*; Mexico City.

Payán, Isidro. Parish priest. October 17, 1987; Ciudad Juárez.

Paz Facio, Alejandro. Director of the *Maquiladora* Association of Chihuahua City. December 9, 1986; Chihuahua City.

Pelaez, Lorenzo. Secretary of the board, Mexican Employers' Confederation (COPARMEX). June 14, 1994*; Mexico City.

Pérez Hernandez, Germán. Magistrate councillor. September 10, 1993; Mexico City.

Pérez, Lorenzo. Director, *Información Procesada de Chihuahua.* September 9, 1988; Chihuahua City.

Pérez Lozano, Juan Francisco. Editor of *Revista Noroeste;* former CDP leader in Cuauhtémoc. April 29, 1987; Cuauhtémoc.

Pérez Velázquez, Guillermo. President, National Chamber of Commerce (CANACO) in Chihuahua. November 19, 1986; Chihuahua City.

Phillips Olmedo, Alfredo. General coordinator of international affairs, PRI. July 5, 1997*; July 8, 1997*; Mexico City.

Pinoncely, Roberto. Member, PAN State Committee of Chihuahua. March 21, 1987; Chihuahua City.

Portillo, Guillermo. Business manager, Duraplay de Parral. May 28, 1987; Parral.

Prieto Luján, Guillermo. President of the PAN State Committee of Chihuahua, 1980–88. November 5, 1986; February 2, 1987; February 16, 1987; September 16, 1988; Chihuahua City.

Quevedo Reyes, Manuel. PRI candidate for federal deputy from Ciudad Juárez, 1988; municipal president of Ciudad Juárez, 1977–80. April 7, 1987; Chihuahua City.

Ramírez, José Baray. Manager, Agricultural Union of Fruit Producers of Chihuahua. With Humberto Cuiltly, ex-president. May 7, 1987; Cuauhtémoc.

Ramos Molina, Humberto. Municipal president of Cuauhtémoc, 1983–86; co-founder of Democratic Peasant Movement (MDC) and the Democratic Electoral Movement (MDE). April 27, 1987; April 28, 1987; March 23, 1988; September 17, 1988; Chihuahua City and Cuauhtémoc.

Rascón, Javier. President, National Chamber of Transformation Industries (CANACINTRA), Chihuahua. November 18, 1986; Chihuahua City.

Rascón, Leopoldo. Business secretary, Mining Association of Chihuahua City; manager, Minera Brenda, SA de CV. December 12, 1986; Chihuahua City.

Rincon Gallardo, Gilberto. Presidential candidate of the Social Democracy Party, 2000. June 20, 2000*; Mexico City.

Rocha, Salvador. PRI representative to the Federal Election Institute (IFE). September 8, 1993*; Mexico City.

Rodríguez, Alfonso. Information director, Economic Development of Ciudad Juárez. With Antonio Ruiz, director. August 23, 1988; Ciudad Juárez.

Rodríguez Caraveo, Salvador. Former president of the PAN District Committee in Cuauhtémoc. With Javier Salinas Cautel. March 14, 1987; Cuauhtémoc.

Rodríguez Guajardo, Victor. President of the PAN Municipal Committee in Cuauhtémoc. April 25, 1987; April 26, 1987; Cuauhtémoc.

Rojas Durán, Alejandro. Member of the PRI's Critical Current. April 30, 1988; September 14, 1990; Mexico City.

Romero, Cecilia. Adjunct secretary general of the PAN. June 14, 1993*; July 5, 1997*; June 16, 2000*; Mexico City.

Romero, Gabriela. Vice-president of the National Civic Feminie Association (ANCIFEM). April 27, 1988; Mexico City.

Rosales, Luz. President, Citizens' Movement for Democracy. July 9, 1997*; June 13, 2000*; June 19, 2000*; Mexico City.

Salazar, Carlos. Director of international relations, PAN National Executive Committee. June 16, 2000*; Mexico City.

Saldaña Rodríguez, Juan. Former president of the PAN in Ciudad Juárez. August 29, 1988; Ciudad Juárez.

Salinas Contel, Javier. Activist in the National Synarchist Union. May 5, 1987; Cuauhtémoc.

Sánchez, Alfonso. President, Christian Family Movement (MCF), Chihuahua City. March 17, 1987; Chihuahua City.

Santos Esparza, José. Former PAN municipal president of Santa Barbara. May 27, 1987; Santa Barbara.

Segura, Jacinto. Delegate to Chihuahua of the Federal Planning and Budget Ministry (SPP). January 30, 1987; Chihuahua City.

Serrano, Jorge. President, National Pro-Life Committee. May 19, 1988; Mexico City.

Serrato Luevanos, Juan. PAN, president of the Directive Committee of the Tierra y Libertad Colony of Delicias. July 1, 1987; Delicias.

Solís, José. Parish priest. October 20, 1987; October 21, 1987; Ciudad Juárez.

Solís, María Jesús. Activist from the low-income Abraham González Colony in Camargo. With José Martínez Bejarano. July 8, 1987; Camargo.

Solís Silva, Alfonso. PAN candidate for municipal president of Camargo in 1986. July 12, 1987; Camargo.

Talamás Camandari, Manuel. Bishop of Ciudad Juárez. October 8, 1987; Ciudad Juárez.

Tarango, Mario. President of PRI in the State of Chihuahua and PRI candidate for municipal president of Delicias in 1983. February 10, 1987; February 12, 1987; September 6, 1988; Chihuahua City.

Terrazas, Patty. President, the United Front of Agricultural Producers (FOPEC). July 3, 1987; Delicias.

Terrazas Torres, Enrique. Member, PAN State Committee of Chihuahua; important businessman. March 16, 1987; Chihuahua City.

Torres, Alberto. President of the PAN Municipal Committee in Ciudad Juárez in 1985. September 25, 1987; Ciudad Juárez.

Torres family. PAN activist family in Magisterial Colony of Parral. March 16, 1987; Parral.

Torres Hernández, Isela. Interim president and secretary general of the PRI in Ciudad Juárez. August 25, 1988; Ciudad Juárez.

Torres Jáquez, Daniel. Leader of the Consumers Front (FEDECO); member of the Mexican Socialist Party (PMS) in Chihuahua City. September 22, 1988; Chihuahua City.

Torres Moreno, Bernardo. Member of the Unified Socialist Party of Mexico (PSUM); public school teacher in Cuauhtémoc. April 30, 1987; Cuauhtémoc.

Tostado, Amador. Secretary general of the Central Campesina Independiente (CCI) in Chihuahua. March 28, 1987; Chihuahua City.

Treviño, Javier. Adviser to the Zedillo campaign. August 24, 1994*; Mexico City.

Treviño Santos, Lorenzo. Municipal president of Delicias for the Authentic Party of the Mexican Revolution (PARM), 1980-83. July 6, 1987; Delicias.

Trevizo, Jorge. Parish priest. October 18, 1987; Ciudad Juárez.

Ugalde, Arturo. Director, Economic Development of the State of Chihuahua. December 5, 1986; Chihuahua City.

Valenzuela, Hector. PAN candidate for senator from Mexico State in 1988; former president of Civilization y Liberty. April 8, 1988; Mexico City.

Vallina, Eloy. President of the Chihuahua Group. September 26, 1988; Chihuahua City.

Vázquez, Dizán. Director of the Diocesan Center of Communication of Chihuahua; official spokesman for the archbishop of Chihuahua. September 8, 1988; Chihuahua City.

Vázquez, Raul. Director, Center for Union Studies, the Mexican Employers' Confederation (COPARMEX). March 15, 1988; Mexico City.

Velazco Arzac, Guillermo. Secretary of the Mexican Employers' Confederation (COPARMEX) council. March 12, 1988; Mexico City.

Vicencio Tovar, Abel. Secretary general of PAN National Executive Committee; PAN national president, 1978–84; PAN parliamentary coordinator, 1988–present. March 17, 1988; Mexico City.

Villalobos, Guillermo. Director, Entrepreneurs' Center of Chihuahua City. November 11, 1986; August 20, 1994; Chihuahua City.

Villalobos, Irma. Former president, National Civic Feminine Association (ANCIFEM), Chihuahua City. November 12, 1986; Chihuahua City.

Villalobos, Oscar. President of the Municipal Committee of PRI in Delicias. July 3, 1987; July 4, 1987; Delicias.

Villanueva, Ignacio. Parish priest. October 12, 1987; Ciudad Juárez.

Villareal, Francisco. Leader of civic groups in Ciudad Juárez; businessman; mayor of Ciudad Juárez, 1993–96. October 26, 1987; October 8,1994; Ciudad Juárez.

Villarreal, Gustavo. PAN municipal president of Parral, 1983–86. May 11, 1987; May 21, 1987; Parral.

Weisel Armendariz, Silvia. PAN activist in Parral. May 21, 1987; Parral.

Woldenberg, José. Citizen councillor. September 18, 1994*, Mexico City. President of the General Council of the Federal Election Institute (IFE). July 9, 1997*; June 14, 2000*; Mexico City.

Zambrano, Jesús. PRD representative to the Federal Election Institute (IFE). September 8, 1993.

Zebadua, Emilio. Citizen councillor, the Federal Election Institute (IFE). June 26, 2000*; July 6, 2000*; Mexico City.

Bibliography

Acción Nacional. *Cambio democrático de estructuras: Memoria de la XX Convención Nacional celebrada del 7 al 9 de febrero de 1969 en la Ciudad de México, D.F.* Mexico: Ediciones de Acción Nacional, 1969.

———. "Proyección de los principios de doctrina aprobados por la XVIII Convención Nacional, mayo de 1965." In *Principios de doctrina*, pp. 35–69. Mexico: EPESSA, 1985.

Acosta, Carlos, Pascal Beltrán del Río, Homero Campa, Elías Chávez, Gerardo Galarza, Oscar Hinojosa, María Esther Ibarra, and Fernando Ortega. "Al final, los priístas, sólos, declararon a Salinas presidente electo." *Proceso* 11,619 (September 12, 1988), pp. 6–13.

Acuña Nogueira, Héctor Manuel, et al. *La Iglesia y lo político: Hacía una caracterización de la jerarquía católica mexicana.* Mexico: Estudios Sociales, A.C., 1987.

Aguayo Quezada, Sergio. "A Mexican Milestone." *Journal of Democracy* 6, no. 2 (1995), pp. 157–67.

Aguayo Quezada, Sergio, and Luz Paula Parra Rosales. *Los organismos no gubernamentales de derechos humanos en México: Entre la democracia participativa y la electoral.* Mexico: Academia Mexicana de Derechos Humanos, 1997.

Aguilar Camín, Héctor, et al. "El caso Chihuahua." *Proceso* 10,508 (July 28, 1986), p. 4.

Aguilar Zinser, Adolfo. *¡Vamos a ganar! La pugna de Cuauhtémoc Cárdenas por el poder.* Mexico City: Editorial Oceano de México, 1995.

Alcocer, Jorge. "Recent Electoral Reforms in Mexico: Prospects for a Real Multiparty Democracy." In Riordan Roett, ed., *The Challenge of Institutional Reform in Mexico*, pp. 57–76. Boulder: Lynne Rienner Publishers, 1995.

Alcocer V., Jorge. "Desvarío panista." *Proceso* 12,677 (October 23, 1989), pp. 30–34.

———. "No al PRD." *Proceso* 13,715 (July 16, 1990), pp. 36–37.

Alduncin, Enrique. *Los valores de los mexicanos: México: Entre la tradición y la modernidad.* Mexico: Fomento Cultural Banamex, 1986.

Alianza Cívica. "La calidad de la jornada electoral del 21 de Agosto de 1994: Informe de Alianza Cívica Observación '94." Mexico City: September 19, 1994.

Almada, Francisco R. *Gobernadores del Estado de Chihuahua.* Chihuahua: Centro Librero La Prensa, 1981.

Almeida y Merino, Adalberto. "Los aspectos éticos de las próximas elecciones: Orientación pastoral." Chihuahua: Arzobispado de Chihuahua, 1988.

———. "Los católicos y el deber cívico." *Norte* (September 24, 1983), p. 3B.

———. Homily of Sunday, July 13, 1986. In Partido Acción Nacional, *Sin más armas: Que la vida misma,* pp. 249–53. Mexico: EPESSA, 1986.

———. *El proceso evangelizador y su organización: Tercera Carta Pastoral.* Chihuahua: Editorial Camino, 1985.

———. *Votar con responsabilidad: Una orientación cristiana.* Chihuahua: Editorial Camino, 1983.

Almeida y Merino, Adalberto, et al. "Coherencia cristiana en la política: A los católicos que militan en los partidos políticos." March, 1986.

———. "Juicio moral sobre el proceso electoral." In Partido Acción Nacional, *Sin más armas: Que la vida misma,* pp. 255–58. Mexico: EPESSA, 1986.

Almond, Gabriel, and Sidney Verba. *The Civic Culture: Political Attitudes and Democracy in Five Nations.* Princeton: Princeton University Press, 1963.

Almond, Gabriel, and Sidney Verba, eds. *The Civic Culture Revisited.* Boston: Little, Brown, and Company, 1980.

Alvarado, Arturo. "Los resultados de la elección para senadores" and "La jornada electoral de 1994: Una larga y circular travesía." In Germán Pérez del Castillo et al., eds., *La voz de los votos: Un análisis crítico de las elecciones de 1994.* Mexico City: Miguel Angel Porrua, 1995.

Alvarez, Luís H. "Radicalización de Acción Nacional." In *Memoria y esperanza: Discursos de Luís H. Alvarez,* pp. 5–11. Mexico: EPESSA, 1988.

———. "Un solo renglón." In *Memoria y esperanza: Discursos de Luís H. Alvarez,* pp. 221–33. Mexico: EPESSA, 1988.

Alvarez, Luís H., Victor Manuel Oropeza, and Francisco Villareal. "Por la verdad en Chihuahua." *Proceso* 10,508 (July 28, 1986), p. 3.

Alvarez, Luís H., and Abel Vicencio Tovar. "Compromiso nacional por la legitimidad y la democracia." *Palabra* 2,7 (January–March, 1989), pp. 62–70.

"Analizará la asamblea de la OEA el informe sobre México." *La Jornada* (May 25, 1990), pp. 1, 6.

Andazola, Juan Manuel. "La relación iglesia-estado y valoración de los sistemas económicos y políticos." *Diario de Chihuahua* (May 22, 1987), p. 15.

Anderson-Barker, Cynthia. *Election Fraud in Mexico: A Case Study of Elec-*

tions in Michoacán State on July 12, 1992. Los Angeles: Loyola Law School, 1993.

"A participar activamente en política, exhortó el Padre Peña a Católicos reunidos en el MBA." *Diario de Chihuahua* (May 10, 1987), p. 2A.

"Apresurado, el PRI se autoproclamó triunfador." *Ahora* 2,82 (July 8–15, 1988), pp. 4–9.

Aragón, Olga. "PRI gana 45 municipios, entre ellos Chihuahua; PAN 19, incluido Juárez." *Diario de Chihuahua* (July 7, 1998).

Arias, Patricia, Alfonso Castillo, and Cecilia López. *Radiografía de la Iglesia en México, 1970–1978.* Mexico: Universidad Nacional Autónoma de México, 1988.

Arquidiócesis de Chihuahua. *La formación sacerdotal y el Seminario Regional del Norte.* 1981.

Arrellano Caracas, Antonio. "Cuestiona Nuñez la viabilidad de la consulta interna para elegir candidatos." *La Crónica* (July 27, 1998).

Arriola, Carlos. "La crisis del Partido Acción Nacional (1975–1976)." *Foro Internacional* 17,4 (April–June, 1977), pp. 542–56.

Arzobispado de Chihuahua. "Declaración del arzobispo y sacerdotes sobre los sucesos violentos occuridos allá." January 28, 1972.

Asociación Nacional Cívica Feminina. *La ANCIFEM.* Mexico: ANCIFEM, [n.d.].

Aziz Nassif, Alberto. "La coyuntura de las elecciones en Chihuahua 1983." In Carlos Martínez Assad, ed., *Municipios en conflicto,* pp. 75–132. Mexico: Instituto de Investigaciones Sociales–Universidad Nacional Autónoma de México, 1985.

———. *Prácticas electorales y democracia en Chihuahua.* Cuadernos de la Casa Chata #151. Mexico: Centro de Investigaciones y Estudios Superiores en Antropología Social, 1987.

———. *Territorios de alternancia (el primer gobierno de oposición en México).* Mexico: Triana Editores, 1996.

Baer, Delal M. "Mexico's Second Revolution: Pathways to Liberalization." In Riordan Roett, ed., *Political and Economic Liberalization in Mexico: At a Critical Juncture?* pp. 51–68. Boulder: Lynne Rienner Publishers, 1993.

———. *The 1991 Mexican Midterm Elections.* CSIS Latin American Election Series, vol. 9, study 1. Washington, D.C.: Center for Strategic and International Studies, 1991.

Bailey, David C. *¡Viva Cristo Rey! The Cristero Rebellion and the Church-State Conflict in Mexico.* Austin: University of Texas Press, 1974.

Bailey, John. "Centralism and Political Change in Mexico: The Case of National Solidarity." In Wayne A. Cornelius, Ann L. Craig, and Jonathan Fox, eds., *Transforming State-Society Relations in Mexico: The National Solidarity Strategy.* La Jolla: Center for U.S.-Mexican Studies, University of California, San Diego, 1994.

Bailey, John, and Leopoldo Gómez. "The PRI and Political Liberalization." *Journal of International Affairs* 43, no. 2 (Winter, 1990), pp. 291–312.

Bailey, John J. *Governing Mexico: The Statecraft of Crisis Management.* New York: St. Martins Press, 1998.

Barranco Villafan, Bernardo, and Raquel Pastor Escobar. *Jerarquía católica y modernización política en México.* Mexico: Palabra Ediciones, Centro Antonio de Montesinos, 1989.

Barrio Terrazas, Francisco. "A pesar de todo lo que tiene preparado el sistema, en Chihuahua ganaremos 2 a 1." *La Nación* 44,1707 (May 15, 1986), pp. 9–10.

Basáñez, Miguel. *La lucha por la hegemonía.* Mexico City: Siglo Veintiuno Editores, 1982.

———. *El pulso de los sexenios: 20 años de crisis en México.* Mexico: Siglo Veintiuno Editores, 1990.

Becerra, Ricardo, Pedro Salazar, and José Woldenberg. *La mecánica del cambio político en México: Elecciones, partidos, y reformas.* Mexico: Ediciones Cal y Arena, 2000.

Beltrán del Río, Pascal. "Dió entrada a denuncias del PRD el Centro de Derechos Humanos, de le ONU." *Proceso* 13,707 (May 21, 1990), p. 26.

Beltrán del Río, Pascal, Homero Campa, and Gerardo Galarza. "El PRI cierra ojos y oídos y aprueba hasta ilícitos: Se encona el Colegio Electoral." *Proceso* 11,617 (August 29, 1988), pp. 6–9.

Berdejo Arvizu, Aurora. "Acuerdo político: Más transparencia y garantías: CSG; 'Revisión al Código Electoral.'" *Excelsior* 72,6 (December 2, 1988), p. 10.

Bilello, Suzanne. "La prensa extranjera y las elecciones en Chihuahua, julio de 1986." In Gerardo Bueno, ed., *México–Estados Unidos, 1986,* pp. 157–69. Mexico: El Colegio de México, 1987.

Blancarte, Roberto J. "Recent Changes in Church-State Relations in Mexico: An Historical Approach." *Journal of Church and State* 35, no. 4 (Autumn, 1993), pp. 781–805.

Blancarte, Roberto J., ed. *Cultura e identidad nacional.* Mexico: Consejo Nacional para la Cultura y las Artes, Fondo de Cultura Económica, 1994.

———. *El pensamiento social de los católicos mexicanos.* Mexico, D.F.: Fondo de Cultura Económica, 1995.

———. *Religion, iglesias y democracia.* Mexico, D.F.: La Jornada Ediciones, Centro de Investigaciones Interdisciplinarias en Humanidades, 1995.

Brachet-Marquez, Viviane. "Explaining Sociopolitical Change in Latin America: The Case of Mexico." *Latin American Research Review* 27, no. 3 (Summer, 1992), pp. 91–123.

Bravo Mena, Luís Felipe. "COPARMEX and Mexican Politics." In Sylvia Maxfield and Ricardo Anzaldúa Montoya, eds., *Government and Private Sector in Contemporary Mexico,* pp. 89–103. San Diego: Center for U.S.-Mexican Studies, University of California, 1987.

———. "La lección de la elecciones." *Palabra* 2,7 (January–March, 1989), pp. 34–46.

Brown, Robert McAfee. "Un comentario." In Wifredo Guinea, ed., *Los documentos del Vaticano II,* pp. 303–11. Mexico: Editorial "El," 1966.

Bruhn, Kathleen. *Taking on Goliath : The Emergence of a New Left Party and the Struggle for Democracy in Mexico.* University Park: Pennsylvania State University Press, 1997.

Bruneau, Thomas C. "Basic Christian Communities in Latin America: Their Nature and Significance (Especially in Brazil)." In Daniel H. Levine, ed., *Churches and Politics in Latin America,* pp. 225–37. Beverly Hills: Sage Publications, 1979.

Burgoa O., Ignacio. "El derecho constitucional del estado con relación a la iglesia." In Conferencia del Episcopado Mexicano, *Sociedad civil y sociedad religiosa: Compromiso recíproco al servicio del hombre y bien del país,* pp. 435–57. Mexico: Librería Parroquial de Clavería, 1985.

Calderón Vega, Luís. *Cuba 88: Memorias de la UNEC.* Mexico: 1959.

———. *Memorias del PAN.* Vol. 1. Mexico: Editorial JUS, 1978.

Camp, Roderic Ai. *Crossing Swords: Politics and Religion in Mexico* New York: Oxford University Press, 1997.

———. "The Cross in the Polling Booth: Religion, Politics, and the Laity in Mexico." *Latin American Research Review* 29, no. 3 (Summer, 1994), pp. 69–101.

Cano, José Dolores, et al. "A la opinión pública." *La Nación* 44,1712–13 (August, 1986), p. 20.

Carr, Barry. *Mexican Communism, 1968–1983: Eurocommunism in the Americas?* La Jolla: Center for U.S.-Mexican Studies, University of California, San Diego, 1985.

"Carta Pastoral del Episcopado Mexicano sobre el desarrollo e integración de nuestra patria en el primer aniversario de la encíclica 'Populorum Progresio,' 26 marzo 1968." In Conferencia del Episcopado Mexicano, *Documentos colectivos del Episcopado Mexicano.* Mexico: Comisión Episcopal de Medios de Comunicación Social, 1985.

Carter Center of Emory University. *The Carter Center Delegation to Observe the July 6, 1997, Elections in Mexico.* Atlanta: The Carter Center, 1997.

———. *The July 2, 2000 Elections in Mexico: A Pre-Electoral Assessment.* Atlanta: The Carter Center, 2000.

———. *Report of the Team Sent by the Council of Freely Elected Heads of Government to Witness the Observation of the Elections in Michoacán and Chihuahua, Mexico.* Atlanta: The Carter Center of Emory University, July 13, 1992.

Carter Center of Emory University and the Council of Freely Elected Heads of Government. *The August 21, 1994, Mexican National Elections: Fourth Report.* Atlanta: The Carter Center of Emory University, November, 1994.

———. *Elections in Mexico: Third Report.* Atlanta: The Carter Center of Emory University, 1994.

———. "Electoral Reform in Mexico." Occasional paper series, vol. 4, no. 1. Atlanta: The Carter Center of Emory University, 1993.

Castañeda, Jorge G. "Can NAFTA Change Mexico?" *Foreign Affairs* (September–October, 1993).

———. "Ferocious Differences." *Atlantic Monthly* 276, no. 1 (July, 1995), pp. 68–76.

———. *México: El futuro en juego.* Mexico: Joaquin Mortiz Planeta, 1987.

———.*Utopia Unarmed: The Latin American Left after the Cold War.* New York: Vintage Books, 1994.

Castillo, Herberto. "Caminar, no morir." *Proceso* 10,510 (August 11, 1986), pp. 20–21.

———. "Izquierda-derecha, discrepancias de fondo." *Proceso* 10,517 (September 29, 1986), pp. 34–37.

Castillo, Leticia. "En secreto, obispo filipino pregona aquí ante disidentes." *Ahora* 1,44 (October 16–23, 1987), pp. 3–4.

Centeno, Miguel. *Democracy within Reason.* University Park: Pennsylvania State University Press, 1994.

Centro Empresarial de Chihuahua. *Proposiciones de COPARMEX para resolver algunos de los problemas de México.* Chihuahua: COPARMEX, [n.d.].

Chand, Vikram K. "Democratisation from the Outside In: NGO and International Efforts to Promote Open Elections." *Third World Quarterly* 18, no. 3 (1997), pp. 543–61.

Chávez, Armando. *Sesenta años de gobierno municipal: Jefes políticos del Distrito Bravos y presidentes del municipio de Juárez, 1897–1960.* Mexico: 1959.

Chávez, Elías. "Acusan trés renunciantes: Conchello dió subsidios para dividir al PAN." *Proceso* 2,76 (April 17, 1978), pp. 10–11.

———. "Conchello se defiende: Hay prominentes panistas que sirven al Grupo Monterrey." *Proceso* 2,76 (April 17, 1978), pp. 6–8.

———. "La desintegración del PAN: Muchos dirigentes son simples oportunistas." *Proceso* 2,75 (April 10, 1978), pp. 13–16.

———. "Historias que a los priístas distinguidos les gustaría olvidar." *Proceso* 14,749 (March 11, 1991).

———. "Jornadas de titubeos del secretario de gobernación." *Proceso* 11,610 (July 11, 1988), pp. 18–23.

Clouthier, Manuel J. "Entrevista del periodista Ricardo Rocha al Ing. Manuel J. Clouthier, candidato del PAN a la presidencia de la república." In *Diálogos con el pueblo,* vol. 1, *Los primeros cien días de campaña,* pp. 13–31. Mexico: EPESSA, 1988.

———. "Mitin. cierre de campaña nacional. Zócalo de la Ciudad de México." In *Diálogos con el pueblo,* vol. 3, *La recta final,* pp. 193–205. Mexico: EPESSA, 1988.

———. "Poder ciudadano y resistencia civil." In *Diálogos con el pueblo,* vol. 2, *A la mitad del camino,* pp. 11–18. Mexico: EPESSA, 1988.

———. "Tarea de articulación de una lucha popular: Eso debe ser la campaña." In *Diálogos con el pueblo,* vol. 1, *Los primeros cien días de campaña,* p. 9. Mexico: EPESSA, 1988.

Collier, George Allen. *Basta! Land and the Zapatista Rebellion in Chiapas.* Oakland: Food First Book, Institute for Food and Development Policy, 1994.

Collier, Ruth Berins. *The Contradictory Alliance: State-Labor Relations and Regime Change in Mexico.* International and Area Studies, research series 83. Berkeley: University of California at Berkeley, 1992.

Comblin, Joseph. *¿Ha fracasado la Acción Católica?* Barcelona: Ediciones Eler, 1963.

Comisión Editorial del Partido Acción Nacional. "Plataforma política y social 1976–1982." In *El México de la oposición: 7 plataformas presidenciales*, pp. 138–61. Mexico: EPESSA, 1986.

Comisión Federal Electoral. *Código Federal Electoral*. Mexico: Talleres Gráficos de la Nación, 1987.

Conchello, José Angel. "Discurso del Lic. José Angel Conchello D., presidente de Acción Nacional." In *8a Asamblea XXIV Convención: Documentos*, pp. 9–29. Mexico: Ediciones de Acción Nacional, 1975.

Confederación Patronal de la República Mexicana. XLVII Asamblea Nacional Ordinaria. *Participar para modernizar a México*. Mexico: COPARMEX, 1986.

———. XLIX Asamblea Nacional Ordinaria. *Modernización o crisis y autoritarismo*. Mexico: COPARMEX, 1986.

Conferencia del Episcopado Mexicano. *La evangelización en el presente y en el futuro de América Latina: Documento aprobado de la III Conferencia General del Episcopado Latinoamericano, Puebla*. Mexico: Librería Parroquial de Clavería, 1984.

———. "Declaración de los obispos mexicanos" (August 19, 1986). In *La Iglesia habla: Orientaciones pastorales de los obispos de México sobre el tema cívico-político*, pp. 217–19. Monterrey: USEM, 1987.

Consejo Permanente del CEM. "Declaración de los obispos mexicanos." In *La Iglesia habla: Orientaciones pastorales de los obispos de México sobre el tema cívico-político 1981–1987*, pp. 217–19. Monterrey: USEM Monterrey, 1988.

Convención Iberoamericana de Estudiantes Católicos. "Convocatoria y conclusiones de la Convención Iberoamericana de Estudiantes Católicos, 12 al 22 de Diciembre de 1931." In Luís Calderón Vega, *Cuba 88: Memorias de la UNEC*, appendix. Mexico: 1959.

Cook, Maria Lorena. *Organizing Dissent: Unions, the State, and the Democratic Teachers' Movement in Mexico*. University Park: Pennsylvania State Press, 1996.

Cornelius, Wayne A. *Mexican Politics in Transition: The Breakdown of a One-Party-Dominant Regime*. 5th ed. La Jolla: Center for U.S.-Mexican Studies, University of California, San Diego, 2000.

———. "Mexico's Delayed Democratization. *Foreign Policy* 95 (Summer, 1994), pp. 53–71.

———. "Political Liberalization and the 1985 Elections in Mexico." In Paul W. Drake and Eduardo Silva, eds., *Elections and Democratization in Latin America, 1980–85*, pp. 115–42. San Diego: Center for Iberian and Latin American Studies, University of California, 1986.

Cornelius, Wayne A., et al. "Overview: The Dynamics of Political Change in Mexico." In Wayne A. Cornelius, Judith Gentleman, and Peter Smith, eds., *Mexico's Alternative Political Futures*, pp. 1–51. San Diego: Center for U.S.-Mexican Studies, University of California, 1989.

Corral Jurado, Javier. "La OEA revisa el caso Chihuahua." *La Nación* 45,1734 (July 10, 1987), pp. 3–5.

Corro, Salvador. "Clouthier lanza huevos y el PRI se muestra cauto: Con pintoresquismo y abstención se afronta el drama de Sinaloa." *Proceso* 11,522 (November 3, 1986), pp. 12–17.

Corson, Fred Pierce. "Un comentario." In Wifredo Guinea, ed., *Los documentos del Vaticano II*, pp. 426–29. Mexico: Editorial "El," 1966.

Creuzet, Michel. *Los cuerpos intermedios.* Madrid: Speiro, S.A., 1977.

Crozier, Michel, Samuel P. Huntington, and Joji Watanuki. *The Crisis of Democracy: Report on the Governability of Democracies to the Trilateral Commission.* New York: New York University Press, 1975.

Cruz Zapata, Raul. *Carlos A. Madrazo: Biografía política.* Mexico: Editorial Diana, 1988.

Dahl, Robert A. *Polyarchy: Participation and Opposition.* New Haven: Yale University Press, 1971.

Daniel Pérez, Camilo, and Victor Quintana. *Sembrando entre la nieve: El Movimiento Campesino Democrático. Su lucha* Zapopxan: EDOC-PRAXIS, 1987.

Dávila Garibi, J. Ignacio. "Biografía: El primer obispo de Ciudad Juárez, Mons. Manuel Talamás y Camandari." *Christus* 22,263 (September, 1957), pp. 713–15.

Davis, Diane. "The Dialectic of Autonomy: State, Class, and Economic Crisis in Mexico, 1958–1982." *Latin American Perspectives* 20, no. 3 (Summer, 1993), pp. 46–76.

———. "Failed Democratic Reform in Contemporary Mexico: From Social Movements to the State and Back Again." *Journal of Latin American Studies* 26, no. 2 (May, 1994), pp. 375–409.

———. "Social Movements in Mexico's Crisis." *Journal of International Affairs* 43, no. 2 (Winter, 1990), pp. 343–67.

"Declaración del arzobispo y sacerdotes de Ciudad Juárez sobre la situación nacional." *Christus* 37,437 (April, 1972), pp. 45–46.

De Janvry, Alain, Gustavo Gordillo, and Elisabeth Sadoulet. *Mexico's Second Agrarian Reform: Household and Community Responses, 1990–1994.* La Jolla: Center for U.S.-Mexican Studies, University of California, San Diego, 1997.

Democratic and Doctrinal Forum. "Our Withdrawal from the National Action Party." *The Other Side of Mexico* 28 (September–October, 1992).

"Democratizar en Chihuahua." *Cuadernos de Nexos* 11 and 12, pp. xiii–xv. *Nexos* 138 (June, 1989).

De Mora, Juan Miguel. *Elecciones en México: ¿Se repetirá el ejemplo de Chihuahua?* Mexico: EDAMEX, 1988.

Deutsch, Karl. "Social Mobilization and Political Development." *American Political Science Review* 55, no. 4 (December, 1969).

Diamond, Larry, Juan J. Linz, and Seymour Martin Lipset. "Introduction: Comparing Experiences with Democracy." In Larry Diamond, Juan J. Linz, and Seymour Martin Lipset, eds., *Politics in Developing Countries: Comparing Experiences with Democracy*, pp. 1–34. Boulder: Lynn Rienner Publishers, 1990.

Diamond, Larry, and Marc Plattner, eds. *The Global Resurgence of Democracy.* Baltimore: Johns Hopkins University Press, 1993.

"Dictámen del jurado popular al pueblo de Chihuahua." *Diario de Chihuahua* (August 8, 1986), p. 12.

Dillon, Sam. "Mexico's New Radical Politics: Primary Elections." *New York Times* (July 22, 1998), p. A1.

Di Palma, Giuseppe. *To Craft Democracies: An Essay on Democratic Transitions.* Berkeley: University of California Press, 1990.

Domínguez, Jorge, ed., *Technopols: Freeing Politics and Markets in Latin America in the 1990s.* University Park: Pennsylvania State University Press, 1997.

Domínguez, Jorge I., and James McCann. *Democratizing Mexico: Public Opinion and Electoral Choices.* Baltimore: Johns Hopkins University Press, 1996.

———. "Shaping Mexico's Electoral Arena: The Construction of Partisan Cleavages in the 1988 and 1991 National Elections." *American Political Science Review* 89, no. 1 (March, 1995), pp. 34–49.

———. "Whither the PRI? Explaining Voter Defection from Mexico's Ruling Party in the 1988 Presidential Elections." Paper presented at the annual meeting of the Western Political Science Association, March, 1991.

Dresser, Denise. *Neopopulist Solutions to Neoliberal Problems: Mexico's National Solidarity Program.* La Jolla: Center for U.S.-Mexican Studies, University of California, San Diego, 1991.

———. "Treading Lightly and without a Stick: International Actors and the Promotion of Democracy in Mexico." In Tom Farer, ed., *Beyond Sovereignty*, pp. 316–43. Baltimore: Johns Hopkins University Press, 1996.

Dussel, Enrique D. *Historia de la Iglesia en América Latina: Coloniaje y liberación, 1492–1983.* Madrid: Editorial Mundo Negro, 1983.

———. *De Medellín a Puebla: Una década de sangre y esperanza 1968–1979.* Mexico: Editorial Edicol, 1979.

El Foro Nacional por el Sufragio Efectivo. "Declaración del Foro por el Sufragio Efectivo." In Juan Miguel de Mora, *¿Elecciones en México: Se repetirá el ejemplo de Chihuahua?* pp. 233–41. Mexico: EDAMEX, 1988.

"El P. Aguilar: Un profeta de nuestro tiempo." *Christus* 42,498 (May, 1977), p. 62.

"Encuestalía: Quien quiere un Papa?" *Nexos*, 148, April, 1990.

"Entrevista de prensa del Lic. Manuel González Hinojosa del Miércoles 4 de Febrero de 1976." Mexico: PAN, 1976.

Equipo de Reflexión de Pastoral. "La muerte del P. Aguilar: Reto a nuestra conciencia cristiana." *Christus* 42,498 (May, 1977), pp. 61–62.

Fazio, Carlos. "El episcopado, contra 'la desinformación' oficial sobre sus actividades." *Proceso* 10,513 (September, 1986), pp. 13–15.

———. "Prigione alienta el conservadorismo con el nombramiento de obispos." *Proceso* 12,648 (April, 1989), pp. 18–19.

———. *Samuel Ruiz: El caminante.* Mexico City: Espasa Calpe Mexicana, 1994.

Federal Electoral Commission of the Government of the United States of Mexico. *Código Federal Electoral.* Mexico: Comisión Federal Electoral, 1987.

Fernández Armendariz, Eduardo. "Dimes y diretes sobre los talleres." *Norte* (January 30, 1987), p. 3E.

————. "Los talleres, búsqueda de la perfección de nuestro sistema demo-crático: Cedic." *Norte* (January 30, 1987), p. 2E.

Fernández Pradel, Jorge. *Acción Católica: Principios—realización.* Quito: Imprenta del Clero, 1939.

Foweraker, Joe. *Popular Mobilization in Mexico: The Teachers' Movement, 1977–87.* New York: Cambridge University Press, 1993.

————. *Theorizing Social Movements.* Boulder: Pluto Press, 1995.

Foweraker, Joe, and Ann Craig. *Popular Movements and Political Change in Mexico.* Boulder: Lynne Rienner Publishers, 1990.

Foweraker, Joe, and Todd Landman. *Citizenship Rights and Social Movements: A Comparative and Statistical Analysis.* New York: Oxford University Press, 1997.

Fox, Jonathan. "The Difficult Transition from Clientelism to Citizenship: Lessons from Mexico." *World Politics* 46, no. 2 (January, 1994).

Frente Cívico Familiar et al. *The Elections in Yucatán, Mexico: Summary and Conclusions of Citizen Observers.* Merida, November 28, 1993.

Frieden, Jeffrey. *Debt, Development, and Democracy: Modern Political Economy and Latin America, 1965–1985.* Princeton: Princeton University Press, 1991.

Fuentes Mares, José. *Y México se refugió en el desierto.* Chihuahua: Centro Librero La Prensa, 1978.

Galarza, Gerardo. "Admite Luís H. Alvarez las discrepancias en su partido y se congratula de ellas." *Proceso* 13,690 (January 22, 1990), pp. 6–11.

————. "Un debate prueba que la reforma electoral dividió a los panistas." *Proceso* 13,689 (January 15, 1990), pp. 20–25.

————. "La dirigencia del PRI niega que hubo compromiso con el PAN sobre reforma política." *Proceso* 13,692 (February 5, 1990), pp. 24–28.

————. "En febrero elegirá dirigente el PAN y el apoyo a la reforma será determinante." *Proceso* 13,689 (January 15, 1990), pp. 20–25.

————. "Salinas 'ha respetado su palabra'; y el PAN sacó adelante la reforma electoral oficial." *Proceso* 12,677 (October 23, 1989), pp. 11–15.

Gallup Organization, Inc. *Eco / Gallup Mexico Pre-Election Survey, Press Release #1.* New York: Gallup, Inc., June 19, 1988.

————. *Eco / Gallup Mexico Pre-Election Survey, Press Release #2.* New York: Gallup, Inc., June 26, 1988.

García Cantú, Gastón. *El desafío de la derecha.* Mexico: Editorial Joaquín Mortiz, 1987.

García Martínez. *U.C.M.: Manual del socio.* Ediciones del Comité Central, 1962.

Garrido, Luís Javier. "Un partido sin militantes." In Soledad Loaeza and Rafael Segovia, eds., *La vida política mexicana en crisis*, pp. 61–76. Mexico: El Colegio de México, 1987.

————. *La ruptura: La corriente democrática del PRI: La intransición mexicana.* Mexico, D.F. : Grijalbo, 1993.

Garza, Luís Angel. "Olvidadas las ilegalidades en su encumbramiento, Sócra-tes Rizzo avanza hacia la gubernatura de Nuevo León." *Proceso* 14,747 (February 25, 1991), pp. 15–17.

Gentleman, Judith. "International Integration and Democratic Development: The Cases of Poland and Mexico." *Journal of Interamerican Studies and World Affairs* 34, no. 1 (Spring, 1992), pp. 59–110.

Gobierno del Estado de Chihuahua. *Chihuahua, proceso electoral, 1986.* Chihuahua: Dirección de Gobernación, 1987.

Gobierno del Estado de Chihuahua. Part 3 of *Código Administrativo,* book 4 of *Los partido políticos y procesos electorales.* Chihuahua: Dirección de Gobernación, 1986.

Golden, Tim. "Mexico Is Shown Paper Trail of Illicit Campaign Spending." *New York Times* (June 13, 1995), p. A3.

———. "Opposition in Mexico Calls Vote Fraudulent." *New York Times* (May 31, 1995), p. A12.

———. "Vote Fraud Fight Flaring in Mexico." *New York Times* (December 6, 1993).

Gómez Morin, Manuel. "Informe a la Asamblea Constituyente de Acción Nacional, rendido el 14 de septiembre de 1939." In *Diez años de México: Informes del jefe de Acción Nacional,* pp. 1–20. Mexico: Ediciones PAN, 1983.

———. "Informe a la nación (respuesta al discurso pronunciado en Chilpancingo por el presidente de la república gral. Lázaro Cárdenas, el día 20 de febrero de 1940)." In *Diez años de México: Informes del jefe de Acción Nacional,* pp. 23–40. Mexico: Ediciones PAN, 1983.

———. "1915." In *"1915" y otros ensayos,* pp. 17–38. Mexico: Editorial JUS, 1973.

———. "La Universidad de México—Su función y la razón de ser de su autonomía." In *"1915" y otros ensayos,* pp. 87–128. Mexico: Editorial JUS, 1973.

———. "La Universidad de México—Su naturaleza jurídica." In *"1915" y otros ensayos,* pp. 79–86. Mexico: Editorial JUS, 1973.

Gómez Tagle, Silvia. "Los adjetivos de la democracia en Chihuahua." *Argumentos: Estudios Críticos de la Sociedad* (June, 1987), pp. 75–106.

Gómez Tagle, Silvia, ed. *Las elecciones de 1991: La recuperación official.* Mexico City: Ediciones La Jornada, 1993.

González Bernal, Jaime. *La lucha política noviolenta: Criterios y técnicas.* 1988.

González Luna, Efraín. *Los católicos y la política en México.* Mexico: Editorial JUS, 1988.

———. "Clases sociales y lucha de clases." In *"Clases sociales y lucha de clases" y otros temas,* vol. 8, pp. 53–71. Mexico: Editorial JUS, 1977.

———. "Deber cívico y política orgánica." In *Humanismo político,* vol. 1, pp. 117–33. Mexico: Ediciones PAN, 1984.

———. "Democracia, vínculo de unidad nacional." In Efraín González Luna, Adolfo Christlieb Ibarrola, Rafael Preciado Hernández, Manuel Gómez Morin, and José González Torres, *La democracia en México,* pp. 9–34. Mexico: Editorial JUS, 1962.

———. "La dignidad del trabajo." In *Humanismo político,* vol. 2, pp. 91–104. Mexico: Ediciones PAN, 1984.

————. "La economía contra el hombre." In *Humanismo político*, vol. 2, pp. 105–11. Mexico: Ediciones PAN, 1984.

————. "El hombre y el estado." In *Humanismo político*, vol. 1, pp. 97–108. Mexico: Ediciones PAN, 1984.

————. "El hombre y el estado (continuación)." In *Humanismo político*, vol. 1, pp. 109–16. Mexico: Ediciones PAN, 1984.

————. "Neurosis de la escaramuza." In *Humanismo político*, vol. 1, pp. 26–37. Mexico: Ediciones PAN, 1984.

————. "La persona, el bien común, y la cultura." In *Humanismo político*, vol. 1, pp. 133–52. Mexico: Ediciones PAN, 1984.

————. "Técnica de salvación." In *Humanismo político*, vol. 1, pp. 15–25. Mexico: Ediciones PAN, 1984.

González Morfín, Efraín. "En AN, un partido dentro de otro partido." *Proceso* 2,76 (April 17, 1978), pp. 8–9.

————. "Concentración o distribución de la propiedad." In *Justicia y reforma social*, pp. 34–48. Mexico: Ediciones de Acción Nacional, 1967.

————. "La doctrina de Acción Nacional." In Efraín González Morfín, José González Torres, and Adolfo Christlieb Ibarrola, *Tres esquemas*, pp. 3–20. Mexico: Ediciones de Acción Nacional, 1969.

————. "El significado de Acción Nacional." In *8a Asamblea XXIV Convención: Documentos*, pp. 118–32. Mexico: Ediciones de Acción Nacional, 1975.

————. *Solidarismo*. Mexico: Ediciones de Acción Nacional, 1974.

"González Morfín: La reforma política fortalece el control sobre los partidos." *Proceso* 2,75 (April 10, 1978), pp. 10–13.

González Ramírez, Manuel R. *La Iglesia mexicana en cifras*. Mexico: Centro de Investigación y Acción Social, 1969.

Granados Chapa, Miguel A. "Talleres de la democracia, un clero relapso, insistente." *Norte* (February 14, 1987), p. 3A.

————. "Talleres de la democracia: Opiniones del clero en Chihuahua." *Norte* (February 17, 1987), p. 3A.

Granados Roldán, Otto. *La Iglesia católica mexicana como grupo de presión*. Mexico: Universidad Nacional Autónoma de México, 1981.

Grayson, George. *A Guide to the 1994 Mexican Presidential Election*. Washington, D.C.: Center for Strategic and International Studies, 1994.

Grindle, Merilee. "Reforming Land Tenure in Mexico: Peasants, the Market, and the State." In Riordan Roett, ed., *The Challenge of Institutional Reform*, pp. 39–56. Boulder: Lynne Rienner Publishers, 1995.

Guinea, Wifredo, ed. "Constitución dogmática sobre la Iglesia ('Lumen Gentium')." In *Los documentos del Vaticano II*, pp. 6–91. Mexico: Editorial "El," 1966.

————. "Constitución pastoral sobre la Iglesia en el mundo actual ('Gaudium et Spes')." In *Los documentos del Vaticano II*, pp. 193–302. Mexico: Editorial "El," 1966.

————. "Decreto sobre el ministerio pastoral de los obispos ('Christus Dominus')." In *Los documentos del Vaticano II*, pp. 392–425. Mexico: Editorial "El," 1966.

Gutiérrez, Alejandro. "Con mi triunfo se demuestra que el PRI no estaba muerto; tampoco puede hablarse del principio del fin del PAN: Patricio Martínez." *Proceso* 1132 (July 12, 1998), internet version.

Gutiérrez Casillas, José. *Historia de la Iglesia en México*. Mexico: Editorial Porrúa, 1984.

"Habrá acontecimientos trascendentales en el Estado de Chihuahua: Barrio." *La Nación* 44,1712–13 (August, 1986), pp. 11–16.

Hansen, Roger D. *The Politics of Mexican Development*. Baltimore: Johns Hopkins University Press, 1971.

Hartz, Louis. *The Liberal Tradition in America: An Interpretation of American Political Thought since the Revolution*. New York: Harcourt, Brace and Company, 1955.

Harvey, Neil. *Rebellion in Chiapas: Rural Reforms, Campesino Radicalism, and the Limits of Salinism*. La Jolla: Center for U.S.-Mexican Studies, University of California, San Diego, 1994.

Herrera González, Marcos Enrique. "1988, nueva versión de 1910: Clouthier." *Poder Ciudadano* 4 (April, 1988), pp. 5–8.

Hibbs, Douglas A., Jr. *Mass Political Violence: A Cross-National Causal Analysis*. New York: Wiley, 1973.

Hinojosa, Oscar. "Discrepancias, aún de priístas, con el acercamiento del estado con la Iglesia." *Proceso* 12,632 (December, 1988).

———. "El episcopado a la carga: 'Se va generalizando el descontento entre el pueblo.'" *Proceso* 10,513 (September, 1986), pp. 12–13.

———. "La misión evangélica ordena dejar la sacristía, afirma Sergio obeso." *Proceso* 10,514 (September, 1986), pp. 10–13.

———. "Naufragaron las promesas de elecciones límpias." *Proceso* 11,610 (July, 1988), pp. 6–17.

———. "Prigione, enlace de Bartlett para reprender a obispos críticos." *Proceso* 10,511 (August, 1986), pp. 6–11.

Hirschmann, Albert. *Exit, Voice, and Loyalty*. Cambridge: Harvard University Press, 1970.

———. *Shifting Involvements: Private Interest and Public Action*. Princeton: Princeton University Press, 1982.

Human Rights Watch. *Human Rights in Mexico: A Policy of Impunity*. New York: Human Rights Watch, 1990.

———. *Prison Conditions in Mexico: An Americas Watch Report*. New York: Human Rights Watch, 1991.

Huntington, Samuel P. *Political Order in Changing Societies*. New Haven: Yale University Press, 1968.

———. *The Third Wave: Democratization in the Late Twentieth Century*. Norman: University of Oklahoma Press, 1989.

Huntington, Samuel P., and Joan Nelson. *No Easy Choice: Political Participation in Developing Countries*. Cambridge: Harvard University Press, 1976.

"Información política y social." *Información Procesada de Chihuahua* (May, 1986), pp. 15–43.

"Información política y social." *Información Procesada de Chihuahua* (July, 1986).

Inglehart, Ronald. *Modernization and Postmodernization: Cultural, Economic, and Political Change in 43 Societies.* Princeton: Princeton University Press, 1997.

———. "The Renaissance of Political Culture." *American Political Science Review* 82 (December, 1988), pp. 1203–30.

Inglehart, Ronald, and Miguel Basáñez. *The North American Trajectory: Cultural, Economic, and Political Ties between the United States, Canada, and Mexico.* New York: Aldine de Gruyter, 1996.

Instituto Federal Electoral. *Código Federal de Instituciones y Procedimientos Electorales.* Mexico City: Instituto Federal Electoral, 1994.

———. *Informe sobre observadores y visitantes extranjeros.* Mexico, D.F.: Instituto Federal Electoral, 1994.

———. *Memorias del proceso electoral federal de 1991,* vols. 1–5. Mexico, D.F.: Instituto Federal Electoral, 1993.

———. *Proyecto de informe a la Camara de Diputados,* Addenda 21, 22, and 23. Mexico City: Instituto Federal Electoral, 1994.

———. *Resultados definitivos de los computos distritales de la elección de presidente de los Estados Unidos Mexicanos.* Mexico City: Instituto Federal Electoral, 1994.

———. *Resultados de elecciones federales de 1997 en Chihuahua.* Mexico City: Instituto Federal Electoral, 1997. (http://www.ife.org.mx/wwworge/chih.htm).

Inter-American Commission on Human Rights. "1990: Resolution No. 01 / 90, Cases 9768, 9780, and 9828 of Mexico, May 17, 1990: Final Report," pp. 97–123. Washington, D.C.: Organization of American States, 1990.

Joseph, Gilbert M., and Daniel Nugent, eds. *Everyday Forms of State Formation: Revolution and the Negotiation of Rule in Modern Mexico.* Durham: Duke University Press, 1994.

Keane, John. "Despotism and Democracy: The Origins and Development of the Distinction between Civil Society and the State, 1750–1850." In John Keane, ed., *Civil Society and the State,* pp. 35–71. London: Verso, 1988.

———. "Remembering the Dead: Civil Society and the State from Hobbes to Marx and Beyond." In John Keane, ed., *Democracy and Civil Society,* pp. 31–67. London: Verso, 1988.

King, Gary, Robert Keohane, and Sidney Verba. *Designing Social Inquiry: Scientific Inference in Qualitative Research.* Princeton: Princeton University Press, 1994.

Klesner, Joseph. "Electoral Politics and Mexico's New Party System." Paper presented at the 21st International Congress of the Latin American Studies Association, Chicago, Ill., September 24–26, 1998.

———. "Electoral Reform in Mexico's Hegemonic Party System: Perpetuation of Privilege or Democractic Advance?" Paper presented at the annual meeting of the American Political Science Association, Washington, D.C., August 28–31, 1997.

———. "An Electoral Route to Democracy? Mexico's Transition in Comparative Perspective." Review essay. *Comparative Politics* 30, no. 4 (July, 1998).

———. "Modernization, Economic Crisis, and Electoral Alignment in Mexico." *Mexican Studies / Estudios Mexicanos* 9, 2 (Summer, 1993).

Knight, Alan. "Historical Continuities in Social Movements." In Joe Foweraker and Ann Craig, eds., *Popular Movements and Political Change in Mexico*. Boulder: Lynne Rienner Publishers, 1990.

Kornhauser, William. *The Politics of Mass Society*. New York: Free Press, 1959.

Krauze, Enrique. *Caudillos culturales en la revolución mexicana*. Mexico: Siglo Veintiuno Editores, 1985.

———. "Chihuahua, ida y vuelta." *Vuelta* 115 (June, 1986), pp. 32–43.

———. *Tarea política*. Mexico: Tusquests Editores, 2000.

Lake, Anthony. "From Containment to Enlargement." Speech at Johns Hopkins University (SAIS), September 21, 1993.

Langston, Joy. *Why Rules Matter: The Formal Rules of Candidate Selection and Leadership Selection in the PRI, 1978–1996*, working paper no. 58. Mexico City: Centro de Investigación y Docencia Económicas, 1996.

Lartigue, François. *Indios y Bosques: Políticas forestales y comunales en la Sierra Tarahumara*. Mexico: Ediciones de Casa Chata, 1983.

Latin American Bishops' Conference. Final Document of Commission 1, Subcommission A, of the Medellín Conference, "Justicia." *Christus* 33,396 (November, 1968), pp. 1026–35.

———. Final Document of Commission 1, Subcommission B, of the Medellín Conference, "Paz." *Christus* 33,396 (November, 1968), pp. 1036–45.

———. Final Document of Commission 6 of the Medellín Conference, "Movimiento de seglares." *Christus* 33,396 (November, 1968), pp. 1080–85.

Leo XIII. "Rerum Novarum." In Jesús Iribarren and José Luís Gutiérrez, eds., *Ocho grandes mensajes*, pp. 19–56. Madrid: Biblioteca de Autores Cristianos, 1971.

Lerner, Victoria. *Historia de la revolución mexicana, 1934–1940: La educación socialista*. Mexico: El Colegio de México, 1982.

Levine, Daniel H. "Assessing the Impacts of Liberation Theology in Latin America." *Review of Politics* 50, no. 2 (Spring, 1988), pp. 241–64.

———. "On Premature Reports of the Death of Liberation Theology." *Review of Politics* 57, no. 1 (Winter, 1995), pp. 105–32.

———. *Popular Voices in Latin American Catholicism*. Princeton: Princeton University Press, 1992.

———. "Religion and Politics, Politics and Religion: An Introduction." In Daniel H. Levine, ed., *Churches and Politics in Latin America*, pp. 16–40. Beverly Hills: Sage Publications, 1979.

Levine, Daniel H., ed. *Constructing Culture and Power in Latin America*. Ann Arbor: University of Michigan Press, 1993.

Linares, Gamaliel. "El clero del norte, bajo constante asedio oficial." *Ahora* 2,65 (March 11–18, 1988), pp. 9–10.

———. "Retiene PRI mayoría en el congreso local." *Diario de Chihuahua* (July 7, 1998).

Lipset, Seymour Martin. *Political Man: The Social Bases of Politics.* New York: Doubleday, 1960.

Lister, Florence, and Robert Lister. *Chihuahua: Stormhouse of Storms.* Albuquerque: University of New Mexico Press, 1966.

Loaeza, Soledad. *Clases medias y política en México: La querella escolar, 1959–1963.* Mexico: El Colegio de México, 1988.

———. "La Iglesia católica mexicana y el reformismo autoritario." *Foro Internacional* 25,2 (October–December, 1984), pp. 138–65.

———. "Notas para el estudio de la Iglesia en el México contemporáneo." In Martín de la Rosa and Charles A. Reilly, eds., *Religión y política en México*, pp. 42–58. Mexico: Siglo Veintiuno, 1985.

———. "El PAN: De la oposición leal a la impaciencia electoral." In Loaeza, *El llamda de las urnas*, pp. 241–71. Mexico: Cal y Arena, 1989.

———. *El Partido Acción Nacional: La large marcha, 1939–1994: Oposición leal y partido de protesta.* Mexico: Fondo de Cultura Económica, 1999.

López Obrador, Andrés Manuel. *Tabasco, víctima del fraude electoral.* Mexico City: Editorial Nuestro Tiempo, 1990.

Lucero, Rafael. "'Juárez será un reto': El sucesor de Talamás." *Ahora* 2,66 (March 19–26), pp. 7–11.

Lujambio, Alonso. *El poder compartido: Un ensayo sobre la democratizacion mexicana.* Mexico: Oceano, 2000.

Mabry, Donald J. *Mexico's Acción Nacional: A Catholic Alternative to Revolution.* Syracuse: Syracuse University Press, 1973.

Marín, Carlos. "Vehículo de la frustración de su directora, 'El Día' le reprocha al PRI todo lo que le encubrió." *Proceso* 14,752 (April 1, 1981), pp. 8–9.

Márquez Terrazas, Zacarías. *Chihuahuenses egregios,* vol. 2. Chihuahua: Editorial Camino, 1985.

Martínez, Oscar J. *Ciudad Juárez: El auge de una ciudad fronteriza a partir de 1848.* Mexico: Fondo de Cultura Económica, 1982.

Martínez Assad, Carlos. *El laboratorio de la revolución: El Tabasco garridista.* Mexico: Siglo Veintiuno, 1984.

Martínez D., Félix. *Historia del seminario de Chihuahua.* Chihuahua: Editorial Camino, 1986.

Maza, Enrique. "Y Salinas de Gortari empezó a desgranar promesas de un México con todo resuelto." *Proceso* 12,631 (December 5, 1988), pp. 12–15.

McCoy, Jennifer. "On the Mexican Elections." *Hemisphere* (Fall, 1994), pp. 26–29.

McCoy, Jennifer, Larry Garber, and Robert Pastor. "Pollwatching and Peacekeeping." *Journal of Democracy* 2, no. 4 (Fall, 1994).

Mecham, J. Lloyd. *Church and State in Latin America: A History of Politico-*

Ecclesiastical Relations. Chapel Hill: University of North Carolina Press, 1966.

Medina, Gerardo. "Las prerogativas de los partidos políticos." *La Nación* (March 1, 1987), pp. 3–5 and 31.

Mendoza, Diana A. "No se ha vendido el voto católico, afirma Prigione." *El Universal* 72,285 (May 9, 1988), pp. 1, 11.

"Mensaje del obispo y presbiterio de Ciudad Juárez, a todo el pueblo." *La Nación* 44,1712–13 (August, 1986), pp. 20–21.

Metz, Allan. "Mexican Church-State Relations under President Carlos Salinas Gortari." *Journal of Church and State* 34, no. 1 (Winter, 1992), pp. 111–30.

Meyer, Jean. *El catolicismo social en México hasta 1913*. Mexico: Instituto Mexicano de Doctrina Social Cristiana, 1985.

———. *La Cristiada*, vol. 1, *La Guerra de los Cristeros*. Mexico: Siglo Veintiuno Editores, 1987.

———. *La Cristiada*, vol. 2, *El conflicto entre la Iglesia y el estado, 1926–1929*. Mexico: Siglo Veintiuno Editores, 1985.

———. *La Cristiada*, vol. 3, *Los Cristeros*. Mexico: Siglo Veintiuno Editores, 1987.

Meyer, Lorenzo. "Democratization of the PRI: Mission Impossible?" in Wayne A. Cornelius et al., eds., *Mexico's Alternative Political Futures*. La Jolla: Center for U.S.-Mexican Studies, University of California, San Diego, 1988.

———. "México o los límites de la democratización neoliberal." Paper presented at the Research Seminar on Mexico and U.S.-Mexican Relations, Center for U.S.-Mexican Studies, University of California, San Diego, May 15, 1991.

Middlebrook, Kevin. *The Paradox of Revolution: Labor, the State, and Authoritarianism in Mexico*. Baltimore: Johns Hopkins University Press, 1995.

———. "The Politics of Industrial Restructuring: Transnational Firms' Search for Flexible Production in the Mexican Automobile Industry." *Comparative Politics* (April, 1991).

Milbrath, Lester. *Political Participation: How and Why Do People Get Involved in Politics?* Chicago: Rand McNally, 1965.

Millet, Richard. "Beyond Sovereignty: International Efforts to Support Latin American Democracy." *Journal of Interamerican Studies and World Affairs* 36 (Fall, 1994), pp. 1–23.

Mizrahi, Yemile. "Dilemmas of the Opposition in Government: Chihuahua and Baja California." *Mexican Studies / Estudios Mexicanos* 14, no. 1 (Winter, 1998), pp. 151–89.

———. "Entrepreneurs in the Opposition: Modes of Political Participation in Chihuahua." In Victoria E. Rodríguez and Peter M. Ward, eds., *Opposition Government in Mexico,* pp. 81–96. Albuquerque: University of New Mexico Press, 1995.

———. "Rebels without a Cause? The Politics of Entrepreneurs in Chihuahua." *Journal of Latin American Studies* 26, no. 1 (February, 1994), pp. 137–59.

Molinar Horcasitas, Juan. "Counting the Number of Parties: An Alternative Index." *American Political Science Review* 85, no. 4 (December, 1991), pp. 1383–92.

———. "Regreso a Chihuahua." *Nexos* 10,111 (March, 1987), pp. 21–32.

———. *El tiempo de la legitimidad: Elecciones, autoritarismo, y democracia en México.* Mexico, D.F.: Cal y Arena, 1991.

Molinar Horcasitas, Juan, and Jeffrey A. Weldon. "Electoral Determinants and the Consequences of National Solidarity." In Wayne A. Cornelius, Ann L. Craig, and Jonathan Fox, eds., *Transforming State-Society Relations in Mexico: The National Solidarity Strategy.* La Jolla: Center for U.S.-Mexican Studies, University of California, San Diego, 1994.

Morales, Sonia, and Rodrigo Vera. "Samuel Ruiz ha resistido, desde 1960, hostigamientos, acusaciones, condenas, agresiones, injurias." *Proceso* 956 (February 27, 1995), pp. 12–17.

Moreno Padilla, Javier, ed. *Constitución política de los Estados Unidos Mexicanos, con una explicación sencilla de cada artículo para su mejor comprehensión.* Mexico: Editorial Trillas, 1986.

Morris, Stephen D. *Corruption and Politics in Contemporary Mexico.* Tuscaloosa: University of Alabama Press, 1991.

———. *Political Reformism in Mexico: An Overview of Contemporary Mexican Politics.* Boulder: Lynne Rienner Publishers, 1995.

National Action Party. *The Democratic Plea of PAN in Yucatán.* Mexico City: PAN, June 27, 1995.

———. Research Secretariat. *Basic Information about the Party.* Mexico City: January, 1994.

National Democratic Institute et al. "Briefing Paper for the National Democratic Institute for International Affairs and the International Republican Institute's Joint International Delegation to the 1994 Mexican Elections." August, 1994.

Nie, Norman H., and Sidney Verba. "Political Participation." In Fred Greenstein and Nelson Polsby, eds., *Nongovernmental Politics,* pp. 1–74. Reading, Mass.: Addison-Wesley Publishing Company, 1975.

Nuncio, Abraham. *El PAN: Alternativa de poder o instrumento de la oligarquía empresarial.* Mexico: Editorial Nuevo Imagen, 1986.

O'Donnell, Guillermo, and Phillipe Schmitter. *Transitions from Authoritarian Rule: Tentative Conclusions about Uncertain Democracies.* Baltimore: Johns Hopkins University Press, 1986.

Olimon Nolasco, Manuel, et al. *Los derechos humanos: Historia contemporánea, doctrina social cristiana y fundamentos teológicos.* Mexico: Instituto Mexicano de Doctrina Social Cristiana, 1987.

Olson, Mancur. *Logic of Collective Action.* Cambridge: Harvard University Press, 1965.

Orozco, Víctor. "Las luchas populares en Chihuahua." *Cuadernos Políticos* 9 (July–September, 1976), pp. 49–66.

Ortiz Pinchetti, Francisco. "A los 112 kilos de peso Clouthier inicia su ayuno:

'Lo único que pido, y por eso estoy sin tragar, es que Salinas cumpla sus promesas.'" *Proceso* 12,633 (December 19, 1988), pp. 12–15.

———. "En Chihuahua parece gestarse una alianza pluripartidista de oposición, por la democracia." *Proceso* 10,510 (August 11, 1986), pp. 18–19.

———. "En Colima, el PRI se mostró en toda su intimidad." *Proceso* 14,752 (April 1, 1981), pp. 6–11.

———. "Los Colimenses lo tomaron en serio e hicieron de de la Madrid un auténtico rival de Socorro Díaz." *Proceso* 14,751 (March 25, 1991), pp. 24–25, 27.

———. "De consumarse el fraude, Baeza tendrá que gobernar sobre tres cadaveres, dicen los ayunantes." *Proceso* 10,509 (August 4, 1986), pp. 10–11.

———. "El foro de defensa del voto logró acuerdos para pasar a las acciones." *Proceso* 10,515 (September 15, 1986), pp. 27–28.

———. "Incipiente organización opositora, respuesta a la política de arrasamiento." *Proceso*, 10,511 (August 18, 1986), pp. 12–21.

———. "Inseguridad y violencia signos del gobierno de Fernando Baeza." *Proceso* 14,769 (July 29, 1991).

———. "Luís H. Alvarez, tres semanas en huelga de hambre: 'Quiero vivir, pero como hombre libre.'" *Proceso* 10,507 (July 21, 1986), pp. 12–13.

———. "El padrón electoral y las casillas, clave del fraude: El PRI ganará en Chihuahua y la única verdad será la suya." *Proceso* 10,503 (June 23, 1986), pp. 16–19.

———. "El PRI ganará en Chihuahua y la única verdad será la suya." *Proceso* 10,503 (June 23, 1986), pp. 16–19.

———. "También la indignación se previó en Chihuahua y se le inutiliza." *Proceso* 10,506 (July 14, 1986), pp. 6–14.

———. "'Vamos por todo, las condiciones están dadas,' asegura Clouthier." *Proceso* 11,578 (November 30, 1987), pp. 10–14.

Ortiz Pinchetti, José Agustín. *La democracia que viene: Ejercicios de imaginación política*. Mexico: Editorial Grijalbo, 1990.

Outler, Albert C. "Un comentario." In Wifredo Guinea, ed., *Los documentos del Vaticano II*, pp. 92–96. Mexico: Editorial "El," 1966.

Pacheco Méndez, Guadalupe. "Un caleidoscopio electoral: Ciudades y elecciones en Mexico, 1988–1994." *Estudios Sociologicos* 15, no. 44, pp. 319–50.

———. *El PRI en los procesos electorales de 1961 a 1985*. Mexico City: Universidad Autónoma de México, 1986.

"Panorama económico." *Información procesada de Chihuahua* (May, 1986), pp. 4–14.

"Panorama económico." *Información procesada de Chihuahua* (July, 1986), pp. 4–22.

"Panorama económico." *Información procesada de Chihuahua* (August, 1986), pp. 4–16.

"Panorama religioso." *Información procesada de Chihuahua* (July, 1986), pp. 118–29.

"Panorama religioso." *Información procesada de Chihuahua* (August, 1986), pp. 80–87.

"Panorama religioso." *Información procesada de Chihuahua* (September, 1986), pp. 69–79.

Partido de Acción Nacional. *Acción Internaciónal* 19 (February 30, 1995).

———. *Acción Internaciónal* 23 (June 30, 1995).

———. *Acción Internacional* 28 (November 30, 1995).

Partido Revolucionario Institucional. Consejo Político Nacional, Acuerdo general para la postulación del candidato a la presidencia de la republica para el periodo 2000–2006. May 17, 1999. http://www.pri.org.mx.

———. "Michoacán: Balance del proceso electoral." *La Jornada* (July 15, 1992).

———. XIV Assamblea Nacional, "Dictamen de la Comisión de Estatutos." In *Participación viva,* pp. 56–69. Mexico: Partido Revolucionario Institucional, 1990.

Pastor, Robert. *Integration with Mexico: Options for U.S. Policy.* New York: Twentieth Century Fund, 1993.

———. *Whirlpool: U.S. Foreign Policy towards Latin America and the Caribbean.* Princeton: Princeton University Press, 1992.

Pastor, Robert., ed. *Democracy in the Americas: Stopping the Pendulum.* New York: Holmes and Meier, 1989.

Paul VI. "Populorum progressio." In Jesús Iribarren and José Luís Gutiérrez García, eds., *Ocho grandes mensajes,* pp. 317–66. Madrid: Biblioteca de Autores Cristianos, 1971.

Pei, Minxin. "Creeping Democratization in China." *Journal of Democracy* 6, no. 4 (October, 1995).

———. *From Reform to Revolution.* Cambridge: Harvard University Press, 1994.

Pequeñas comunidades cristianas. Chihuahua: Editorial Camino, 1988.

Pérez del Castillo, Germán, et al. *La voz de los votos: Un análisis crítico de las elecciones de 1994.* Mexico City: Miguel Angel Porrua, 1995.

Pérez-Díaz, Victor. *The Return of Civil Society: The Emergence of Democratic Spain.* Cambridge: Harvard University Press, 1993.

Pérez Mendoza, Jaime. "Luís H. Alvarez no ve motivo para desistir; 'Yo creo que va a morir pronto,' dice su sacerdote." *Proceso* 10,510 (August 11, 1986), pp. 14–15.

———. "Por petición de Bartlett el Vaticano ordenó que hubiera misas en Chihuahua." *Proceso* 10,509 (August 4, 1986), pp. 6–13.

Philip, George. *The Presidency in Mexican Politics.* New York: St. Martins Press, 1992.

Pius XI. "Quadragesimo Anno." In Jesús Iribarren and José Luís Gutiérrez, eds., *Ocho grandes mensajes,* pp. 63–120. Madrid: Biblioteca de Autores Cristianos, 1971.

Pomerleau, Claude. "The Changing Church in Mexico and Its Challenge to the State." *Review of Politics* 43, 4 (October, 1981), pp. 540–59.

Popkin, Samuel. *The Rational Peasant: The Political Economy of Rural Society in Vietnam.* Berkeley: University of California Press.

Presidencia de la República. "Licencia al gobernador de Chihuahua." In *Las razones y las obras: Gobierno de Miguel de la Madrid, tercer año.* Mexico: Presidencia de la República, Fondo de Cultura Económica, 1986.

Puig, Carlos. "Informe de la Comisión de Derechos Humanos de la OEA, ante denuncias del PAN." *Proceso* 13,694 (February 19, 1990), pp. 18–21.

Putnam, Robert. *Making Democracy Work: Civic Traditions in Modern Italy.* Princeton: Princeton University Press, 1993.

Quintana Silveyra, Victor M. "La protesta social en Chihuahua en los ochentas." In Rubén Lau and Victor M. Quintana, eds., *Movimientos populares en Chihuahua.* Ciudad Juárez: Universidad Autónoma de Chihuahua, 1991.

Ramos Cortés, Victor M. *Poder, representación, y pluralidad en la Iglesia.* Guadalajara: Universidad de Guadalajara, 1992.

Rascón, Marco A., and Patricia Ruiz. "Chihuahua: La disputa por la dependencia." *Cuadernos Políticos* 47 (July–September, 1986), pp. 25–39.

Reding, Andrew. *Democracy and Human Rights in Mexico.* New York: World Policy Papers, 1995.

Reed, Nelson. *The Caste War of Yucatán.* Stanford: Stanford University Press, 1964.

Revueltas, Armando. *Así fué, Cd. Juárez, Chihuahua 1986: Una historia digna de contarse.*

Riding, Alan. *Distant Neighbors: A Portrait of the Mexicans.* New York: Vintage Books, 1986.

Robles, Manuel. "Barrio, Clouthier, Bátiz, estrategia y lenguaje nuevos: Que la gente aprenda que puede devolver los golpes." *Proceso* 11,532 (January 12, 1987), pp. 13–15.

———. "Furibunda reacción contra el PAN, por llevar sus protestas a Washington." *Proceso* 10,511 (August 18, 1986), pp. 12–13.

———. "Subsidios a los partidos: Al más fuerte, más dinero." *Proceso* 11,547 (April 27, 1987), pp. 18–20.

Rodríguez, Enrique. "El PRI obtuvo mayoria en elección de diputados y PAN en la de senadores." *Diario de Chihuahua* (July 11, 1997).

Rodríguez, Enrique, and A. Gutierrez. "Entregan constancia de mayoria a Patricio." *Diario de Chihuahua* (March 11, 1998).

Rodríguez, Victoria E. "Municipal Autonomy and the Politics of Intergovernmental Finance: Is It Different for the Opposition?" In Victoria E. Rodríguez and Peter M. Ward, *Opposition Government in Mexico,* pp. 153–72. Albuquerque: University of New Mexico Press, 1995.

Rodríguez, Victoria E., and Peter M. Ward. *Political Change in Baja California: Democracy in the Making?* La Jolla: Center for U.S.-Mexican Studies, University of California, San Diego, 1994.

Roett, Riordan, ed. *The Mexican Peso Crisis: International Perpectives.* Boulder: Lynne Rienner Publishers, 1996.

Romero, Miguel Angel. "Chihuahua: Laboratorio político." *El Cotidiano* 6, 30 (July–August, 1989), pp. 16–19.

Rossiter, Clinton, ed. *The Federalist Papers.* New York: Penguin Books, 1961.

Rubin, Jeffrey W. *Decentering the Regime: Ethnicity, Radicalism, and Democracy in Juchitán, Mexico.* Durham: Duke University Press, 1997.

Rubio, Luís. "Economic Reform and Political Change in Mexico." In Riordan Roett, ed., *Political and Economic Liberalization in Mexico: At a Critical Juncture,* pp. 35–50. Boulder: Lynne Rienner Publishers, 1993.

Rubio, Luís, et al. *México a la hora del cambio.* Mexico, D.F.: Cal y Arena, 1995.

Rustow, Dankwart A. "Transitions to Democracy: Towards a Dynamic Model." *Comparative Politics* 2, 3 (April, 1970), pp. 337–63.

Sachman, Ignacio. *Operación Chihuahua: Vanguardia de la modernización política nacional.* Mexico: El Nacional, 1989.

Sahagún, Alfonso. "Talleres de la democracia: Una iniciativa de cambio político pacífico. Dimensión social de la fe." *La Nación* 45,1733 (June 15, 1987), pp. 21–24.

Saldierna, Georgina. "Reconocimiento oficial del PRI al triunfo de Ruffo." *La Jornada* (July 5, 1989), p. 12.

Salinas de Gortari, Carlos. "La precisión del cambio." *Nexos* 136 (April, 1989).

———. "Los retos de la democracia." Reprinted in Carlos Salinas de Gortari, *El reto,* pp. 37–58. Mexico: Editorial Diana, 1988.

Sánchez Gutiérrez, Arturo. "La elección de la Cámara de Diputados." In Germán Pérez del Castillo et al., eds., *La voz de los votos: Un análisis crítico de las elecciones de 1994.* Mexico City: Miguel Angel Porrua, 1995.

Saragoza, Alex M. *The Monterrey Elite and the Mexican State.* Austin: University of Texas Press, 1988.

Schmitter, Phillipe. "Dangers and Dilemmas of Democracy." *Journal of Democracy* 5 (April, 1994).

Shaiken, Harley. *Mexico in the Global Economy: High Technology and Work Organization in Export Industries.* San Diego: Center for U.S.-Mexican Studies, University of California, 1990.

Shaiken Harley, with Stephen Herzenberg. *Automation and Global Production: Automobile Engine Production in Mexico, the United States, and Canada.* San Diego: Center for U.S.-Mexican Studies, University of California, 1987.

Sistema integral de evangelización, instructivo para pequeñas comunidades. Mexico: Comunicaciones Nueva Vida.

Sota García, Eduardo, and Enrique Luengo González. *Entre la conciencia y la obediencia: La opinión del clero sobre la política en México.* Mexico City: Universidad Iberoamericana, 1994.

Staudt, Kathleen, and Carlota Aguilar. "Political Parties, Women Activists' Agendas, and Household Relations: Elections on Mexico's Northern Frontier." *Mexican Studies / Estudios Mexicanos* 8, no. 1 (Winter, 1992), pp. 87–106.

Talamás y Camandari, Manuel. *¿Cuál es su excusa?* Mexico: Ediciones Paulinas, 1986.

Taller sobre los católicos y la democracia: Segundo documento de trabajo. Chihuahua: Arquidiócesis de Chihuahua, 1987.

Tangeman, Michael. *Mexico at the Crossroads: Politics, the Church, and the Poor.* Maryknoll, N.Y.: Orbis Books, 1955.

Tannenbaum, Frank. *Mexico: The Struggle for Peace and Bread.* New York: Alfred A. Knopf, 1950.

Tarrow, Sidney. "Making Social Science Work across Space and Time: A Critical Reflection on Robert Putnam's *Making Democracy Work.*" *American Political Science Review* 90, no. 2 (June, 1996), pp. 389–98.

———. *Power in Movement: Social Movements, Collective Action, and Politics.* Cambridge: Cambridge University Press, 1994.

———. "Struggle, Politics, and Reform: Collective Action, Social Movements, and Cycles of Reform." Western Societies Program, occasional paper 21. Ithaca: Center for International Studies, Cornell University, 1989.

Terrazas Sánchez, Filiberto. *La Guerra Apache en México.* Mexico: Costa Amic Editores, 1977.

Tocqueville, Alexis de. *Democracy in America.* Ed. J. P. Mayer. Garden City, N.J.: Anchor Books 1969.

Unidad de Asistencia Electoral. *Posibilidades de apoyo a organizaciones no gubernamentales de observadores electorales en México.* Mexico City: UN Mission, May 23, 1994.

Valenzuela, Arturo. "Latin America: Presidentialism in Crisis." *Journal of Democracy* 4 (October, 1993).

Vallier, Ivan. *Catholicism, Social Control, and Modernization in Latin America.* Engelwood Cliffs, N.J.: Prentice-Hall, Inc., 1970.

———. "Religious Elites: Differentiations and Developments in Roman Catholicism." In Seymour Martin Lipset and Aldo Solari, eds., *Elites in Latin America,* pp. 190–232. New York: Oxford University Press, 1968.

Vásquez, Dizán. *El compromiso ecuménico de la Iglesia católica y el problema de las sectas en América Latina.* Caracas: Acción Ecuménica, 1988.

Venegas, Lilia. "Women on the Border: The *Panista* Militants of Tijuana and Ciudad Juárez." In Victoria E. Rodríguez, ed., *Women's Participation in Mexican Political Life.* Boulder: Westview Press, 1998.

Vera, Rodrigo. "La aceptación del subsidio convierte al PAN en partido multimillionario." *Proceso* 12,629 (November 21, 1988), pp. 20–23.

Verba, Sidney, Norman H. Nie, and Jae-On Kim. *Participation and Political Equality: A Seven-Nation Comparison.* Cambridge: Cambridge University Press, 1978.

Villarreal, René. "The Policy of Import-Substituting Industrialization." In José Luis Reyna and Richard S. Weinert, eds., *Authoritarianism in Mexico,* pp. 67–107. Philadelphia: Institute for the Study of Human Issues, 1977.

Von Sauer, Franz A. *The Alienated "Loyal" Opposition: Mexico's Partido Acción Nacional.* Albuquerque: University of New Mexico Press, 1974.

Ward, Peter. "Policy Making and Policy Implementation among Non-PRI Governments: The PAN in Ciudad Juárez and in Chihuahua." In Victoria E. Rodríguez and Peter M. Ward, *Opposition Government in Mexico,* pp. 135–52. Albuquerque: University of New Mexico Press, 1995.

Wasserman, Mark. *Capitalists, Caciques, and Revolution: The Native Elite and Foreign Enterprise in Chihuahua, Mexico, 1854–1911.* Chapel Hill: University of North Carolina Press, 1984.

Whitehead, Laurence. "Mexico's Economic Prospects: Implications for State-Labor Relations." In Kevin Middlebrook, ed., *Unions, Workers, and the State in Mexico.* La Jolla: Center for U.S.-Mexican Studies, University of California, San Diego, 1991.

Wilkie, James W., and Edna Monzon de Wilkie. *México visto en el siglo XX: Entrevistas con Manuel Gómez Morin.* Mexico: Editorial JUS, 1978.

Williams, Edward J. "The Resurgent North and Contemporary Mexican Regionalism." *Mexican Studies / Estudios Mexicanos* (Summer, 1990).

Zaid, Gabriel. *La economía presidencial.* Mexico City: Vuelta, 1986.

Zald, Mayer, and John D. McCarthy, eds. *Social Movements in an Organizational Society: Collected Essays.* New Brunswick: Transaction Books, 1987.

Zebadua, Emilio. *Banqueros y revolucionarios: La soberanía financiera de México, 1914–1929.* Mexico: Fondo de Cultura Económica, 1994.

Zubek, Voytek, and Judith Gentleman. "Economic Crisis and the Movement toward Pluralism in Poland and Mexico." *Political Science Quarterly* 109, no. 2 (Summer, 1994), pp. 335–60.

Index